DOROTHY S. AINSWORTH Editor, Professor Emeritus, Smith College

MARION R. BROER Professor, University of Washington

ELIZABETH J. CULVER Instructor, University of Washington

GERTRUDE GOSS Associate Professor Emeritus, Smith College

JANE A. MOTT Director of Physical Education, Smith College

FLORENCE M. RYDER Associate Professor, Smith College

JEAN CAMPBELL TUGMAN Formerly Assistant Professor, Smith College

INDIVIDUAL SPORTS

ARCHERY

BADMINTON

BOWLING

FENCING

GOLF

RIDING

SWIMMING

FOR WOMEN

TENNIS

FOURTH EDITION

ILLUSTRATED BY

VIRGINIA DIX STERLING
Hugh C. Pape
Anne Fisher Tatlock

W. B. SAUNDERS COMPANY

PHILADELPHIA AND LONDON

W. B. Saunders Company: West Washington Square,
Philadelphia, Pa. 19105

12 Dyott Street
London, W.C.1

Reprinted May, 1964, June, 1965, June, 1966 and May, 1967

Individual Sports for Women

 Made in the United States of America. Press of W. B. Saunders Company. Library of Congress catalog card number: 63–9475.

PREFACE TO THE FOURTH EDITION

The publication of the Fourth Edition of *Individual Sports for Women* indicates the very lively and increasing interest in the field of women's sports. More and more girls throughout the country are eager for individual sports and are selecting them for their Physical Education programs. This is not surprising for these sports carry over to the after school hours and to games with boys and men, which gives these sports (which are enjoyable in themselves) an added social value. These activities can be enjoyed long after school and college days are past, and can increase the pleasure of holidays and vacations. Their exercise fills the need for a feeling of physical well-being. Practice in individual sports can, moreover, make a solid contribution to the national Fitness Program, which is of such concern and importance to educators today. Proficiency in individual sports is highly regarded today.

This edition has three new authors. The badminton chapter has been rewritten by Jane Mott, Director of Physical Education at Smith College; the bowling chapter by Elizabeth Culver, Instructor of Physical Education at the University of Washington in Seattle; and the riding chapter by Jean Campbell Tugman, formerly Assistant Professor of Physical Education at Smith College. The chapters on riding and bowling have been completely rewritten; the badminton chapter has many additions and changes involving attention to strategy, equipment, and points to emphasize in teaching.

All the other chapters have been revised by their original authors, Miss Broer, Miss Goss, and Miss Ryder, who have made very valuable additions, both in aids to teaching and in bringing each sport up to date with respect to changes in regulations and modern emphases in teaching. We believe that such changes have greatly increased the value and usefulness of the book.

We continue to use many of the excellent and beautiful illustrations drawn by Virginia Dix Sterling from our earlier editions. There are also new drawings for the bowling chapter by Mr. Hugh C. Pape and for the riding chapter by Anne Fisher Tatlock. We are pleased with and proud of all these illustrations, and believe they will guide our readers to a better visual understanding of the text.

This book is written primarily for the teacher, but the intelligent player may also gain much from it. There are explanations of equipment, terminology, technique, and progressions in learning the various skills. The sportswoman can greatly improve both her understanding and her skill through reading and practicing the lessons taught in the various chapters.

Certain individual sports, such as archery, swimming, riding, and even golf and bowling, can be enjoyed either alone or with others. Other sports require an opponent, such as badminton, fencing, and tennis. In all sports companionship and competition are important. Although a certain proficiency must be attained to enjoy any sport, the pleasure of keen competition can be found at almost all levels of ability. The authors recognize that sports are played for competitive as well as recreational values, and they feel that this book will be equally useful to those who look to sports for personal recreation and those who prefer competition.

We hope that this Fourth Edition will help make individual sports more meaningful for many persons and that it will lead both the teacher and the student to know and enjoy even more the sports described therein.

DOROTHY S. AINSWORTH
Northampton, Massachusetts

CONTENTS

1

TEACHING INDIVIDUAL SPORTS

1

TEACHING INDIVIDUAL SPORTS

Marion R. Broer

While the eight individual sports discussed in this book appear to be very different and are in fact very different in the actual structure of the sport, in facilities and equipment demanded by each, and, in the case of swimming, even different in the medium in which the sport takes place, they have many common elements. The most effective teacher will be the one who takes maximum advantage of this fact.

There are not only many previously learned understandings that are basic and can be applied to all or several of them but also many previously acquired movement patterns which can be called upon and adjusted somewhat as required by specific equipment and purpose. Effective use of this past experience can speed learning. In teaching, advantage can be taken of these similarities, so that in each learning situation the student builds on previously acquired movement patterns and knowledge.

TRANSFER

Transfer is the name education has given to the process of effective utilization of past experience in meeting new situations. In developing skill in sports this means seeing relationships not only in actual movement patterns but also in the principles of equilibrium and of force production and application so that these can be applied intelligently to gain the specific purpose demanded by the new sport. *TRANSFER IS NOT AUTOMATIC.* The teacher must help the student gain insight into the relationships between various movement situations and into the broad application of basic understandings and basic movement patterns. The teacher must help the student develop the habit of making use of previously learned skills and knowledge. This is one of the essentials of good teaching.

In considering the understandings that are basic to these individual sports, those which first come to mind have to do with equilibrium, since the force of gravity is ever present and must be considered in all movements. Whether one wishes to assume a very stable position on the ground as in archery, fencing, and golf; or to maintain the upright position and yet be able to move rapidly, as in bowling, tennis, and badminton; or to maintain equilibrium in the medium of water without contact with the solid earth, as in swimming; or to maintain equilibrium on a moving supportive surface, as in riding; the force of gravity and the principles by which the body adjusts to it must be understood.*

Most of these principles have been learned through trial and error at a very young age. If a small child is observed as he is learning to walk, this is obvious. Although a child learns to walk in general through imitation, many mechanical principles involved in equilibrium are learned at this tender age by trial and error. How does the baby first walk? Because he has lifted his center of gravity and narrowed his base considerably, his problem is one of equilibrium. How does he cope with the force of gravity? He holds his arms outward, unknowingly applying a principle of leverage to aid in balancing. He walks with his feet wide apart and although this makes it necessary to waste effort in moving his weight from side to side as well as forward, it helps him accomplish his purpose of maintaining sideways equilibrium. He then finds that he is likely to fall forward or backward, and therefore he frequently runs before he walks. He has learned some basic leverage principles, the relationship between size of base and stability, the importance of the relationship of the center of gravity to the base, and a way to use gravity to advantage to help him walk.

Can teachers help students in learning skills so that they need not take the "bumps" the baby takes in his trial and error learning, but still can learn as much as possible about their bodies and the principles that govern movement? Can teachers help students understand these principles that they have learned through trial and error as children and help them gain insight into their broad application? A physical educator who understands the basic principles of movement can teach knowledge and develop understandings important to all skills through *any* specific activity. Besides the principles of equilibrium, which apply to all activities, there are many other principles common to these individual sports.

Archery, badminton, bowling, golf, and tennis have the common purpose of projecting an object. Therefore, in learning these activities, the principles that apply to projectiles must be understood; and, if learned in one of these activities they can be applied in the others. The effect of the force of gravity on a moving object must be considered, and the angle of force application must be adjusted according to purpose. The vertical component of the force applied varies with the different activities and with the distance of projection.

In archery, the vertical component of force increases as the archer moves from 30 to 50 yards from the target, since gravity has more time to work on the

*For a discussion of these principles the reader is referred to Marion R. Broer: *Efficiency of Human Movement*. Philadelphia, W. B. Saunders Company, 1960.

arrow. Certainly at 50 yards the vertical component of the force applied in archery must in general be greater than in badminton or tennis, although in the latter sports one must consider the distance which gravity can lower the ball or shuttle and still have it high enough to clear the net. Obviously, then, the vertical component of the force applied to the ball or shuttle will depend on the distance of the player from the net and the speed with which the object is hit. Although the golf ball must travel even farther than the arrow, the vertical component of the force is lessened to increase horizontal force, since more force must be expended to move the ball forward against the tremendous air resistance that results from the great speed of the golf ball.

The importance of air resistance is also obvious in the flight of the badminton shuttle which, because of its light weight, irregular shape, and high speed, causes so much air resistance that its horizontal force is dissipated long before gravity has had time to pull it to earth. Its forward progress is thus halted, and gravity being the only force acting on it, the shuttle falls directly downward.

Although bowling and golf seem to be very different, many of the same understandings are involved. Force is applied to an object that is at ground level at the time of projection. Because the weight of the bowling ball is impossible to control far from the body (length of the extended arm) by pure muscular power, the effective use of the force of gravity in assisting the muscles must be understood. Use of a vertical swing which does not interfere with the effective action of gravity and centrifugal force is as important in golf as in bowling. While in golf the club is not as heavy as the bowling ball, the length of the lever makes control difficult, if not impossible, without the aid of gravity.

In badminton, tennis, bowling, and golf, the force applied to the projectile depends on the speed that can be built up at the end of the various lever lengths. The student must understand the contribution of steps and/or weight transference, of length of backswing, of bringing the large trunk muscles into the swing, of applying force at the center of the arc of the swing when the end of the lever is moving at its fastest, of sequential action, of interaction between the feet and the supporting surface, to the speed which can be produced. While in bowling, the object is held in the hand and therefore the direction of the movement of the hand at the moment of release is the most important factor in control of the direction of the projected object; in the striking activities (badminton, tennis, golf), the factor of angle of striking surface must be considered also, and in the activities involving an oncoming object (tennis and badminton), still other factors, those of direction of object approach to the striking surface and relative speed of object and racket are important considerations.

In all of these activities, very similar general body movement patterns are employed. All of them make use of the underhand pattern of movement, although it is somewhat modified in golf because of the necessity for using two hands to control the long implement. In addition, tennis and badminton employ the overhand and sidearm patterns of movement.

These are but a few examples of the broad application of basic principles and movement patterns to individual sports.

Each student involved in any teaching situation will have had many previous movement experiences. The principles basic to human movement and various general movement patterns will have been encountered over and over in many varied types of movement situations. Therefore, every teacher has readily available for the tapping, a wealth of student experience on which to build new understandings and motor skills. Although the student frequently is unaware of the fact, she has previously acquired many understandings and movement skills that can help her in the new learning situation. The teacher's problem becomes that of structuring learning situations which will cause the student to become aware of understandings and skills she already possesses, and guide her in gaining insight into their application to the new sport.

LEARNING

All that is known substantiates the fact that learning is an active process, and there is no reason to believe that this is less true of the learning of motor skills than of any other learning. The physical education teacher cannot transfer her motor skill to the nervous system of a student any more than the mathematics teacher can pour his understanding of calculus into his student's mind. Learning takes place as insight dawns. For effective learning in any skill, the student must be involved beyond the point of simply going through a movement described and demonstrated by the teacher. She must see the relationships herself. She needs to be involved in deciding for herself the movement or movements that have the greatest possibility for producing the best results according to her purpose.

ESTABLISHING PURPOSE

Too frequently the teacher forgets that a student learns according to her own purpose and that this purpose may not necessarily coincide with the purpose of the teacher. This points up the importance of guiding the student in the establishment of her purposes. For example, if a student's purpose is simply to get the tennis ball into her opponent's court, the learning of a forceful serve undoubtedly will be retarded. How often has a teacher of tennis had the experience of working with a student on the complete pattern of movement required for a forceful serve only to find that the moment her back was turned, the student swung the racket forward and upward and, with a bent arm, "popped" the ball high over the net into her opponent's court? Obviously, this student's purpose and that of the instructor were not the same. Greater understanding of the game of tennis as a whole may help this student gain the insight that will change her purpose. But she herself must actually *see* the relationship of a forceful serve to the game. The teacher must help the student establish intermediate purposes, the accomplishment of which will lead to the larger goal.

TEACHING

Whether the teacher is attempting to guide the student in the establishment of well defined purposes or helping her gain insight into the movements that will give the most effective results in terms of these purposes, the teacher's task is to carefully structure learning situations that will make obvious to the student relationships to previous experiences and the movement she must choose and the reasons for its superiority over another. Her task may be to suggest various possibilities for accomplishing the purpose and to guide the student's thinking so that the application of previous understanding to the new situation will be apparent and the student will see for herself the advantages and disadvantages of each method for reaching her goal. In this type of teaching, the teacher sets the situation so that the student must use previous background skills and knowledges or must use a certain movement to gain insight into the new situation.

This type of teaching will not lead to students who look alike or who look like their instructor as they perform any skill. This is as it should be, since no two students have the same physical mechanism with which to work.

CAUSES OF INEFFECTIVE PERFORMANCE

In helping students perfect their movements, it is important that the instructor look for *basic* causes for ineffective performance. It does no good to tell the student of bowling that her ball went too far to the left. The student does not need an instructor to point out this fact. She needs help in understanding *why* the ball went to the left and what can be changed to correct this.

A small experiment with a light ball (tennis ball or softball), in which the student moves the ball along a right to left arc drawn on the floor and attempts to release it so that the ball hits a target straight ahead, and then moves the same ball along a straight line on the floor and releases to send the ball to the target, will demonstrate to the student whose ineffective performance was caused by a circular swing the importance of a straight swing more effectively than will the words "You swung the ball in an arc; swing it in a straight line backward and forward." If this student's curved swing is caused by lack of sufficient strength to control the heavy ball when it is far from her body in a straight backswing, no amount of telling her or of demonstrating the importance of a straight swing will be of assistance since, even when she understands the contribution of the straight swing to accuracy, she lacks the strength necessary to control this weight unless it is close to her center of gravity. Obviously the teacher must in this case give the student a lighter ball and suggest exercises to strengthen the arm, shoulder girdle, and trunk muscles. She also must help the student to see for herself the necessity for strengthening these muscles if she is to carry through a strengthening program that will help her in reaching her bowling goal. In other words, she must help the student establish this intermediate purpose.

If a student in badminton is constantly missing the shuttle as she attempts to serve, it does little good to reiterate descriptions of the "correct form." The student in all probability needs help in developing a concept of the speed with which the shuttle falls through the air, since because of its light weight and shape, air resistance is a greater factor and therefore the speed with which the shuttle drops is different from that of the more familiar object, the ball.

If a student of badminton or tennis continues to hit the shuttle or ball with a bent arm, thus reducing the force she can produce, perhaps the *basic* cause is that she has not yet developed the spatial concept of the distance of her reach elongated by the racket. Do teachers take for granted that such new concepts are developed immediately and automatically? Too frequently the answer to this question must be in the affirmative. Yet, actually many students, perhaps the majority, do not develop these concepts automatically and therefore, time taken to help them understand these differences will be well invested.

It is possible that the basic cause for this fault, hitting the drive with a bent arm, may be lack of strength to withstand the force of the tennis ball as it contacts the racket at the end of the long lever. If so, the teacher must attack the strength problem directly, guiding the student toward an understanding of her problem, helping her develop the intermediate strength development goal and suggesting ways that strength can be developed.

TEACHING IN "WHOLE" AND IN "PART"

In all of education, and physical education is no exception, there has been considerable discussion of "whole" versus "part" teaching. Is it possible to perceive the whole by noting and adding together its various parts piece by piece? Consider Figure 1.1. It includes all of the parts of a whole well known to every physical educator; yet it is not easy to see the whole. However, only a glance at Figure 1.2 is necessary to perceive the whole immediately. This is an example of the Gestalt psychologists' statement that squareness is perceived only from looking at a square not from seeing four lines. It follows that the breast stroke in swimming is more than certain arm movements plus certain leg movements plus breathing. It is all of these performed together in a well coordinated whole. A complex whole depends on the *interrelationship* of the separate parts.

Learning is a total response to a situation that frequently is complex. Therefore,

"PARTS" OF A WELL KNOWN "WHOLE"

FIGURE 1.1

it appears reasonable that skills should be presented in their entirety. The learner must get an idea of the skill as a whole. After practicing the whole it may be desirable to isolate, for special attention, a certain part with which the student is having particular trouble, but only after the student has a concept of the total skill. Even then, the part should be put back into the whole very rapidly. Although there appears to be some conflict in the conclusions drawn from various research studies dealing with this question of whole or part teaching, much of this conflict results from a difference in definition of the words "whole" and "part." Some research workers have defined "whole" as the whole game, for example the whole game of tennis, and claim that they are teaching by the "part method" when they isolate for specific attention a skill involved in the game, such as, in tennis, the forehand drive, backhand drive, or serve. Others define the "whole" as the complex of movements involved in a skill, such as the tennis serve, in which case the parts are considered to be the toss, the backswing, the forward swing with its follow through. It is obvious that the student trying to learn tennis does need to gain a general concept of the game in order to understand the interrelatedness of the smaller wholes (the skills) that will be learned. Without this, the learning of the specific skills will lack motivation. However, the whole upon which the student should concentrate her attention for a period of time must be the largest concept that she is capable of comprehending fully and practicing at one time. This, in a game like tennis, is a complete stroke.

When the "whole" is so defined there is little conflict in research results. Therefore, it would appear to be advisable first to help the student gain a general concept of the entire activity, and then gain insight into the complete movement pattern involved in each skill. Parts of a skill, such as the toss for the tennis serve, that cause particular difficulty for a student, may need to be isolated and practiced briefly, but should be put back into the total pattern as quickly as possible. The part that needs to be isolated for particular attention will vary from student to student according to the particular difficulty encountered by each individual. It may also change as the skill level of the student advances.

DEMONSTRATIONS

When using demonstration, the teacher must remember that perception is an individual matter. No two students will see exactly the same thing as they watch the demonstration. Furthermore, it is impossible to watch all of the small details of the movement demonstrated. What is seen is the movement as a whole: the general pattern, not specific details. This is actually fortunate since if each student in a class attempted to reproduce all of the specific movements of the instructor, most would be very frustrated by basic differences of body build that would make this impossible.

In an attempt to make detail more obvious to students, teachers sometime demonstrate in slow motion. Comparison of slow motion pictures of skills performed up to time with pictures of the "same skill" performed slowly indicate that the movement is not the same. Therefore, teachers are not demonstrating the skill as it must be performed if they use the slow motion technique, unless they use slow motion pictures of skills performed at normal tempo.

The fact that a movement performed at a slow tempo is not the same as when performed up to speed has implications for the teacher beyond those involved in demonstration. In many individual sports, both accuracy and speed are important elements. Since research findings agree that accuracy developed at a slow tempo is lost when the movement is speeded up, but that there is little loss of speed when accuracy is emphasized, it would appear unwise to teach a movement at a slow tempo in order to concentrate upon accuracy. Rather, a movement should be learned up to tempo, with accuracy being emphasized at the same time. It may be expedient for a student to go through a movement slowly in order to gain an understanding of the sequence, but continued practice at a slow tempo has been found to be a waste of time.

Speed of movement varies with individuals and therefore the optimum tempo for a movement will vary from student to student. Some individuals habitually move rapidly, others slowly. Some can adjust easily to a superimposed rhythm; others have great difficulty. For example, a student who moves with ease when skiing and swimming may appear unskilled on the dance floor where she is required to adjust to an outside rhythmic stimulus. *When movement to a set tempo is not necessary to the purpose of the activity,* the teacher would do well to allow students to develop skill at their own tempos determined through experiment.

The use of music in teaching swimming and bowling as well as such skills as the golf swing and tennis drive has been advocated by some, and certainly, if well chosen, music may be helpful in inducing a relaxed movement as opposed to a tense, percussive one. However, it seems unwise to continue the music for long or to insist that all students maintain its tempo. Also, it must be remembered that in demonstrating, the teacher moves according to her own optimum tempo, which will not be the most effective one for all of her students.

All of this does not mean that teacher demonstration is useless or that the instructor should never demonstrate. It simply means that, when demonstrating, the teacher should guide the student's observation toward the basic movement pattern rather than the specific positions of various parts of the body at particular points in the movement. Also, skills should be demonstrated at the speed that is necessary for the teacher's accomplishment of purpose.

PROBLEM SOLVING

Perhaps demonstration would be more meaningful if given *after* the student has had an opportunity for personal experimentation, since she then would have a foundation on which to place her obsertion and, as a consequence, the demonstration would be of greater help to her in building her total concept of the movement pattern. Students need an opportunity to determine for themselves, through experimentation, just what they have to do to accomplish their purpose. This does not mean that the teacher hands the student a bowling ball and tells her to discover for herself how to strike down all the pins. Instead, she sets small problems that will guide the student step by step into seeing for herself how the body can, while maintaining equilibrium, produce force that moves the ball in various ways. At the same time, these small problems should make obvious the method that will be most effective in accomplishing the student's purpose.

What is problem solving teaching? This method has been used successfully in edu-

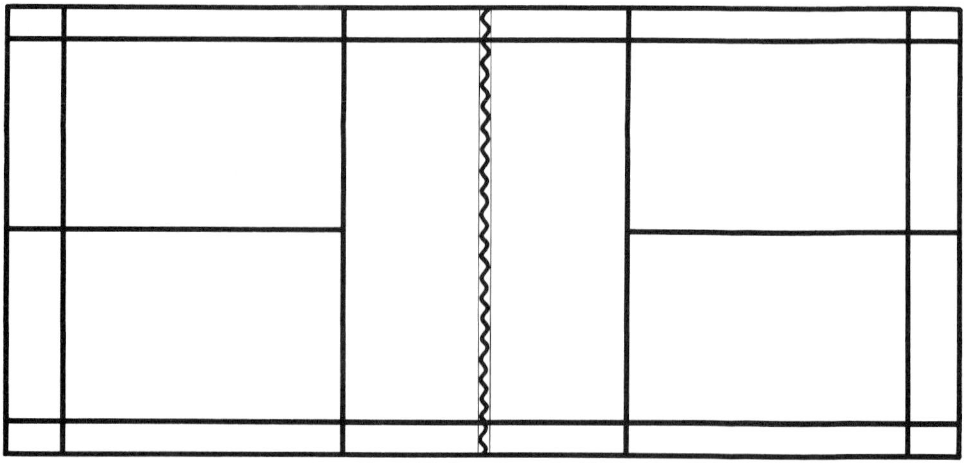

FIGURE 1.2

cation for some time, and it can be applied to the teaching of a motor skill. In fact, physical education offers as many or more opportunities for this kind of teaching than do other disciplines. Problem solving teaching simply involves defining the problem in terms of purpose (the student's purpose, which has been established through careful guidance). The student, *through meaningful exploration structured and guided by the teacher,* determines the method for accomplishing this purpose most consistently, with the least strain and the least expenditure of energy.

The student learning to float could determine the body adjustments which would more nearly balance her body weight around her center of buoyancy (normally her lungs unless her legs are large with adipose tissue) if she first experimented on land with balancing some long narrow object (block of wood) on a fulcrum which was placed at various points under the object. The relationships between the long narrow object and the body, and between the body's chest area and an area marked on the object which would approximate the position of the chest in the body when in its normal, hands at sides position, need to be made clear to the student (Figure 1.3a). Once the student sees the lack of balance when the "chest area" is over the fulcrum (Figure 1.3b) and notes that, if balance is to be attained, the distance of the "head end" of the object from the fulcrum must be longer than the distance from this end to the "chest" area, and that the leg end of the object must be shortened (Figure 1.3c), her attention can be turned to methods of accomplishing this type of lengthening and shortening of the two ends of the body itself. Since she cannot change the fulcrum about which the body will rotate in the water (the center of buoyancy) she must move various parts of the body in such a way that the body above the chest is lengthened and that below the chest is shortened. She will not need to be told to extend her arms on the water above her head and draw her feet toward her body. She will be able to determine for herself that this adjustment is necessary.

Obviously, the teacher must be ready with astute questions to guide the student's thinking, but the student will have the experience of insight into the solution of the problem—of having the final solution come from within. Learning will have taken place. Of course, previous to the above learning situation, the student will have needed an opportunity to experiment with the law of buoyancy. A student experimenting with putting into the water objects of the same weight and different sizes and objects of the same size and different weights will quickly see the law that is operating. Again knowledge will come through insight, rather than from hearing the words of an instructor, and will therefore, have more meaning for the student.

The swimming student can quickly determine through experimentation such important relationships as those between size of surface area and resistance offered by the water, between speed of movement and resistance of water, and between direction of movement and direction of water resistance and thus direction of movement of the body. Simple experiments such as immersing the hand in the water, turning it sideways, and pulling it back at a certain speed and then repeating the movement *at the same speed* with the palm facing the direction of the movement illustrate the importance of surface area. The speed of pull can then be varied, keeping the area constant, and so forth.

In such experiments it is important that, whenever possible, only the one factor which the instructor is attempting to make obvious to the student be varied. If two or more are varied, the student cannot conclude which is responsible for the different result. If, in the small experiments just described, the student pulled the hand sideways through the water at a certain speed and then pulled it palm leading through the water at a faster speed, she would have no basis on which to conclude whether surface area, speed, or both were causing the obviously greater resistance of the water to the hand movement.

Some problem solving situations will, of necessity, be more complicated than these examples, and it will be difficult or impossible to isolate a single factor. However, experiments can be structured so that the factor or factors important to the particular understanding are obvious to the student so that insight can result. The possibilities for experimental situations in the learning of motor skills are limited only by the ingenuity of the teacher. Teaching of this type is highly individualized, since each teacher develops different experimental techniques for making obvious to her students the basic principles and movements involved in the skill to be learned. It is the direct opposite of the kind of teaching that describes a detailed stereotyped pattern of movement, which, because it was observed in some highly skilled player's performance, has been written in a book as "the form" for a particular skill. "Good form" in any of the individual sports does not involve various set patterns of movement that will be the same for all students, but rather the movements that will accomplish the purposes most consistently and with the least strain and the least expenditure of energy.

In summarizing literature dealing with motor learning, Hellebrandt wrote: "There are many ways in which the same goal can be reached, and man unconsciously picks and chooses among the gamut of those available, easing the burden of fatigue . . . and thus extending the range and sensitivity of his movement vocabulary. The physical therapist, shop foreman, physical educator or coach may wish to impose upon the human subject

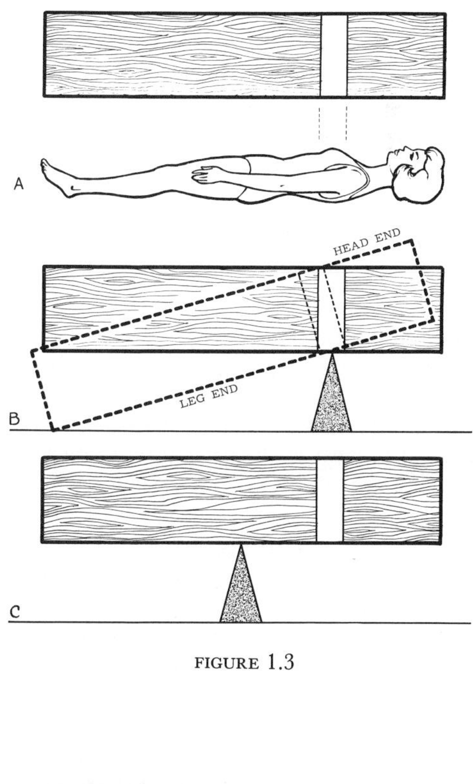

FIGURE 1.3

some precise and specific technique of movement but an infinitely wise living machine . . . makes its own autonomous adjustments. *Instead of suppressing these, we would do well to study them*" (italics added).* The instructor of an individual sport who teaches through student problem solving can learn much from studying her students as they move in the solution of structured problems.

Johnson stated: "It should be pointed out that good form is subject to change as we further our understanding of scientific principles, experiment with new methods and techniques . . . improve equipment, and take advantage of changes in game rules." † She further stated that the search for better methods continues even at high levels of skill, which accounts for the variations in movements of champion performers.** Their movements frequently are observed to vary considerably from the described "form" as well as from movements of other champions in the same sport. Close observation, however, reveals that they all apply the basic mechanical laws that are essential to success and that it is in the superficial aspects of their styles that they vary. Unfortunately, these superficial aspects of their movements are the more easily noted and frequently are incorporated into the accepted definition of "good form." Teachers of individual sports must look beyond the styles of champions to determine the essentials for the accomplishment of the particular purpose.

EVALUATION OF PERFORMANCE

So long as the student's style does not interfere with the basic mechanics, her little individual mannerisms are unimportant. Because of differences in body build, physiological rhythms, emotional make-up, and so forth, students cannot and should not look alike as they perform any given skill. Evaluation, therefore, cannot be based on what the student looks like. In some sports, such as bowling and archery, evaluation of success is no problem, because objective evidence is readily available. It is possible, although in many teaching situations not as simple, to obtain objective evidence in golf. Various objective tests have been suggested in the areas of tennis and badminton and for some strokes in swimming. However, there is little to help the teacher in much of her evaluation of student accomplishment in swimming, and nothing in fencing and riding.

It is important that the teacher structure her evaluative procedures in terms of the basic factors important in accomplishing each purpose. For example, a rating scale for swimming might be based on such basic factors as relaxation, rhythm, and power (the relationship of movement through the water to energy expended). If the instructor feels that it is necessary to evaluate actual movements, only factors basic to efficient force production should be considered: for example, such things as the size of the surface area presented to the water in the direction opposite to desired movement (drive) and in the direction of desired movement (recovery).

Obviously, the only valid evaluation of the results of learning under instruction that recognizes individual differences and the importance of student involvement in the learning situation must be in terms of effective accomplishment of purpose. There is no *one* way to perform any skill. There are certain basic principles that must be followed if the movement is to be efficient, but individuals varying in body build and emotional make-up will move differently.

SUMMARY

Numerous basic understandings and general movement patterns apply to many

* F. A. Hellerbrandt: "The Physiology of Motor Learning." *Cerebral Palsy Review, 10*:4–13 (Jul.–Aug.) 1958.

† Joan Johnson, "Motor Learning of High Skilled Students." *The Physical Educator 17*:46, May 1960. (In Aileene Lockhart, et al.: "The Care and Treatment of the Skilled.")

** *Ibid.*, p. 47.

of the individual sports discussed in this book. When these have been learned through one activity, they are available for application in another if the student has gained a broad understanding and insight into relationships.

Learning is a highly individualized, active process. It depends on the concepts formed by the student. The good teacher of individual sports must, therefore, guide students in setting their purposes—both the more distant larger goals (such as learning the game of badminton) and the smaller intermediate purposes (such as developing skill in the serve, clear, or smash). It follows logically that the student must first gain a concept of the "whole" toward which she is striving, and then attack the learning of the smaller "wholes," isolating only briefly any part that may be causing her difficulty and putting it back into the total movement pattern as quickly as possible.

The teacher must structure learning situations that will allow students to experiment with various possible methods for reaching their goals and that guide the students' thinking so that they can see for themselves the principles that are basic to successful accomplishment of their purposes. The teacher must look for *basic* causes of ineffective performance, and structure situations that will give the student insight into both the basic cause of failure and the method of correction. If the basic cause is lack of strength or a failure to develop new spatial concepts, and so forth, this must be corrected before the movement can be successfully performed.

Because of basic individual differences, students cannot perform any skill in exactly the same way. Therefore, they will not, and should not, look alike. Differences in style that do not interfere with basic mechanics are unimportant: success must be evaluated in terms of ability to accomplish the purpose most consistently with the least strain and least expenditure of energy.

There is no doubt that problem solving teaching, which helps students gain insight offers to each student a truly "learning" situation and to the teacher a challenge to be creative and an opportunity to guide and develop the students' thinking rather than simply to supervise their routine practice.

Suggestions for Further Reading

Broer, Marion R.: *Efficiency of Human Movement.* Philadelphia, W. B. Saunders Company, 1960.

Brownell, Clifford L. and E. Patricia Hagman: *Physical Education—Foundations and Principles.* New York, McGraw-Hill Book Company, Inc., 1951.

Cowell, Charles C. and Hilda M. Schwenn: *Modern Principles and Methods in Physical Education.* Boston, Allyn and Bacon, Inc., 1958.

Davis, Elwood C. and John W. Lawther: *Successful Teaching in Physical Education.* New York, Prentice-Hall, Inc., 1948.

Davis, Elwood C. and Aileene Lockhart: *References on Motor Learning and Motor Performance.* Washington, D. C., American Association for Health, Physical Education, and Recreation, 1960.

Frazier, Alexander, ed.: *Learning More About Learning.* Washington, D. C., Association for Supervision and Curriculum Development, NEA, 1959.

Hellerbrandt, F. A.: "The Physiology of Motor Learning." *Cerebral Palsy Review, 10:*4–13, July–August, 1958.

Kozman, Hilda C., Rosalind Cassidy and Chester O. Jackson: *Methods in Physical Education.* Philadelphia, W. B. Saunders Company, 1958.

Lockhart, Aileene, et al.: "The Care and Treatment of the Skilled; Do We Practice What We Know About Motor Learning?" *The Physical Educator, 17:* 43–53, May, 1960.

Lockhart, Aileene and Bonnie Purdy: "Retention and Relearning of Gross Motor Skills after Long Periods of No Practice." *Research Quarterly, 33:* 265–272, May, 1962.

2

ARCHERY

Florence M. Ryder

Archery's popularity is on the march! Increasing enthusiasm for the sport is apparent throughout the country; more and more people are becoming interested in archery, not only as a temporary hobby, but as a continuing recreational outlet. It offers one of the most satisfactory fields of activity for individual, dual, or group competition and fun. Furthermore, for students with certain physical handicaps, archery offers a safe field for competition and recreation.

Numerous books have presented the fascinating history of archery. An increasing number of stimulating articles are appearing—all of which describe the sport as an unusual recreational experience. Most novices are not interested in historical facts until they have become somewhat proficient in the sport itself. However, something can be done to stimulate such an interest by presenting a summary of the place archery has taken in the sports history of the United States. References can be given and further interest thus aroused. If the instructor is well versed in the historical and romantic aspects of archery, she will easily influence her group to explore both the past records and the present trends in this sport. A list of suggested readings at the end of this chapter includes only a few of the many excellent references available for more detailed information on archery. All in all, archery has had, and will continue to have, an established and deservedly popular place in physical education and recreation programs in schools and colleges.

RANGE AND EQUIPMENT

Before the actual teaching of archery can be discussed, several other important considerations must be taken up. The question of *laying out the range* must be studied. This involves matters of safety, correct lighting, ground covering, the dimensions of the field and indoor range, and the equipment.

I. LAYING OUT THE RANGE

A. Safety.

1. The Backstop—Behind the Targets (For Safety and Time Saving).

a. MOST DESIRABLE. A well turfed, closely cropped terrace or hill is the ideal backstop for arrows.

b. LESS DESIRABLE. 1. Bunkers of straw, bound by burlap or canvas, placed well back in the field. 2. Burlap or felt curtains (at least two), one to be hung 10 yards behind the other, braced at either end by posts made of soft wood to prevent arrow breakage.

c. LEAST DESIRABLE. An open, unused space, 25 to 30 yards behind the target line. (If no bunker or backstop is available, an additional 25 yards behind the targets is necessary. This area should be kept well mowed.)

2. Protection at Sides of Range to Prevent Crossing.

a. Barberry hedging is a desirable safety measure for the sides of the range. This may be planted from the shooting line to a point 10 yards behind the target line if there is an open space behind the targets.

b. This same area may be roped off to prevent people from strolling across the range.

c. White lines can indicate the enclosure, but are the least adequate as a safety measure.

d. There should be a clear area of at least 20 yards on each side of the range.

3. One Shooting Line for All Archers Using Range. Staggering of targets has been practiced in some situations where individual anchors for targets are used. With secure individual anchoring, targets may be moved up or down the field, allowing all archers to shoot from the same line, regardless of their distance from their individual targets. Figure 2.1 illustrates such an arrangement.

B. Correct Lighting.

1. For morning shooting only, targets should be at the western end of the field.

2. For afternoon shooting only, targets should be at the eastern end of the field.

3. For all day shooting, targets should be at the northern end of the field.

C. Ground Covering.

1. Good turf, well cropped and well raked will prevent loss of arrows. All stones should be removed.

2. Good drainage is most essential.

D. Dimensions of Range.

1. Length.

a. The 60 yards of the National and American rounds and the 50 yards of the Columbia round necessitate having a range that is at least 65 yards long. The

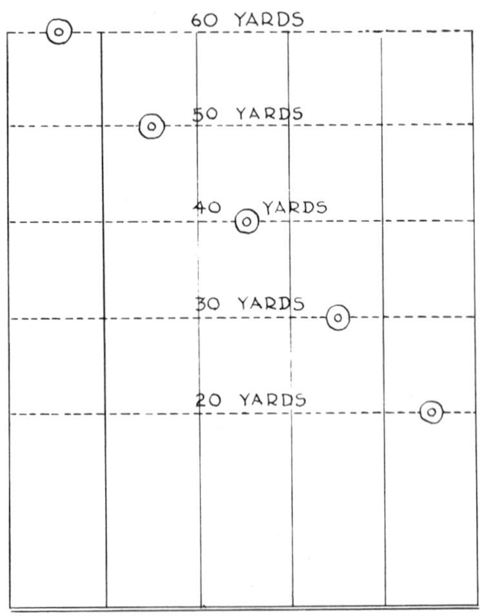

FIGURE 2.1 *Staggered ranges for safe shooting.*

given dimensions are for the actual length of range from the farthest shooting line to the targets.

b. If there is space, and if men are to use the range, there should be at least one lane 100 yards long.

2. Width. Width of minimum range for one target is 6 yards. For more than one target, measure 6 yards distance from the center of the gold to the center of the gold of the next target.

3. Laying Out the Indoor Range.

a. Dimensions. At least 35 yards long, 20 yards wide, and 9 feet high—thus sufficient for Olympic round.

b. Safety and prevention of arrow breakage.

1. A backstop, behind the targets, may be made of strips of loosely hung burlap, light carpets, felt, or bales of straw.

2. No approach to this end of the shooting area should be left unlocked.

E. Equipment for Outdoor Range.

1. Stationary quivers are placed directly opposite each target. These are placed on each shooting line (i.e., at 30, 40, and 50 yards from the target). These quivers should be set up just forward of the archer's stance at the shooting line.

2. Movable quivers may be used on either side of the stationary quiver.

3. Target and target stands, described under "Tackle" on page 20.

4. Bow stands and arrow racks for storage of tackle between classes, described on pages 18 and 19.

5. Bow racks, with a spiked end, that can accommodate at least four bows.

F. Equipment for Indoor Range.

1. Movable quivers sufficient in number for targets used.

2. Regulation targets, 36, 24, or 16 inches in diameter; stands as described on page 20.

3. Targets may be attached to burlap-covered bales of straw secured together and set on a "dolly" for easy movement.

4. Targets also may be set on old automobile tires with support in back.

5. Adequate indirect lighting that produces no glare on the targets is important.

II. ARCHERY TACKLE

Archery equipment, called *tackle,* includes various types of bows, arrows, and accessories. A bow, 6 to 8 arrows adapted to use with that bow and to the individual's specifications, an arm guard, shooting tab or glove, and, if needed, a movable quiver, a point of aim, and a pair of toe markers are required.

The initial expense of the tackle may seem large, but, considering the number of archers using it, it is relatively inexpensive. If the instructor insists that the equipment receive good care, if she teaches correct form, and if she requires immediate minor repairs, the cost of upkeep of the equipment is relatively small. The tackle provided should serve a class of from 10 to 15. It is well to remember that good tackle, though not cheap, will outlast poorer, less expensive equipment. Also, it is wise to find a dependable tackle maker and continue to work in cooperation with him.

BOWS

There should be *at least* one bow on hand for each student in a class. For an average class of 15 students, it is wise to provide 20 bows from which to choose. If financially practical, 30 bows will give a more accurate choice.

Material and Types. Until recently, most authorities agreed that yew, Osage, or lemonwood was the best material for bows, lemonwood being the least expensive of the three. This is still true of wood bows. Currently, a good quality of Fiberglas developed especially for bow material is being used successfully, and Fiberglas bows are becoming more and more popular because of their durability and faster cast. Whether laminated or solid, this new material offers a most usable and dependable bow. These are manufactured in both straight-end and recurve bows. The tips of the working recurve bow form a more graceful outline and also flow into the curve of the bow on the draw. On release the rebound to the original position adds cast to the bow. The tips of the static recurve describe sharp angles with the limbs, and each curve is rigid and does not bend with the limb on the draw. For classes where the equipment is used by many individuals during a given season, the purchase of Fiberglas working recurve or static recurve bows might wisely be staggered to include a few each year until there is a balance between the straight-end and recurve varieties. The preference of the classes—as well as the strain on the budget—can then determine which to replace in the future.

Lengths. Select a very few 5-foot bows, a few 5-foot 3-inch bows, and a majority of 5-foot 6-inch bows. It is becoming increasingly common among manufacturers to make all bows of the same length and suitable for a 27-inch arrow. This eliminates breakage by overdrawing. Also, a bow that draws 24 pounds at 27 inches will draw considerably less at 24 inches, thus giving a wider variation in drawing weight. Shorter bows are certainly more desirable for younger girls. The bows for such a group may be ordered on the basis of the average height of the group. Individually, of course, it is wise to own a bow approximately equal in length to one's own height.

Weights. Depending on the average strength of the students in the group, 18 to 28 pounds pull is a good average range in weight, with the majority around 22 pounds. Eighteen to 22 pounds should be provided for beginners; 20 to 24 for intermediates; 24 to 28 for advanced archers. It may be well to allow beginners to use lighter bows until good form is achieved.

Handles. Those affording long wear and good grips are of cordovan leather. Cord or cork also are acceptable. Some bows have laminated built-up wooden handles, which may be fitted to the hand. Fiberglas also is used.

Arrow Rest. An arrow rest, a built-up shelf attached to the bow above the handle at the side, should allow an arrow to leave the bow at an exact location with every draw. (It is more important in sight aiming than when the point of aim method is used.)

Other Requisites. A new bow should be examined for even and equal bend in both limbs, from nocks to handle; return to nearly straight outline when unstrung; equal division of the entire length of the belly when the bow is strung; smoothly grooved nocks.

BOW STRINGS

Extra strings, at least equaling in number the bows used, should be ordered and kept in a tin box. Occasionally it is difficult and expensive to obtain good linen strings, but synthetic strings of Fortisan or Dacron stand up very well under hard use. These should be light in weight, well waxed, and should have good servings. They may be ordered either in lengths to fit bows purchased or in 6-foot strings adjustable at the lower nock to the various bow lengths. Strings should be strong enough to prevent breakage, which slows up shooting time. A small knot of thread should be placed on the serving to mark the spot at which the archer nocks his arrow. The knot should be placed so that the arrow is at right angles to the string as its nock rests against this knot.

BOW STANDS

Stands or racks can either be purchased or made locally, and will vary widely in price. Each should accommodate 12 bows on either side. The number of bows used daily will determine the number of racks needed for class use. The stands are similar in appearance to a portable coat rack. They can be made easily and according to specific directions by the school or local carpenter. They must be light enough to be moved comfortably, and should be supplied with canvas bands or other supports at the top so that the bows will not be blown off between classes. Hooks at each end are useful for arm guards, gloves, and tabs. These racks are for daily class use. The storage of bows is discussed on page 21.

Where transportation of equipment requires time and energy, an archery cart on small wheels may assist in the facility of handling tackle. It can be made to hold all equipment needed on the range except the targets. Such a cart is described in an article in the *Journal of Health, Physical Education, and Recreation,* March 1954.

ARROWS

	Required number	
Fair	Good	Excellent
72 (6 doz.)	144 (12 doz.)	240 (20 doz.)

Material. Most authorities agree that for the hard usage that school or club equipment receives, Port Orford cedar or Norwegian pine is the most acceptable and satisfactory wood for self arrows. They are usually 5⁄16 of an inch in diameter. Matched arrows of wood should have a footing, either of two- or four-point variety, which greatly lengthens the life of the arrows. Aluminum arrows and Fiberglas arrows have become increasingly popular. Wood and metal arrows are sold in matched sets with great variation in price. Matched sets are preferable, but in many situations probably are better for personal rather than school or club purchase. There is no doubt that matched sets improve scoring and thus reduce discouragement, so it may be wise progressively to increase the number of matching sets for a given situation. They should be guaranteed to be range or flight tested, or to have accurate technical specifications as to spine and weight in grains, and balance point of the completed arrow.

Economy of Purchase. The best method of purchasing arrows is to buy them in lots of 2, 4, or 6 dozens in sets of 8. Divide the amount alloted to the purchase of arrows between good cedar arrows of the dowel variety and medium-priced aluminum or Fiberglas arrows.

Lengths. Twenty-two to 24-inch arrows are necessary for short-armed girls who use shorter bows. Twenty-five-inch arrows are a good average. Twenty-six-inch arrows are much in demand; 27-inch arrows are for taller, longer armed girls.

Markings. If practical, arrows may be labeled as to length with India ink and the mark then covered with lacquer. This facilitates correct choice and accurate replacement after use.

Other Requisites. Samples of arrows presented for approval or rejection should be examined closely, but more important to the instructor is the fulfillment of her order by the tackle-maker according to given specifications. A new order should be examined for:

FINISH AND CREST. A lacquered, well-polished wooden arrow withstands use and weather well. Lacquer is preferable to varnish because it stays cleaner. A brightly colored crest helps to locate lost arrows and thus decreases scoring and retrieving time. The crest also establishes ownership.

SHAFT. The shaft must be completely round and straight as one looks down its length.

NOCKS. The material used for nocks varies with the tackle-maker, but replaceable nocks are commonly used. Some form of reinforcing at the nock increases the length of life of the arrow.

FEATHERS. Feathers should be checked from the nock end to see if the feathers are placed symmetrically and if the cock feather is at right angles to the nock for three-vaned arrows. The type of vane varies with the fletcher but has little effect on accuracy. The feathers are commonly slightly spiraled on the shaft for target shooting and may be either real or synthetic. Plastic vanes have much to recommend them, but many prefer turkey feathers. Four-vaned arrows recently have become popular. These are set with 90 degrees between each two vanes, or they may be paired with 75 degrees between the vanes of the top and bottom pairs and 105 degrees between the others at the sides (Figure 2.2).

PILE. The pile or tip is the covered point of the arrow and is important on two counts for target shooting. It should be of the parallel type and must be strongly attached.

ARROW RACKS

A rack, approximately 40 by 28 inches, holding at least 12 individual sets of 8 arrows each, may be made by the local carpenter and seems the best way of storing arrows. The rack also provides an easy means of transporting the arrows to the shooting range from the equipment room. There should be 12 lines of holes, ½ inch in diameter, bored at 3-inch intervals, 8 in a line across the width of the rack. This is duplicated by a second level, 10 inches below the first and 6 inches above the base, with identical holes bored directly below those on the upper surface. Below the two levels is the base, upon which are rows of matching cups placed directly below the holes to receive the arrow tips. Such an arrangement keeps the arrows neatly in place in their own sets. End handles on such racks make carrying easier, and these handles can be marked at 6 to 10-inch intervals so that string-to-handle distance can be measured by them. Each arrow set should be marked at the end of its row by a bit of adhesive tape on which the length of that arrow set is written with indelible pencil.

QUIVERS

There are four usable types. On the range a *stationary quiver* may be placed opposite each target at each shooting line. Wooden stakes painted green are sunk in the earth far enough for good support. A wire ring for arrows and a

FIGURE 2.2 *Two types of four-vaned arrows.*

wire hook for the bow are attached to the stake. Iron *movable ground quivers* also are practical and may be bought reasonably. These should have tight fitting rubber tubing around the bow hook or other means of holding the bow without damage. This type can be made easily and inexpensively from wire coat hangers and bound with friction tape. *Movable indoor quivers* often are made of cardboard tubing or bamboo mounted on a square of wood so that they may stand alone for indoor shooting. *Leather wearable quivers* can be worn on the belt or over the shoulder for roving, clout shooting, archery golf, and rabbit hunts. Such quivers may be bought at varying costs.

Other Suggestions. Cardboard mailing tubes sealed with large corks, mounted squares of synthetic fiber or large open-mouthed jars may be used as substitutes if budget curtailment is necessary.

TARGETS AND TARGET STANDS

Regulation 4-foot targets approximately 50 inches in diameter are required. They should be about 4 to 5 inches thick and made of roped straw well bound and sewed spirally. Cheap targets are not economical. When targets have been shot thin, they may be reinforced with a backing of 4 or 5 layers of ordinary corrugated paper from large packing cartons. A stiff backing, such as heavy cardboard or building board, will support the target when placed behind it. This prevents the typical sagging of the target on the stand.

Stands also can be made locally, and thus will vary widely in price. The regulation standard consists of 3 soft pine boards, 3 inches wide by 1 inch thick and 6 feet long. The lower end of each of the 3 boards should be cut at a slight angle to act as a ground spike. A 4-inch bolt through holes bored at the upper ends of the uprights holds them together. Lengths of rope to keep the tripod from spreading apart are valuable aids in setting out the targets. Three hooks are generally used on the tripod, 1 at the top to receive the target above, and 1 for each of the 2 front legs, about 3 feet 9 inches from the top, on which to rest the target. The target face should be inclined backward 12 to 18 degrees with the vertical. The center of the gold should measure 51 inches from the ground. The legs of the tripod should be covered with discarded bicycle tires painted green. This removes some of the necessity of withdrawing arrows from the legs of the standard, as most arrows will rebound from the rubber. It also increases the length of life of the tripod itself. As substitutes for rubber, lengths of burlap or of corrugated paper painted green may be used. It is wise to tie the target stand securely to the ground with rope and ground hooks. This prevents tipping and thus arrow breakage.

TARGET FACES

Preferably faces should be of light canvas or sized muslin painted with a gold or yellow center 9.6 inches in diameter, surrounded by 4 concentric circles, each 4.8 inches wide. The outside edge beyond the white outer ring should be at least 1 inch in width, and is known as the "petticoat." If targets are to be left out in inclement weather, they should be protected by a covering. A waterproof canvas hood approximately 52 inches long serves very well.

FINGER PROTECTION

Finger protection varies with the individual archer, but protection must be provided for any amount of shooting. A shooting *glove* is efficient but relatively expensive for class use. Light, smooth cordovan *leather finger tabs* may be purchased or made. Such tabs also may be cut from a discarded inner tube. *Tips* cut to fit individual shooting fingers usually are made of light, smooth leather and are cooler to wear than a glove or tab. A glove's 3 middle fingers may be reinforced by stitching on durable but pliable leather tips. Shooting gloves should be marked with the athletic association's mark or some other form of identification to prevent inadvertent removal from the range.

ARM GUARDS

Arm guards or bracers should be of thick, pliable leather, 7 to 8 inches long, and either laced to encircle the forearm or made striplike and buckled on. These also should be marked for identification purposes. One should be provided for each archer and always should be worn during shooting.

REPAIR KIT

A compact repair kit should contain pliers for pulling out embedded arrows from trees; beeswax; box for extra bow strings; Duco cement and wax; scissors; jackknife; heavy linen thread for servings; pen and indelible ink; ½-inch wide adhesive tape; glass headed pins if inexpensive, homemade sights are to be used; 12-inch ruler; bits of leather for rubbing bows and strings after waxing.

SCORE CARDS

Two types of cards, daily tally cards and tournament record cards, are used. If there are many enrolled, the score cards can be multigraphed and pasted on cardboard for each target for each section. This is not so satisfactory to the individual archer, however, and should be avoided if possible. To keep the individual score cards from blowing away, the students usually hook them on the bow hooks of their stance quivers. The cardboard group record may be kept in the possession of one named scorer for each target, or it may be tied to the back of the targets by the instructor before class. Unused score cards may be left in a box; labeled and used ones for each section may be clipped or bound together.

MISCELLANEOUS EQUIPMENT

A neat compartment box can be made, approximately 20 by 18 inches, which can accommodate all the necessary "extras." This should eliminate the forgetting of some bit of equipment needed on the range. The arrangement of the compartments would be based on the size of the things to be stored therein: points of aim, pencils, pliers, score cards, and bottle caps or golf tees for "toe markers."

QUIVER RACKS

If many movable metal quivers are used, a rack to support them is worth having for neatness in the equipment room. Such a rack can be made of two endboards connected at the base and top. The base should have a deep curb to prevent the points from slipping out, and the top should have two 1-inch slots to catch and hold the rings of the quivers.

III. ARCHERY TACKLE ROOM

The room known as the Tackle Room should be the meeting place of both advanced archers and beginners. The dimensions of an adequate room are 6 feet in width by 12 feet in length by 9 feet in height. Three wide shelves may occupy the full length of one side, leaving wall space for hanging bows on two of the other walls. The bottom shelf should be high enough so that the arrow racks may stand below it. The shelves may hold boxes for "extras," a box for arrows in need of repair, special equipment, such as box targets for archery golf, and quivers. There should be sufficient wall space for a bulletin board and the daily "scoring" target.

The room temperature should be kept as nearly at 65 degrees as possible, and a humidifier should be used to keep the bows from drying out; no radiator is needed within the room itself. In summer the arrows should be covered and kept in a dry room with moth balls to protect the feathers.

The wall bow rack may be constructed by using a series of rubber-covered pegs consecutively placed and about 6 feet from the floor. The distance between pegs is 8 inches. Above each peg should be a bit of adhesive tape numbered in indelible pencil. Each bow should be marked with the number of its peg. The bows should be classified from the lightest to the heaviest, and a bow may be reclassified whenever it loses cast. If there is no provision made for hanging the shooting gloves and tabs and arm guards on the field bow racks, boxes for these articles should be placed within easy reach. The repair kit does not have to be taken to the range each day, but it should be kept adequately filled during the shooting season. The miscellaneous equipment box should be on the shelf ready for the instructor of the first class of the day. If such is not used, the "extras" should be taken out individually by the first instructor of the day and returned by the last one.

CLASSES

I. SIZE AND CALIBER OF CLASSES

In planning the actual teaching of archery, one must determine the number of students in one class somewhat by the number of targets, bows, and arrows available. But from the point of view of the number who will learn most in one hour from one instructor, it is obvious that a small group is preferable. Ten girls for a like number of targets is ideal, and it is wise to provide no fewer than 5 targets for 15 archers. Interest should not be discouraged, however, as a larger number can be handled. The course can be greatly aided by the assistance of the advanced archers in the student body. In both schools and colleges, these student coaches can help in instructing and increase their own interest in the sport by so doing.

As in other sports, the classes should be arranged according to the varying ability and experience of the students. The novice or *beginners* classes should be separate from those for intermediates, if possible. *Intermediate* archers are those who have had the groundwork in elementary form and enough shooting experience to be placed beyond the novice group. Usually classes have to be of mixed caliber, but the instructor should have beginners as well as intermediates cover material planned for a given week. Instructions for the *advanced* archers, those with superior ability and previous experience in the sport, follow on pages 40 to 44.

II. OTHER CONSIDERATIONS IN ARRANGING CLASSES

Preliminary

A. Allot free time on the range for practice and competition.

B. Arrange for class meetings indoors on rainy days when lectures, movies, and demonstrations of use and care of equipment can be given, if no indoor range is provided.

C. Stress safe conduct of all the class—e.g., all shooting at once, the recovery of arrows at one time, proper use of equipment, and so forth.

D. Check the equipment after each class, and replace it in good order and condition—e.g., see that the bows are unstrung, the arrows are clean, and that no frayed strings are used.

E. Report any breakage or loss of equipment, and put aside anything that needs repairs.

Having considered these preliminary steps, we may now turn to the actual teaching of archery. Outlines for a suggested 8 weeks' course of 16 lessons for beginners, intermediates, and advanced archers are presented. The lesson period is planned for 50-minute duration. The schedule is elastic and should be adapted to varying conditions according to the ability and progress within the group. Detailed explanations may be found directly after the outlines.

SUGGESTED OUTLINES FOR CLASS PROCEDURES DURING CLEAR WEATHER

I. BEGINNERS

A. First Week.

1. Bows already braced for number of beginners in each class.
2. Instructor's choice of tackle for each student.
3. Teaching of parts of bow and arrow, names of miscellaneous equipment.
4. Elementary care of all equipment.
5. Stressing of safety.
6. Practice in fundamental positions without tackle and with tackle.
7. Shooting at 20-yard range, or possibly at 15 yards.

B. Second Week.

1. Checking by instructor of tackle chosen.
2. Reviewing of parts of tackle and of safety procedures.
3. Practice in stringing and unstringing bow. braces
4. Explanation of point of aim, the range finder, and adjustment necessary to correct point of aim.
5. Shooting at 20-yard range; at 30 yards if ready.
6. Demonstration of retrieving arrows, from target; from grass.
7. Corrections of individuals' points of aim.
8. Lesson in scoring.

C. Third Week.

1. Review of point of aim method and use of range finder.

2. Explanation of use of bow sight (optional).

3. Shooting at 30-yard range in unison and remaining ends under observation. (Shooting time divided between 20- and 30-yard ranges.)

4. Correction of off-center groupings.

D. Fourth Week.

1. Working in pairs with correction of partner's form while shooting trial end at 40 yards.

2. Taking of photographs in groups of three.

3. Explanation of individual faults by instructor. See page 38.

E. Fifth Week.

1. Shooting of at least two ends at 50 yards.

2. Discussion and explanation of photographs in groups of three.

3. Starting of the daily ladder tournament.

F. Sixth Week.

1. Beginning of the first Columbia round.

2. Individual coaching for those needing more attention.

G. Seventh Week.

1. Recording of the first Columbia round in two days.

2. Continuation of ladder tournament.

H. Eighth Week.

1. Challenge tournament for those below the finalists.

2. Announcement of class winners in various sections.

The eight weeks' plan presented above will now be considered in detail:

A. First Week.

1. Two wise procedures are to have the bows braced beforehand by the instructor and to use arrows longer than necessary to draw to anchor point. Extra bows not used by the class should be quickly unstrung by the instructor.

2. As the class lines up according to height, the instructor can readily pick out the length and weight of the bow and length of arrow adaptable to each. This is accomplished by judging the girl's strength so that she will not be "overbowed." The length of arrow is measured from the center of the chin, (with the head turned to the left) to the left fist, (raised to the side at shoulder level with the left elbow almost extended). For beginners, a quick approximation of required arrow length can be made by holding a yardstick at shoulder level against the breastbone at the base of the neck with the fingers reaching forward along the stick. Note the numbers of inches at the end of the fingers. This gives the measurement of the arrow needed in relation to the arm length. An arm guard and finger protection of some sort should be fitted. As the equipment is given out, the instructor can quickly state the reasons for the weight and length of bow and length of arrows for each student and the meaning of the weight of bow.

3. Teaching the parts of the bow and arrow (upper and lower limbs, back, belly, nocks, arrow rest, arrow plate; pile, shaft, foreshaft, shaftment, crest) as well as the adjustment of finger and forearm protection, comes next. (Figures 2.3, 2.4, and 2.5).

4. Instruction in the correct handling and care of tackle should include emphasis on its beauty and its cost. Besides the admonitions about the bow, which are stressed in the safety rules, students should be taught to:

a. Avoid dropping or leaning on the bow; avoid shooting with the bow over- or under-strung, or with the string twisted.

b. Rest the *bow* rather than the string on the bow hook, with the bow at right angles to the shooting line.

c. Prevent breakage by turning in any bow that has a frayed serving or string.

d. Request directions for adjusting the bow string if it is over- or under-drawn.

e. Check to be sure that an arrow of the correct length is used.

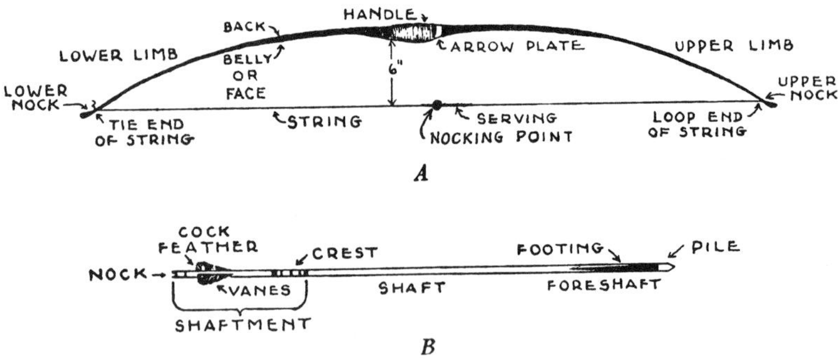

FIGURE 2.3 *A, Parts of the bow. B, Parts of the arrow.*

f. Place the cock feather at right angles to the string when nocking the arrow.

g. Place the arrows loosely in the arrow ring of the quiver between shots.

h. Carry arrows at their tip ends, (preferably between the fingers) with the feathers separated.

i. Wipe the arrows clean for shooting as well as for return to the arrow rack at the end of class.

j. At the end of the period, return accessory equipment (gloves, tabs, arm guards) to the storage box or hook provided for them. The file number of the bow, according to the weight, should be attached to the bow below the handle by means of a small bit of adhesive tape on which the number has been written with indelible pencil or ink. This number should be memorized so that that particular bow may be used repeatedly if it proves satisfactory—or avoided if not desirable.

5. The next step is to stress safety. The necessary rules should be as few as possible, and also direct and positive.

a. Leave the shooting line *only* on signal from the instructor.

b. Draw the bow *only* after being shown how.

c. Draw the bow *only* with an arrow on the string.

d. Draw the bow *only* when no one is in front of the shooting line.

e. Draw the arrow up to the tip but *not* within the bow.

f. Be responsible for the safety of your fellow archer as well as your own.

g. Use arrows of the correct length for the given bow. These safety rules should be quickly reviewed at the beginning of each lesson with a beginning group.

6. When the instructor is confident that the students understand the safety rules and know the parts of the bow and arrow by name, then she may proceed with teaching the fundamental positions.

The following description of method is specifically for a right-handed person. For a left-handed person, the reverse of all described procedures should be followed. Place any left-handed students at the left end of the shooting line with their backs to the remainder of the class. It is best to have the students line up on the shooting line, place their equipment in the ground quivers, and await directions. The first instruction is given without bows.

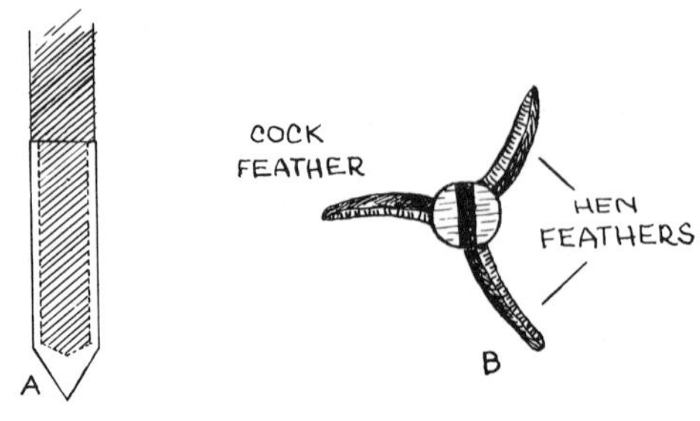

FIGURE 2.4 *A, Parallel pile. B, Spacing of feathers.*

a. **Position of Body and Feet.**

(*1*) The addressing of the target. An easy stance: feet about 10 inches or so apart; the weight evenly divided between the two feet; heels about opposite the center leg of the tripod, straddling the shooting line.

(*2*) The left shoulder pointing directly at the target but *not* elevated. A good test of whether the individual is in line with her target is to have her stretch out her left arm directly from her side toward the center of the target, then turn her head to check. If she is not in line, a slight adjustment in position, forward or backward, can correct it. Place toe markers at tip of each shoe to show foot placement.

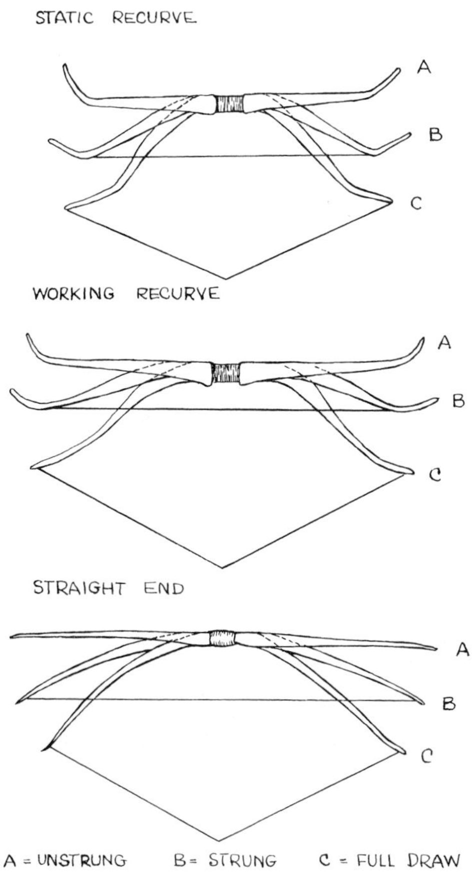

FIGURE 2.5 *Three types of bows.*

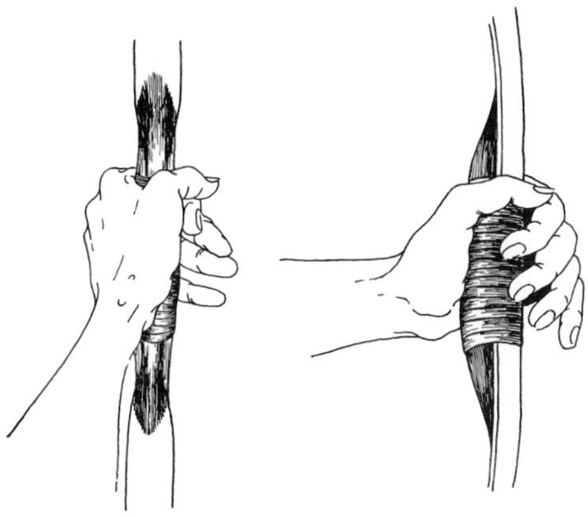

FIGURE 2.6 *A, archer's view of bow hand. B, side view of bow hand.*

(*3*) Turning of the erect head to the left, the only change from the body's right angle position in relation to the target. No other part of the body turns toward it. Eyes should be level.

The class should rest a minute, moving their feet freely, and then repeat the correct stance with the bow arm extended toward the target to check each position. At this time the instructor should watch for uneven balance and incorrect placement of feet.

Instruction from here on should be with tackle.

b. **Bow Hand and Arm.**

(*1*) The *bow hand* should grasp the bow handle with the flat of the left fist at the top of the handle; the fingers and thumb holding the bow firmly but not tightly; the first thumb knuckle nearly to the center of the inside surface of the handle as shown in Figure 2.6.

Watch for: (a) Incorrect position of thumb and wrist. (b) Swinging outward of the palm.

(*2*) The *bow arm*. With the bow hand placed as directed above, the bow arm is elevated sideways toward the target to shoulder height, with a very slight "give" at the elbow. This causes the elbow to point backward, and produces a decided lowering of the shoulder, which relaxes tension throughout the arm.

Watch for: (a) Hunching of the left shoulder. (b) Pushing throughout the arm, which causes the left elbow to be straightened dangerously, bringing it within the string. (c) "Rolling" of the arm, which tends to make the elbow point downward instead of backward-downward. (d) Insufficient extension of the left elbow. The correct form should be practiced with a bent, but undrawn, bow several times until each student has attained an acceptable position in which to hold the bow at full draw.

c. **The String Hand and Arm.**

(*1*) The bow is held horizontally at the side (upper limb forward, the string toward the thigh) by the bow hand.

(*2*) Without an arrow, the right hand is brought toward the string, palm up, index finger separated slightly from the two center fingers.

(*3*) The three fingers, quite straight, reach under and at right angles to the string, the last joints flexed over the string. The distal finger cushions should be pushed toward the finger tips by the "roll" of the string.

(*4*) The hand and wrist are flat, continuing a direct line to the elbow.

Under strict observation, a draw of a few inches may be allowed, but the admonition of never drawing a bow and never releasing the string without an arrow should be stressed. The repetition of the draw even for a few inches will give the novice a feeling for the direct pull, which is important. Correct stance at full draw is illustrated in Figure 2.7.

d. **Nocking.** This is the next step after training in fundamental positions. The nocking method described involves the minimum number of changes in hand positions (Figure 2.8).

(*1*) The arrow is grasped at the nock end by the three shooting fingers and the thumb.

(*2*) It is placed over the string and over the bow, resting on the arrow plate.

(*3*) The arrow is drawn backward until the nock reaches the string.

(*4*) It is twirled until the cock feather is "up," that is, at right angles to the string, and the string is slipped into the nock with the arrow against the nocking point.

FIGURE 2.7 *Correct stance at full draw.*

(*5*) The fingers automatically drop into shooting position on the string with the index finger above the arrow and the second and third fingers below. Then the student is ready for the draw. The movement should be repeated until the fingers are accustomed to the new coordination.

The bow elevation and point of aim may change, but the nocking point is always constant.

(*6*) The fingers should just "feel" the arrow, not grasp it. If the fingers hold the arrow, it will tend to roll away from the bow.

e. **Continued Movement of String and Bow Arms.**

(*1*) With the arrow nocked and the fingers of both hands in correct position, the draw is started from the side until the left hand is approximately at shoulder height and aiming directly at the target, shoulder low, elbow slightly bent, as previously directed.

(*2*) The string hand pulls the string back slowly, close to the left arm, until the index finger of the right hand is directly under the jaw, with the tip of the index finger touching under the chin. This is the low anchor recommended for target shooting.

(*3*) The thumb is folded just parallel to the index finger and should lie close in against the archer's throat.

(*4*) The tip of the chin, not tilted upward, should be the definite spot which the tip of the index finger should touch on each and every draw. This point is known as the *anchor point* of the drawing process and must always be reached.

(*5*) The string should touch the center of the chin and the tip of the nose.

(*6*) The arrow is drawn its full length until the tip is just at the left side and forward edge of the bow. The length of the draw is the same for each range.

(*7*) The elbow, as it is pulled backward, should be at shoulder level, so that a direct line of stress is applied.

NOTE: The draw has been analyzed by parts, but actually happens in a well-coordinated movement of the two arms started at the side and completed at shoulder level.

Watch for: (a) Shifting of the body weight. (b) Any change in head position, except the complete, direct turn to the left looking over the left shoulder. (c) Any poor drawing of the string that would endanger the left breast.

***f.* Holding, Aiming, and Loosing.** These are difficult for the beginner and, although closely allied, must be analyzed separately.

(*1*) With the bow full-drawn, the student must be told to "hold" the

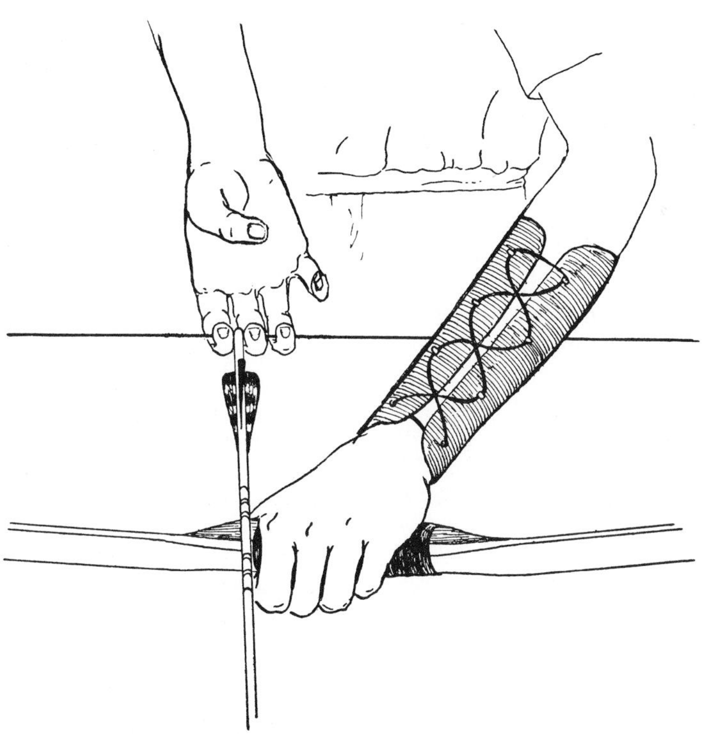

FIGURE 2.8 *Correct nocking position showing cock feather.*

draw until the act of aiming is completed. The length of time required for holding depends on the adjustment necessary in the aiming process, but should not be hurried. A conscious check for lack of motion of the bow arm should be made.

When too rapid draws are repeated, the class may be asked to draw slowly and to hold until the instructor says "loose." Each individual releases after a different period of time, but at the start, this suggested "holding" of the draw is often realized only by controlling it in unison.

(*2*) The *point of aim method* is agreed upon as being practical for target shooting. "Sights" are usually not practical for beginners' use immediately, but may be introduced as soon as acceptable form is achieved. The important idea to instill in a beginner's mind is that the pile of the arrow must be held on a particular spot (the point of aim), which is in vertical line with the gold. This differs from range to range.

NOTE: Details in the point of aim method of aiming are discussed under the procedure during second week for beginners, page 32. Sight aiming is discussed on page 34.

(*3*) Loosing is a much debated question, but again simplicity and directness in releasing the string at full draw is the best method. With the string hand at the anchor point, thumb against the throat, as soon as the aiming process is over the fingers should release their pull by opening simultaneously to complete extension. This allows the string to roll off the fingers smoothly and evenly; they alone move on releasing. Any sideward movement of the fingers on the release pulls the string away from its forward path.

Watch for: (a) Creeping (forward movement of string hand or backward swing of bow arm). (b) Relaxing (letting either arm and shoulder, or both, move).

NOTE: Some teach a loosing technique as a continuation of the movement of the two arms in the direction established at the time of release. This provides a smooth loose with the fingers drawn across the throat from anchor point backward approximately two inches. This may be taught at the time of teaching the release, or later when a more accurate anchoring has been acquired.

7. Shooting at 20-yard range:

Have the beginners, with their equipment, lined up on the 20-yard line. Directly in line with the center of each target and about 5 yards in front of it, a piece of wood (painted white and with a nail at one end) should be stuck in the ground. Under the observation of the instructor and the student assistant, have two students come to full draw position; their left eyes should be closed or partly closed, and sighting made with the right eyes. If each has the string hand and arm in correct alignment, with the anchor point at the chin held firmly and the bow arm in easy position, she can give attention to focusing the tip of the arrow on the white bit of wood. This should show just above the arrow tip. Wherever the hits may be, the student should keep concentrating on that spot, the "point of aim." She should get as good an arrow "grouping" as possible; that is, a close proximity of the arrows when shot. Each one shooting, as well as those awaiting their turns for instruction, will learn a great deal in observing this "grouping."

The shooting of at least three arrows should be observed by the instructor; another three may be shot independently. The instructor and assistant should proceed on down the shooting line, repeating the same method with each student. On a signal from the instructor, the class should rest their bows with the backs against the bow hooks and pointing at the targets. Then each retrieves her arrows.

With the aid of the instructors, the piece of wood used as point of aim may be adjusted as necessary, but always should be placed directly in a vertical line with the gold. If the arrow grouping is low, the bit of white wood should be placed behind the center leg of the tripod. If not visible there, the student may use the center spot where the target meets the central leg of the tripod, or a central spot on the target. If the grouping spot is high, the learner should bring her point of aim out from the target toward the shooting line about 3 or 4 feet. The important result from the first shooting attempts is to have the arrows grouped closely. The fact should be stressed that grouping is much more important at the start than hitting the target at random, for it proves that the archer is using steady, consistent form. If the six arrows are found "all around the clock," and sometimes even on a neighbor's target, the archer is not remembering the fundamentals of form, or is not "holding" on her point of aim.

As the second "end" is shot, the instructor and the student assistant, starting from the center and moving outward on the line, should assist in the shooting of at least two arrows by each member of the class. Students should be allowed to shoot the remainder by themselves; or they may wait for the instructor to return if they require help. It should be emphasized that the archer should never look up from her point of aim until she has heard the hit, and that she should analyze others' shots as she waits. After the first end has been shot, the class should be grouped together and allowed to analyze their mistakes and to tell what should be done to correct them. They should understand that differences "up and down" the target may be due to incorrect points of aim or to other faults, but that differences right and left are due primarily to errors in form. These are listed on page 46.

The clock system of describing hits on the target is interesting and practicable in assisting correction of shooting. The target face can be considered the face of a clock. The hits are described as though they had been shot into a clock's face. For example, a twelve o'clock red would be a hit that had reached the target just directly above the center and in the red ring. By having a shooting partner note the positions of certain hits, slight corrections may be made that will increase accuracy in shooting.

Each day students should replace tackle in good condition and in an orderly manner so that it will become a natural habit. Each student should unstring her bow, and place it on the bow rack. Arrows should be wiped clean and replaced in correct positions on the arrow stand. Auxiliary equipment (such as gloves, bracers and points of aim) should be in their designated places also.

B. Second Week.

1. At the first meeting, the students should choose their own equipment, but their choice should be passed upon by the instructor. They should have all the required equipment they used during the previous week, plus their white points of aim, and also a score card and pencil. Assistance should be offered in putting on arm guards and finger protection. The equipment, except for the bows, should be placed up at their quivers.

2. Returning in a group, the students should review the parts of the bow and arrow, as well as their responsibility for equipment and safety.

3. Then they are ready to learn how to string and unstring the bow, and, with the group in a shallow semicircle around the instructor, this may be demonstrated. This must be done slowly, and each step should be carefully explained.

a. The bow grasped at the handle with the left hand, with the back of the bow toward the archer, the bow string hanging down. The hand must not be moved from the handle until after the completion of the stringing or unstringing.

b. The string not twisted around the bow and hanging directly down from the bow.

c. The nock of the lower limb held against the instep of the left foot, not on the ground; the bow held diagonally across the body from left to right (Figure 2.9).

d. The "heel" of the right palm placed on the bow just below the eye of the string, the index finger and thumb reaching just lightly to the eye.

e. The actual "bracing" of the bow is the result of a *pulling* by the *left* hand and a *pushing* by the *right.* With

FIGURE 2.9 *Position for bracing.*

sufficient slack in the string, the eye is slipped into the nock by the finger tips.

NOTE: At first, the class should try just that: pulling and pushing simultaneously so that the strings hang loosely away from the bows. Some instructors teach the stringing in reverse of the directions just given, i.e., handle in right hand, and so on. If taught and practiced as described above, a change of hand is not necessary since the bow hand is used at the handle in the bracing process. Otherwise there seems to be no greater benefit from one method than from the other.

Observe: That the fingers are not pushing. That each arm is doing its share of the work.

When the students have the feeling for it, they should be taught to reach lightly to the eye of the string with the fingers and slip it ahead of the pushing "heel" of the hand and into the nock. The fingers should not be on the inside of the bow for, if they are, a painful pinch may result. Also the string should be centered. At this time it should be explained what a *fistmele* is—the approximate 6-inch measurement offered by the width of the palm with an extended thumb. This is used to measure the distance between the bow at the handle and the string. However, the distance will vary with individuals and thus be inaccurate. A greater distance between handle and string usually is found in a strung recurve bow. The distance used here is from 8 to 10 inches, rather than the 6 inches with a straight end bow. This is measured from the back of the bow to string. The same method of bracing can be used for the recurve bow unless it is too heavy. The manufacturer's directions should be followed. If the bow is too rigid, a jig should be used rather than the "step-through" technique for the average girl (Figure 2.10).

If 6 to 10-inch bits of doweling have been provided, or if the handles of the bow rack have been marked in 6 to 10-inch lengths, each student may measure her own more satisfactorily. The unstringing (or unbending) is the reverse process of stringing. The bow should be held precisely the same as for stringing and the pushing-pulling process should continue until there is slack in the string. This time, however, the index finger actually "pulls" out the eye from the nock.

The class now should be ready for a review of the fundamental positions of bow and string arms and hands and of stance. They should return to the shooting line and take the correct standing position. The entire class should replace the equipment on the quivers, take the funda-

FIGURE 2.10 *Bracing recurve bow. A, Step-through method. B, By use of bow-bracing jig.*

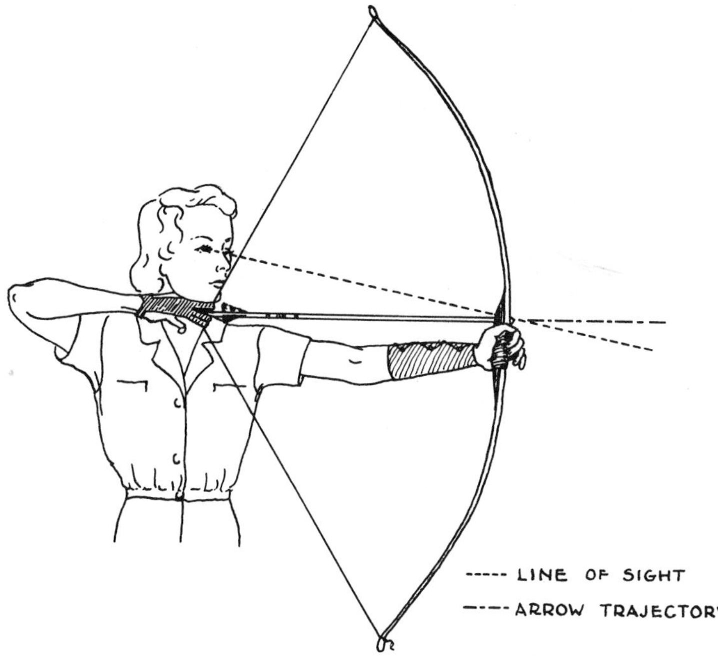

FIGURE 2.11 *Relation of string to nose, chin and anchor point. This is the low anchor used in target shooting.*

FIGURE 2.12 *High anchor used in instinctive method.*

mental position for the beginning of the draw, and without the use of the bow and arrow continue into a full draw, observing all requirements of good form. They should then take the full draw position of the bow hand and arm, pointing the index finger of the bow hand at the point of aim.

Next the nocking of an arrow and holding it in correct shooting position with the right hand should be passed upon by the instructor or by the student coach. Those who have difficulties should be paired and should practice *finger shooting* with partners, criticizing each other's form as well as release. In finger shooting, the archer's partner faces her and offers her right index finger pointing upward as the "string." This should be placed about at the middle of the archer's elevated forearm. The archer reaches to the "string" with her three string fingers and pulls it up to anchor point. When at full draw and offering resistance, the "string" is allowed to roll off the archer's fingers, as shown in Figure 2.13.

4. Aiming in general should be presented at this time. Many prefer to teach beginners the point of aim method. Others believe in presenting the use of sights immediately. Most authorities believe that, for beginners, either of these two should be taught. Those who are enthusiastic about field archery claim that, with the accomplishment of good form, the field archery method of aiming should be taught. Although this usually is practiced at shorter ranges and for a variety of uses (hunting, fishing, novelty shoots, and games), it can be taught easily in class by changing certain aspects of form. It should also adapt itself to use in a small indoor range. For the average beginner, however, it has been found that the point of aim and/or bow sight method is preferable for target shooting.

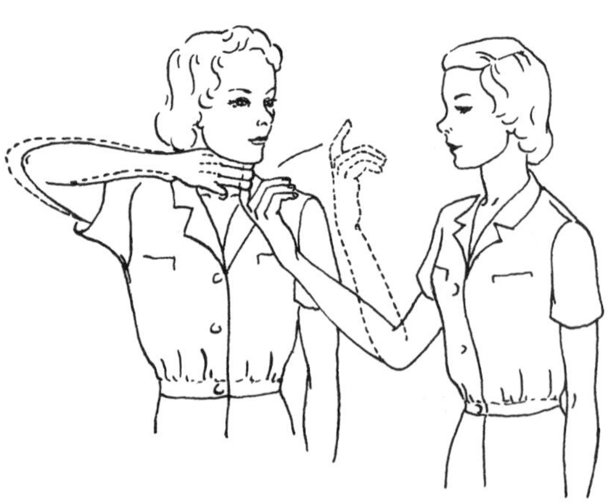

FIGURE 2.13 *Finger shooting.*

(*a*) Point of Aim. First the point of aim method can be offered. This use of an auxiliary spot at which to aim is essential to make the necessary adjustment between the straight line of vision and the trajectory of the arrow (Figure 2.14). This may be determined by use of the range finder discussed. For each bow and its matching set of arrows, there is a *point blank range,* one spot from which an individual may hit the gold while aiming directly at its center; this may or may not be the range from which the individual is shooting. If the archer changes her shooting distance, as from range to range, she must also change her point of aim. For if she continues to aim at the center of the gold at different ranges, her arrow will fall short or fly behind the target, depending on her distance from the target. Use of a point of aim at varying distances from the target is necessary because of the difference between the line of vision and the trajectory of the arrow. At close range the arrow flies in a less curved path; at a greater range it describes a greater arc in flight. At close range the eye sights the arrow tip well below the gold of the target. The difference in levels between the eye and the anchor point is several inches. These facts must be recognized in learning to aim. In sighting, the right eye focuses on the arrow tip by looking to the right of the string and to the left of the bow and holding the arrow tip directly on the point of aim. If using a sight, it must be held directly on the center of the gold, disregarding the tip of the arrow.

The use of the perpendicular bow with the string bisecting the gold and aiming

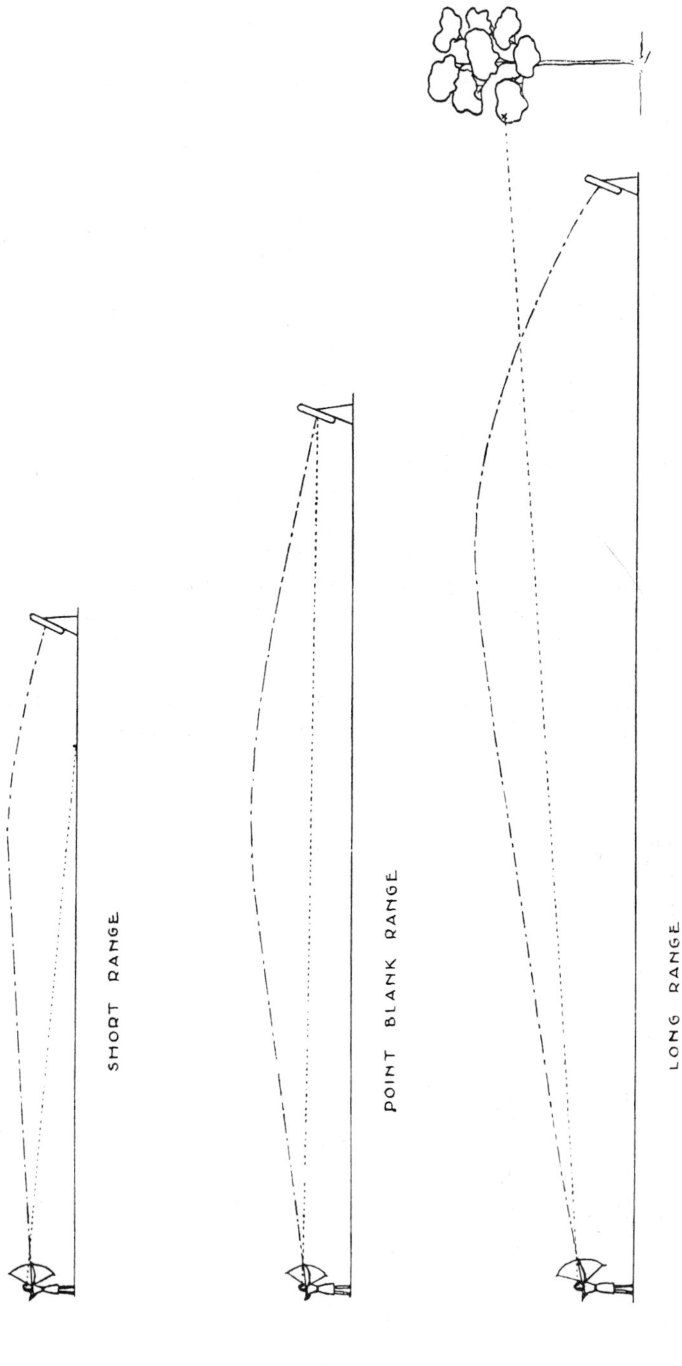

FIGURE 2.14 *Diagrammatic explanation of point of aim.*

with the right eye, as in shooting, is the most accurate way of determining whether the spot used for the point of aim is in line with the center of the target. If the low point of aim for the nearer range and the higher points of aim for the farther ranges appear on the string, then the particular spots chosen for points of aim are correctly centered. The arrow tip must be aligned directly on the point of aim at full draw and during the "holding" required in aiming.

If the arrows are landing high on the target, or consistently beyond, the point of aim must be lowered, i.e., brought nearer the shooting range or the sight raised very slightly. If the arrows are flying low or below the target, the point of aim must be raised or the sight lowered very slightly. A definite object should be placed at the given auxiliary spot; it is called the point of aim.

One method of consistently finding one's point of aim at different ranges is through the use of the *range finder* (Figure 2.15). Use any convenient short stick, such as a tongue depressor squared off at the top. When the stick is held perpendicularly at arrow's length in correct stance, the left hand corner of the stick should be held on the gold of the target. The holding hand should be adjusted so that the top edge of the thumb will coincide with the point of aim for that particular range. At this point on the stick, make a mark indicating the given range. One to three arrows should be shot to prove the hold and aim. With the range finder or arrow, "measure" the distance from the hit on the target to the point of aim. Change the tip of the range finder from the hit to the gold. The new location of the point of aim should be checked. If necessary, the students may adjust the point of aim for their partners when first trying this method. Each student, after she has determined her points of aim, should mark each on her own range finder. She should keep her range finder with her name on it and use it with the same bow and arrows at each practice session. Theoretically the point of aim method is difficult, but practically it is easy to apply. It can be worked out progressively in the class procedure.

(*b*) SIGHTS. Because many archers improve through the use of sights, a number of authorities have taught the

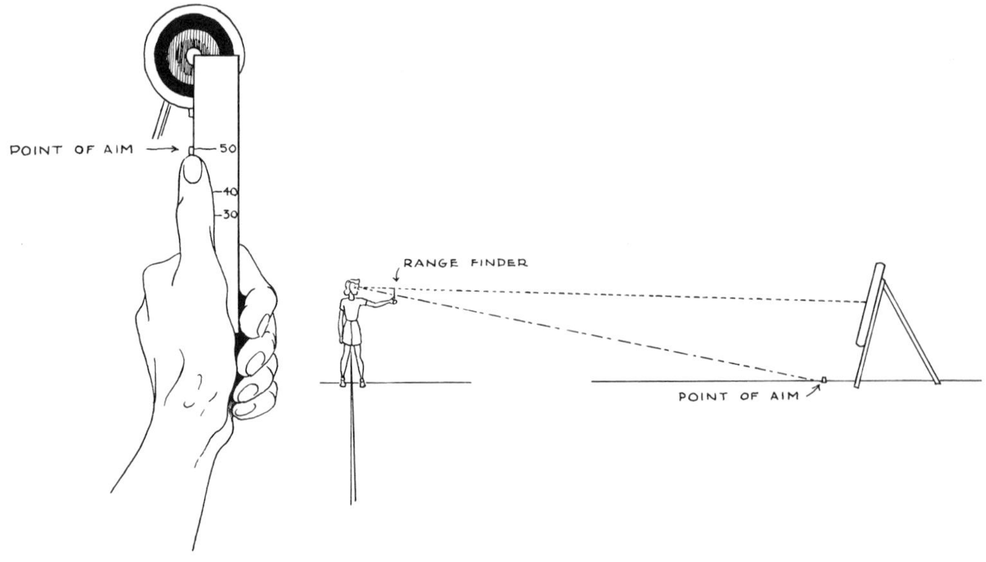

FIGURE 2.15 *Use of the range finder.*

use of sights to beginners early in the season. This direct method of aiming is perhaps slowly replacing the point of aim, or indirect method. For many, it works unusually well.

A sight is a device used to achieve an aim that is always on the gold of the target. Many types of mechanical bow sights are available, but for school, college, and camp use an adhesive strip attached to the back of the bow on the upper limb just above the arrow rest, plus a map pin with a large head, serves very well. The pin is pushed into the tape from left to right; it should be held directly on the center of the gold. The location of the pin sight for various ranges is marked on the tape; any horizontal correction needed on a particular day can be made by drawing the pin in or out. A slight correction at the bow makes for a marked correction at the target.

If the arrows land consistently to the right or left of center, other things being equal, a horizontal adjustment is necessary. If the grouping is to the left of center, the pin should be drawn out from the side of the bow. If the arrows are landing to the right of center, push the pin in slightly. This change in the relationship of the pin to the side of the bow (the distance the pin projects from the side) allows the archer to correct for windage, too.

If a mechanical bow sight is used, the aperture should, of course, be held on the center of the target. A sighting is taken through it to the exact spot of aim. Corrections are identical to those made for pin sights.

(*c*) INSTINCTIVE AIMING. A method of aiming—although really a method of shooting—that is practiced commonly today, especially by field archers, is "instinctive aiming." Actually, it is not new, nor is it practiced by instinct. Our American Indians used it, and it is based on a highly developed judgment of distance and elevation, not on guesswork. Most instructors of archery seem to agree that this method is best applied after the fundamentals of good target shooting have been mastered. Others start beginners at short ranges with no direction on aiming, but with strong emphasis on draw, anchor, release, and positioning of the bow arm. The high anchor of this method is its point of greatest difference from the target aiming method (Figure 2.11).

Usually the arrow is drawn so that the index finger comes to the corner of the mouth as an anchor point. This brings the hand against the cheek, with the length of the forefinger directly under the cheek bone. With this high anchor, the head is tilted slightly forward after its original turn toward the target. This places the sighting eye over the arrow. The bow also is canted slightly forward (clockwise as it faces the target), which allows greater visibility of the target. Aiming is accomplished primarily by feeling the correct elevation of the bow arm and the exactness of pointing the arrow at a given target. This "definite" feeling for the correct height of the arrow in relation to the target must be developed, just as accuracy in a ball-throw to a given spot must be practiced persistently to produce an efficient throw. Consistent performance, therefore, requires repeated practice.

The shortness of the range used means that less consideration of the effect of gravity on the flight of the arrow is necessary. If time and space make field archery events possible in the school or college, this method is worthwhile and should be taught, either during the first terms or in subsequent sessions. It also provides an introduction into the fascinating experience of bow hunting or fishing.

The important thing in aiming is to keep the tip of the arrow on the point of aim (in the indirect method) or the sight on the center of the gold (in the direct method). Beginners seem to find this difficult to practice. No one method of aiming can be considered the "best." Each has its advantages, depending both on the situation and the preference of the individual archer.

5. With their points of aim placed up, or their sights adjusted, the entire group should shoot their first "end" at 20 yards. At a given signal the group goes up to retrieve the arrows. They should be warned about "shorts," arrows that fall short of the target, and those that may have "snaked" their way into the grass. If the group has progressed well, an end or two at 30 yards will be challenging.

6. Removal of arrows from the ground and target can be demonstrated by the instructor with the class grouped about one target (Figure 2.16).

a. Back of left hand flat against target with arrow between index and second fingers.

b. Right hand grasp of arrow shaft close to target surface.

c. Push with the left hand against target and, with a firm pulling motion, draw the arrow with the right hand directly backward.

d. Place tips of arrows under thumb, leaving feathers free. When an arrow has become embedded in the straw up to its crest, it should be continued on slowly through the straw and withdrawn from the back of the target.

e. An arrow that has been forced deeply through the grass parallel to the ground so that it is almost hidden should be removed with a forward motion through the grass unless the feathers are free. If the feathers are not embedded, the arrow may be withdrawn backward, but never pulled straight up at right angles to the ground.

f. Each member of the class should retrieve her own arrows. Students should be reminded to carry them in the fingers at the tip ends, feathers, in fan formation, wide apart.

7. Advice also may be given at the targets on the necessary corrections of individual points of aim. On the return to

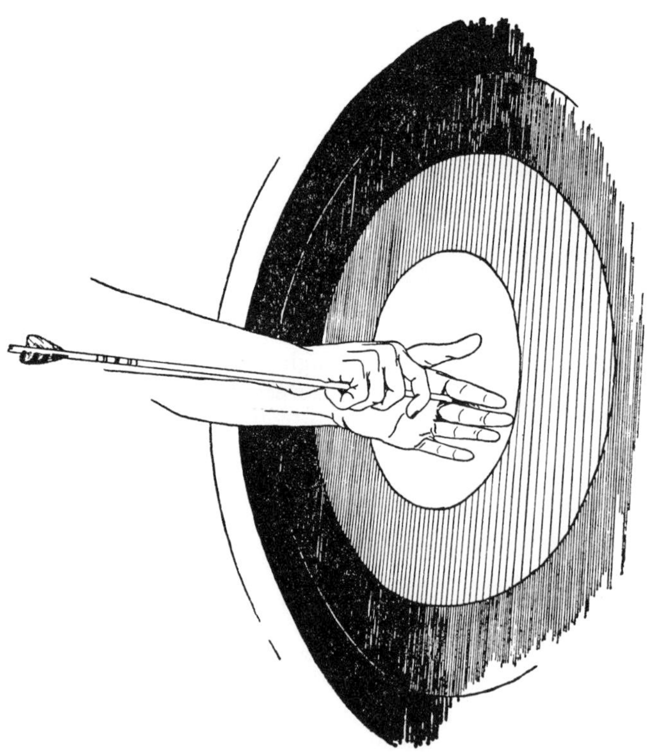

FIGURE 2.16 *Method of drawing arrows from target.*

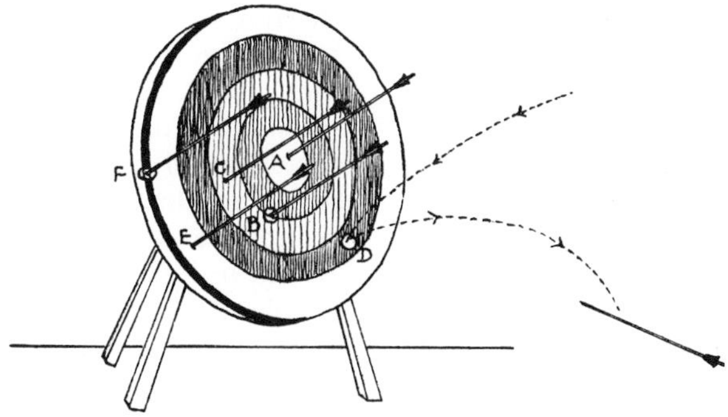

FIGURE 2.17 *Explanation of scoring of a given six arrows:*
A. Gold 9 points
B. Split 7 points —(higher valued ring always recorded)
C. Blue 5 points
D. Rebound (7) points —(from any part of scoring surface if shot from 60 yards or less)
E. White 1 point
F. Petticoat 0 points
NOTE: *During this particular end, no arrow hit the red ring, 7, nor the black, 3; nor struck through the scoring surface from 60 yards or less.*

the shooting line the second six arrows at 20 yards should be shot.

8. After this end, the class should bring up their pencils and score cards for the lesson in *scoring*. Again, group them around one target, and explain scoring in general. By using the 6 arrows present (or placed) in the target, the recording of the score and the value of each ring should be taught (Figure 2.17). Scores are always recorded with the highest score first, no matter which arrow scored which hit. If the first two shots are missed and then a gold, red, white, and black are made, in that order of shooting, on the score card it should be recorded as 9, 7, 3, 1, 0, 0. On the same line as the recording, total hits and total score are written for that end: in this case, 4-20. A hit on the part outside the white, known as the petticoat, counts as neither a score nor a hit. A hit that cuts two colors is given the higher value. A rebound, that is, an arrow that hits and bounces off a scoring part of the target or an arrow that hits the scoring surface of the target and goes clean through the target, are both given a score of 7, with a circle around it, *if* the arrow was shot from 60 yards or less. A score of 5, with a circle around it, is given *if* the arrow was shot from a distance over 60 yards. (This is according to the Official Tournament Rules of the N. A. A.) The enclosing circle differentiates the scores from the usual red 7 and blue 5. An arrow dropped from the bow that the archer cannot reach without moving her feet, counts as a shot.

After questions are answered, each student should record her own score, which should be kept continuously from then on. The instructor should also at this point observe how the arrows are retrieved and how carried back to the quivers, correcting those students who fail to conform. Here it may be necessary to have a more open class discussion of point of aim and the use of sights with a more detailed explanation of them. Before the third end at 20 yards, the instructor should ask where the point of aim should be for a 30-yard range. Then the class should decide how each one should place up or find her point of aim. The third end should be shot off. While retrieving the arrows and scoring up that end, the bits of wood should be placed up for a 30-yard shoot or the sights adjusted. One or two ends at 30 yards should be shot off. A discussion of any necessary corrections of point of aim or levels of sights would be helpful now. Each member of the class should total the score for the day and hand in her score card. These should be checked by the instructor so that she can correct any mistakes in scoring at the start. An easy check on the arithmetic is that the hits and score must both be either odd or even numbers. An incorrect score would read 42 hits, 125 score; a correct one, 42 hits, 128 score.

C. Third Week. This week will go more smoothly and more enthusiastically if the instructor has faithfully required diligent effort from the class in striving to perfect form. The choice of equipment and the stringing of the bows should still be observed by the instructor.

1. Before the class starts to shoot, point of aim theory and use of sights should be reviewed with discussion about necessary correction of trial points of aim and adjustments of the sight pins. If range finders have worked, they will be time savers from now on for those who use point of aim method.

2. The class may be started by helping, individually, one or two who may be having difficulties. The class should shoot the first end at 30 yards, preferably in unison. During the second end, the student assistant or the instructor should observe each student shoot at least two arrows, the second after the correction of the first. The second day's time should be divided between 20- and 30-yard ranges.

3. At the targets a discussion by the class of "groupings" of arrows and correction necessary if the groupings are "off-center" should prove stimulating. On completion, the instructor should check on retrieving, scoring, and carrying of arrows. During the third end, individual faults and explanation of how they may be overcome should be stressed.

D. Fourth Week. 1. On the first day of the fourth week, after checking on the choice of equipment and the stringing of the bows, the class should be divided in half, or individuals may choose partners. On a trial end at 40 yards each group should take turns in correcting the other's shooting form. 2. Photographs, taken with an ordinary camera while the small groups are shooting, should be arranged. As natural conditions as possible are desirable so it should be announced that some pictures will be taken during the class, but that no attention should be given to the photographer. If a camera is used that develops the pictures on the scene, interest is sparked immediately. If not, the archers may see them later.

It is well to have the student assistant take the pictures if possible. Not more than three girls should be photographed at one time. Others may appear in the picture, but the three should be in correct focus to facilitate analysis of any faults in shooting form.

3. On the second day of the week, the class should become acquainted with the 40-yard range, shooting as many ends as possible, with correction. At the end of the classes each day, the total scores should be recorded, and the unstringing of the bows and replacing of the equipment should be observed.

As the students go to retrieve the arrows shot at 40 yards, the bows should be carried to the 30-yard quivers. On the first end at 30, each student should shoot two arrows and hold four, the latter to be shot under the observation of the instructor or the student coach. At this time, it is well for the two who are teaching the class to change halves of the shooting line so that they may become familiar with each individual's progress. They should observe the shooting of two arrows, one without criticism and one with—first from behind the archer and then from the side. On the second day of the week, reference to the more common faults in technique should be made to the group and individually as needed. While the tackle is being put away on each day, and while scores are being tallied, more individual coaching, criticism, and encouragement may be offered, together with definite made of wool) often adds gaiety to the final roundup of the class. While the tackle is being put away, the group may be advised generally or specifically about buying their own equipment as well as shooting at home or on local ranges or at summer camps. For the most advanced, attendance at one of the archery camps may be proposed.

This is, of course, but a suggested procedure for novices for an eight-week term with clear weather. A greater variety can be introduced, but the basic outline of procedure we believe to be sound in theory and practice.

II. INTERMEDIATE

A separate schedule for an intermediate group has not been prepared in detail, because the suggestions made for the beginners and for advanced groups can be modified from both extremes so that a happy balance of progress and interest may be obtained. Such repetition of material and methods as is found in the following clear weather schedule for intermediates is given in outline form so that the instructor can know at a glance whether each group has been planned for, and the material covered from week to week.

A. First Week.

1. Review of safety laws.
2. Review of fundamental positions.
3. Summary of care of equipment.
4. Stringing and unstringing of bows and nocking under observation.
5. Start shooting at 40-yard range, standing between the beginning and the advanced groups, or use targets adjusted as described on page 16.

B. Second Week.

1. Review point of aim method or the use of pin sights.
2. Shooting at 50-yard and then at 40-yard range.
3. Recording of score from now on.

C. Third Week.

1. Shooting of "short" Columbia Round.
2. Discussion of difficulty with point of aim or adjustment of pin sights, as well as side groupings.
3. Individual correction of faults.

D. Fourth Week.

1. Correction of form in pairs on trial end at 50 yards.
2. Continuance of Columbia Round.

E. Fifth Week.

1. Rules given out for archery golf to be run in open hour.
2. Starting of first counting of Columbia Round.

F. Sixth Week. Balloon or William Tell shooting at far end of range.

G. Seventh Week.

1. Completion of Columbia Rounds for class team competition.
2. Suggestion to shoot Columbias for Intercollegiate Telegraphic Meet or Interscholastic Mail Match in open hour.

H. Eighth Week. Challenge tournament for those not on class, school, or college teams.

III. ADVANCED

A. First Week.

1. Review of safety laws, parts and choice of equipment.
2. Checking on tackle used and care of equipment.
3. Review of point of aim and bow sight methods of aiming; use of the range finder.
4. Start of shooting at 50 yards for a "short" Columbia Round.

B. Second Week.

1. Discussion of point of aim method and use of pin sights with necessary adjustments.
2. Beginning of day's shooting at 50-yard range, recording of scores from now on.

C. Third Week.

1. Posting of highest scores of Columbia Rounds.
2. Discussion of faults and methods of correction, first as a group and then individually.
3. Shooting of second Columbia Round.

hints to be practiced during the next lesson or in an open hour. Better form and scoring should be noticed at this time.

E. Fifth Week.

1. Shooting time may be divided between 30- and 40-yard ranges, but at least two ends should be shot at 50.

2. After the second end is shot off, and scored, the photographs should be shown. The three students whose pictures appear together should be grouped, and their errors or excellences in form should be pointed out to them individually; meanwhile the remainder of the class, under the guidance of the student coach, should continue shooting. Such discussions of each photograph can prove very helpful, for the picture is a graphic description of certain peculiarities of form that often must be visualized to be appreciated

3. A ladder tournament for the class is stimulating and very easily planned. Anyone on the ladder may challenge any other person on the ladder. With only 10 to 14 in the group, limiting it to a given number above is not necessary. Number four challenges number two for the total of the day's score. The one with the higher daily score has her name established in the higher place. Challenges must be accepted in the order received. In other words, number one can be challenged only by the first person who approaches her, not by two or three archers on the same day. The final day for completion of the tournament in class must be announced in advance. The concentration on achieving the best scores will be stimulation enough during class, but correction in details of form should be offered constantly. While observing the putting away of tackle, individual questions having specific bearing on some student's difficulties or misunderstanding should be answered.

F. Sixth Week.

1. Begin the first recorded and completed *Columbia Round.* It is generally impossible to finish a Columbia in one class period. Do as much as possible the first day, and finish on the second. Practice arrows should be allowed at 50 yards only; on the second day, no practice rows should be allowed.

2. If there are one or two stude in the group who seem to be unabl keep up to the pace of the class and have difficulty in making hits at 50 ya they should be kept working at 40 30 yards for form and accuracy. T should be placed at the right end of range as they face the target; those sh ing Columbias should take their st toward the left end. Either the stu coach or the instructor should be sponsible for the slower group and sh strive to find the real cause of each dent's difficulties. Some will alway slower in progress than the average they should not be neglected.

G. Seventh Week.

1. On the first day all those who not completed their Columbia Ro should do so. The ones in the slower g should start at least a "short" Colu Round and finish it during the wee a "short Columbia," we mean 12 a each, instead of the usual 24 at 50, 40 30 yards. The score cards shoul marked "Short Columbia."

2. On the second day, the class start a challenge tournament in pa the semi-finals of the ladder tourna The students with the two highest on the last day of the seventh week s shoot in the finals the last week.

H. Final Week. This week w very full indeed, for both the Colu and the finals in the ladder tourna must be finished off. After the first this week, there should be a meet the instructors in the different sec where the highest Columbia Round in each section and from all the se is determined from the score cards. are made for announcing them classes on the last day. The indi winner of the ladder tournament in class, as well as the highest daily from the recordings for the ladder nament, also should be determined. may be planned but are not nec Awarding a pail of lollypops or a peppermint stick or a golden tassel

D. Fourth Week.

1. Choosing of class team material.

2. Shooting of first counting Columbia Round.

3. At one end of range, Popinjay Shoot.

E. Fifth Week.

1. Giving out of multigraphed rules for archery golf to be run off in open hour during sixth and seventh weeks.

2. Continuation of Columbia Rounds.

F. Sixth Week.

1. Archery golf contest in open hours.

2. Working on Columbia Rounds to be used for telegraphic or mail meet and class competition.

G. Seventh Week.

1. By staying after class hour if possible, completion of Columbia Rounds.

2. Practice at the range most difficult for each individual.

H. Eighth Week.

1. Final competitions.

2. Open challenge tournament.

3. Plans for archery picnic.

This eight weeks' plan, in detail, would be as follows:

A. First Week. This is the time to get the advanced group off to a fast start.

1. and 2. As quickly as possible review safety laws, parts, and choice and elementary care of the equipment. Although this may be covered during the two days in order to allow for more shooting time each day, details of such a review should not be neglected.

3. Before any shooting is done, however, point of aim method should be reviewed, pin sights discussed and "instinctive method" explained. To have point of aim clearly understood is most important, especially if the advanced archers have received their fundamental training at some other institution. Despite differences in form, point of aim is basic but should not be insisted upon. The type of sight used and the vertical and horizontal sight adjustments that may be required should be discussed in general terms. The "instinctive method" also should be demonstrated and explained, so that the students may observe how it differs from the other two methods of aiming. This way, they will be able to decide which method they prefer, and which one they want to perfect. It is helpful with a new group of advanced archers, some of whom are unfamiliar to the instructor, to inquire about the types of rounds and tournaments entered previously. According to the findings, the students may be classified into two groups: *A*, the more experienced; and *B*, the less experienced. Divided into these classifications they may take their places at the shooting line quivers.

4. Shooting the first day should be at the 50-yard range, with individual corrections given immediately. The form of an archer who has learned the "relaxed" method or any other variety of draw or release should not be changed. It is confusing, and there is no real reason for change if the archer is consistent. With those who have learned the method described for the beginners, assistance should be given in perfecting small details of form. Once form is consistent, effort should be directed toward accuracy. On the second day the shooting should be divided among the 50-, 40-, and 30-yard ranges.

B. Second Week. Set the goal for Columbia Round or Junior Columbia. The class should be acquainted with the highest score ever recorded at their institution for a Columbia and a National and be given the best score recorded in interclass competition and in any former telegraphic intercollegiate or interscholastic mail meet. This sets goals for the season.

1. On the first day, a "short" Columbia should be shot off to get in training, especially for adjustment of point of aim and sights. This should include a practice end, then two ends each at 50-, 40-, and 30-yard ranges. This may be repeated if time allows.

2. On the second day, a recording should be made of a completed Columbia or the better part of one. Scores should be recorded regularly.

3. On either day, the use of sights should be explained in greater detail and discussed. Sights are nearly as numerous in kind as the archers who use them. An increasing number of tournament archers are sight shooters. Many attribute their higher scores to the use of sights. Mechanical sights vary in price. A simple one that will serve student purposes adequately may be made by sticking a 6-inch strip of ½-inch adhesive tape marked with ¼-inch spacings upward from the handle of the bow, on the back, and thrusting a glass-headed map pin crosswise through the tape. The pin should be placed in the tape to the left of the bow, and remains as far out from the bow as may be found necessary (Figure 2.18).

To use the sight, find by trial the exact distance from the side of the bow at which the head of the pin must be so that, when shooting in consistent form, the head of the pin is held steadily "on the gold." After loosing, the arrow should strike there, other factors being equal.

The "average" location of the 50-, 40-, and 30-yard ranges should be marked prominently on the tape, with wider lines. The individual student must learn and memorize the exact location of the pin above or below the "average" lines for his own shooting with the use of that bow. This has been described on page 35.

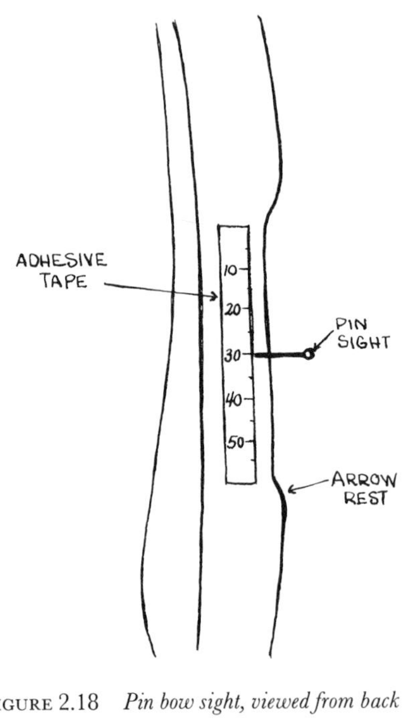

FIGURE 2.18 *Pin bow sight, viewed from back of bow.*

C. Third Week.

1. The best scores of completed Columbias in each section should be posted on the bulletin board in the archery equipment room and also announced in class. A method of stimulating better scores that has worked well is the recording of individual scores, made either in class or during open hour practice, on a large cardboard target posted in the tackle room. This method is described in greater detail under means of stimulating interest, page 47.

2. Discussion of faults and methods of correction. This should be done first with the group, then individually. Arrow groupings give indications of errors in technique. In correcting an archer's performance, the instructor should not confuse her by suggesting too many things on which to work. Rather, she should see that one fault is eliminated before another is noticed.

D. Fourth Week.

1. The instructor should watch out for material for *class teams*. The names of possible candidates, plus any who have proved to be worthy of consideration even though in the beginners' or intermediates' groups, should be assembled by the instructors and, with the aid of the student coaches, placed on tentative class team rosters. After the second day of the week, the final judgment on the class members can be reached, either by majority agreement of all the instructors and the student manager or by the agreement of the head of archery and the student manager.

2. Each member of the class teams may shoot off her best Columbia Round within a given time, but the score must be recorded and certified by another person, who also signs the score card.

3. A competition that is fun and calls for great accuracy is the Popinjay Shoot (p. 48), a modification of the traditional wand shoot, which can be shot off during the fourth week.

E. Fifth Week.

1. Rules for Archery Golf competition, which have been simplified and multigraphed, should be distributed.

2. Any member of the advanced or intermediate group may enter and should be urged to practice shooting at short ranges in an open hour. The class teams should be announced in class as well as in the student paper and on the Archery bulletin board.

3. As much of a completed Columbia Round as possible should be shot off each day.

F. Sixth Week.

1. Before the beginning of the sixth week, the student coaches should be called together, and they should plan to assist in running off the archery golf tournament. This may be arranged by challenging the best golf players in college or school to play off several holes of golf in competition with the shooting off of the same number of "holes" in archery during a designated open hour. The archer's "hole" consists of a wire ring 4½ inches in diameter (miniature golf, 2½ inches). The arrow must fly through the opening.

Less planning is necessary if, instead, the players shoot at 9 or 18 small targets made of strong, 8- by 10-inch pasteboard boxes placed at intervals over a wide field, such as a hockey field. The shooting proceeds from one target to another, as from hole to hole in golf. The object is to see who can score on each target with the least number of trials.

An approach shot may be taken from a given distance toward the individual target; the following shot must be taken from wherever that arrow landed, with the target, of course, turned to face the archer. The boxes should be held down with a forked stick or croquet wicket, easily removed from the ground but strong enough to offer resistance to breezes. If a smaller target is desired to require greater accuracy, small circles of 3 inches in diameter may be painted on the centers of the boxes. Many handicaps or changes in procedure can be managed from year to year to keep the interest in this type of archery alive.

In these two days, the three lowest scorers will be considered for the finals to be run off the following week.

2. For the class time, Columbia Rounds or a National Round should proceed during the two days, so that the scores may be used, if possible, for a telegraphic or mail meet or class competition. If preferred, some form of field archery may be tried if the archery area is safe. Here those who may have developed the high anchor and slightly different form of the "instinctive method" may distinguish themselves.

G. Seventh Week. A serious effort should be made to complete a Columbia Round during class so that it may count for class competition, for intercollegiate or interscholastic competition should be encouraged, if it has not been accomplished previously. During open hour, the finals of the archery golf competition, with the three lowest scorers competing, should be supervised by the student manager of archery. It is well at this time to have each student practice shooting several ends at the range most difficult for her.

H. Final Week.

1. Class competition results and recorded scores for the annual Intercollegiate Telegraphic Meet or the annual Interscholastic Mail Match, which are organized by the National Archery Association, should be handed in, certified by official scorers.

2. An open challenge tournament for each day is fun for those not competing otherwise.

3. Plans should be laid for the archery picnic. The picnic is an excellent time to announce the winners of Columbia Rounds, class competition, and highest individual scores in the Intercollegiate

Telegraphic Meet or the Interscholastic Archery Mail Match for High Schools. It is at such moments that the carry-over of interest is stirred. It is surely a high point at which to close the season.

SUGGESTED OUTLINES FOR CLASS PROCEDURES DURING INCLEMENT WEATHER

Inclement weather is the greatest handicap known to archers. It can play havoc even with the most advanced archer's form. In localities where rain is more than likely to force classes indoors, it is necessary to plan for such contingencies in advance so that as little time as possible is lost from an all too short season. However, if the class is to meet indoors and no indoor range is available, a combination of archery theory and exercise must be planned for. This will of necessity vary according to the situation, but the schedules that follow may offer suggestions or tentative outlines of a plan for a term for those who have no indoor range.

I. BEGINNERS

For *beginners* it really is no great hardship, even though a disappointment, to be indoors during the *first one or two weeks,* for much of the routine and fundamentals can be taught indoors. If a rainy day or two comes then, an excellent opportunity is afforded to teach or review parts of the bow and arrow, fundamental positions, care of the tackle both when not in use and in use, and to practice finger shooting in pairs.

If the weather closes in during the *third week,* practice in stringing and unstringing the bow under observation of the instructor is worth while. It may be practiced even for speed. One admonition that must be stressed is to be sure that the lower nock is against the instep and makes no contact with the floor. Nocking also may be practiced, so that the coordination is mastered. On one of these two days a motion picture on archery may be shown to the class, stopping it wherever required to emphasize a point. Finger shooting and exercises to strengthen scapular and upper spinal muscles can be practiced at this time.

During the *fourth* or *fifth week* if it is necessary to meet the group inside, the photographs that were taken previously may be discussed. First, the most prevalent mistakes of the group should be analyzed; then individual faults should be explained while the remainder of the class bowls, plays deck tennis, badminton, shuffle-board, or ping-pong—or whatever is at hand to play. At some schools there may be a reflectoscope or delineoscope, which may be used to enlarge the picture of the group and to show individual form. This is the most graphic means of showing the students right and wrong methods.

A second motion picture on archery may save the day during the *sixth* or *seventh week* if there is bad weather, or the one shown previously may be repeated. If repeated, comments by the class should be encouraged, for by now they should be keener in analysis of correct and incorrect form. Here, too, the instructor may offer reasons for learning the sport thoroughly and continuing it another term and during and after school days. This showing and discussion takes only part of the period; the remainder should be given over to informal sports. Where there are those whose physical condition precludes participation in the individual sports at hand, have a good book on archery from which to read to them.

By the *eighth week,* which is the most trying week of all to handle indoors, there is much that the class can do to assist the instructor. The first day may be given over to adding, averaging, and recording class scores, and individual and college or school competitions. On the second day, those who do not wish to exercise may help in cleaning the arrows, wiping off the bows, and learning more about the care of tackle when not in use. To clean arrows, use fine steel wool before waxing. Beeswax should be used on the string, except for the serving; this should be waxed with paraffin. In replacing servings and nocking points, dental floss or carpet thread should be used.

II. INTERMEDIATE AND ADVANCED ARCHERS

For *intermediate and advanced archers,* the loss of shooting time is more disappointing than for beginners. However, if managed efficiently, much of the sport can be learned off, as well as on, the range. If rain comes during the *first two weeks,* parts of the bow and arrow and care of the tackle should be thoroughly reviewed, as well as the fundamental positions of shooting. Before the informal sports are played, finger shooting should be checked by the instructor to insure a consistently perfect release, even by advanced archers. Emphasize the equal pull of all three fingers. The ring finger is often "lazy."

When bad weather comes during the *third week,* it is advantageous for the instructor to show a motion picture. She may use the film to stimulate suggestions from this better group of archers about how the film may be improved upon another year and from what angles the best "still" picture can be taken to show correct and incorrect form. This discussion and planning will consume the entire period for those sufficiently interested; the others can play at their favorite informal sports. Privately owned films and Kodachrome slides and projectors can be located by applying to local and state officers of archery associations. Such owners are almost invariably willing to lend them. If feasible from a financial standpoint, a teaching film can readily be produced and can be used for several years. Incidentally, the taking of the film adds great interest and stimulates better form in those being photographed.

If pictures have been taken previous to the *fourth* or *fifth week,* as they should have been, the individual's as well as the group's most common faults and difficulties may be analyzed here from the photographs. This could be done individually, or, with the use of a delineoscope, the group could criticize the enlarged pictures together.

If the local motion picture has already been shown on some other rainy day, plan during the *sixth* or *seventh week* to have on hand another film on archery obtainable from the National Archery Association or from a neighboring school or college. The class also could be motivated to produce a crossword puzzle of archery terms, which could then be given to another group to solve.

During the *eighth week,* tabulation of scores can be completed and checked, and the tackle cleaned. On one of these two days, a glossary "bee" is fun to spring on the group. Divide the class as evenly as possible according to ability and run the competition much like an old-fashioned spelling bee. This is also a good time to discuss the type of equipment to buy for personal use.

There is not a sufficiently great difference between the rainy day material for beginners and for the *intermediate-advanced group* to make another schedule necessary for a mixed group. The instructor can best plan what to include and what to ignore according to the ability of the class and their progress. Those with physical handicaps may need special consideration, and the division of the class should result in as close competition as possible.

III. INDOOR RANGE

An indoor range can be established without too much effort for use during inclement weather. If it can be permanently set up for use all year, there is much advantage offered. The dimensions of an indoor range, the special equipment needed, and safety measures required are all listed on page 17. For indoor shooting, a smaller target usually is preferred, but a regulation 48-inch target may be used, counting only the hits on the three inner rings. Another easy plan is to use bales of straw, on which target faces of 16, 24, or 36 inches are attached. As a substitute for outdoor shooting, it should be explained that shooting from a 20-yard range at a 24-inch target is similar to outdoor shooting at a 40-yard range with a 48-inch target.

An indoor range also offers an excellent opportunity to practice at least the high anchor of the instinctive method of aiming. Much can be accomplished indoors to improve form, especially with beginners. One device worth noting is the elastic bow string. This gives the students the feel of the correct draw without the resistance of the bow. The stance, draw, and hold can be improved materially through its use. Of course the string is also usable outdoors, but is an excellent rainy day indoor learning aid.

COMMON FAULTS IN ARCHERY FORM

Certain common faults in archery form have been recognized individually and in groups. If classified by the location of the hits, some errors are clearly understood. Unfortunately, with beginners especially, more than one fault may be demonstrated at the same time. It is this combination of mistakes that requires both keen analysis on the part of the instructor and an observant shooting partner. It must be pointed out that errors in shooting form may cancel each other and produce an acceptable hit. Others may be combined to increase the degree of difficulty, which results in a very poor hit or in a miss. In general, mistakes may be made that cause the arrow's flight to deviate in one of four directions: up, down, to the right, or to the left. Agreement about the recognition of all such important errors in form has never been made, but the following is at least a partial listing of the most outstanding ones.

FACTORS THAT CAUSE THE RELEASED ARROW TO RIDE HIGH

1. Riding the bow (extension of bow arm on the release).
2. Increasing slightly the pull on the string just before release.
3. Lifting the bow arm on the release.
4. Lifting the index finger of bow hand.
5. Nocking the arrow low on the string.
6. Allowing the third finger to "slip" on the string.
7. Dropping the elbow or string hand just before release.
8. "Peeking" at short ranges.
9. Poorly determined point of aim (too far) or lifting from point of aim.
10. Inaccurate anchor against open mouth or "reaching" jaw.
11. A strong wind toward the target.

FACTORS THAT CAUSE THE RELEASED ARROW TO RIDE LOW

1. A "creeping" release.
2. Not reaching or not holding at anchor point.
3. Dropping bow arm.
4. Reaching forward with chin to string.
5. Nocking the arrow high on the string.
6. Using understrung bow, which causes string to hit wrist.
7. Holding low on bow handle.
8. "Peeking" at longer ranges.
9. Poorly determined point of aim (too near) or lowering from it.
10. Too high an anchor.
11. Holding too long, so that fatigued muscles "give" too quickly.
12. A head-on wind.

FACTORS THAT CAUSE THE RELEASED ARROW TO VEER TO THE RIGHT

1. Throwing bow arm to the right.
2. Plucking the string on release.
3. Tilting the bow to the right.
4. Failing to align the point of aim with the center of the target—too far to right.

5. Failing to allow for wind from the left.
6. Head tilt to the right.
7. Pulling fingers off string too quickly, whether from lack of protection or soreness.
8. Weight on the toes or toward the forepart of the foot.
9. Gripping the bow string too high on the fingers.
10. Using arrows with too weak spine.

FACTORS THAT CAUSE THE RELEASED ARROW TO VEER TO THE LEFT

1. Throwing bow arm to the left.
2. Fingers tightly gripping the arrow.
3. Tilting the bow to the left.
4. Anchoring out from the cheek.
5. Failure to align point of aim with center of target—too far to left.
6. Failure to allow for wind from the right.
7. String touching hunched left shoulder.
8. Using left eye to sight.
9. Weight on heels or swaying slightly toward heels.
10. Head dropped backward rather than rotated to left.
11. Too tight a grip on bow.
12. Sighting to left of string.
13. Using arrows with too stiff spine.

Recognition of these difficulties in form and correction of one at a time as they appear make for improvement in form, and thus lead to better scores. It is wiser not to note many mistakes at once, for the correction is confusing for the archer. Eliminate one before beginning to work on another. Be alert to their presence, and if two or more are complementary, of course call attention to them only as one relates to the other. Perhaps posting a list of such causes would help some archers to recognize a specific error or two and thereby help correct them before the mistake becomes a habit.

STIMULATING INTEREST IN ARCHERY

Variety in shooting is a means of stimulating continued interest in the sport. Any ingenious instructor who really loves the activity can arrange the seasonal schedule so that the special occasions well spaced throughout the year will catch the interest and effort of many an archer. Indoor shooting during the winter is an excellent stimulus toward maintenance of good form and the ability to maintain accuracy even under changes of range and size of target. During the season, clout shooting, flight shooting, archery golf, balloon shoots, wand shoots, field archery, roving, play days, exhibition shoot, recreational archery with mixed doubles in competition, Willian Tell or Popinjay shoots, ending the term perhaps with a challenge mail or telegraphic meet or a rabbit hunt in the woods, all add gaiety and variety to weeks of straight target work. In midseason, a "funday" may be a pleasant surprise. Have the archers, especially the intermediate and advanced, shoot in unexpected ways: standing on one foot, kneeling on one knee, using the nondominant hand, shooting alternately in pairs, marking time around the clock—one arrow on each hour in a specific color ring.

Suggesting the purchase of tackle for personal ownership, wherever possible, is a stimulus to maintaining keenness for the sport. Visual aids in addition to motion pictures often are more useful in stimulating interest and building background than in the study of technique. A full length mirror is helpful in creating an awareness of stance and form. A smaller mirror held close by the instructor makes it possible for the student to see and correct her head position, anchor point, and finger position at the throat. For the rest, the teacher of archery is thrown on her own initiative in the making of diagrams and charts which will supplement instruction. These can readily give analytical, detailed demonstration of the steps in shooting.

A *weekly check* on *individual scoring* can be made by use of a target posted in the archery room. A cardboard arrow with the individual's name and pencilled score is attached with a thumb tack in the tip. This target, 30 inches in diameter, painted with five regulation colored rings, has each of the five rings labeled in the hundreds. The white equals 100; the black, 200; the blue, 300; the red, 400; and the gold, 500. The majority of arrows perhaps will remain in the blue, but great enthusiasm is demonstrated when an arrow can be moved up into the red. With the short season that is necessary in many eastern schools, the 500 gold ring is still only a goal to be realized. If working with younger girls, the same system with modified scoring can be established.

The *Popinjay Shoot* is a colorful adaptation of the *Wand Shoot*. Onto a flat lath, 2 inches wide and 10 feet above the ground, at 1-foot intervals are tacked into place six birds jigsawed out of lathing, three on each side, with the seventh bird perched on the top—the Popinjay. The pattern for these can be a 6- to 8-inch long garden bird decoy. The "side" birds may be painted various colors that show up well in the light—yellow, blue, white, red. The Popinjay should be an inch longer, preferably with a crest on his head and painted in a variety of colors. Shooting at the birds in competition, in alternation, at 30 yards, each using two consecutive arrows, the score of seven goes to anyone who hits a bird, nine to the Popinjay hitter, and one to those who hit the upright. This may be shot off by sides, chosen as one chooses sides by counting off as in children's games or by dividing the class as equally as possible according to their Columbia Round scores, one high and one low on each side until all are placed. This livens up the class or group a bit and calls for accurate aim. It is often so popular that there is a demand for it during open hour, individually or in groups. Other events can be added and modified from year to year for continuation of interest in archery.

ARCHERY TERMS

Larger volumes have more inclusive glossaries. The one that follows is intended only to define the terms used in this chapter.

Addressing the Target. Standing ready for target shooting with the body at right angles to the target, feet straddling the shooting line.

American Round. For women, 30 arrows at 60, 50, and 40 yards each.

Anchor Point. A definite spot on the face to which the index finger of the string hand must come consistently in drawing.

Archery Golf. An adapted roving game, played on a real or simulated golf course, using the bow and arrow.

Arm Guard. Usually a leather protection worn on the lower bow arm to prevent string abrasions.

Arrowplate. An insert of hard material designed to prevent injury to the bow, set into the bow where the arrow crosses it on release.

Arrow Rest. On some bows, a shelf on the side of the bow on which the arrow rests in drawing and holding. Important in sight shooting.

Back. The flat of the bow; the side away from the string.

Backed Bow. A bow that is strengthened by a thin strip of wood, rawhide, or other strong material glued on the length of the back.

Belly. The surface of the bow that faces the string; also called *face*.

Boss. The straw backing of a target to which a target face is attached.

Bow Arm. The arm, the hand of which holds the bow during shooting.

Bow Sight. A device on the bow used for aiming.

Bow-stave. A piece of wood from which a bow can be made.

Bowyer. A maker of bows.

Brace. To string a bow; to put the string's eye into the bow's upper nock.

Bracer. An arm guard.

Butt. Straw bale to which target face is attached when bale is used as target backing.

Canted. Tilted slightly forward from the vertical.

Cast. The distance a bow can shoot; the release

of the drawn string, which sends the arrow outward.

Chrysal. A pinched spot or crack that has been caused by repeated compressions, which develops in the belly of the bow.

Clout. A mark placed on the ground for long distance shooting.

Clout Shooting. A definite round, usually 36 arrows, 180 yards for men, 140 and 120 yards for women, shot at a 48-foot target laid flat on the ground.

Cock Feather. The feather set at right angles to the arrow nock, generally of a different color from the hen feathers.

Columbia Round. A round, usually shot by women or girls, consisting of 24 arrows shot at each of 50-, 40-, and 30-yard ranges.

Composite Bow. A bow that consists of various layers of material.

Creeping. A "give" forward with the string hand at the moment of release.

Crest. The identifying marks on the arrow at the feathered end.

Double Round. A round shot twice in succession.

Draw. The pulling back of the bowstring; also the distance to which the bow is drawn.

Drawing Weight. The force in pounds used to bring bow to full draw.

Drift. A sideways deviation of an arrow in flight due to the wind.

Elevation. The required height of the bow hand while aiming.

End: American. Six arrows which are shot in succession or in two groups of three; *English:* three arrows shot consecutively.

Eye. A loop woven into each end of the string that is fitted into each nock when the bow is strung; singly, a loop attached to the upper nock of the bow.

Face. Of the bow. See *Belly.*

Field Archery. The use of the bow and arrow in shooting at animate and inanimate objects, at unknown, unannounced, and not predetermined distances.

Field Captain. Person in charge of a tournament.

Finger Shooting. Method of practicing release of the string by using partner's index finger as the "string."

Finger Tip or Stall. Protection from the string, usually of leather, worn on the string fingers.

Fistmele. An old English term describing the approximate height of the fist with the thumb raised, used in measuring the distance from string to braced bow. Inaccurately, 6 inches.

Fletch. To secure feathers to an arrow.

Fletcher. One who secures feathers to an arrow; a device for securing feathers to an arrow.

Flight Shooting. The effort to shoot an arrow the farthest possible distance.

Follow the String. The tendency of a bow to retain the same curves unstrung that it holds when strung.

Footed Arrow. An arrow with a wooden shaft reinforced with a splicing of hard wood at the pile end, giving added strength and weight.

Foot Marker. A pair of flat markers that may be inserted in the ground to mark stance, against which the toes are placed on the shooting line.

Grouping. The clustering in close proximity of arrows that have been shot.

Handle. The mid-section of the bow that the bow hand grips.

Head. Point, tip, or pile of an arrow.

Hen Feathers. The two feathers on the shaftment that are not at right angles to the nock and are similar in color. See *Cock Feather.*

Hereford Round. For women, 72 arrows at 80 yards, 48 at 60 yards, 24 at 50 yards.

Hit. To strike the target on its scoring surface.

Holding. Steadily keeping an arrow at full draw before its release; the pause at full draw before the arrow's release.

Horns. The reinforcements of horn on ends of upper and lower limbs on some bows, into which parts the nocks are set.

Instinctive. A method of shooting in which no formal aiming device is used.

Jig. A device for securing feathers to the arrow shaft, or for bracing a bow.

Junior American Round. For boys and girls, 30 arrows each at 60-, 50-, and 40-yard ranges.

Junior Columbia Round. A beginner's round, shot by both boys and girls, consisting of 24 arrows shot at each of 40-, 30-, and 20-yard ranges.

Lady Paramount. The lady in charge of a women's tournament.

Laminated bow. A bow consisting of layers of different types of metal, Fiberglas, or wood, or a combination of these.

Let Fly. To release an arrow for flight.

Limbs. Upper and lower parts of the bow, divided by the handle.

Loop. See *Eye.*

Loose. To release the fully drawn bowstring.

National Round. For women: 48 arrows shot at 60 yards and 24 arrows at 50 yards.

Nock. The groove in the end of the arrow for the reception of the string; the groove at each end of the bow for the reception of the string;

the reinforcements at each end of the bow; the act of placing the arrow on the string.

Nocking Point. The point on the string at which the nock of the arrow should be placed.

Over-bowed. Using too strong a bow.

Over-drawn. For the arrow, to draw it so that the pile is within the belly; for the bow, to draw beyond the required length of the arrow.

Perfect End. Six consecutive arrows shot into the gold. If witnessed and attested to, official recognition is offered by the N.A.A. The goal of every archer!

Petticoat. The edge of the target face beyond the white ring.

Pile. The pointed metal tip of the arrow.

Pinsight. A device adjustable on the bow, used for acquiring and holding proper aim.

Point Blank Range. The distance, for any given bow, at which the point of aim is the center of the gold.

Point of Aim. A mark, used when sighting, upon which the tip of the arrow is aimed, not more than 1½ inches square or in diameter and not more than 6 inches above ground level according to N.A.A. ruling.

Quiver. A holder for arrows; three types: stationary at given ranges; ground, which is movable; and one worn on the belt of the archer, or over the shoulder.

Range. Shooting distance; an archery ground, indoors or out.

Range Finder. A device by which varying points of aim may be easily determined.

Recurve Bow. One having its limb ends bent forward (away from the face of the bow). Has two general types: one in which the bow tips remain *static* on being braced and one in which they flow more flexibly into the contour of the bow when it is braced, (*working* recurve). There are many slight differences and combinations of these, but the working recurve seems the most popular at present.

Round. The name used to describe shooting a definite number of arrows at specific distances. All rounds recognized by the N.A.A. are described in its Official Tournament Rules, drawn up in April 1961.

Roving or *Rovers.* An archery game consisting of shooting a certain number of shots at given distances over an outdoor course.

Self-arrow. An arrow made from a single piece of wood without the reinforcement of a footing.

Self-bow. A bow made of one kind of wood.

Serving. The "whipping" or wrapping of thread around the bow-string in the center of the string which receives wear from nocking and drawing.

Shaft. The main part of an arrow.

Shaftment. The part of the arrow holding the crest and the feathers.

Shooting Line. The line that marks a specific distance on the range.

Sight. An aiming device usually attached to the back of the bow above the handle, used so that aiming may be directly on the gold.

Spine. A characteristic of an arrow's strength and resiliency.

Stave. A length of wood from which a bow is made.

Stringing. Bracing the bow; securing string correctly in nocks.

Tab. A protection for the string fingers, usually made of leather.

Tackle. An inclusive term for archery equipment.

Target Face. The front cover of a target, painted with the regulation colored rings.

Tassel. A bunch of yarn for wiping off of arrows, usually worn on an archer's belt.

Timber-hitch. The knot used in securing the bow-string to the lower limb.

Toe marker. A flat device used to mark the archer's stance at any range.

Toxophilite. One who has studied the history as well as mastered the art of shooting with bow and arrow.

Trajectory. The path the arrow describes in flight.

Under-bowed. Using too light a bow.

Vane. A feather of an arrow (natural or plastic).

Wand Shoot. Shooting at a narrow upright stick. The distances and dimensions vary. N.A.A. ruling calls for stick two inches wide with six-foot height above ground for both men and women archers.

Weight. The total pull, measured in pounds, required to draw a bow the length of its arrow; of an arrow, actual weight in grains.

Whipping. See *Serving.*

Wide. Term to describe the flight of an arrow to either side of the target.

Windage. The possible influence of wind upon an arrow in flight.

Suggestions for Further Reading

Craft, Dave and Cia: *The Teaching of Archery.* New York, A. S. Barnes & Co., 1936.
Duff, James: *Bows and Arrows.* New York, The Macmillan Co., 1927.
Elmer, Robert P.: *Archery.* New York, A. S. Barnes & Co., 1929.
———: *Target Archery.* New York, Alfred A. Knopf Company, 1936.
Elmer, Robert P. and Nabih A. Faris: *Arab Archery.* Princeton, New Jersey, Princeton University Press, 1945.
Forbes, Thomas A.: *New Guide to Better Archery.* Harrisburg, Pennsylvania, The Stackpole Co., 1961.
Hochman, Louis: *The Complete Archery Book.* Greenwich, Connecticut, Fawcett Publications, Inc., 1957.
Lambert, Arthur W., Jr.: *Modern Archery.* New York, A. S. Barnes & Co., 1929.
Reichert, Natalie and Gilman Keasey: *Archery.* New York, The Ronald Press, 1961.
Rounsevelle, Philip: *Archery Simplified.* New York, A. S. Barnes & Co., 1931.
Schmidt, Marvin: *Introduction to Archery.* Chicago, Ziff-Davis Publishing Co., 1946.
Stemmler, L. E.: *Essentials of Archery.* Queens Village, New York, L. E. Stemmler Co., 1937.
Sumption, Dorothy: *Archery for Beginners.* Philadelphia, W. B. Saunders Company, 1932.
Thompson, Maurice: *The Witchery of Archery.* Pinehurst, North Carolina, The Archers Co., 1928.
Wiseman, Howard: *Tackle Archery This Way.* London, Stanley Paul & Co., Ltd., 1959.
Yocum, Rachael B. and H. B. Hunsaker: *Individual Sports for Men and Women.* New York, A. S. Barnes & Co., 1947.

PERIODICALS AND HANDBOOKS

Archers' Magazine. Official publication of the National Archery Association. A monthly magazine on sport, crafts, and hobbies of target archers, field and target shooters, and bow hunters.
Archery. A monthly magazine on hunting and field archery.
Archery Handbook of the Boy Scouts of America. Merit Badge Series.
Archery Handbook. Eloise Jaeger, Department of Physical Education, University of Minnesota. Published by The Athletic Institute, 209 South State Street, Chicago 4, Illinois.
Briggs, Lawrence E.: "Archery Enhances a Camp Program." Published in *Archers' Magazine.* Available in mineographed sheets from the National Archery Association.
National Bowhunter. A monthly magazine for bow hunters.
Practical Aids for Archery Instructors. Compiled by Mrs. Myrtle K. Miller, Director of Teela-Wooket Archery Camp, Roxbury, Vermont.
Technique Chart on Archery. Division for Girls and Women's Sports, American Association for Health, Physical Education, and Recreation, 1201 16th Street, N. W., Washington 6, D. C.

ASSOCIATIONS

National Archery Association. Mrs. Helen Huck, Secretary-Treasurer, 20-A Yale Avenue, Buffalo 26, New York.

National Field Archery Association. Mr. John L. Yount, Secretary, Box 514, Redlands, California.

Camp Archery Association. Mr. Fred D. Stern, Secretary, 200 Coligni Avenue, New Rochelle, New York.

3

BADMINTON

Jane A. Mott

Badminton played by experts is one of the fastest and most demanding of the racket games. At the competitive level it demands great agility, superior endurance, lightning-quick reactions, and masterly strategy. Fortunately for the novice and backyard player, however, one of the major values of the sport is that sufficient skill for enjoyment can be acquired quickly. Moreover, the space required for badminton is relatively small (44 × 20 feet). The court can be set up indoors or out, and for informal play no special surface is necessary. Since the pace and complexity of the sport easily can be geared to the abilities of the participants, it is not surprising that the surge in the popularity of badminton has been equalled by few other sports. As a novice comes to master fundamental techniques, she finds that the game presents new challenges at a higher level of performance.

The exact origin of badminton is not known, but the appeal of the game has endured for hundreds of years. British royal court records of the 12th century mention a form of the sport, and similar games are believed to have been played in China and in Europe before the 18th century. A game played by British army officers at Poona, India, during the middle 1800's usually is credited with being the immediate ancestor of modern badminton. Under the name, *Poona,* the sport was brought to England by army officers, who demonstrated it there during a social gathering at the Duke of Beaufort's country estate, "Badminton House," in Gloucestershire. On that day, "badminton" became the accepted name for the game.

The first rules were printed in India in 1876, and these governed the sport until 1887, when the Bath Badminton Association of England was formed. This group standardized the equipment and playing rules. In 1895, the English Badminton Association was established, and it then took over the printing of the official rules.

From England, badminton spread to Canada and the United States. Although the Canadian Badminton Association was not founded until 1922, and the American Badminton Association was established even later, in 1937, the sport was played in the two countries long before those dates. In fact, the New York Badminton Club, which was formed in 1879, has the distinction of being the world's oldest club of its kind.

Few sports have enjoyed such rapid growth throughout the United States. This growth has been shown by the number of badminton clubs formed, by the many sectional tournaments, and by the increasing numbers of schools and colleges that offer badminton as a curricular and extracurricular activity in physical education programs.

Instruction in badminton techniques in schools and colleges is doing much to foster the continued popularity of the sport. In badminton, as in any other game, proficiency encourages participation. The primary aims of the instructor in relation to technique are to give the learner a clear picture of the necessary skills and an opportunity for intelligent, guided practice and competition with others of approximately similar ability.

The information about playing badminton given in this chapter is grouped by topic for convenience in reading; it is not arranged in a suggested order of presentation to the learner. Selection and care of equipment are discussed first. Specific techniques are analyzed, then strategy and etiquette are described for doubles and singles games. General suggestions, practice formations, and sample lesson plans follow in the section on class instruction. Here sample teaching progressions are outlined. Finally, tournaments and methods of evaluation suitable for badminton classes are discussed.

THE EQUIPMENT

Well-kept equipment is essential for good play. Student cooperation in the care of equipment can best be gained by stressing its importance early in the course and by informing players of the cost of rackets, shuttlecocks, and nets.

I. Rackets

To be sure of good construction, it is important that rackets be purchased from a reliable manufacturer, since badminton rackets are not guaranteed. It is a mistake to invest in the cheapest rackets on the market—or in the most expensive tournament rackets for general class use. A price a little higher than average should buy good, serviceable rackets that can be restrung many times.

Most badminton rackets are approximately 26 inches long and are made of ash, beech, or hickory (Figure 3.1). A few rackets are now made of Fiberglass, but, as yet, these are not widely used. Some of the more expensive frames have steel shafts, which offer less wind resistance than wood. Wooden shafts, on the other hand, cause the shuttlecock to rebound more rapidly. The choice of a wooden or a steel shaft is a matter of individual preference. In purchasing a frame, consideration should be given to the weight, handle size, grip, and balance. The *weight* range of strung rackets varies from 4 to 6 ounces; a weight of approximately 5 ounces is considered best for the majority of players. The variation in *handle sizes* is from 3 to 4 inches, and the average size, 3½ to 3¾ inches, seems best for class use. The length of an individual's fingers is a factor in the choice of handle size, shorter fingers requiring a smaller circumference.

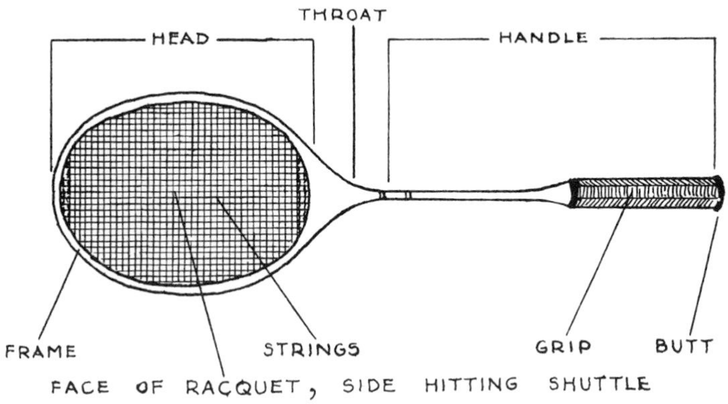

FIGURE 3.1 *The parts of the racket.*

The handle measurement includes the encasing *grip,* which covers the four flat sides or *plates* of the handle. The grip is preferably of perforated leather. Usually, the *balance* of a strung racket is centered to make the weight distribution even. This is preferred by most players; but, since some like a racket with more weight in the head, a number of rackets with this balance should be purchased for classes.

Two types of stringing material are suitable for badminton rackets: lamb's gut and nylon. Different qualities and weights of each type are available, but in general nylon is less expensive and outlasts gut. Nevertheless, skilled players prefer gut for its *touch* and approximately 20 per cent greater resiliency. Twisted nylon is the best buy for class use, whereas 20-gauge gut is a very satisfactory choice for an individually owned racket. Delicate 21-gauge gut is for top tournament play; 19-gauge is heavy-duty weight. In buying rackets for school use, particularly if orders are placed well in advance of the badminton season, it is desirable to purchase unstrung frames. Stringing immediately before use ensures proper tension of 15 to 20 pounds, for, as time passes, strings become slack or "dead." Expert hand stringing is superior to that done by machine. Gut tends to fray in the center of the racket, and nylon often breaks where it is cut by the stringing grooves. Regardless of the type of string used, the edges of the grooves should be filed smooth.

The badminton racket is the most fragile of all sports rackets, and consequently it requires good care. When not in use, it should be kept in a press of even tension, hung between pegs in a dry place. If a racket is used throughout the day, it should not be placed in a press until the end of the day. If corner screw presses are used, students must be taught to give only a few turns at a time to each screw and to continue the procedure until all screws are tight. Equal pressure at the four corners of the press will then be exerted. Students also should be trained to examine a racket closely, both before play and at frequent intervals during play, in order to discover a broken string as soon as it occurs. If the student puts the racket aside immediately after breaking a string, it is possible to replace the one string without having to restring the racket completely.

II. Shuttlecocks

In general, there are two types of shuttlecocks suitable for class use. The first is the official tournament bird, with a cork base and 16 evenly matched feathers. These birds weigh 73 to 85 grains; the heaviest ones are used for outdoor play. For indoor play, the average weights are 76 grains for birds with pointed feather tips and 79 grains for those with rounded ends. As room temperature increases, heavier shuttlecocks are required.

It takes one goose to provide enough sturdy, well-balanced, straight-spined feathers for just one first-quality shuttlecock. The expense of feathered shuttlecocks makes proper care of them extremely important. The feathers must be straightened after every rally; the bird should be put in play by hitting it underhand rather than tossing it up and hitting it overhand; it should be picked up by hand from the floor—never hit or kicked along the floor. Before the feathered shuttles are used, they should be placed in a container at a temperature of 60 to 65 degrees Fahrenheit and a relative humidity of 70 to 75 per cent for at least one hour. This treatment prevents the feathers from becoming brittle and breaking.

Birds of a second type are made of plastic. These are less expensive than good quality feathered shuttles, and they remain in good condition longer. The only care required is to avoid stepping on them. Plastic birds do not simulate exactly the flight of feathered shuttlecocks, nor do they sound the same when hit. They may, however, be used for both wall and court practice, which is an important advantage in large classes. If students use plastic birds first and feathered shuttles later, they are apt to be careless in handling the feathered shuttlecocks unless reminded of the great difference in fragility.

III. Court and Net

The rules specify the width and color of the lines that make up a badminton court. Ideally, the floor surface and walls should be dark—forest green being the favored color. The ceiling should afford a minimum clearance of 30 feet, and 40 is preferable. Artificial lighting is more satisfactory than sunlight, since nonglare lamps can be used.

Nets are standard in size but vary in quality. The higher priced ones wear considerably longer. Students should be instructed *not* to lean on the nets or to pull on them.

TECHNIQUES

GENERAL TECHNIQUES

Techniques are presented in this section under three topics: use, analysis, and presentation, including points to emphasize. Practices are sometimes suggested. The analysis is given in terms of a right-handed player.

I. Forehand Grip

A. Use

This grip is used for all strokes taken on the right-hand side of the body, for all serves, and for round-the-head shots.

B. Analysis

The grip is much like the Eastern forehand grip in tennis. The V of the thumb and forefinger is very pronounced and is on the top plate of the handle (Figure 3.2). The forefinger is diagonally across the back of the handle and hooked under it and ahead of the thumb. The racket is grasped by the fingers, with the butt held by the little finger. The handle does *not* rest in the palm of the hand.

C. Presentation to Beginners

The students are grouped in a semicircle around the instructor. Each student should hold the throat of her racket with her left hand. After demonstrating the

FIGURE 3.2 *The forehand grip.*

FIGURE 3.3 *The backhand grip.*

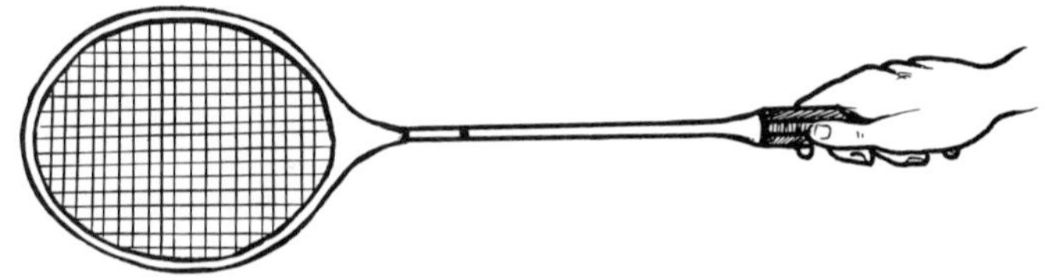

correct grip, the instructor has the students place their right hands on the racket handles in the forehand grip position. After the grip of each player has been checked, the rackets are returned to the left hand. The class then should practice the correct forehand grip several times, and each practice grip should be checked by the teacher. The importance of a proper grip should be stressed, for effective wrist action, which is the most important single element in badminton, depends on the player's holding the racket correctly.

D. Emphasis

1. With the racket held out in front, the student should see the knuckles of the four fingers (three if the hand is very small).

2. The grip is with the fingers, not the palm.

3. The forefinger must be wrapped *around* the handle, not extended up the handle.

4. The thumb is *around,* not up, the handle.

II. Backhand Grip

A. Use

The backhand grip is used for all strokes executed on the left side of the body (Figure 3.3).

B. Analysis

This grip is similar to the Eastern backhand grip in tennis. With the racket face perpendicular to the floor, the right hand is placed on the handle, with the first knuckle of the forefinger on the top plate. The thumb is extended along the back plate of the handle, at a slight diagonal across it. Although this extended thumb position limits wrist action to a small degree, it permits the thumb to add force to the wrist movement. The little finger grasps the butt of the racket, and the V of the thumb and forefinger is somewhat more *closed* than is the case in the forehand grip.

C. Presentation to Beginners

The backhand grip, like the forehand grip, is demonstrated and practiced with the students in a semicircle. The instructor assumes the forehand grip with her right hand and holds the racket throat with her left hand. She then raises the racket high where it can be seen easily and turns her back to the class. While holding the racket throat stationary, she demonstrates the shift to the left of the hand and fingers that results in a proper backhand grip. After the students have practiced assuming the grip in this manner several times, and after their hand positions have been checked, they should practice the change back and forth between the forehand and backhand grips without using the left hand to support the racket.

D. Emphasis

1. The thumb is up the racket (for good leverage on the hit).

2. The forefinger is close to the other fingers.

III. Wrist Action

A. Use

The importance of wrist action in badminton cannot be overstressed, for the wrist is involved to some extent in every stroke. In comparison with tennis and squash rackets, the badminton racket is light in weight and its handle small. This permits the wrist to perform the whip action necessary to impart great force to an object constructed of feathers and cork.

B. Analysis

Wrist action is the term used to describe the movement of the wrist from the backward, cocked position (extension) to the flexed position. The speed with which this action is performed determines the speed of the bird. Correct grips are essential for free wrist action. For players with very strong wrists, whip action of the backhand can be increased if the thumb remains wrapped around the handle, much as it is in the forehand. This thumb position is not recommended, however, for most women players.

C. Presentation to Beginners

After the forehand grip has been taught on the first day of class, the instructor demonstrates wrist action by hitting the bird toward the ceiling, starting with little taps and continuing to hit the shuttle higher and higher until the full arm and wrist actions are used. She then gives one bird to each couple and stations the students far apart for practice in the manner demonstrated. Attention may be called to the *swish* of the racket when it is properly whipped through the air. This technique drill is more difficult than it may sound, and it is excellent warm-up practice for any player. If students tend to play with wrists stiff, practice with the racket held by the left hand may help. The fine wrist coordination is absent in the left arm, and a stiff, awkward motion usually results. When changed back to the right hand, the awareness of better wrist control and freer action may cause the student to use a wrist snap.

D. Emphasis

1. A tight grip should be avoided (for free wrist action).
2. The racket head comes through last (for wrist snap).
3. The racket should *swish* through the air (for good acceleration).

IV. Footwork and Stance

A. Use

The terrifically fast pace of a well played badminton game requires the competitor to cover the entire court and to make numerous stops, starts, and changes of direction. Good footwork patterns must become habitual, for there is no time to think *how* to move.

B. Analysis

In general, the footwork in badminton is similar to that in tennis. For forehand strokes the right arm and left leg are forward, with one or two exceptions: drop shots from the right front corner of the court are returned with the right foot forward, and some players prefer this stance for the short serve. The weight is carried on the balls of the feet, and small steps usually are taken. To cover short distances, the slide or hop step is used.

For the forehand strokes, the body faces the right sideline; the left foot is toward the net, with the right foot back. The body weight shifts from the rear foot to the forward foot as the stroke is made. The more power desired, the farther the body turns toward the sideline on the backswing.

For the backhand strokes, the body

FIGURE 3.4 *The ready position.*

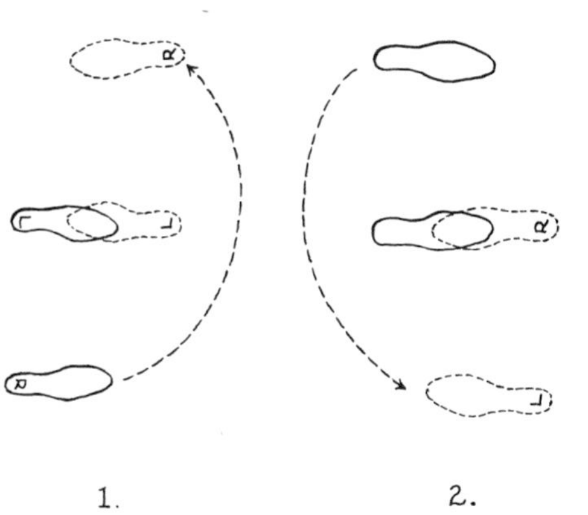

FIGURE 3.5 *Pivot from position for forehand, to position for backhand. 1, pivot on left foot. 2, pivot on right foot.*

faces the left sideline. The body weight shifts from the rear foot (left) to the front foot (right) as the stroke is made. In returning very deep shots, a longer swing and greater resultant force can be achieved by starting the stroke in a position almost facing the rear of the court rather than the sideline.

For forehand and backhand strokes requiring much power, there is considerable knee flexion of both legs on the backswing and of the forward leg on the hit.

The *ready* position (that which the player assumes when receiving the serve and during the rally between strokes) is the starting point from which plays are made (Figure 3.4). The position is an alert one, facing the net, with the left foot slightly ahead of the right. The knees are *easy,* the weight evenly balanced on the toes, with the racket held well up in front of the body, its head pointing toward the opponent. This high position of the racket makes possible quick, overhead returns of the bird, which are preferred to the slower, defensive underhand strokes.

C. Presentation to Beginners

Stance and body position are taught as parts of each stroke. Footwork drills can be practiced, but always with the racket in hand and in conjunction with a stroke. For example, after the forehand drive has been introduced, footwork practice ending with a forehand drive from several parts of the court can be presented and practiced.

D. Emphasis

1. The racket is held high while waiting (for a quick return).
2. For powerful strokes, the side is turned to the net on the backswing.
3. The player should start to move quickly (to get into stroking position soon enough).
4. The player should be standing still as she hits (to assure effective stroking position).

Two elementary footwork practice formations are:

1. Change from forehand to backhand body position. With the left foot forward: (a) step forward with the right, pivoting on the left or (b) step back with the left, pivoting on the right (Figure 3.5).
2. Change from backhand body position to forehand. With the right foot forward: (a) move the left foot ahead; or (b) pivot on the left foot and place the right foot back (Figure 3.6).

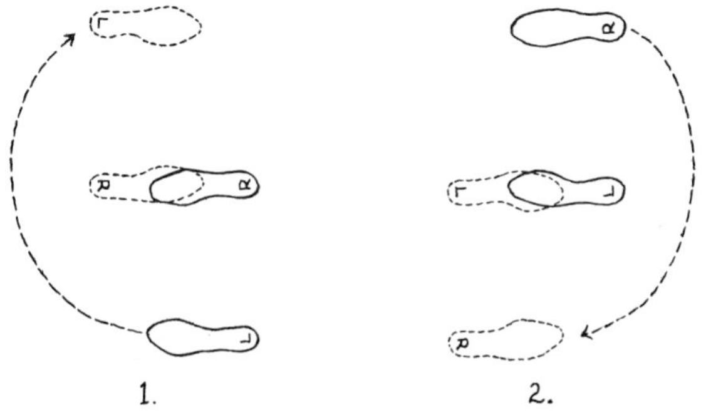

FIGURE 3.6 *Pivot from stance for backhand to stance for forehand stroke. 1, moving the left foot forward. 2, moving the right foot back.*

The Serves

Three types of serve can be used to put the shuttle into play at the beginning of each rally: the long high, the short low, and the drive. According to the official rules, only the server may score a point; therefore, these three strokes are very important, and much time must be devoted to mastering them. The serves are defensive strokes because they must be executed underhand. Specifically, the serving rule states that, at the moment of impact with the bird, the top edge of the racket head must be below the level of the wrist, and contact with the bird must be below the waist level.

A wily player disguises her intent to use a particular serve so that her opponent cannot anticipate the best location from which to receive. The backswing and body position therefore, are, the same for the three serves. Differences in execution lie in the movement of the wrist at the time of impact and in the force given to the shuttlecock.

V. Long High Serve (Underhand Clear)

A. Use

This serve is a basic one for singles play and is used occasionally in doubles as a surprise shot. The long, narrow singles service court encourages the execution of this deep serve, which forces the opponent to the rear of the court. On the other hand, the short doubles service court, and the presence of a partner to *cover,* weaken the effectiveness of the long high serve.

The long high serve technique not only is used to start play but also during rallies to return shots that cannot be hit overhead. The technique is known in these instances as the *underhand high clear,* which is a defensive stroke that forces the opponent to the back boundary line and thus gives the stroker time to return to an advantageous court position.

B. Analysis

The bird is hit so as to reach a maximum height near the rear of the court and to fall sharply to a point within a few inches of the back boundary line.

1. Grip. The forehand grip is used.

2. Stance. The player stands with the body slightly bent forward and both knees somewhat flexed. The left foot is ahead and pointing toward the net; the right foot is back, with the toe at about a 45-degree angle with the net. This position allows for the forward transfer of body weight just before impact, which is necessary to impart force to the hit.

3. Action. With the elbow slightly bent and the wrist cocked, the arm is swung downward and backward until the face of the racket is parallel to the floor and at hip height behind the body. Although more difficult for some beginners to master, a circular backswing that starts upward may be substituted profitably, since it yields greater momentum and disguises more effectively the type of serve to be executed. On the forward swing, the body weight is shifted to the left foot, and the wrist is uncocked and whipped into the stroke just before impact with the bird. The follow-through carries the racket above the head and in line with the point of aim (Figure 3.7).

The only essential difference between the techniques of the long high serve and the underhand high clear is that the intention in executing the clear is to contact the bird at a higher level than is legal in the serve. At the start of the serving stroke, the forefinger and thumb of the left hand grasp the base of the shuttlecock. As the backswing begins, the bird is tossed upward lightly, ahead and to the right of the forward foot. Beginners may prefer simply to drop the shuttlecock, in which case the drop should occur at the end of the backswing.

C. Presentation to Beginners

Students are on one side of the badminton court in several lines with space for swinging rackets; the instructor stands in front of them. This formation is used throughout this section for the introduction of all new strokes to beginners and is not described again.

The instructor explains the purpose of the long high serve, indicates the service

FIGURE 3.7 *The toss service. A, backswing. B, point of contact. C, follow-through.*

court, and demonstrates the technique. The students practice the stroke mimetically and then move to playing positions on the courts. After a few initial attempts to serve are made, the instructor explains the rules governing the execution of the stroke. Verbal analysis of the technique, further demonstration, and correction of errors are employed as needed during the practice session.

D. Emphasis

1. The bird is tossed or dropped well out in front (to make contact despite the length of the racket and arm).

2. The player should lean into the hit (to avoid shifting weight backward at impact).

3. The player should cock the wrist and whip the arm (for proper racket acceleration).

4. The point of aim is the ceiling (to obtain good height and a vertical drop).

Two suggested practices are:

1. One bird per pair of students. The player on one side of the net stands about one yard behind the short service line and serves straight across to her opponent, attempting to make the bird land in the back alley. Opponent lets the bird drop, then picks it up, moves to serving position, and serves back. There is no rallying during this practice. Three pairs can practice on one court. One pair can practice between courts (Figure 3.8).

2. Two birds per court. One player from the right court and one from the left serve simultaneously to the back alley of the court diagonally opposite. Receivers let the birds fall to the floor, then serve back. There is no rallying. Rear court players move forward, and forward players move back after the first five serves. After the second five serves, players in the right court change places with those in the left, and the entire practice is repeated (Figure 3.9).

VI. Short Serve

A. Use

This is the basic serve for doubles play and is intended to force the receiver to use a defensive upward hit for the return. The short serve also is used as a surprise play in singles, particularly when the opponent stands in a deep court position to receive.

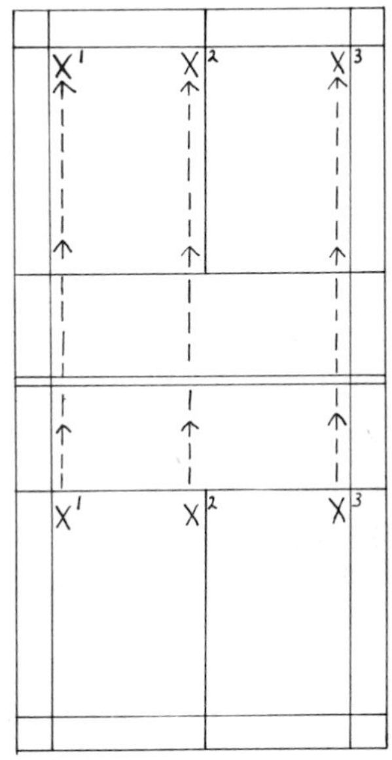

FIGURE 3.8 *Long serve practice formation.*

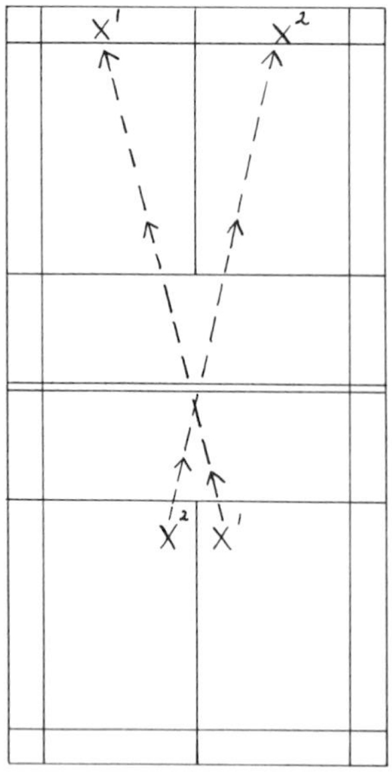

FIGURE 3.9 *Long serve practice formation.*

B. Analysis

The bird is stroked so that it barely clears the net in a flat line of flight and lands close to or on the short service line.

1. Grip. The forehand grip is used.

2. Stance. Same as for the long high serve. (Some players prefer a stance with the right foot forward, believing that this position places the server in an advantageous position to prepare to receive the return.)

3. Action. When the stance is with the left foot forward, the motion for the stroke is the same as for the long high serve until just before impact with the shuttlecock. At that time, the racket speed is slowed by checking the uncocking of the wrist and by relaxing some of the muscular tension in the arm and shoulder. The bird is stroked gently, with the wrist uncocked just enough to form a straight line with the forearm. There is little follow-through. The bird is held and tossed as for the long high serve.

C. Presentation to Beginners

It is the same as for the long high serve.

D. Emphasis

1. The backswing is strong and forceful (to disguise intent to make a short serve).

2. The player should toss or drop the bird well out in front (to make contact despite the length of the racket and arm).

3. The player should reach with the wrist and guide the shuttlecock toward the point of aim (to avoid uncocking wrist too much and so causing a high, short hit).

Two suggested practice drills are:

1. One bird per pair of students. The player stands one yard behind the short service line and attempts to serve straight across to her opponent so that the bird falls just beyond the short service line. The opponent lets the bird hit the floor and then serves back. The formation is similar to the one in Figure 3.8.

2. Two birds per court. The players serve into the service courts diagonally opposite. The receiving players let the birds fall to the floor and then serve back. The formation is similar to the one in Figure 3.9. After each player has served five times, right and left court positions are exchanged, and the practices are repeated.

VII. Driven Serve

A. Use

This serve is used occasionally as a surprise in doubles play and, for the same purpose, but more infrequently, in the singles game. The intention is to send the bird past the opponent before she can react effectively. A driven serve may be angled so that it flies above the wrong service court until the last moment, when it crosses the center line to drop into the proper court. This flight sometimes deceives the opponent into holding her stroke in the belief that the serve will be a fault. The serve is difficult to execute well, however, and should be attempted by experienced players only.

B. Analysis

The stroke combines the power of the long high serve with the low height of the short serve and is aimed to fall deep in the service court.

1. Grip. The forehand grip is used.

2. Stance. It is the same as for the other serves.

3. Action. The motion is the same as for the other serves until just before impact. The wrist then is uncocked and whipped through forcefully. The follow-through is rather flat and toward the net at about chest height, rather than high as for the long high serve, or low as for the short serve. The toss of the shuttlecock and the timing of the toss are the same as for the other serves.

C. Presentation

This serve should be taught only to students who have mastered the other two serves and who have had much experience in playing the game. The stroke is presented in the same manner as the other two serves.

D. Emphasis

1. The racket is swung underhand (to avoid a sidearm action, which results in an illegal serve).

2. The bird should be hit hard enough to pass the opponent before she is ready.

The formations shown in Figures 3.8 and 3.9 can be employed for practice on the driven serve.

THE FOREHAND OVERHEAD STROKES

I. Overhead Clear

A. Use

This stroke is of the greatest importance; it is the most frequently used technique in the singles game and also is the basic stroke in women's doubles. The fast low clear is an offensive tactic used to put the bird just over the opponent's head. The long, high clear is a defensive tactic used to send the bird to the baseline with tremendous height, which gives the player who made the clear time to recover a good court position.

B. Analysis

The bird rises high over the net, continues in an upward flight, and drops almost vertically.

1. Grip. The forehand grip is used.

2. Stance. The left foot is forward at about a 45-degree angle to the net; the right foot is in a comfortable position behind the forward foot.

3. Action. The preparatory part of the stroke includes a high, quick backswing with the flexed elbow leading as the knees bend and the body leans away from the net. The backswing ends with the racket behind the head, the right shoulder dropped and rotated back, the right elbow bent and pointed toward the floor behind the body, and the wrist fully cocked. There is no pause at the completion of the backswing. On the forward swing the weight transfers to the ball of the forward foot as the elbow is moved to point ahead; the racket is lifted rapidly and the arm is extended. While the elbow is still slightly flexed, the bird is contacted as high as possible at a point just ahead of the body and in line with the right shoulder. The follow-through carries the arm to a full stretch upward and forward (Figure 3.10).

C. Presentation to Beginners

It is the same as for the long high serve.

D. Emphasis

1. The racket should whistle on the hit (for whiplike arm and wrist action).

2. The player should stretch to hit the bird as soon as possible (for a quick and forceful return).

3. The elbow should lead as if throwing the racket (for whiplike arm and wrist action).

4. The player should assume the proper stance, pause with the racket up and forward, and then swing-back-and-hit in one motion (for strong acceleration of the racket head and to keep the opponent uncertain of the player's intentions until the last moment).

5. The point of aim is the ceiling (for good height and a vertical drop).

Elementary practices are:

1. One bird per pair of students. Partners stand directly opposite each other and rally, using high clears. Each attempts to force the other behind the

FIGURE 3.10 *The overhead clear. A, backswing; B, point of contact; C, beginning of follow-through.*

back boundary line. Three pairs per court and a pair between courts can practice simultaneously.

2. Rally in rotation. One bird per court in same formation as for 1. Player 1 starts the bird with a long serve to player 2, who clears to player 3, who clears to player 4, and so on. Player 6 clears to player 1, and the rally continues in rotation. Competition may be set up among the courts by having the players on each court count the number of times the bird is hit consecutively without a miss (Figure 3.11).

3. Two birds per court. Rear court players hit overhead clears to each other. Forecourt players stand with their toes on the short service line and attempt to intercept the birds. (The forecourt players may not take more than one step backward.) The players reverse their court positions after five minutes so that all of the players have an opportunity to practice clears (Figure 3.12).

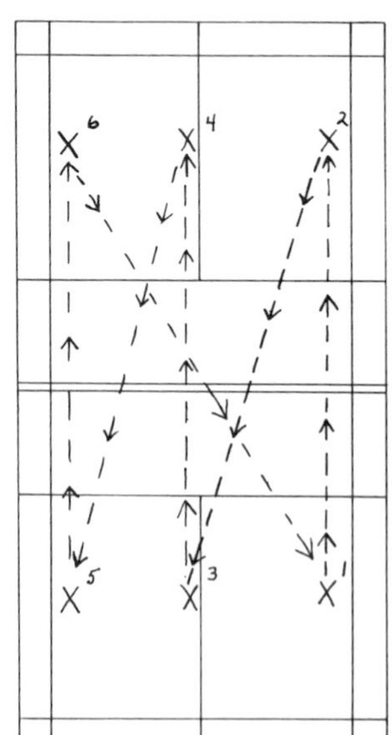

FIGURE 3.11 *Rally in rotation.*

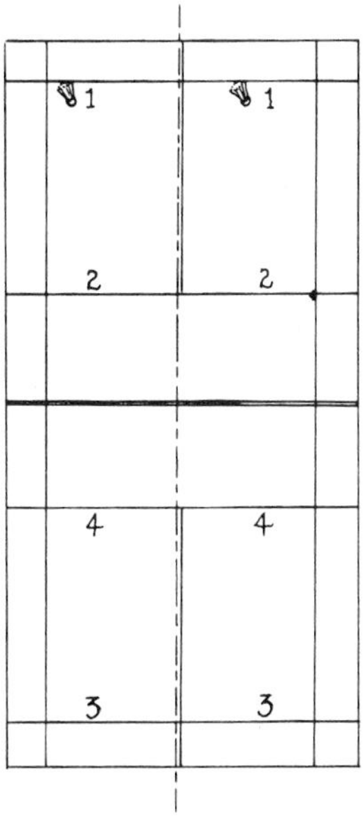

FIGURE 3.12 *High clear practice formation.*

II. Smash

A. Use

This is the principal offensive stroke in badminton. The smash is used more in doubles play than in singles, and is especially effective in men's doubles. The purpose of the stroke is to conclude a rally decisively and to the advantage of the smasher.

B. Analysis

The bird is hit so that it travels with great speed in a downward direction, just clearing the net.

1. Grip. The forehand grip is used.

2. Stance. It is the same as for the forehand overhead clear.

3. Action. The preparatory phase and the transfer of body weight are the same as for the forehand overhead clear. The point of contact with the bird is ahead of the forward foot and in front of the right shoulder, with the arm at full extension. As the hit is made, all of the power of the wrist, arm, and, indeed, the entire body, is brought into the stroke by a downward hit. The follow-through continues downward and diagonally past the left leg.

A variation of the stroke that may be described as a *flick smash,* sometimes is used to return a poor short serve. Because the receiver who has rushed a serve is too hurried and too close to the net to employ a full arm swing, the smash effect in this instance is achieved primarily through strong wrist action. There is little backswing or follow-through of the arm (Figure 3.13).

C. Presentation to Beginners

The stroke is introduced to the class in the same fashion as the preceding strokes. The differences in the execution of the overhead clear and smash (position of bird

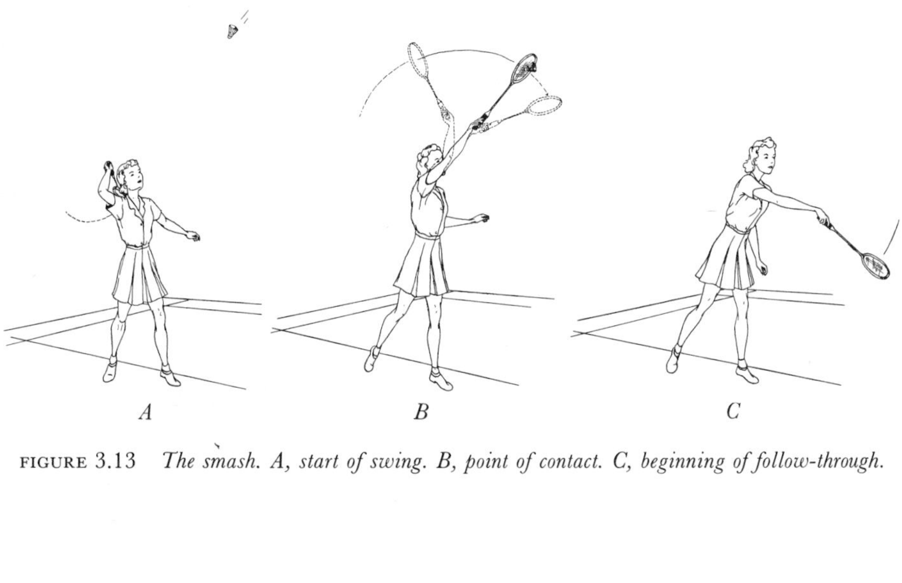

FIGURE 3.13 *The smash. A, start of swing. B, point of contact. C, beginning of follow-through.*

and arm at point of contact and follow-through) are explained and demonstrated.

D. Emphasis

1. The player should reach to hit high and well in front (for a sharp, downward hit).

2. The player should hit hard and snap the wrist (for power and good direction).

3. The stroke is finished with the racket on the left (to avoid the fault of *carrying the bird,* caused by rolling the wrist inward and following through past the right hip).

Suggested practices are:

1. Two birds per court. The player on one side hits the bird high to the player standing in the center of the opposite court. The receiver returns the bird with a smash. There is no rallying. Players change roles after a few hits. In the second practice session, the player attempts to return the smashes, and the rally continues until one opponent is successful in finishing the point (Figure 3.14).

2. Same formation. The student practices the smash from a position very close to the net and then from slightly farther back.

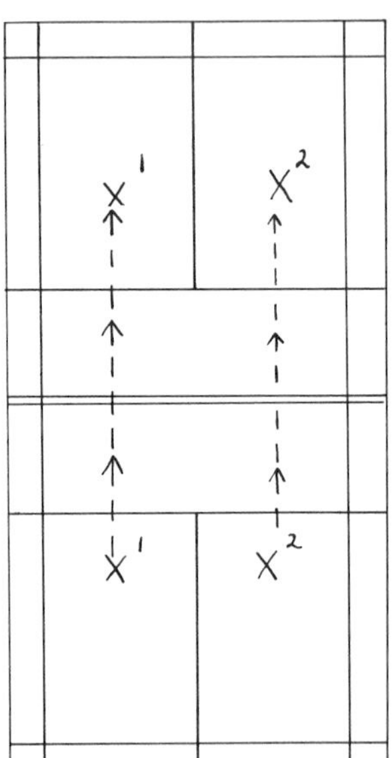

FIGURE 3.14 *Smash practice formation.*

III. Overhead Drop

A. Use

This stroke is used instead of the smash or clear for a sudden change of pace when the opponent is caught in the rear court, or when the opponent anticipates a deep shot. The overhead drop is particularly effective in singles play.

B. Analysis

The bird is hit so that it floats from the racket, skims the top of the net, and lands in the foremost part of the court. A perfect drop shot is one that teeters on the top of the net, then falls gently down the net into the opponent's court. Such a shot is almost impossible to return.

1. Grip. The forehand grip is used.

2. Stance. It is the same as for overhead clear and smash.

3. Action. In order to deceive the opponent, the preparatory action is identical to that of the overhead clear and smash. As the shuttlecock is contacted at a point high and well in front of the body, the speed of the swing is checked, and the bird is stroked gently. There is no powerful acceleration as in the other two overhead strokes. The wrist starts to uncock gently just before impact and continues to extend in order to direct and control the flight of the bird. The follow-through is short (Figure 3.15).

C. Presentation to Beginners

Using the same type of organization as for the previous strokes, the instructor introduces the overhead drop shot with an explanation of its use and its similarity to other overhead strokes.

D. Emphasis

1. The player should reach as she hits (to avoid dropping the right shoulder on contact and thus causing an upward or flat direction of flight).

2. The player should swing as if she were about to smash, until the last moment (to disguise the stroke).

3. The hit is made as soon as possible (to hurry the opponent and to avoid striking the bird at a point behind the body, which sets up the bird for the opponent to smash).

FIGURE 3.15 *The overhead drop shot. A, start of stroke. B, point of contact. C, follow-through.*

Suggested practices are:

Several students can practice this stroke simultaneously on one court, since the bird and the racket travel slowly, and there is little danger to the students. The players on one side of the net stand close to it and set up high shots to their opponents, who stand in the first third of the court (same formation as in Figure 3.8). The opponents return the birds with overhead drop shots. After ten practice shots, the pattern is reversed, and the players who were executing drop shots set up to their opponents. As the students become proficient, they should practice this stroke from positions deeper in the court.

IV. Round-the-Head Stroke

A. Use

This is a particularly useful stroke which can be substituted to advantage for certain backhand shots, especially for those directed to the left side of the head or shoulder. The round-the-head stroke, however, is an advanced technique and should not be presented to novices.

B. Analysis

The stroke is an overhead shot in which the shuttlecock is hit on the backhand side of the body with the forehand face of the racket.

1. Grip. The forehand grip is used.

2. Stance. Preferably, the left foot is forward.

3. Action. The preliminary swing is like that of any overhead, forehand stroke. The forward swing is a circular motion in clockwise direction starting behind the head. The circular movement carries the racket to the backhand side of the head as the elbow extends. Until the moment of impact, the opponent should not know whether the return will be a clear, smash, or drop shot. At impact, for a clear, the arm and wrist take the racket up and out to the right. For a smash, the arm and wrist forcibly whip the racket downward past the right leg. For a drop, the arm movement is checked, and the wrist controls the flight direction with very little follow-through (Figure 3.16).

C. Presentation

This stroke is a difficult one, and should not be presented until the class has mastered all the other strokes.

D. Emphasis

1. The shuttlecock should be met as high as possible (to hurry the opponent and to give a freer choice of the type of shot that can be made).

2. The player should lean well back before stroking (for power).

Each of the three types of return (clear, smash, drop) can be practiced in the same

FIGURE 3.16 *Round-the-head stroke at point of contact.*

formations suggested for the other overhead strokes.

THE BACKHAND OVERHEAD STROKES

A. Use

In the game of badminton, a player avoids deep backhand shots whenever possible and, instead, favors the forehand. There are times, however, when a clear, flick, or drop from the deep backhand corner must be used as a defensive measure.

B. Analysis

1. Grip. The backhand grip is used.

2. Stance. The body is turned so that the back is toward the net and the rear foot (left) is parallel to the baseline.

3. Action. For the three strokes, the right arm is swung high across the face and backward, with the racket head pointing directly downward and with the wrist cocked. As the stroke is made, the elbow leads, and the weight of the body passes from the rear to the forward (right) foot.

CLEAR. As the arm and body weight move toward the net, the stroke is accelerated, and the wrist whips the racket head through. The bird is contacted in front of the body, at full extension of the arm, and with the weight on the forward foot at the time of impact. The follow-through is upward and outward.

FLICK AND DROP. The acceleration is less than for the clear, and the wrist is used to direct the shot just over the net. For the flick, a stronger wrist motion is required than for the drop, but the flight of the bird as it passes over the net is much the same for both strokes. The flick lands a little deeper in the forecourt than does the drop, and usually is directed down the sidelines. The arm and racket do not follow-through so far as for the clear. The swing is checked just before impact with the bird, and the follow-through is a downward motion. For the flick, it is an abrupt, sharp downward arc; for the drop, a slow, gentle arc.

C. Presentation to Beginners

The backhand strokes can be introduced to the class in the same manner as the forehand overhead strokes.

D. Emphasis

1. The back must be to the net (for a free swing).

2. The elbow is aimed at the target (to avoid merely flipping the forearm forward with little wrist action).

3. The thumb pushes the racket (for good leverage).

Practice of the backhand clear, drop, and flick can be organized in formations similar to those used for the corresponding forehand strokes.

THE UNDERHAND STROKES

This category of strokes includes the underhand high clear, the underhand drop shot, and the flick clear. Full descriptions seem unnecessary here, since the strokes closely resemble others analyzed earlier. In this section, the reader is referred to the relevant parts of the text, and supplementary information is supplied where needed.

Comments on the *forehand underhand clear* may be found under the long high serve, which is essentially the same technique.

The *backhand underhand clear* is a purely defensive shot to be employed only as a last resort. It requires the same grip and stance used for other backhand strokes. The preparatory action is like that used for the overhead clear, except that the backswing is taken at a lower level and is completed with the knees well bent and the racket head close to the floor. The point of contact with the bird is in front of the body at about knee height. The forward swing and follow-through are similar to the action of the backhand overhead clear.

The *flick clear* is analyzed with other net strokes. The *underhand drop shot* can easily be understood by comparing it with other drop shots and other underhand techniques.

THE DRIVES

I. Forehand Drive

A. Use

This stroke can be used offensively to pass an opponent, or defensively for the return of a smash. The drive should be used sparingly and as a surprise shot, usually down a sideline. The technique is seen more often in doubles than in singles, especially in men's doubles; but even in doubles play, badminton, unlike tennis, is never based on drives.

B. Analysis

The bird skims rapidly over the top of the net.

1. Grip. The forehand grip is used.

2. Stance. The left side is toward the net; the right foot is back.

3. Action. A circular backswing or a straight one at chest height can be used. For either, the wrist is cocked, the elbow is slightly bent, and the body weight is transferred during the swing to the rear foot. On the forward swing, the racket travels parallel to the floor, the elbow straightens, and the wrist whips into the stroke. The body weight is transferred to the left foot during the forward swing and is on that foot just prior to the hit. The bird is contacted forcefully at a point opposite the left foot, whereupon the arm and racket follow through toward the net at shoulder height (Figure 3.17).

C. Presentation

The stroke can be presented in the same manner as the long high serve.

D. Emphasis

1. The racket should *swish* (for strong wrist action).
2. The player should hit at chest height (to avoid having to reach down, which results in lifting the bird high).
3. The elbow leads; the wrist comes through last (for the flexible arm movement necessary for power).

The same formations described for practice of the smash can be used for the drive. Each pair attempts to rally with drive strokes (two birds per court).

II. Backhand Drive

The use, presentation, and points of emphasis are the same for the backhand drive as for the forehand drive. The backhand grip is used, and the stance is reversed; that is, the right side of the body is toward the net and the right foot is nearer to the net than the left. The ex-

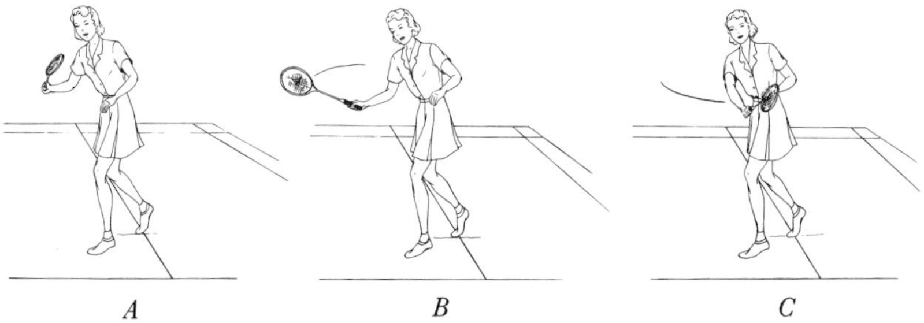

FIGURE 3.17 *The forehand drive. A, backswing. B, point of contact. C, follow-through.*

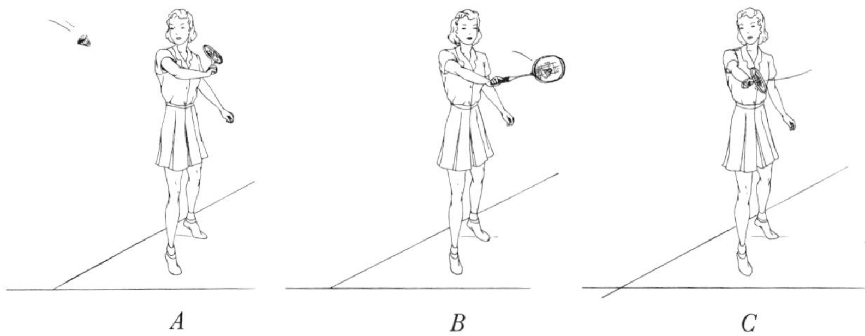

FIGURE 3.18 *The backhand drive. A, beginning of stroke. B, point of contact. C. follow-through.*

ecution of the stroke is similar to that of the forehand drive (Figure 3.18).

NET SHOTS

These strokes are executed at the net. They are used to return drop shots that cannot be hit with an overhead stroke because the defender does not reach the bird in time or because the drop shot was an excellent one in which the bird just skimmed the net tape. One type of net stroke is a drop shot, which goes straight or in a crosscourt direction and lands as close to the net as possible. The second type of net stroke is an underhand clear, which can travel in the same two directions but should land deep in the court.

III. Straight (Hairpin) and Crosscourt Net Strokes

A. Use

These are defensive strokes, generally, but can be used effectively when well placed and well timed.

B. Analysis

1. Grip. The grip may be forehand or backhand, depending on the side of the body from which the stroke is made.

2. Stance. For forehand net shots, the right foot is often forward. Since very little body action is required for this shot, weight transfer is unimportant. The main concern is *reach,* and by stepping with the right foot toward the shuttlecock just prior to the shot, the racket side of the body is brought closer to the bird.

3. Action. There is practically no backswing and only a slight wrist cock, since time does not permit, and a delicate touch is required. The bird is met near the top of the net in order to be returned as quickly as possible, with the racket face turned up and at arm's length. The stroke is made with wrist motion only, so that the bird topples over the net band. The wrist movement determines the direction of the flight, straight or crosscourt. There is no follow-through, but the racket face is pointed toward the spot where the bird was sent. (Figure 3.19).

C. Presentation

The instructor should introduce the hairpin stroke through demonstration, and the students should practice the technique on the court, in pairs. Very little will be gained by having students practice the stroke mimetically. The *touch* of the bird on the racket must be experienced. The footwork, however, can be tried with the racket in hand (see preceding section on footwork drills).

D. Emphasis

1. The bird is met as high as possible (to reduce the danger of misjudging the force necessary to clear the net, and to hurry the opponent).

2. There is no backswing (for speedy return and gentle hit).

Suggested practices are:

1. One bird per pair of students, and several pairs per court. Players stand close to the net (about two feet back) and hit straight drop shots to each other (Figure 3.20).

FIGURE 3.19 *The hairpin net stroke.*

2. One bird per pair, and no more than three pairs per court. Players stand close to the net and hit diagonal or cross-court drop shots to each other (Figure 3.21).

IV. Flick Clear from Net Position

A. Use

This stroke is particularly effective when the opponent is near the net. It should be remembered, however, that a really good drop shot, which barely skims over the top of the net and then clings to the side of the net as it falls, cannot be returned by any type of clear but must be met by another drop shot.

B. Analysis

The flick clear is a variation of the drop shot return and can be either a forehand or backhand shot. The flick clear is executed with the same technique as is the drop shot, except that the wrist whips into the shot at the last moment and the point of aim is higher. Little arm action is needed, because the shot is executed in the forecourt, and the bird has only half the distance to travel to reach the opponent's baseline as compared with a clear hit from the rearcourt.

C. Presentation

This stroke is introduced in the same way as the other net strokes. Also, the same practice formations are suitable. One player can start with a drop shot from close to the net; the other can attempt to clear. Rallying is not satisfactory when there are more than two pairs of students per court.

THE GAME

The actual game of badminton can be introduced early to novices with profit, and the terms and rules should be pre-

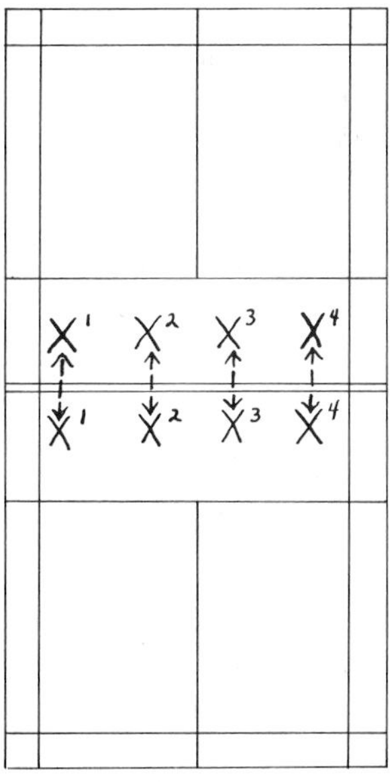

FIGURE 3.20 *Net shot practice formation.*

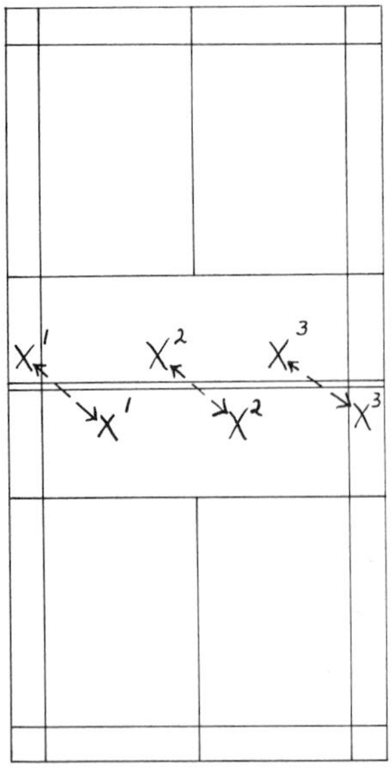

FIGURE 3.21 *Diagonal net shot practice formation.*

sented as they are called for in the play. Official rules can be found in the current edition of the *Tennis-Badminton Guide,* published by the Division for Girls and Women's Sports of the American Association for Health, Physical Education, and Recreation. Only a few of the game terms are included here:

In Side. The side which is serving.

Out Side. The side which is receiving the serve.

One Down or *One Hand Out.* The indication that one partner has finished her turn of serving.

Inning. The turn of service for one side.

Fault. A player's error in which the shuttle fails to fall in the proper court, or the shuttle is hit illegally.

Point. The unit of scoring. Only the serving side may score points (similar to volleyball). A fault by the serving side does not give the receiving side a point, but causes the server to lose her turn of service.

Game. The required number of points to win: in ladies' singles—11 points; ladies' mixed, men's doubles, and men's singles—15 or 21 points. Generally, doubles games involving women are 15 points in length; men's games are 21. In either case, the number of points to be played is determined before the game begins.

I. Doubles Game

In the doubles game there are four players, two on each side of the net. The service rules, the team play, and the strategy distinguish the game from badminton singles (Figure 3.22).

A. Service Rules

These are introduced on a blackboard or by having four players demonstrate while the instructor explains the service court boundaries and the serving order. The player in the right court of the serving, or "in," side serves first and continues to serve, alternating between the right and left courts, until her side fails to win the point. Her partner serves next until the side again fails to score. The shuttle then goes to the opponents, and both of

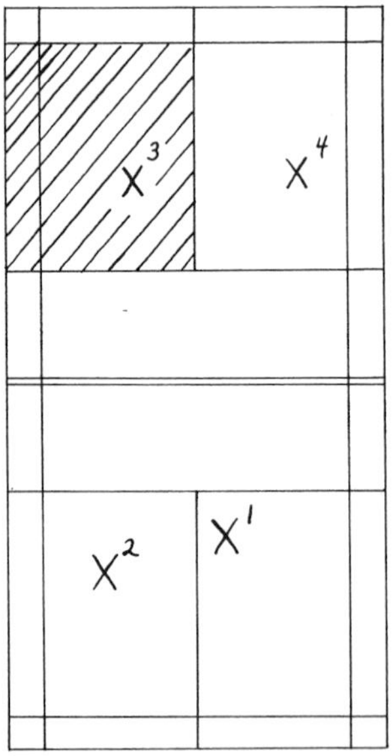

FIGURE 3.22 *The doubles court.* X^1 *the server.* X^1 *and* X^2*: the "in" side at start of the game.* X^3 *and* X^4*: the "out" side. Shaded area: the service court in doubles.*

those partners have turns at serving before their side is "out." For example, X^1 serves from the right court and makes a point (Figure 3.22). She then serves from the left court; she or her partner makes a fault, and she loses her turn of service. X^2 then continues to play from the right court, although it is not her original court. In this way, the serve is delivered from alternate courts. When the serving side next makes a fault, the shuttle is given to the opponents, and so on. In the next inning, the player in the right court serves first. There is one exception to this order of service. The side serving first in the game is permitted to have only one of the partners take her turn to serve before *side-out* is called.

B. Team Play

Partners may choose one of several *systems,* or methods of sharing the responsibility for covering the court. The ones most frequently seen are the parallel (or side-by-side), the up-and-back (or forward and back), the rotation, and the in-and-out.

1. Parallel System. Each player is responsible for her own half of the court, dividing it lengthwise from the center of the net to the center of the back boundary line. All the shots down the center should be taken by the left court player since she can make the return on her forehand. Partners should call to each other before the return of the bird, *mine, yours,* and so forth, so that doubtful shots will be covered with minimum confusion.

The parallel system is the simplest for beginners to understand, and the actual game and scoring should be introduced to a class of beginners by using this type of team play. This system also requires speedy footwork in moving forward and backward, and these techniques should be developed in novices.

A major problem with beginners is to get them to hit the bird *away* from their opponents. The tendency is to return the bird to midcourt, the very spot where the opponent probably is standing. When side-by-side team play is first tried, a suggestion for helping the students to vary their shots is to have each player hit a clear and a drop shot alternately. The next step is to have them mix these two shots and then, of course, to add the smash when it is an appropriate return. Shots directed down the center of the court sometimes are more effective than sideline shots against parallel team play. Any apparent weakness of the opponents should be attacked, however, regardless of general rules.

2. Up-and-Back System. The partners cover the court from side to side, with one player standing in the center of the forecourt with her feet on the short service line, and the other in the center of the rearcourt about a yard in front of the long service line. The forecourt player covers the first third of the entire court (all net shots and weak returns). Her partner covers the remainder of the court (two-thirds). The mixed doubles game uses the up-and-back system almost exclusively, with the woman always playing the net (Figure 3.23).

In order to assume the up-and-back positions in games other than mixed doubles, three plans can be followed.

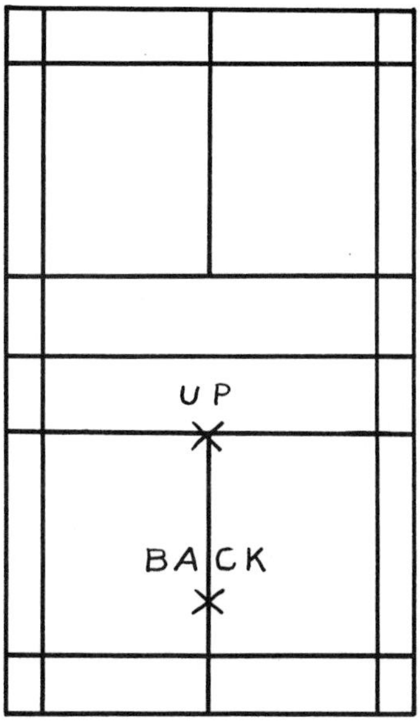

FIGURE 3.23 *Position of players in the up-and-back system.*

a. Elementary. The player serving or receiving always moves into the front position, and the partner into the rear. It is wise to introduce this type of team play first, since it requires few decisions.

b. Intermediate. After the elementary system has been experienced successfully, the intermediate should be presented. This consists of the same court coverage for the serving team (server up and partner back), but the type of serve determines the court positions of the receivers; that is, if the serve is a short one, the receiving player returns the shuttle and then covers the front court; her partner moves to cover the rear. If the serve is long, the receiver moves to the rearcourt, returns the bird, and then takes her position in rear center as her partner moves into the forecourt position.

c. Advanced. After players have experienced all types of team play systems, it may be that certain combinations of partners should play fixed positions when using the up-and-back method. A combination of a strong and weak player always should play with the strong player in the rearcourt and the weak player in the front. The rearcourt player must have a powerful clear and smash. The forecourt player is responsible for making drop shots and returning net shots and should develop these skills. The majority of the shots should be directed down the sidelines. Medium-length drives sometimes are difficult to handle in this system, because the rearcourt player is pulled forward or the forecourt player is forced back.

3. Rotation System. In rotation play, the right court player covers the forecourt, and the left court player the rearcourt. When a player crosses the halfcourt line, or center line, to return a shot, she continues on and changes places with her partner. Thus, they rotate positions, and each becomes responsible for the area previously covered by the other. Obviously, this necessitates quick movement, interchange, and complete cooperation. Rotation for right-handed players is in counterclockwise direction; for left-handed players it is in clockwise direction (Figure 3.24).

This system should be taught only to advanced players of equal ability. It will not function unless a variety of shots is used, including diagonal drops and crosscourt clears. Since beginners and low intermediate players do not always make such distinctive shots, the rotation system interchange will not be needed often in their games. Therefore, the parallel type of play will result automatically from attempts to use the rotation method. Even if all strokes have been taught, until they are well learned this type of play is too difficult for students, because they spend more energy and effort in thinking of where they should be than in actually hitting the bird. The strengths of the rotation system lie in the fact that players move into shots, not away from them, and openings are being closed continually.

There are certain vulnerable spots on the court, and these are shown in Figure 3.25. The four corners are the problem areas, but this is true for all types of team

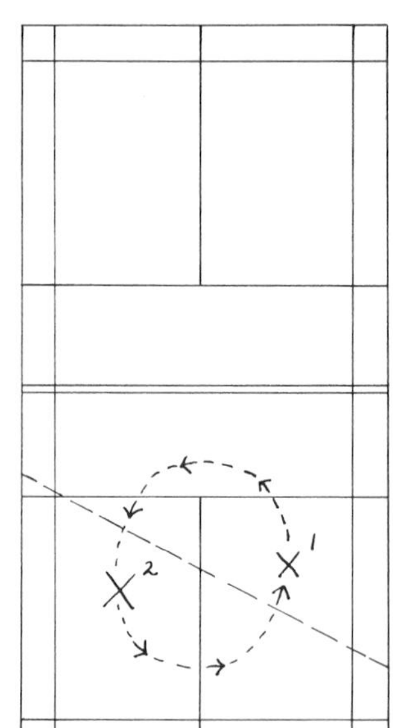

FIGURE 3.24 *The rotation system.*

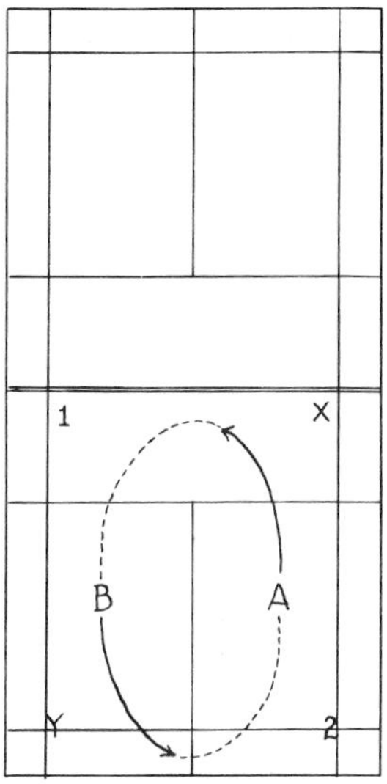

FIGURE 3.25 *Vulnerable spots in the rotation system.*

play. Shots to points X and Y do not cause partners to rotate; but shots to 1 and 2 do make partners change positions.

The success of this system depends on the alertness of the players: not moving until the exact moment, not rotating unless pulled into the diagonal, then moving quickly into position. This system takes much practice and very often is not popular with students when first tried. With practice and experience, however, the rotation can become exciting and fun.

4. In-and-Out System. This plan combines all other methods of court coverage and is the preferred advanced system of team play. Very simply, its principle is that partners play up-and-back when they are on the offensive and side-by-side when they are on the defensive.

When a player smashes or drops, she and her partner move into an up-and-back formation. If in an advantageous position, the player follows her own smash or drop forward toward the net. If, however, she has stroked from deep in the court, it is her partner who should cover the net immediately. When a player clears, the partner at net moves back to whichever court is directly behind her, while the clearing player takes a parallel position in the unoccupied court.

The procedure for the serving team is for the partners to maintain the side-by-side formation until they can assume the offensive.

The in-and-out system is highly sensitive to the demands of the moment. By permitting the partners to move freely, it renders them less vulnerable to the opponents' tactics than do systems that define static boundary lines of responsibility for court coverage or prescribe the direction of rotation. Nevertheless, the in-and-out system is not recommended for beginners or intermediates. Skillful anticipation of the play, harmonious coordination of partners' movements, and dependability of strokes are all necessary for mastery of the in-and-out system and are possible only for advanced performers who play together frequently.

C. Strategy and Tactics of Doubles Play

1. Serving Positions and Placement of the Serve. In doubles, the serving position for intermediate and advanced students depends on the system of team play that the partners are using and the court from which the serve is made. In parallel play, the server can afford to stand nearer the sidelines, since she has only one-half the court to cover; but in forward-back the preference may be for a position nearer the center, in readiness to make a return from either sideline.

Beginners, however, must be told where to stand when they practice the serve, for a habitual position prevents confusion and permits consistency in the stroke. A position about two feet from the center line and one and one-half feet behind the short service line is recommended for beginners (Figure 3.26).

The two front corners of the court are effective targets for the short serve, which is used primarily for the short and wide service court of the doubles game. An occasional placement to the rear corners is recommended also, particularly to the backhand corner when serving from the

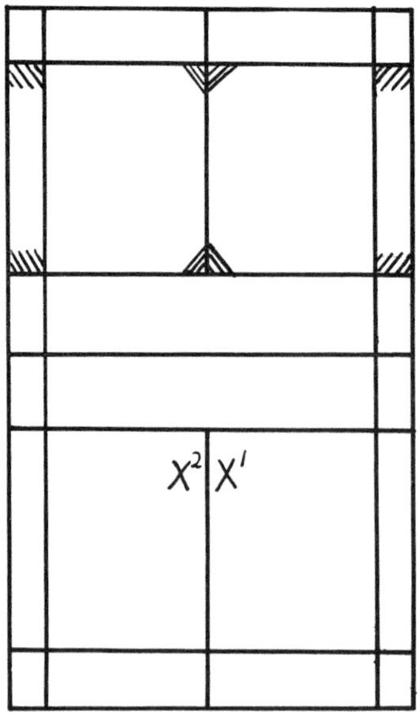

FIGURE 3.26 *Serving positions and placement of the serve in doubles.*

right service court. In mixed doubles, a long serve to the woman sometimes draws her out of position.

2. Receiving Positions and Return of the Serve. The novice should stand approximately two yards behind the short service line to receive, but as her skill improves she should move farther forward. She must always be ready to move back quickly under a long serve. The backhand is avoided as much as possible in receiving by taking a stance somewhat to the left of the center of the receiving court so as to take most of the serves on the forehand.

A poor short serve should be rushed and met before it enters the service court. When the serve is rushed, the partner of the receiver drops back. If, however, a serve is well placed, it cannot be smashed or driven, and the receiver must use an underhand clear or an underhand drop. Generally, these returns should be directed to one of the four corners of the doubles court. If a high, long serve is received, the return should be an overhead stroke (a clear, drop, or smash), again to one of the four corners. Whenever in doubt, a clear to the backhand corner is a safe and intelligent return (Figure 3.27).

3. General Strategy for Doubles Play. Drives and half-court shots (those which go to the alleys and are just deep enough to pass the net player) often are effective, especially against an up-and-back system.

Crosscourt shots, which give the opponents more time for the return, are mostly to be avoided in the doubles game, since covering the width of the court is not especially difficult for the two players.

When the up-and-back system is used and an opponent is smashing from a back corner, the net player should go to the net corner diagonally opposite to the smasher to block a possible crosscourt shot.

When there is a good opportunity for a player to smash, her partner should go to the forecourt opposite the opponent who will receive the smash.

II. Singles Game

The singles game, played by two opponents, can be extremely strenuous and is almost always more so than doubles. In

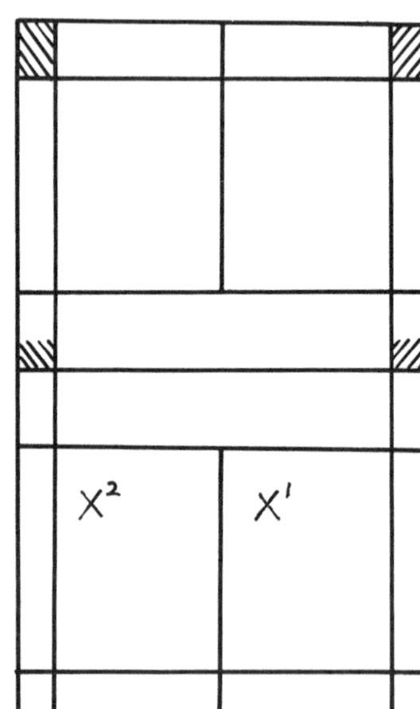

FIGURE 3.27 *Receiving positions and placement of service returns in doubles.*

certain respects, however, singles play is less complicated, because there is neither teamwork with a partner nor the action of two opponents to consider.

A. Service Rules

As in doubles, these rules may be introduced on the blackboard or by demonstration. At the beginning of the game, the server delivers from the right court. As long as she wins the rallies, she continues to serve (alternating courts) and to score points. When the server commits a fault, her term of service ends, and her opponent becomes the server. The court from which the serve is made depends on the server's own score: when it is even (0, 2, 4), she serves from the right court; when the score is odd (1, 3, 5), from the left.

B. Strategy and Tactics of Singles Play

1. Serving Positions and Placement of the Serve. In singles, the server stands somewhat farther back in the court than in doubles: about a yard and a half behind the short service line. The position for either the right or left court is close to the center line (Figure 3.28).

The long high serve is used predominantly, since the singles service court is long and narrow. The two rear corners of the singles court are vulnerable, the backhand corner the more so. Occasionally, the short serve should be used for variety, and in that case either of the two front corners is the target.

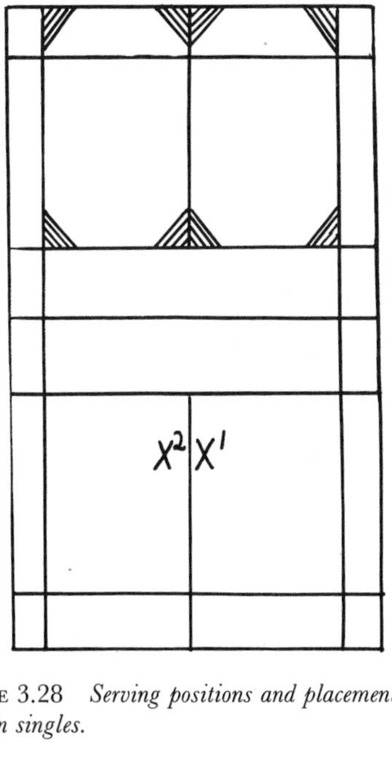

FIGURE 3.28 *Serving positions and placement of the serve in singles.*

2. Receiving Positions and Return of Serve. The receiver stands halfway back and on the left side of the service court so as to take the serve on the forehand. It is necessary to be ready to move forward for a short serve, but the majority of the returns will be from deep in the court, so one cannot afford to stand in the same receiving position as in doubles.

The return of the serve undoubtedly will be an overhead shot, except on the rare occasions when a short service is received. The return can be a smash, clear, or drop. If the serve is somewhat short, a smash should be the answering shot; otherwise a clear to the deep backhand is strategically sound. The four corners of the court are the targets for the returns. The purpose of the receiver is to put the server on the defensive and to force her out of position.

3. General Strategy for Singles Play. Since singles is a more defensive game than doubles, the clear and the drop shot are of prime importance.

When the opponent is near the net, a low clear may pass her before it can be hit.

A crosscourt drop from the forehand, which was hit so that it can be reached speedily, often is best returned with a straight underhand drop.

A straight forehand overhead drop down the sideline usually is best played with a quick crosscourt drop.

When clearing from the sideline, the hit should be straight ahead so that the opponent cannot smash to the extreme far corner of the forecourt.

III. General Court Strategy for Singles and Doubles Play

A. Coaching Points

1. The player should be alert, with

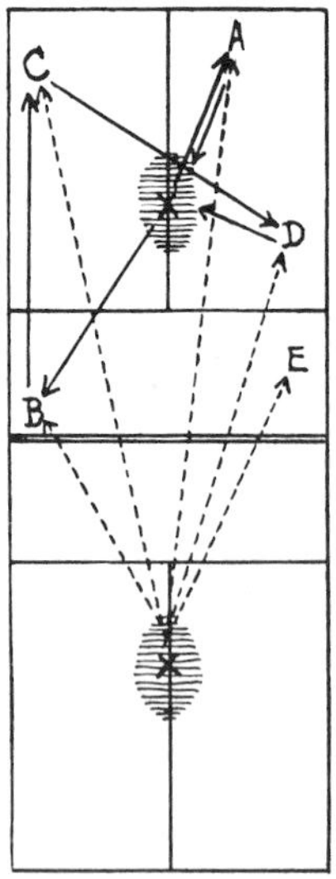

FIGURE 3.29 *Strategy 1. Shaded areas, X, indicate the best waiting positions.*

- - - - Flight of shuttle.
——— Course of player.

the racket held in ready position and the weight on the toes.

2. The player should return to home base quickly between shots. Home base is the center or slightly to the left of center of the area it is the player's responsibility to cover. Home base may shift a little with play. It moves forward after a drop shot and, in singles, it changes to about three feet to the left after a hit to the opponent's forehand.

3. Every bird should be hit with an overhead stroke if possible.

4. The smash is used whenever possible.

5. Deep backhand shots should be avoided by running around them or using round-the-head strokes.

6. The player should use deception in all strokes in order to avoid "telegraphing" the shots.

7. It is important to analyze opponents' weaknesses and play them.

8. If the opponent "telegraphs" shots, the player should anticipate the placement and move in that direction. This practice, however, is dangerous against expert players, because the stroke can be changed at the last moment.

9. The player should use a variety of shots and keep the opponent on the move.

B. Examples of Singles Strategy. (The same principles are effective in doubles)

1. To change the pace (speed) of the bird as well as the direction (Figure 3.29).

a. High clear, to force opponent back.

b. Drop shot.

c. High clear.

d. Smash *or* drive.

e. Crosscourt net stroke.

2. To catch the opponent running in the wrong direction (Figures 3.30, 3.31, 3.32).

a. Three net strokes. Y returns net stroke A by using net stroke B and then starts to move back to position, since the whole court is open. O immediately sends the third net stroke C to the spot vacated by Y (Figure 3.30).

b. Long-short-long-long: to catch opponent running forward. Opponent runs from A to B to C and then starts back

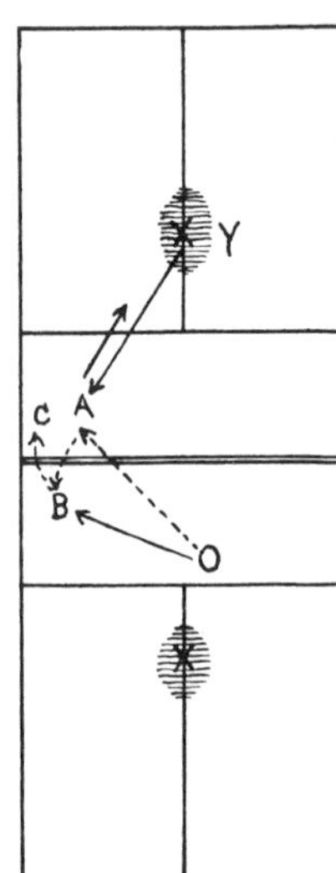

FIGURE 3.30 *Strategy 2a.*

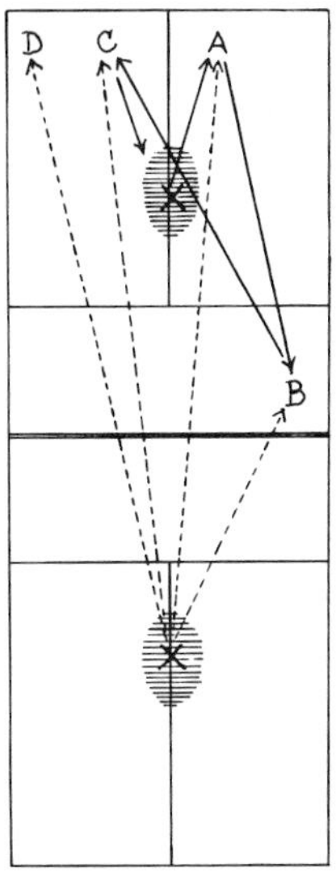

FIGURE 3.31 *Strategy 2b.*

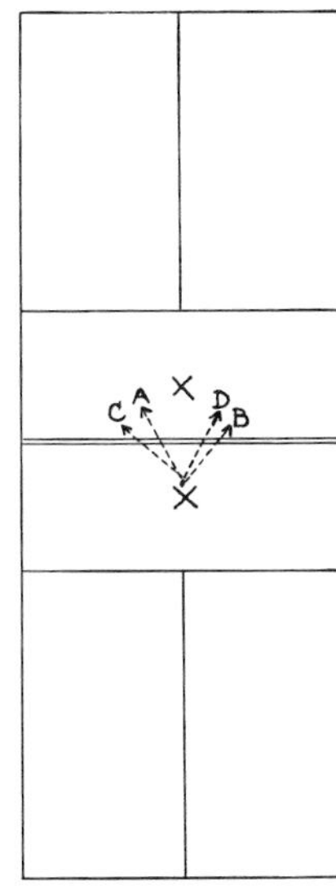

FIGURE 3.33 *Strategy 3.*

to center, expecting another short shot (Figure 3.31).

c. Long-short-short: To catch opponent running back.

d. Side-to-side. Opponent runs from A to B to C and then starts back to center before D is hit (Figure 3.32).

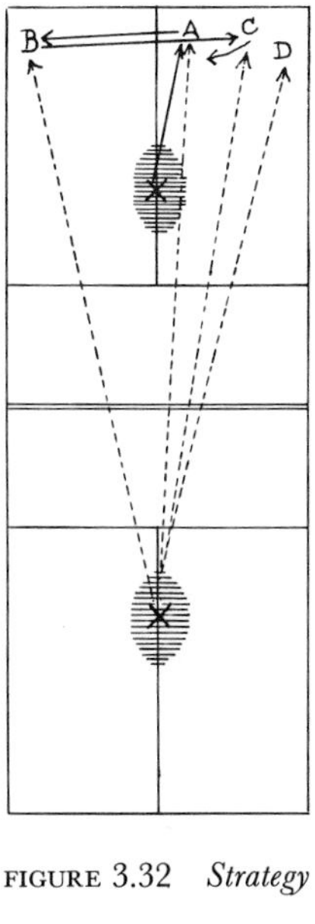

FIGURE 3.32 *Strategy 2d.*

3. To make opponent return alternate forehand and backhand strokes, particularly when near the net (Figure 3.33).

a. Various net strokes.

b. Drop shots.

c. Drives.

NOTE: In these examples the opponent conveniently returns the shuttle to the ideal spot. In actual play this is unlikely, and accuracy is difficult to attain. One must think quickly while moving and executing each shot.

ETIQUETTE

Etiquette in badminton involves good court manners and sportsmanlike behavior. The following specific courteous practices should be taught:

The players always should warm-up with high deep clears, never with smashes or drops. This practice is a matter of etiquette but also one of common sense as far as muscular conditioning is concerned.

If there is no official, the player should call wood shots and *carries* on herself, but not on the opponent, unless the errors are perfectly obvious. The player also should call any other faults on herself, such as hitting the net or committing a fault in serving.

It is courteous to acknowledge the opponent's good shots but not to overdo the practice. For example, if the player sets up a shot that, because of her own poor play, causes the opponent to win the rally, congratulations are not in order.

One never should walk across an occupied court. If it is necessary to enter a neighboring court to retrieve the shuttlecock, or to walk behind the court, the player should wait until the rally is over.

The server calls the score and the number of hands out (or down) before serving.

Congratulations and *thank yous*, but no excuses, are in order at the end of a match.

If the courts are crowded, they should be surrendered to waiting players after two games. Doubles matches take precedence over singles.

CLASS INSTRUCTION

ORGANIZATION OF THE PLAYERS

Ideally, there should be no more than four students per court in a badminton class, and all the players should be of the same general level of ability. Since this arrangement often is impossible, however, the instructor must use ingenuity in organizing the class so that all have equal opportunities to practice and play.

If necessary, a single court can accommodate as many as eight students, provided the area within which each player must practice is clearly defined. Additional space for work on skills can be utilized by stretching pieces of old net from the net post of one court to the net post of the next. The short service line, long service line, and baseline can be drawn with chalk on these *in between* courts. Smooth wall space on which the net height is marked can furnish a third practice area. Rallying against a wall is very difficult for beginners, but it is excellent practice in timing and wrist action for intermediate and advanced players. Also, there may be one or two students in a beginning class who have difficulty in coordinating and contacting the bird when attempting to serve. These individuals should benefit from service practice against a wall where they are working alone and are not conspicuous by their lack of skill. Finally, open floor space can be utilized for mimetic practice of the strokes for footwork drill, for racket control in striking the shuttlecock, and for instruction on rules and strategy.

Although a badminton class may have been arranged to include only one level of ability—beginning, intermediate, or advanced—gradations in skill always are represented. It is helpful to both instructor and students if players are assigned to particular courts on the basis of ability. Where classes are large, a rotation system can be used on each court so that the practice and playing time are fairly apportioned to everyone. From time to time, court reassignments should be made in recognition of changes in the relative proficiencies of the students and of the desirability of competing some of the time with opponents of various degrees of skill.

With an ability grouping type of arrangement within a single class, the instructor need not have all players work on the same techniques simultaneously. Instead, more advanced strokes and more complex drills may be practiced on some courts.

SAMPLE LESSON PLANS

The following lesson plans for each level—beginning, intermediate, and advanced—are offered as suggestions only and may be used as a guide to the order of presentation of the various aspects of badminton. Total course content and the material of any one lesson must be determined by the time limits, class enrollment, and the progress of the group concerned. Also, good results may be achieved with progressions that differ in order from the ones given here.

AN OUTLINE OF 18 LESSONS FOR BEGINNING PLAYERS (35 TO 40 MINUTE PERIODS)

All formations used are those included under the section on techniques. The order of presentation in the plans is forehand overhead clear, long high serve, backhand underhand and overhead clears, short serve, drop shot, and smash. Side-by-side and up-and-back systems of team play are taught.

Lesson 1.

Briefly introduce game, including essentials of equipment care. Present forehand grip, wrist and elbow action (compare with tennis), how to hold bird, drop it, and pick it up. Have class members practice hitting bird to self. Present overhead clear and ready position. Have class rally on courts, bird started by a toss from one player to another.

Lesson 2.

Review and check grip. Class practices hitting bird to self. Review ready position and overhead clear. Present long serve. Players first engage in long serve practice with no rallying; then rally, starting bird with a long serve.

Lesson 3.

Explain similarity of long serve and underhand clear. Teach backhand grip and backhand, underhand, and overhead strokes. Lead class in mimetic practice in changing grip and stance for forehand and backhand, overhead, and underhand clear strokes. Have class engage in court practice of forehand and backhand underhand strokes. Players then rally on courts.

Lesson 4.

Present short serve. Have players practice short serve, first letting bird fall to court, then clearing serve but not rallying. Review backhand strokes. Introduce half-court game.

Lesson 5.

Review short serve. Players practice serve to court diagonally opposite. Class members then practice clearing to partner straight across, two birds to court. This is followed by rallying from backcourt with underhand strokes to opponent in forecourt, who uses overhead strokes. A half-court game completes the lesson.

Lesson 6.

Review underhand strokes and short serve. Have class play half-court game.

Lesson 7.

Introduce drop shot from middle of court. The class members practice with partners. Set-ups must be high and short. Introduce game and parallel doubles play. Include some scoring and terms but not setting.

Lesson 8.

Have class engage in warm-up rally. Review drop shots from middle of court and then introduce hairpin and crosscourt strokes at net. Review simple game rules. Short games are played during the last part of the period.

Lesson 9.

Emphasize hairpin and crosscourt net strokes while class rallies to warm up. Give additional game rules, including setting. Have class play regular games.

Lesson 10.

Introduce smash. Have partners practice, one clearing short to middle of court, other smashing (two birds to a court, hitting straight across). Rallying and games conclude the lesson.

Lesson 11.

Review smash, underhand clears, and drop shots. Present up-and-back doubles play. Have class play games using up-and-back system.

Lesson 12.

Review long and short serves (announcing that they will be tested at next class meeting). Have class play games using up-and-back system.

Lesson 13.

Test short and long serves subjectively (each player serving 10 to 20 birds, depending on the time available). Wall practice during testing for one-half class. Have players change places when testing finished for first group. Games follow if time permits.

Lesson 14.

Start the lesson with wall practice for everyone and completion of serve testing for absentees. Discuss simple tactics and strategy that have not yet been covered. Have class play games.

Lesson 15.

Have a brief wall practice for everyone. Discuss badminton etiquette. Emphasize tactics and strategy during game play. Announce wall volley skills test next lesson and written test for Lesson 17.

Lesson 16.

Present singles game and review other rules. Have wall volley test conducted by students for one-half class. Observe and rate abilities of other half playing singles. Have players change places when testing completed for first half.

Lesson 17.

Administer written test on rules, techniques, etiquette, and strategy. Permit singles play to start as soon as individual students complete test. Continue subjective evaluation of abilities until all have been rated.

Lesson 18.

Conduct progressive bridge tournament. Give out tallies. Play periods of 5 to 7 minutes are suitable. Winners advance to next court and change partners. Winner of tournament is player winning most times.

AN OUTLINE OF 18 LESSONS FOR INTERMEDIATE PLAYERS (35 TO 40 MINUTE PERIODS)

The intermediate level usually contains the widest range of abilities, and because of this fact any set of lesson plans can be only tentative. The rate at which the lessons are covered will depend on the students' ability to master the fundamental techniques. With some intermediate groups, the lesson plans for beginners can be followed. Others may achieve the status of advanced players early in the season.

The strokes and order of presentation are the same as for the beginning group. The flick smash, driven serve, forehand and backhand drives, and flick clear are the new strokes introduced.

Lesson 1.

Discuss care and use of equipment. Have a student-conducted wall volley test for one-half class while other half rallies. Rate abilities of those on courts. Have players change places when first group completes test.

Lesson 2.

Assign students to courts on basis of wall test and subjective judgment. Review overhead and underhand clears and long high serve. Let players practice combinations of strokes. Check on court assignments and make any desired changes.

Lesson 3.

Review short serve. Have class practice long and short serves. Stress deception. Rallying and doubles play using parallel system conclude the lesson.

Lesson 4.

Review short serve and footwork. Let class rally and then play parallel system.

Lesson 5.

Review and have group practice hairpin and crosscourt drop shots at net. Introduce flick smash and practice in combination with short serve. Students then play game using parallel system.

Lesson 6.

Review etiquette and doubles rules. Review up-and-back system and introduce intermediate method of determining position. Class then plays doubles using this system.

Lesson 7.

Review and have group practice drop shots from rear court. Players should mix returns of drops and clears (practice deception). The lesson ends with doubles play using up-and-back system.

Lesson 8.

Present drive serve and have class practice it. This is followed by doubles play using up-and-back system.

Lesson 9.

Review smash using elementary formation. Stress deception while class practices smash, drops, and clears from rearcourt. Let students play doubles using up-and-back team play.

Lesson 10.

Review rules and strategy for singles game. Class members then play abbreviated games of 7 points, so that each student has opportunity to play.

Lesson 11.

Present and have class practice forehand and backhand drives. Review driven serve. Doubles play using up-and-back system follows.

Lesson 12.

Review drives and driven serve. Introduce and have students practice flick clear. Rotate players between wall practice and singles play.

Lesson 13.

Discuss strategy of up-and-back and parallel systems of doubles play. Review flick clear and have class practice the stroke in combination with drop shots. Students then play doubles, first with one, then with other system. Announce wall volley test for next time and written test for Lesson 15.

Lesson 14.

Student-conducted wall volley test for one-half class while instructor rates abilities of other half of class during singles play. Students change places when first group completes test.

Lesson 15.

Written test on rules, techniques, etiquette, and strategy. Singles play starts as soon as individual students complete test. Complete wall test for absentees and continue subjective evaluation of ability until all students have been rated.

Lessons 16 to 18.

Informal doubles tournaments. Different partners each class meeting. Each pair should use system of team play best suited to own strengths and weaknesses.

AN OUTLINE OF 18 LESSONS FOR ADVANCED PLAYERS (35 TO 40 MINUTE PERIODS)

No more than four students per court should be registered in advanced classes, since more time is devoted to play and less to stroke practice than at the elementary and intermediate levels.

All strokes are reviewed and practiced with emphasis on placement and deception. The truly advanced class can cover the basic techniques rapidly, and class time can then be devoted to singles and doubles strategy and tournament experience. The round-the-head stroke and the rotation and in-and-out systems of team play are added to the previously learned techniques.

Lesson 1.
Discuss care and use of equipment. Student-conducted wall volley test for one-half class while other half rallies. Rate abilities of those on courts. Have players change places when first group completes test.

Lesson 2.
Assign students to courts. Review the three types of serve. Emphasize deception and placement as the class practices. Doubles play using parallel system completes the lesson.

Lesson 3.
Review footwork. Review returns of serves. Have class play doubles using parallel system.

Lesson 4.
Review overhead strokes (clear, drop, and smash). Class plays doubles using parallel system.

Lesson 5.
Present round-the-head stroke and have group practice the technique. Doubles games using up-and-back system are played for the remainder of period.

Lesson 6.
Review drop shots from net. Introduce rotation system and then have class members play doubles using it.

Lesson 7.
Review drives. Discuss doubles tactics. Partners play games using rotation system.

Lesson 8.
Review round-the-head stroke. Discuss singles tactics. Alternate players between wall practice and singles games.

Lesson 9.
Let players practice weakest strokes. Discuss officiating. Alternate students between singles play and officiating practice.

Lesson 10.
Introduce in-and-out system and have class members play doubles using it.

Lesson 11.
Discuss in-and-out system strategy more fully. Class plays doubles using this system.

Lesson 12.
Let players practice weakest strokes. Partners play doubles using in-and-out system.

Lessons 13 to 18.
Schedule a round-robin tournament followed by a singles elimination-consolation tournament. Instructor makes up doubles teams. Partners decide which system of team play to use throughout tournament. During these lessons, students who are waiting for matches serve as officials, take the wall test, and on the 17th day take a written test.

SUPPLEMENTARY PRACTICES FOR STROKES AND GAME SKILLS

Practices to be used when a skill is first presented were suggested with the analyses of specific strokes. This section includes a variety of additional practices to be used primarily for review of strokes. Several of the drills are devised to accommodate large groups, either on or off the courts. Some drills are planned to provide practice in using certain sequences of techniques, and other drills call for stroke work under gamelike conditions.

I. Off Court Practices

A. For Correct Grip And "Feel" of the Equipment

1. Hitting to Self.

a. Player stands where she will not interfere with court play. Racket is held in forehand grip, face up and parallel to the floor. Shuttle is bounced on strings. Height of the bounce is increased as player gains control. The number of successive hits without a miss is counted.

b. Player engages in the same

practice using backhand grip with racket face toward the floor.

c. Player shifts racket back and forth from forehand to backhand grip as quickly as can be done accurately.

d. Player holds racket in forehand (or backhand) grip with racket face vertical to floor. The racket is moved rapidly backward and forward by wrist action while the arm is held motionless.

B. For Overhead and Underhand Clears and Wrist Action

1. Wall Volley. A chalk or tape line is placed on a smooth wall 7½ feet above and parallel to the floor. Player stands behind a line 10 feet from the wall. Player rallies against the wall. All hits striking above the 7½ foot line may be counted as successful strokes. A practice shuttlecock with a sponge rubber base is best for wall practice.

2. Couple Practice.

a. Couples stand facing and approximately 30 feet apart. The bird is rallied back and forth. One couple may practice between the sidelines of adjacent courts. Other couples may be placed at the sides and ends of the room if space permits. Old nets or string indicate the net height.

b. Couples rally as above, holding arms extended forward and trying to stroke with wrist action only.

C. For Serves

1. Short Serve to Wall. A line is marked on the wall at net height, and a short service line is marked on the floor. Player stands behind the short service line and serves to the wall. Practice may be adapted to skillful players by marking several narrow lines at two-inch intervals above and below the one at net height. The player's serves may then be scored according to their proximity to the net line.

2. Short or Long Serve to Partner. Chalk lines to indicate the position of short and long service lines are placed on the floor between courts or on other free floor space. Player serves to partner, who lets shuttlecock fall to floor before retrieving it and serving it back.

D. For Footwork

1. Boxer's Drill. Player stands on balls of feet, knees slightly bent and feet parallel. She then steps forward left, brings the right foot up beside the left with a quick change of weight to the right and then makes another quick change of weight back to the left foot without altering the position of the feet. The rhythm is long, short, long. The same pattern is done next in a backward direction starting with the right foot, then to one side, and then to the other. The sequence is repeated with gradually increasing tempo.

2. Rope Jumping with Individual Ropes.

3. Lunge Step. Three parallel lines at approximately two-foot distances are marked on the floor. Player stands on the center line. At a signal, she pivots on the right foot and lunges diagonally forward to step across the right hand line with her left foot. She then returns to starting position. The lunge is repeated rapidly to alternate sides and may be combined with a change from forehand to backhand grip.

II. Court Practices

A. For Overhead and Underhand Clears and Smashes

Eight players to a court, two in the rear and two in the forecourt on each side of net; two birds. Rearcourt players clear the shuttles to their partners directly across the net. Forecourt players, with feet on short service line, intercept hits and smash when possible. Rotate positions after several minutes (Figure 3.34).

B. For Drop Shots and Clears

1. Eight players per court and four birds. Same formation as for clear and smash practice. Forecourt players practice drop shots to net partners directly across. Rearcourt players practice clears. Players change positions to practice other stroke after a few minutes.

2. Eight players per court and two birds. Same formation as for clear and smash practice. The court is divided in half lengthwise. The four players on one half play independently. The bird is

started with an underhand clear from a forecourt player to the opposite rearcourt. The rearcourt player sends an overhead clear to the opposing rearcourt. The player there does an overhead drop over the net to the forecourt, and the forecourt player makes a drop shot to return the bird to the forecourt where the play started. This sequential rally continues until each player has hit successful shots from her position; then players in the rearcourts exchange places with those near the net. Eventually, each player should have practiced from each of the four positions.

C. For Serves

Mark shaded areas A and C on the court (Figure 3.35).

1. Serve to areas A or C in the doubles court. Allow the shuttle to drop to the floor. 1 serves to 3's court, 2 to 4's, and 3 and 4 serve back: five serves to each; A's then do the same.

2. Score successful serves for accuracy. Allow shuttle to drop to the floor. Using above procedure, each player serves in turn from the right and left courts. Five serves to A: 5 points each. Five serves to C: 5 points each. Possible score: 50 points in each court, or a total of 100 points.

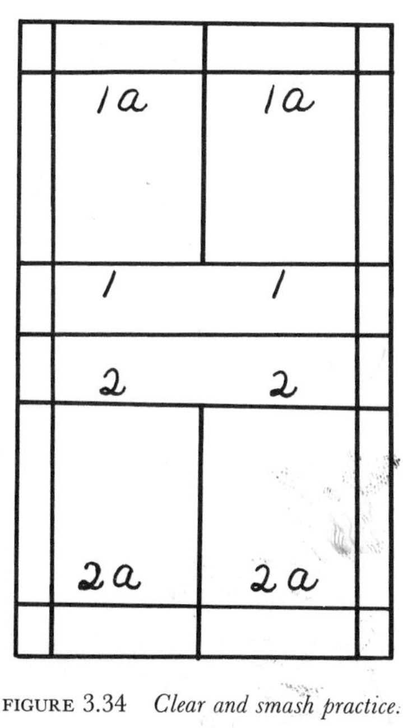

FIGURE 3.34 *Clear and smash practice.*

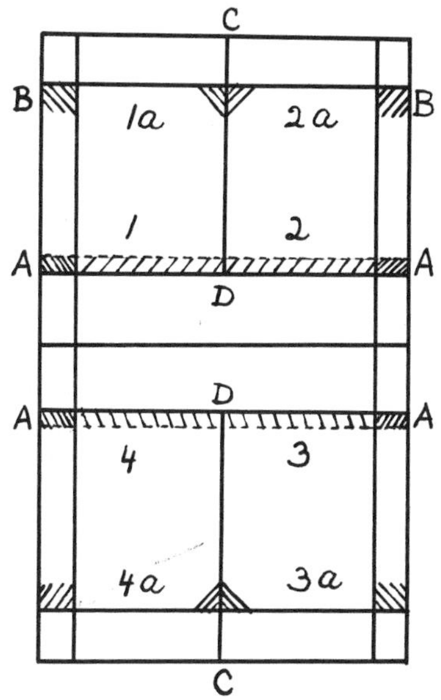

FIGURE 3.35 *Doubles service practice.*

3. Serve and return of service diagonally. 1 plays with 3, and 2 plays with 4. Example: 1 serves to 3, who returns it successfully. They rally until there is a fault. 3 then serves to 1 and they rally. Next, 1A and 3A proceed as above.

(Although 2 and 4 are playing at the same time as 1 and 3, there is not undue confusion if concentration and placement are stressed. While not participating, the other four watch for illegal serves and help coach their partners.)

Mark shaded areas B, C, and D. Area D is 1 foot wide.

Score successful serves to these areas as above. (See Figure 3.36.)

Mark shaded areas A and B in singles service court. Score successful serves to these areas as above.

D. For Net Shots

Four players to a court (Figure 3.37). Players stand in positions near sidelines and close to the net. Player 1 hits diagonal net shot to 2, who hits straight across to 3, who hits a diagonal drop to 4, who returns bird with drop to 1. After adequate practice, reverse order of hitting

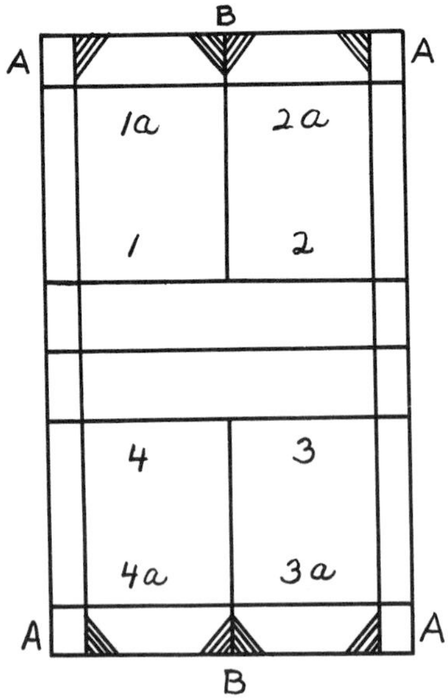

FIGURE 3.36 *Singles service practice.*

so that 2 and 4 hit diagonal net shots and 1 and 3 hit straight across. Four extra players on court can practice same way in rear of the courts without nets. (Figure 3.37).

E. For Practice in Game Form

1. Half-Court Game. Two birds per court; the court is divided in half lengthwise, and each half court plays independently of the other half. Game is similar to table tennis in order of service and scoring: 21 points constitute a game. Forecourt player on serving side steps out of court until serve is made. Each player serves five times, and a point is scored at the end of every rally. After five serves by first player, forecourt player on other team serves. Then, when second player on first team becomes server, she changes positions with partner, etc. Players may use any stroke but must keep bird in half of court bounded by outside alley line and extension of midcourt line. (See Figure 3.38.)

2. Eight-Player Badminton. One bird per court; two forecourt and two rearcourt players on each side of net. A regulation badminton game is played, with these exceptions; forecourt players are restricted to space between net and short service line, backcourt players receive the serve, and forecourt players serve. Net players may not touch the bird during service. They should stand near

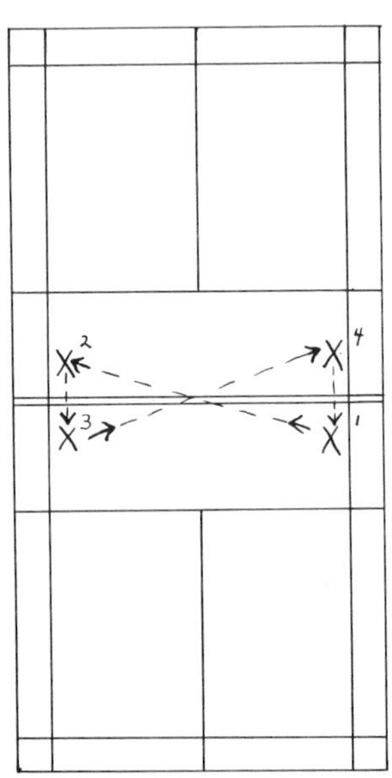

FIGURE 3.37 *Net shot practice.*

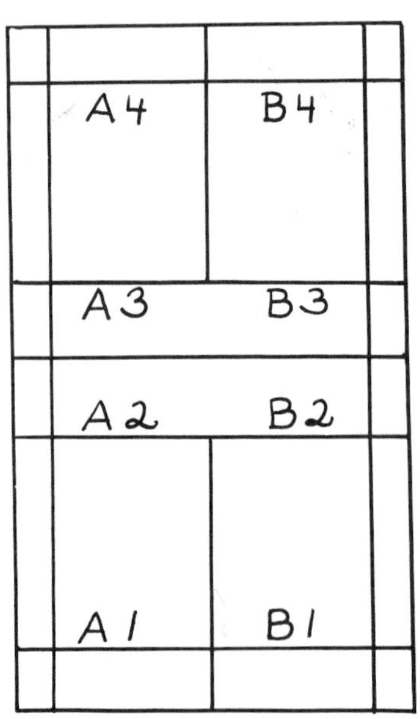

FIGURE 3.38 *Half-court game.*

the sideline to be out of the way. Net players exchange places with those in the backcourt upon receipt of service (when their inning starts). (See Figure 3.34.)

3. Six-Player Badminton. One bird per court; two players in the rear and one in the forecourt on each side. Rearcourt players are servers and receivers of the serves. Player at net exchanges position with one person in rearcourt when serving inning starts. The order of playing net is established before the game (one player always is first, another second, and the third last). The game is scored and played according to the regulation doubles rules. (See Figure 3.39.)

4. Progressive Badminton. The players are divided into two equal groups and are lined up as indicated (Figure 3.40). One player with a racket stands on each side of the net. One of these players starts the shuttle by hitting it across the net. As soon as a person has hit the shuttle, she gives the racket to the next player in her line, and then goes to the end of the other line. Anyone who fails to hit the bird starts it for the next player and then drops out of the game. When only two opponents are left, instead of running

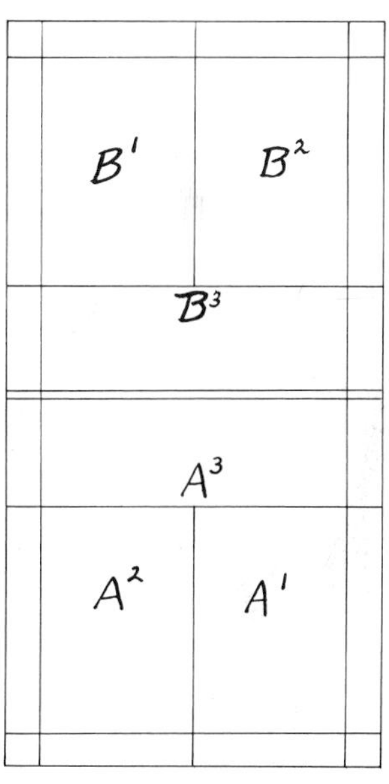

FIGURE 3.39 *Six-player badminton.*

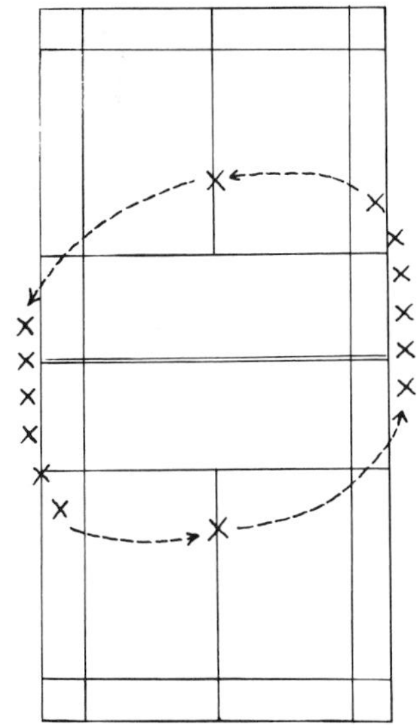

FIGURE 3.40 *Progressive badminton.*

around they rally until one makes a fault. No smashes are allowed.

TOURNAMENTS FOR CLASS USE

I. Rotation (Team)

This is an informal tournament for a single class period. It is particularly well adapted to intermediate and advanced groups.

The class time is divided into five 7-minute periods, or four 8-minute periods, or any convenient time division. Players choose their partners, challenge another team and start to play a game. At the end of the first 7-minute period, the instructor calls time, and teams move one court to their left, except that one team on the end court moves to the opposite side of the same court and plays the team from the next court. If there is an uneven number of teams and too few courts, the team on the end court can rotate off and umpire for one period, then step into the opposite side of the court which they had vacated for the next period.

If there is an odd number of teams and a sufficient number of courts, a singles game can be played on the end court. The couple moving to the end court plays singles, then moves as a team to the next court. Teams keep the same partners throughout the hour. The winning team is the one that has won the greatest number of times at the end of the class period, or the team that has totaled the most points.

II. Rotation (Individual)

This tournament is conducted in the same way as the one just described, except that partners change after every move, and individual players keep a score of their own wins and losses. Unless the class is small and there is ample supervision, this type of tournament is likely to be confusing.

III. Bridge

For the last class of the season, when something different is desired, this tournament is popular.

Tallies, prepared before the class meeting, are marked Court 1, Couple 1; Court 1, Couple 2; and so on. The courts are numbered for as many courts as there are available. Students draw tallies and then go to the proper courts to find their partners. At the end of a given period of time (the class period is divided the same as for the rotation tournament), the winning pairs advance toward the head court (No. 1); the losing pairs stay on the same courts. The losing pair at the head court moves to the foot court. The teams change partners after every move, and each player records the wins and losses on her tally or the number of points won. The winner is declared at the end of the class period.

A less formal team bridge tournament can be organized without tallies. The players are allowed to choose their partners and to play against any team for the first period. Then, the tournament proceeds as described above. Another variation is to allow players to choose their partners and keep the same partners throughout the entire tournament.

IV. Two-Way Elimination or Elimination-Consolation

This tournament can be planned for the last part of the season after the strokes are learned and tournament experience is desirable. Play covers several periods and can be either singles or doubles, depending on the size of the class.

The players can choose their partners, or the instructor can pair them off for teams. The draw is made before the class meeting and with a consideration to seeded players; in this way, the better teams will not meet until the semifinals and finals. The elimination and consolation brackets are arranged according to the usual method. As soon as a team loses, it moves into the consolation bracket. Each team should play one match every class period. Each team will play at least two matches before being eliminated completely, and then the losing teams can play each other outside the tournament. Matches should consist of two out of three games of 15 points each, if the class period is 35 to 40 minutes long. If the period is shorter, one game of 21 points can be played.

V. Ladder

This tournament can follow an elimination tournament if the season permits the time. The tournament gives an opportunity for the teams that lose to challenge the teams that defeated them.

The order of the ladder is determined by the results of the elimination tournament. The winners are placed at the top, runners-up are second, etc. Any team may challenge the team directly above or two above, but no higher. If the lower team wins, it changes places on the ladder with the losing team. Otherwise, the teams maintain their positions.

VI. Round-Robin

This tournament is particularly useful in a class that contains more than one level of ability. If there are two levels represented (intermediate and advanced), the players can be divided into two groups, and two round-robin tournaments can be in progress at the same time. The competition usually requires several class periods.

The players can choose their own partners, or the instructor can pair them off for teams. The tournament schedule is arranged so that each team plays every other team. This is a single round-robin tournament. If each team plays every other team twice, it is a double round-robin tournament. The schedule can be posted on the bulletin board, so that teams know who their opponents are for each class meeting. Matches should consist of two out of three games of 15 points each.

EVALUATION IN BADMINTON

The instructor consciously or unconsciously evaluates the students' progress during each class period. Generally, although such ratings are informal and subjective in nature, they have an important bearing upon future lesson planning and grades.

Occasionally, a class period should be devoted to the testing of specific strokes, the students having been informed of this plan in advance. The tests may be either subjective or objective. The choice of tests will depend on the strokes to be tested, the number of students in class, and the time allowed. When the administration of objective tests is feasible, the scores of an individual student should be combined with the teacher's subjective evaluation for best results. No test yet published is sufficiently discriminating to be used as the sole basis for grading badminton players. Also, although new objective tests are continually being developed, there are no acceptable ones at present for some of the strokes. In these cases, the instructor must rely entirely on her own rating of performance.

The Miller Badminton Wall Volley Test* (a revision of the Lockhart-McPherson test) is one of the standardized objective tests for badminton. It consists of three trials of volleying a bird against a wall for 30 seconds and has a reliability coefficient of $.94 \pm .008$ and a validity of $.83 \pm .047$. This test is based on the ability to execute the stroke most important to success, the clear, and is a measure of general proficiency in the game. The scores can be used for classification, motivation, and overall achievement.

Other objective tests are reported by Scott and French.† Tests for the short serve, long serve, clear, and wall volley are given with directions, coefficients of reliability and validity, and T-scales. These tests can be used individually to evaluate a specific stroke or as a battery for overall ability. The Miller Test is quicker to give and very satisfactory for a general estimate of performance, but it does not diagnose serving weaknesses.

* Miller, Frances A.: "A Badminton Wall Volley Test." *Research Quarterly of the AAHPER, XXII* (203–13), May, 1951.

† Scott, M. Gladys and Esther French: *Evaluation in Physical Education.* Dubuque, Iowa, William C. Brown Company, 1959, pp. 144–150, 155–158.

Suggestions for Further Reading

Badminton Association of England: *Know the Game Badminton.* New York, Sport-Shelf (distributors), 10 Overlook Terrace, 1956.

Bourguardez, Virginia and Charles Heilman: *Sports Equipment: Selection, Care and Repair.* New York, A. S. Barnes & Co., 1950, pp. 208–215.

Davidson, Kenneth R. and Lealand R. Gustavson: *Winning Badminton.* New York, A. S. Barnes & Co., 1951.

Davidson, Kenneth R. and Lenore C. Smith (consultants): *Badminton, Instructor's Guide.* Chicago, The Athletic Institute, 1950.

Devlin, J. F.: *Badminton for All.* New York, Doubleday, Doran & Co., 1937.

Grant, Doug: *Badminton, the International Textbook of the Game.* Montreal, Graphic Publishing Co., 1950.

Jackson, Carl H. and Lester A. Swan: *Better Badminton.* New York, A. S. Barnes & Co., 1950.

Radford, Noel: *Badminton.* London, Pitman Publishing Corp., 1954.

Tennis-Badminton Guide. Washington, D.C., Division for Girls and Women's Sports, American Association for Health, Physical Education, and Recreation. Published biennially.

PERIODICALS

Bird Chatter. 1122 East Palmer, Glendale, California. Published quarterly. Address changes with change of editor.

4

BOWLING

4

BOWLING

Elizabeth J. Culver

Possibly the first bowler in history was a cave man who rolled a boulder down a hill on top of an enemy. In his case a strike meant the game—and there were no spares!

Records reveal that a primitive form of bowling was played by the ancient Egyptians. When the tomb of an Egyptian child, sealed in 5200 B.C., was opened, a set of implements for a game like tenpins was found. In accord with ancient beliefs, they had been included in the tomb to insure amusement for the child in the next world.

Modern bowling, or tenpins, originated as a religious ceremony in Germany during the 3rd century A.D. The name "kegler," which still is used in referring to bowlers, dates back to that time, when a small wooden club, or kegel, was carried to be used for recreation, as a weapon, and as a part of a religious ceremony. Priests often required men to prove their honor by having them attempt to knock down the kegel with a round stone. If a man was successful, he satisfied the priest that his life was an honorable one. Eventually the recreational value of this practice was recognized, and it became a popular part of European recreation.

During the Middle Ages many variations of the game developed throughout Europe. Ninepins was played in Holland, boccie in Italy, skittles and lawn bowls were introduced in England, curling in Scotland, and keys and billiards were popular variations in France.

The Dutch brought the ninepins game

to New Amsterdam, later New York, in 1623. At this time the ninepins were set in a diamond formation. Ninepins increased in popularity quite rapidly, but in the early part of the 19th century it provided the basis for a great deal of gambling, and laws declaring ninepins illegal were passed in New York, Connecticut, and Massachusetts. In order to evade such laws, one more pin was added, and the ten pins were placed in the present triangular formation. Bowling, as tenpins, has realized a very fast growth ever since.

The American Bowling Congress was organized in 1895. This Congress assumed the responsibility for standardizing the lanes, equipment, and rules of the game. The women's counterpart of this organization, the Women's International Bowling Congress, was organized in 1916.

Today over 20,000,000 Americans bowl. The biggest source of bowling enthusiasts is among people in industry. Ninety-seven per cent of United States industrial firms sponsor bowling activities.

Automatic pin setters have made the sport more attractive, faster and more accurate. The more recent emphasis on convenience, comfort, and wholesome atmosphere also has been most instrumental in attracting people to bowling establishments. This new atmosphere has certainly made bowling more suitable for women and children.

The fact that bowling offers exercise and enjoyment to young and old alike, from 8 or younger to 80 and often over, to the family as a group, and to many handicapped people, has been decisive in its becoming the nation's number one participant sport in this age of increased leisure time.

EQUIPMENT

A student should be given information concerning the alleys and pins in order to be familiar with all aspects of the game and to have a knowledge of the specific terminology related to the equipment involved. She also should receive specific instructions concerning proper clothing and shoes and the selection of an appropriate ball.

I. THE ALLEY (LANE)

The alley and its approach are constructed of wood (Figure 4.1). The alley consists of the following parts.

A. Approach. The approach is a level runway extending back from the foul line's outer edge for a minimum distance of 15 feet.

B. Foul Line. A foul line of not less than three-eighths of an inch nor more than one inch divides the end of the approach and the beginning of the alley bed.

C. Alley Bed. The part of the alley upon which the ball is rolled is the alley bed. It is 42 inches wide; and its length from the foul line to the pin deck is 60 feet, and to the edge of the pit is 63 feet. It is constructed of strips of maple and pine set on edge. The first third of the alley bed and the pin deck are made of hard maple; the intervening section is made of pine, a softer wood. This surface is leveled to insure that no section is more than four-hundredths of an inch lower or higher than any other section.

D. Gutters (Channels). The gutters run parallel to each side of the alley bed and extend from the foul line to the pit. They measure nine to nine and one-half inches in width.

E. Pin Deck. The pin deck is the three-foot area at the end of the alley bed on which the pins are set.

F. Pit. The pit is a cushioned area at least nine and one-half inches below the alley level. It extends 30 inches beyond the end of the pin deck and gutters.

II. THE PINS

Regulation bowling pins are a finely-turned form made either of one solid piece of maple wood or of laminated wood. They must be 15 inches high and

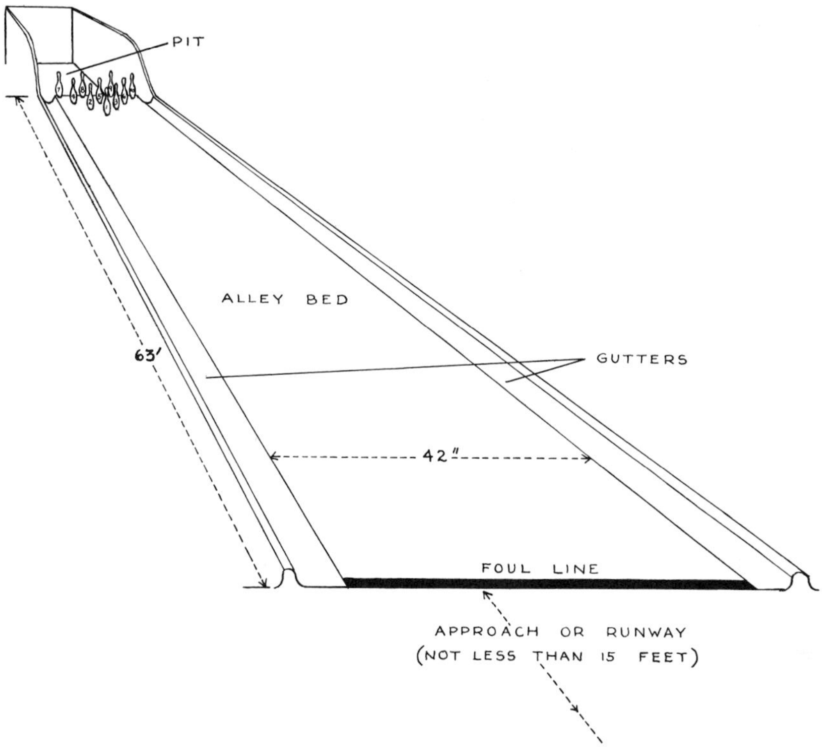

FIGURE 4.1 *The alley.*

must weigh between 2 pounds, 14 ounces and 3 pounds, 10 ounces.

The pins stand on the pin deck in a triangular formation and are spaced 12 inches apart from center to center. They are numbered consecutively in rows from left to right as the bowler faces them.

III. COSTUME

The student's clothes should allow freedom of motion. For example, a loose fitting blouse and a pleated skirt might be worn. Flared skirts or skirts with too straight a cut are a hindrance to movement. Shorts and slacks are taboo at most modern bowling lanes.

IV. SHOES

Special bowling shoes are available at bowling lanes for a nominal rental fee. However, if a student is going to do a great deal of bowling, she should be encouraged to buy a pair of bowling shoes, for she will feel more comfortable in her own shoes. These can be purchased at most bowling lanes and at sporting goods stores.

For right-handed people, the sole of the left shoe is leather and the right sole is rubber with a leather strip at the toe. The opposite is true for left-handed people, and they should be sure to mention that they are left-handed when renting or buying shoes.

The leather sole allows the bowler to slide smoothly on the last step of the approach at the time the ball is released. The rubber sole helps prevent slipping when the bowler pushes strongly with that foot as the slide or fourth step is started; the leather strip at the toe allows the foot to slip backward behind the bowler after the strong push-off has been made. For right-handed bowlers, a stocking on the left foot and a rubber soled shoe on the right could be used when bowling in a gymnasium or hallway, or when practicing the approach at home.

V. THE BALL

Bowling balls range in weight from 9 to 16 pounds; the circumference must be 27 inches. Most girls use balls weighing from 10 to 14 pounds, but the weight used is a matter for individual decision depending on a student's size and strength. Each student should use the heaviest ball that she can control at a medium speed without strain, in order to allow the force producing factors of gravity and momentum to act naturally and in order to minimize the amount of deflection as the ball hits the pins.

Bowling balls are made of various materials—predominantly natural and synthetic rubber, which withstand long and hard use. Most balls have three holes, but some are made with only two holes. The thumb and middle finger are used in gripping a two-hole ball; the third finger is added in gripping a three-hole ball. It is suggested that girls be encouraged to use three-hole balls, because they are easier to hold and control.

The ball is the most important piece of equipment, for it is the implement the bowler uses to knock down the pins. The bowler can direct and control the ball only if she feels comfortable with it. Therefore, it is very important that the ball fit the hand perfectly. A perfect fit can be assured only when a student buys her own ball and has it fitted by a professional. However, a variety of balls are available at bowling establishments, and usually one can be found that will fit reasonably well and feel comfortable.

The following instructions should be given to students selecting a ball, and special care should be taken to see that a proper fit is made.

A. In order to test the size of the holes, slip the thumb and the second and third fingers in and out of the holes. They should fit tightly enough to maintain contact with the edges of the holes, but loosely enough for comfort and easy withdrawal (Figure 4.2, *A*).

B. In order to check the span of the distance between the thumb hole and the finger holes, put the thumb into its hole and extend the fingers across the finger holes. The line of the second joints of the two fingers should fall approximately one-fourth inch inside the finger-hole edge closest to the thumb hole (Figure 4.2, *B*). The span should allow the hand to fit the ball comfortably. A common check for proper span is to insert a pencil between the ball and the palm of the hand, holding the ball with the hand on top of the ball. The pencil will fit snugly if the span is correct (Figure 4.2, *C*).

FUNDAMENTALS

The problem confronting the bowler is to make ten attempts to successfully and consistently knock down ten pins by roll-

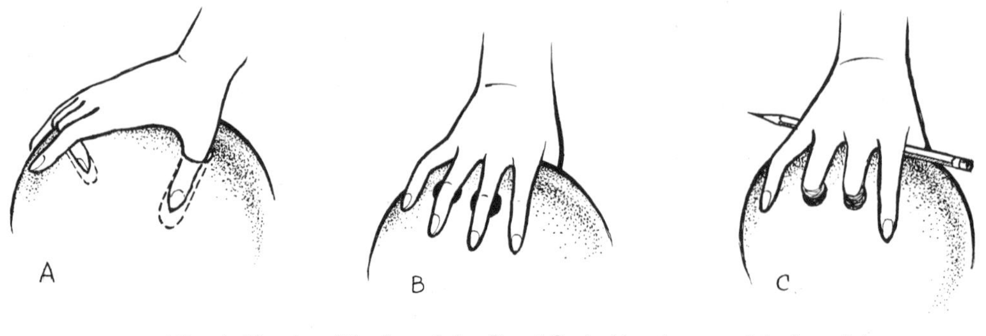

FIGURE 4.2 *A, The size of the finger holes; B and C, checking the span of the finger holes.*

ing a ball a maximum of two times during each attempt. The technique that has been developed to accomplish this task involves the familiar underhand pattern of movement in combination with several approach steps.*

The actual skill of rolling the ball is not a new one, and it should not be confusing to students if they realize that it is merely a variation of a familiar movement pattern that most have used many times when throwing a ball underhand. The biggest problem most beginners have in coordinating the arm swing with the approach steps is in learning to handle the weight of the ball. Many are successful with their coordination without the ball, but become quite frustrated when they try to execute the same coordination with the additional weight. This problem takes time to overcome. If it persists over a considerable length of time, it may be that the ball is too heavy, and the student should experiment with a lighter one. However, the ball should be as heavy as the student can control, in order to allow the force producing factors of gravity and momentum to act naturally. If the ball is too light, it can be pushed or pulled too easily from its natural swinging arc.

Both the arm swing and the approach steps contribute to the production of the force imparted to the ball when it is released. The amount of force produced, of course, varies with the individual bowler. However, students should realize that a great amount of force can bring as poor results in bowling as can too little force. When an extremely fast-moving ball hits the pins they are knocked directly backward into the pit area before they have a chance to knock down other pins. On the other hand, a ball that moves too slowly does not hit the pins hard enough to cause them to knock down many pins not hit by the ball itself. A ball rolled with moderate speed is the most desirable; it has enough force and allows enough time for the pins hit directly to knock down other pins not hit by the ball. This happy medium, rolling the ball with moderate speed, can be accomplished most easily by consistently utilizing the force-producing factors of gravity and momentum, which are inherent in an underhand pattern in combination with a moving base.

I. GRAVITY

Since gravity is a constant force that acts directly downward, it will act continually on the bowling ball throughout the swing. Unless restricted, gravity actually will cause the arm and the bowling ball to swing in a pendular fashion. The amount of force attained by the use of gravity depends on the time and the distance it is allowed to work on the ball. These factors vary according to the starting position of the ball, the distance the ball is pushed outward by the individual at the beginning of the swing (the pushaway), and the height of the backswing.

At the starting position, the ball commonly is held somewhere between the shoulders and the waist. The higher the starting position of the ball, the more force attainable through the use of gravity, because there is a greater distance and more time for gravity to act on the ball. The time and distance also can be lengthened by the use of a pushaway that allows the arm holding the ball to be fully extended before the downward swing of the ball begins. Also, a high backswing promotes more force for the forward swing through the use of gravity, as the time and distance for it to work on the ball are proportionately increased.

A high starting position, a long pushaway and a high backswing take full advantage of the force of gravity. However, these *extremes* demand a great deal of arm, shoulder, and trunk strength if one is to control the great amount of force built up by the pull of gravity. Since gravity is at work throughout the swing, it is necessary to stabilize the shoulder of the swinging arm in order to be sure that the pendular action is straight backward and forward, and thus in line with the path the ball is to take when it is released.

*Directions are given for right-handed bowlers and should be reversed for left-handed persons.

FIGURE 4.3 *Different ball positions with the stance.*

FIGURE 4.4 *Different pushaway distances.*

Thus the factors of the height of the ball in the starting position, the length of the pushaway, and the height of the backswing become individual matters; each student should be given an opportunity to experiment with them and to find which are most appropriate for her strength and abilities (Figures 4.3, 4.4, 4.5).

II. MOMENTUM

Gravity alone, even when properly used, will not contribute enough force to roll a bowling ball down a lane with the speed necessary to knock down the pins successfully and consistently. Therefore, an approach must be developed that uses several steps to build up the momentum to be imparted to the ball.

When considering the development of momentum through the use of an approach, time and distance again become important factors. The greater the time and distance over which momentum is developed, the greater the force imparted. However, it must be remembered that time and distance should be developed in such a way that they enhance coordination, control, and accuracy.

Approaches using three, four, or five steps commonly are used for the purpose of building up momentum. The four-step approach seems to be preferred for teaching beginners, as it appears to be easier for most students to coordinate four steps with the pushaway, arm swing, and release. Also, since the first step of the four is taken on the right foot, the base is more directly under the bowling arm at the moment when the weight of the dropping ball must be resisted. If experienced students are successfully using a three- or five-step approach, they should not be made to change just for the sake of class conformity, because they are satisfying the purpose of the approach in gaining momentum. An effort should be made to

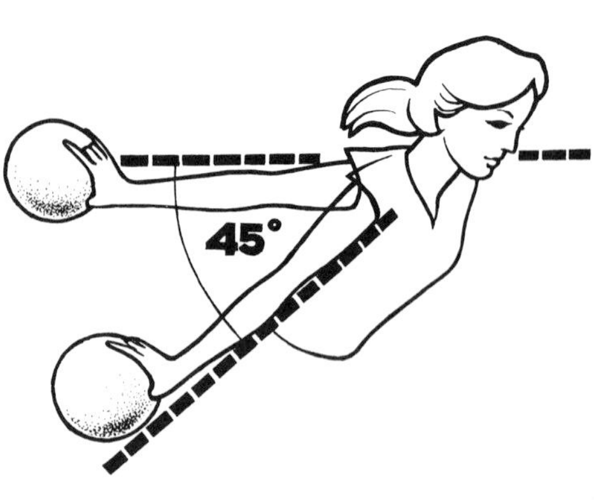

FIGURE 4.5 *Different heights of backswing between 45 and 90 degree angles.*

help these students develop their existing skills further.

Regardless of the number of steps used, it is extremely important that the approach be as smooth as possible, so that all the energy exerted is effective in building up forward momentum and so that the arc of the swing is not disturbed. Any force applied in opposition to the forward movement will decrease both the forward momentum and the efficiency of the approach.

In developing an approach, the student should be encouraged to allow her body weight to be shifted forward from the ankles and carried forward throughout the approach. This will place the center of gravity ahead of the pushing foot, thus increasing the forward component of the force produced by the feet and building up maximum forward momentum with relative ease. A forward position throughout the approach helps promote a forward position over the bent left knee at the end of the approach or at the time the ball is released. A position with the body shifted over a bent left leg allows the arm to swing forward and outward toward the target and thus to impart the built-up momentum to the ball at a point in front of the left foot. Since the ball is traveling fastest at the center of its swinging arc, the greatest momentum is imparted to it by releasing the ball at this point. With the body in a forward position the center of the arc is ahead of the body and the arm swing is able to continue forward over a longer period of time to give the ball a definite direction (Figure 4.6).

If the body weight is held back at the beginning of the approach it is extremely difficult to shift it to a forward position during the remainder of the approach and thus the final position often is one with the weight held back, hampering the arm swing and decreasing mometum. From such a position the ball is released behind or beside the left foot as the center of the arc of the swinging arm is shifted backward proportionately to the backward shift of weight. The remainder of the swing is upward and some control of direction is lost (Figure 4.7).

Another common deviation of the body position is one in which the hips remain high with an extreme bending over at the

FIGURE 4.6 *A good ball release position and the resulting follow-through.*

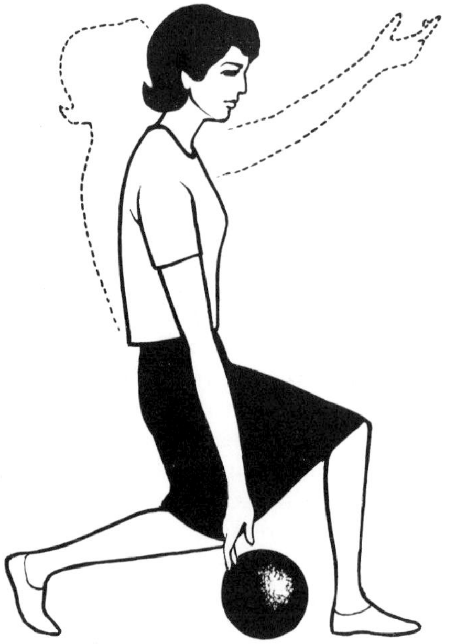

FIGURE 4.7 *A poor ball release position and the resulting follow-through.*

waist. This position promotes strain on the back and also alters the arm swing, directing all of the force downward into the floor. A bent over position might result from the bowler's not bending the left knee as the slide is made (Figure 4.8). In order to maintain balance and impart maximum momentum to the ball it is necessary to lower the center of gravity and keep it centered over the base. This can be done by bending the left knee as the slide is made and carrying the weight of the body in a forward position over the left leg.

The position of the feet and the body should be considered throughout the entire approach. The feet should toe straight ahead so that the force of the pushing feet is directly backward. The movement of the feet and body should be straight ahead in order to allow all the momentum to be built up and released in the direction of the target.

If a student needs to increase the force of her ball, she should be encouraged to experiment with the various force-producing factors involving gravity and momentum. However, she should be closely supervised while doing so to be sure that coordination, control, and accuracy are not sacrificed.

Coordination of the steps and arm swing during the approach are of the utmost importance in order for the forces built up through the use of gravity and momentum to be joined for their maxi-

FIGURE 4.8 *A poor ball release position and the resulting follow-through.*

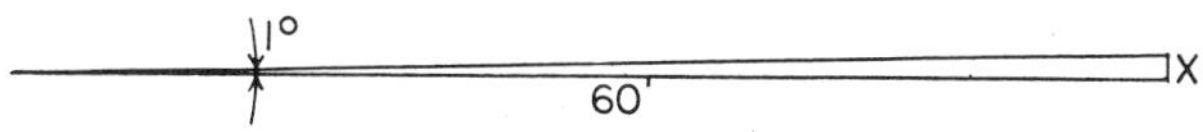

$$\tan 1° = \frac{X}{60}$$
$$0.01746 = \frac{X}{60}$$
$$X = 1.05'$$

FIGURE 4.9 *Distance a ball will angle-in after traveling 60 feet when bowled at an angle of one degree. (From Broer,* Efficiency of Human Movement, *1960.)*

mum efficiency at the point at which the ball is released. A suggested coordination to accomplish this purpose is given later in this chapter.*

III. ACCURACY

Success in bowling can only be realized by an accurate use of the force produced throughout the approach. By maintaining a body position that is always parallel with the target and is always moving straight toward the target throughout the approach, many left or right errors can be eliminated. The direction of the arm swing is very dependent upon the upper body position and it is therefore extremely important that the shoulders be held parallel to the target throughout the approach and release. If the arm swinging the ball moves in a straight backward and forward path in relation to the target, more accuracy will be insured because the ball will be moving continually in line with its intended path and if the point of release should vary slightly from time to time the results will not be drastic. It is suggested that the ball be held to the right as the bowler prepares to make the approach so that when the ball starts its backward swing it will not have to be moved to the right, which could promote a circular swing. Instead, from the position on the right, it can move straight forward, downward and backward, thus helping to promote a straight swing.

A very small change in the angle of the body or arm swing will cause the bowler to miss her target. For example, a change of one degree will result in changing the path of the ball by one foot in the sixty feet it travels from the foul line to the pins (Figure 4.9).

A. Hand Position. The hand position in relation to the ball at the point of release is the most important single factor in determining accuracy. The hand position to be used should be assumed before the approach is started and should remain constant until after the release. In this way undesirable spin to the right or left is avoided. If the hand has to move into a position after the approach is started, a right or left motion will be promoted and will often cause the ball to spin right or left after it is released.

It seems easier to develop control and consistency by rolling a ball straight because it is easy to visualize the beginning and end of its path. On the other hand, a ball that has a curve or hook is somewhat bewildering in that the path it will take is not always easily perceived and the amount of hook or curve varies for each individual. Although a straight ball has only a forward spin and enters the one-three pocket at a smaller angle than does the hook or curve, and, therefore, does not cause the pins to be scattered as much as does the hook or curve ball with side as well as forward spin, it is suggested that, for the purpose of developing control and consistency, beginners be taught to roll a straight ball.

1. Straight Ball. The hand position for a straight ball delivery is assumed by having the palm of the hand face forward toward the target throughout the swing. In looking down on the ball, the thumb of the right hand should be pointing to the very top (12 o'clock) of the ball and thus toward the pins at the point of release. This position puts the hand directly under the ball as it drops downward, and

* See coordination of the four-step approach.

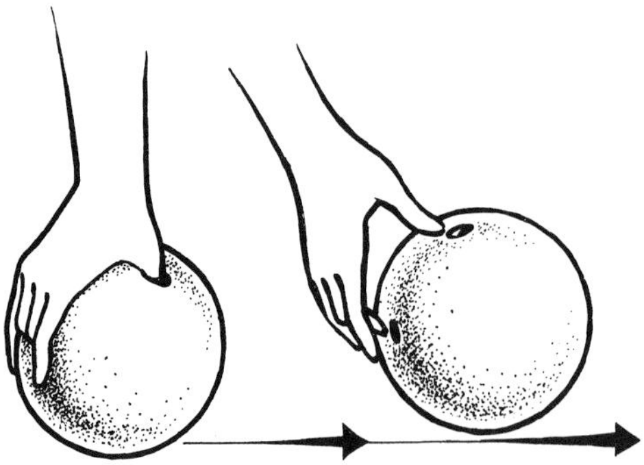

FIGURE 4.10 *Straight ball—hand position and release.*

in a forceful position behind the ball, during the forward swing. When the ball swings forward and starts upward during its pendular swing, the thumb comes out of its hole first, and, as the hand continues forward and upward, the fingers put a forward spin on the ball as they come out of their holes. This forward spin adds speed to the ball as the spin force is in a backward direction against the floor and this pushes the ball forward faster (Figure 4.10).

2. Hook Ball. The hook ball is more effective than a straight ball because it has an additional spinning force and because it increases the angle at which the ball rolls into the pins, making it possible for the ball itself to contact more pins. Therefore, as soon as a considerable amount of consistency has been realized with the straight ball, as should be the case with intermediate and advanced bowlers, a hook ball should be taught.

An off-center force must be applied to the right of the ball to cause the ball to have left spin and thus hook to the left as it approaches the end of its path. This can be effected by changing the hand position so that the palm of the hand faces the side of the body as it swings backward and forward. This is the position of the hand when the arm is hanging relaxed at the side of the body. Again, this position should be assumed before the approach is started and should remain constant throughout the swing. When the hand is in this position the fingers in the ball are to the right of the center of the ball, and, since the thumb comes out of its hole first, the fingers apply an off center force on the right of the ball as the swing continues forward during the release. The result is a right to left force applied to the ball, which causes it to spin to the left. If the hand is cocked upward at the point of release, a hook will be assured as the force exerted by the fingers on the right of the ball will be made greater (Figure 4.11). This cocking action is like the movement used when drinking water from a glass, and is often referred to as a *lift*.

Since the left spin force applied to a hook ball is weaker than the forward force applied by the momentum of the hand and body, the left spin is not effective until the ball has been slowed down by friction to the point of an equalization of forces at which time left spin force is equal to forward force. At the equalization point, the left spin force becomes effective and causes the ball to hook to the left. The slower the ball is rolled, the sooner the forces will become equalized, and a very large hook may be the result. A hook may not be evident in an extremely fast-rolling ball.

3. Back-up Ball. The back-up ball is the reverse of a hook ball, in that it curves to the right, owing to a left to right spin put on the ball at the point of release. The back-up ball is executed by turning the hand and forearm to the

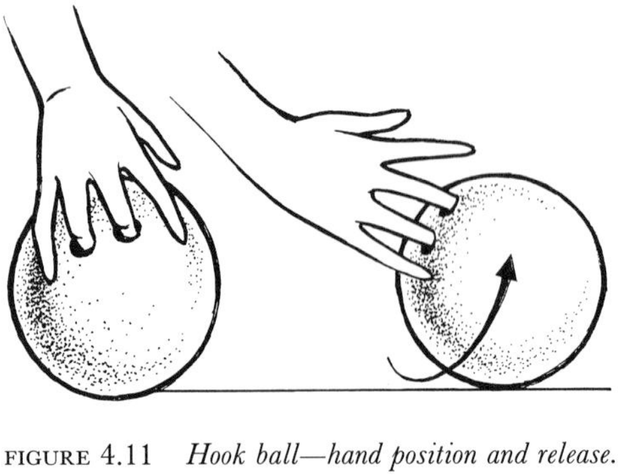

FIGURE 4.11 *Hook ball—hand position and release.*

right as the ball is released from a straight ball hand position. This causes a force to be applied to the left of the center of gravity of the ball. As it is necessary to impart the same amount of spin at an exact point each time, it is extremely difficult to achieve a high degree of consistency with a back-up ball. Therefore, as a back-up ball appears in a student's game, she should be encouraged to eliminate the cause by stabilizing the position of the hand and forearm throughout the swing and release.

4. Curve Ball. A curve ball also involves applying a spin force to the ball at the point of release. It can be executed in two ways. The more common method is to turn the hand and forearm to the left when releasing the ball from either a straight ball or hook ball hand position. In this way a strong force is imparted to the right of the center of gravity of the ball. Another method, seen more often among beginning bowlers, is to swing the entire arm in a circular path around the body as well as to turn the hand and forearm to the left at the point of release. This second method probably should be considered a faulty swing rather than a desirable skill. It is usually found among students who lack the strength to control the ball when it moves very far from the body. In an attempt to gain control of the ball, a student will often swing the ball around her body in order to keep it close to her center of gravity. The turn of the hand and forearm to the left usually accompanies the circular swing around the body as a normal action.

Either method used to roll a curve ball, whether intentional or unintentional, is extremely difficult to control, for there is only one point at which the ball can be released and still travel in the desired direction. If it is released too soon it will go too far to the right of the intended target; if it is released too late it will go too far to the left. If an inconsistent curve ball appears in a student's game, she should be encouraged to overcome it by stabilizing the position of her hand and forearm throughout the swing and release; or, if the curve is due to lack of strength, the student should try a lighter ball. She should also be given some exercises that help to develop arm, shoulder, and trunk strength.

The curve ball and the back-up ball are seen often, but, because they are are so extremely difficult to control, it is suggested that they not be taught.

B. Point of Aim. The target itself must also be carefully scrutinized when attempting to develop accuracy. Before the approach is started, the bowler should focus her eyes on a point of aim and maintain that focus througout the approach and until after the ball has been released. Such focusing helps to maintain balance and a straight line of movement.

The two most popular methods of aiming are known as pin bowling and spot bowling. In *pin bowling* the focal point is on the pin or pins that the bowler is attempting to hit with the ball, while in *spot bowling* the eyes are focused on a spot on the alley that is on a line from the point of release to the pin or pins that are to be hit with the ball. Many bowlers contend that spot bowling is more effective than pin bowling because it is easier to hit a close target than one sixty feet away. The actual length of the alley is rather distorted when several alleys are built side by side, making it more difficult to judge the path the ball must take in order to enter the one-three pocket when looking at the pins. Because of this distortion, a truer judgment can frequently be made by focusing the eyes on a spot much closer to the point of release.

Looking at the pins seems to be more natural for some people and the temptation to do so always is great. Therefore, students should be given full knowledge of both techniques and should be allowed to experiment with them. Usually it takes longer to become accustomed to spot bowling than to pin bowling; therefore, before making a decision as to which method to use, students should be encouraged to try spot bowling over a long enough period to realize the results it can achieve. Each student should then make a decision as to which method she is going to develop. Once a decision has been made, the student should put all her efforts into developing her accuracy through the use of that single method. Changing from one method to the other will only hamper her progress.

COORDINATION OF THE FOUR-STEP APPROACH

In order to utilize the foregoing fundamentals efficiently, it is necessary to coordinate the arm swing with the four steps of the approach so that the force-producing factors of gravity and momentum will be accurately combined when the ball is released. A great deal of concentration is necessary to accomplish this, and the following points should be checked and rechecked throughout the performance of the approach (Figure 4.12).

I. BASIC CONSIDERATIONS

A. To insure that sufficient force production is directed forward toward the target:

1. The arm swinging the ball should be allowed to swing freely under the force of gravity in a line perpendicular to the floor.
2. The body should maintain a forward position by shifting the weight forward from the ankles.
3. The upper body should maintain a relatively upright position facing the target, with the shoulders parallel to the pins to be hit.
4. The feet should point straight ahead on each step.

B. To insure that the force produced is utilized for accuracy:

1. The hand position should remain constant in relation to the ball and the target throughout the swing.
2. The arm should swing in a straight line backward and forward.
3. The approach should be made in a straight line forward.
4. The eyes should maintain a constant focus on the point of aim.

II. STANCE

The position assumed before the movement of the approach begins is referred to as the stance. It predetermines the success of the approach. Therefore, it is important to assume a consistent stance before each approach is started.

Since there is no actual forward movement or time limitation involved, the time taken to assume the stance should be used to think through the approach, the release of the ball, and the path the ball is to take, as well as to position the body so that it will be in an advantageous

FIGURE 4.12 *A coordinated four-step approach.*

position for the approach. The following points should be considered when taking a stance position.

A. Assume an erect standing position with the weight evenly distributed over both feet.

B. Point the feet straight ahead with the left foot slightly ahead of the right foot, in preparation for the right foot to be brought forward for the first step.

C. Face the entire body toward the target with the shoulders parallel to the pins to be hit.

D. Assume an exact hand position for either a straight ball or a hook ball.

E. Position the ball between shoulder and waist height and hold it to the right with the left hand supporting the ball.

F. Focus the eyes on a *definite* point of aim (the pins or a spot).

III. PUSHAWAY AND WEIGHT SHIFT

The forward movement should start by pushing the ball outward in line with the target while the left hand still is helping to support the ball. As the ball is pushed away, the weight should shift forward from the ankles to the forward part of the feet in preparation for the first step.

IV. FIRST STEP

A. Take a small step on the right foot.

B. Complete the pushaway to a controllable distance and allow the ball to start its downward path.

C. Move the left arm away from the ball toward the left to help maintain balance as its movement compensates for the movement of the right arm swing.

V. SECOND STEP

A. Take a step with the left foot slightly larger than the first step.

B. Allow the ball to continue its downward and backward path.

C. Extend the left arm farther from the body and diagonally forward as a compensating action.

VI. THIRD STEP

A. Take a step with the right foot larger than the second step.

B. Allow the right arm and ball to continue and complete its backward and upward swing.

C. Swing the left arm farther forward for the proper compensation for the right arm swing.

VII. FOURTH STEP (SLIDE AND RELEASE)

To be completely effective, this final phase of the approach must allow for a summation of the forces produced through the use of gravity and momentum. This summation is accomplished through the use of sequential movement that starts with the push of the right foot and moves through the body and arm, ending in the fingers holding the ball.

A. Allow the downward and forward swing of the ball to start as the right foot pushes forward and the left foot starts its slide.

B. Bend the left knee to lower the center of gravity and to allow the weight of the body to move forward with no restriction over the left leg.

C. Allow the ball to continue to swing forward throughout the slide.

D. Swing the extended left arm backward as the right arm swings forward in order to balance the off-center force on the body.

E. Since the ball is traveling at its fastest speed at the center of its swinging arc, release the ball when the right arm is at the bottom of the swinging arc, which will be slightly ahead of the left foot.

VIII. FOLLOW-THROUGH

After the ball has been released, the right arm and upper body should be allowed to continue their movement forward in the direction of the target in order to decelerate naturally and avoid the risk of muscular strain that could be caused by a quick stop. In order to make a quick stop, a force opposing the forward force would be necessary and thus there would be a slowing down of the forward movement before the release of the ball as well as a possible change in the direction of the arm swing.

THE STRIKE BALL

It is impossible to hit all ten pins with the ball, but the bowler should try to direct the ball in such a way that it will hit as many pins as possible. It is generally agreed that the best place to hit the pins for a strike is between the one and three pins (or between the one and two pins for a left-handed bowler). This area is commonly referred to as the *pocket*. However, to have the ball hit these two pins successfully does not always result in a strike. If the ball is rolled down the center portion of the alley straight into the pocket, it hits the one pin first and is immediately deflected to the right, away from the center of the triangular pin formation. Therefore, the angle at which the ball enters the pins determines the success of the hit. If the ball rolls into the pocket at an angle from the right, it will be rolling toward the middle of the pins and it will hit the three pin soon enough after it hits the one pin to avoid being deflected very far to the right. The three pin will then direct the ball back toward the center area of the pin formation.

Since the alley is only 42 inches wide, the angle at which the ball can be rolled into this pocket is limited. There is, however, sufficient space for an effective angle.

The five pin becomes the *key pin* when rolling a strike ball, as it stands in the middle of the triangular formation; if it is hit by the ball as it passes through the one-three pocket, a strike normally results. On the other hand, if the five pin is not hit by the ball, it will very often remain standing. Therefore, the ball should be rolled into the pocket at an angle that will allow the ball to hit the five pin. It is often a helpful teaching device to refer to the one, three, and five pins as the *pocket pins*, so that the students will think beyond the pins that are visible and will concentrate on trying to get the ball through the one and three pins to knock down the five pin.

I. STRAIGHT BALL

If a straight ball is to approach the pins at an angle, it should roll on a slight diagonal from the right side of the alley into the pocket area and toward the five pin. This can be accomplished by executing the approach on the right side of the approach lane and allowing the arm to swing the ball toward the point of aim and follow through in the direction the ball is to roll.

For consistent results, it is important to develop both a consistent standing position and a definite point of aim. On modern bowling lanes, there are markings on the approach areas and on the alleys that can be used to the bowler's advantage. These are the seven dots on the approach side of the foul line and the seven darts located on the alley between 14 and 15 feet from the foul line (Figure 4.13).

Regardless of which method is used for aiming, it is suggested that the student of bowling be encouraged to execute her approach for the strike ball with her right foot in line with the second dot from the right on the approach side of the foul line. By bowling the ball from this position she will be able to roll it into the pocket at an appropriate angle.

When pin bowling, the student should maintain a focus on the one-three-five pocket throughout the approach, release, and follow through. When spot bowling, a focus on the second dart from the right on the alley bed for the strike ball is suggested. If a line were drawn from the second dot from the right at the foul line to the one-three pocket, it would cross the second dart from the right. A visual demonstration of this can be given by

FIGURE 4.13 *Seven dots on the approach and seven darts on the alley.*

and concentration to roll the ball parallel and rely on spin to carry it into the appropriate pocket area.

When rolling a hook ball, it is necessary either to move the point of *aim* slightly to the right of that used for a straight ball, or to move the *stance* slightly to the left. The amount of change necessary will be determined by the degree of the curve of the individual's hook ball.

The student's scores will be lower as they go through the learning process for the hook ball and they may be tempted to go back to the straight ball, especially with the second ball. When learning the hook, the student should be encouraged to practice it exclusively for a long period

running a string from the foul line to the one-three pocket. The student should focus on that dart throughout her approach, release, and follow through, until the ball has rolled over it (Figure 4.14).

II. HOOK BALL

The angle at which the hook ball hits the pocket area is greater than that of a straight ball, because the hooking action causes the ball to turn to the left at the end of its path. Therefore, the hook ball enters the pins at a greater angle, which causes it to hit more pins directly than does a straight ball. This, coupled with the spin of the ball, makes the hook much more effective than the diagonal straight ball.

The biggest change necessary when converting from a straight ball to a hook ball, aside from the hand position during the swing, is in the path the ball takes as it rolls down the alley. As the ball is released it should roll parallel with the channel, thus allowing room for the hooking action at the end of its path that will bring it into the pocket area (Figure 4.15). After rolling the straight ball diagonally, it takes a great deal of practice

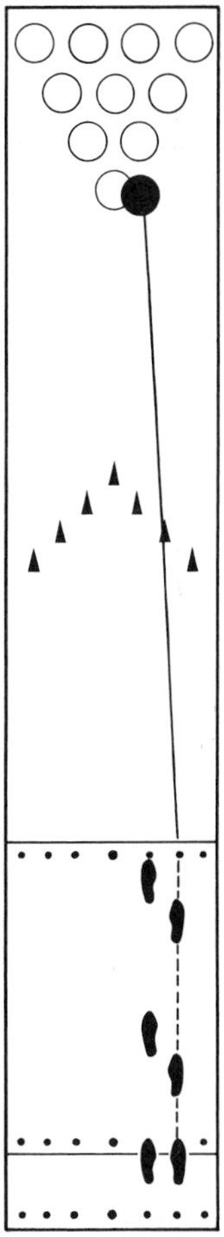

FIGURE 4.14 *The path of a diagonal straight ball.*

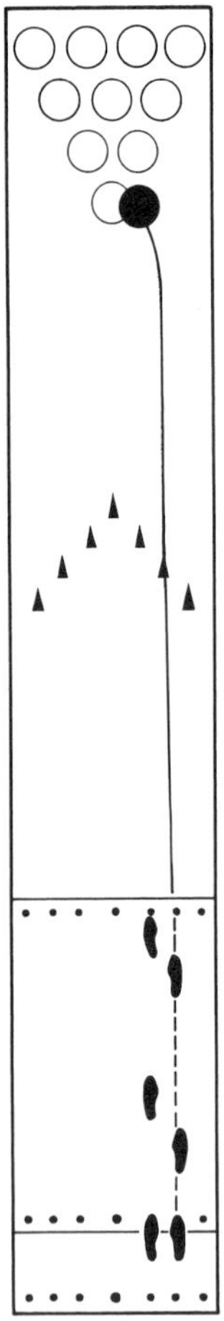

FIGURE 4.15 *The path of a hook ball.*

of time, to develop her skill with it. Each student should then be allowed to make a decision as to whether she wishes to roll a straight ball or a hook, and she should then spend her time and energy developing that specific skill.

THE SECOND BALL

When pins are left standing after rolling the first ball, the bowler is given an opportunity to try to knock them down by rolling a second ball. Three factors that should be considered before rolling the second ball involve the pins that the ball should hit, the path that the ball should take in order to hit them, and the stance and aim that the bowler should take in order to roll the ball along the appropriate path.

I. PIN AND BALL DEFLECTION

The ball should hit as many of the remaining pins as possible. One should never rely on pins to knock down other pins unless absolutely necessary. If just one pin is left standing it is obvious that the ball must hit it in order to have it fall. However, when two or more pins remain standing, the bowler must consider whether the ball can hit them all or whether she must rely on pin deflection to knock down some of the pins. Both ball and pin deflection must be considered. Although the ball, because of its greater weight, will not deflect as much as will the pins, its path will be altered to some degree as it makes contact with the pins. The deflection of a slow-rolling ball will be greater than will that of a fast-rolling ball and a light ball will deflect more than will a heavier one.

The action of the deflected ball and pins is determined by the point of contact and the direction of the force exerted by the ball. The angle at which a pin is deflected from a ball with no right or left

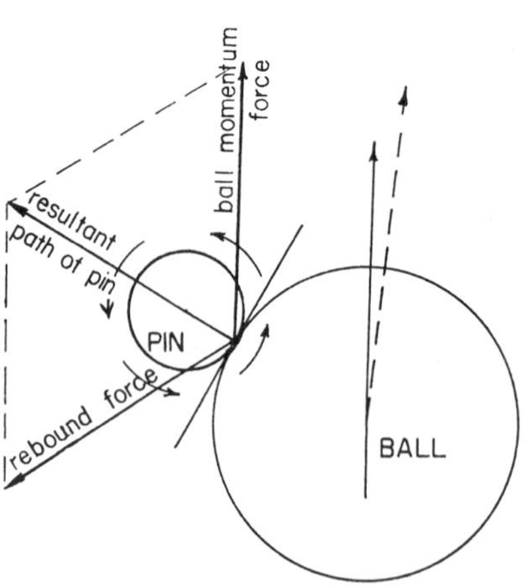

FIGURE 4.16 *Direction of pin rebound from a bowling ball with no side spin. (From Broer:* Efficiency of Human Movement.*)*

spin (a straight ball) is perpendicular to the direction of the ball movement at the point that the ball contacts the pin (Figure 4.16). The hook ball, with left spin, will cause the deflection to be somewhat left of this perpendicular (Figure 4.17). The ball will deflect in the opposite direction, the amount and angle being dependent upon its speed, spin and weight.

II. PATH OF THE BALL

The ball should roll across the alley so that it is rolling toward and through the remaining pins. Cross-alley bowling involves rolling the ball from the right side of the alley when pins remain standing on the left side, and from the left when pins remain standing on the right. Exactly how far the bowler should move to the right or to the left depends upon the pins that are to be hit and the type of ball that the bowler rolls.

III. STARTING POSITIONS AND POINTS OF AIM

When rolling a straight ball and using the pin-bowling type of aim, the bowler

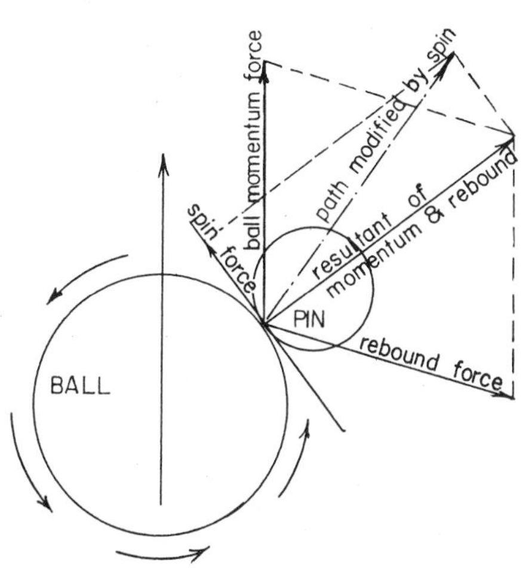

FIGURE 4.17 *Change of path of pin rebound caused by a ball with left spin. (From Broer:* Efficiency of Human Movement.*)*

should focus her eyes on the exact area of the pin or pins she intends to hit and maintain that focus throughout the approach, the release, and the follow through. When spot bowling, the point of aim must change according to the location of the pins. The standing position will vary for both pin and spot bowling, the amount and direction depending on which pins are to be hit.

When pins are left standing in the center of the alley, or in the strike ball area, the bowler should use the same standing position and, if spot bowling, the same point of aim as used when rolling the strike ball. Other situations involving pins on the right or left of the alley require that the standing position and point of aim be changed in order to roll the ball at an angle toward and through the pins. Table I summarizes the starting positions and points of aim that cover the basic areas of the alley.

Figure 4.18 shows the path of the ball as it is rolled from the various starting positions while using the corresponding point of aim.*

When teaching a bowling class, definite starting positions and points of aim should be suggested, but the teacher should be alert to individual differences and suggest changes when they appear to be necessary.

IV. HOOK BALL

The same factors apply to the second hook ball. As with the strike ball, it is necessary to allow for the hooking action at the end of the path. Therefore, when attempting to hit pins on the left of the alley, the ball should not have as large a diagonal path as does a straight ball; but, for pins on the right of the alley, the ball should have a larger diagonal path to allow the hook to turn into the pins.

As with the strike ball, the student rolling a hook ball must either move the point of *aim* slightly to the right of that

* Kidwell, Kathro and Paul Smith, Jr.: *Bowling Analyzed.* Dubuque, Iowa, William C. Brown Company, 1960, p. 41.

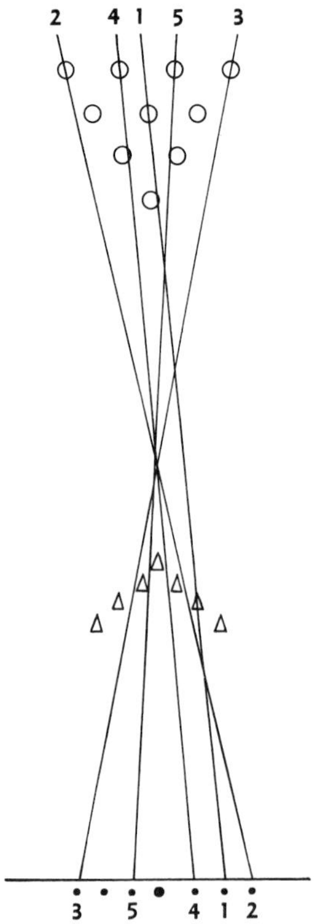

FIGURE 4.18 *The pathways of a diagonal straight ball rolled from the various starting positions across the corresponding point of aim.*

used for a straight ball, or move the *stance* slightly to the left.

SCORING

Each game or line of bowling consists of ten frames (Figure 4.19).

A bowler is allowed to roll her ball two times during each frame in attempting to knock down all ten pins. The recorded score is cumulative; this means that the score of a specific frame is found by adding the number of pins knocked down in that frame to the score of the preceding frames (Figure 4.20).

I. STRIKE

If all ten pins are knocked down with the first ball, the bowler has made a *strike* and she does not roll a second ball in that frame. A strike is indicated by a cross (**X**) placed in the small square in the corner of that frame. The bowler making a strike receives a bonus in that the frame in which the strike is made is scored as ten, the number of pins knocked down for a strike, *plus* the number of pins knocked down with the *next* two balls the bowler rolls (Figure 4.21).

II. SPARE

When all ten pins are knocked down with the two balls allowed within one frame, the bowler has made a *spare.* This is marked with a diagonal line (/). A bonus is also given to the bowler making a spare but it is smaller than the one given for a strike. A spare is scored as ten *plus* the number of pins knocked down with the *next* ball rolled by the bowler making the spare (Figure 4.22).

III. TENTH FRAME

If a bowler makes a spare or strike in the tenth or last frame she receives a bonus ball or balls. If a spare is made she is allowed one extra ball, and if she makes a strike she may roll two extra balls. Therefore, as many as three balls may be rolled in the tenth and last frame. Figure 4.23 illustrates the scoring of a complete game.

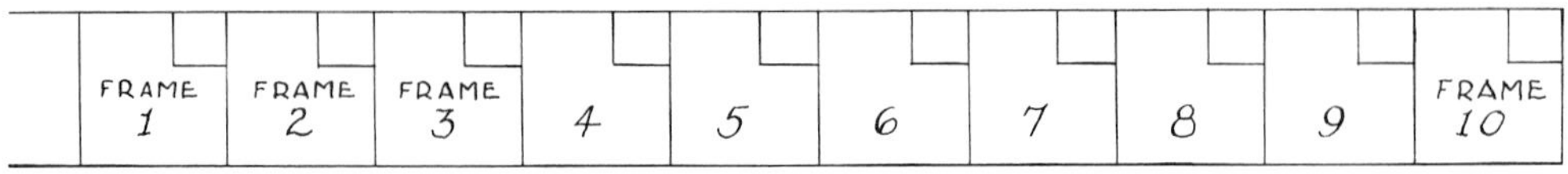

FIGURE 4.19

Table I. Starting Positions and Points of Aim for Covering Basic Alley Areas*

PIN POSITION	BOWLER'S POSITION	POINT OF AIM
Extreme left	Right foot in line with first dot on the right	Between the second and third darts on the right
Extreme right	Right foot in line with first dot on the left	Between the second and third darts on the left
Slightly left of center	Right foot in line with third dot from the right	Between the third and fourth darts from the right (right of center dart)
Slightly right of center	Right foot in line with third dot from the left	Between the third and fourth darts from the left (left of center dart)

*Left-handed bowlers should use the points of aim outlined, but should use the *left* foot to establish the starting positions in relation to the dots.

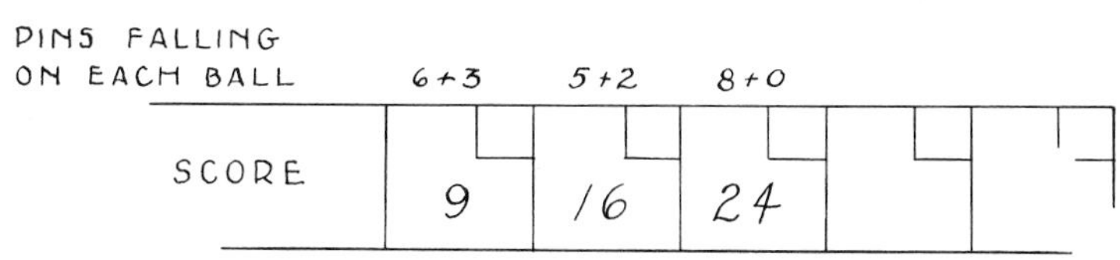

FIGURE 4.20

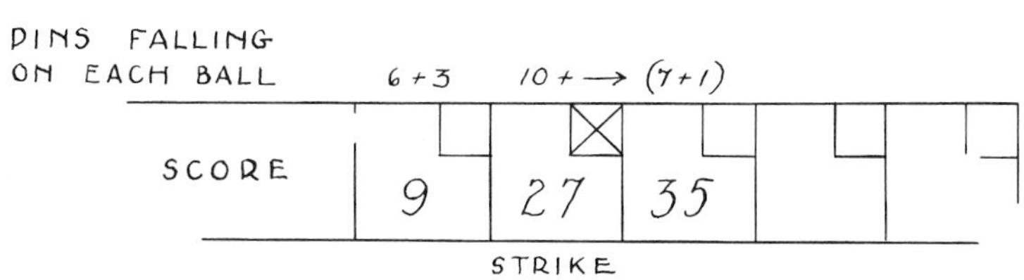

FIGURE 4.21

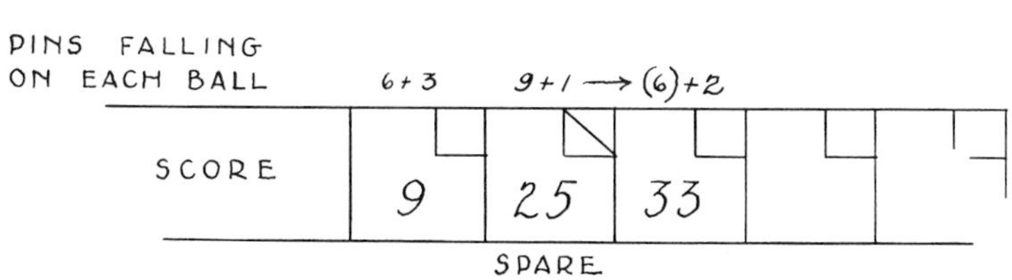

FIGURE 4.22

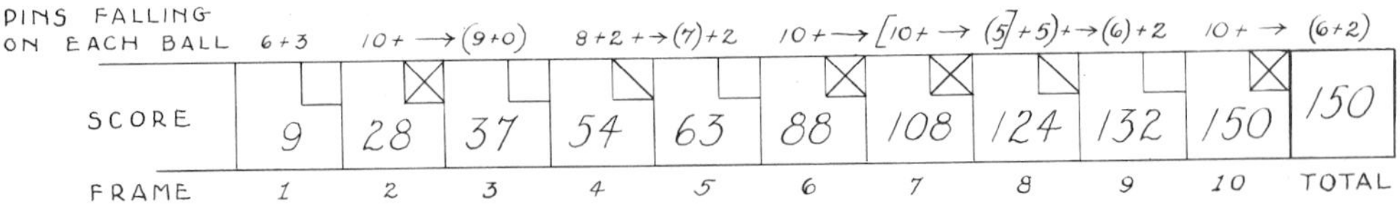

FIGURE 4.23

IV. ADDITIONAL SYMBOLS

A. Split (Railroad). A split (O) is made when the head pin is not standing and the pins in front of and in between the remaining pins have been knocked down.

B. Blow (Error). A blow (—) is made when all ten pins are not knocked down with two balls, unless a split is involved.

C. Foul. For a foul, an F is placed to the left of the small square in the frame. It occurs when any part of the body touches the alley beyond the foul line. If a foul occurs when rolling the first ball, the pins knocked down do not count and the bowler must roll her second ball at all ten pins. If it occurs when rolling the second ball, the pins knocked down with the first ball are the only ones scored for that particular frame.

D. Gutter Ball. For a gutter ball, a G is placed to the left of the small square in the frame. This symbol is registered only when the first ball rolls into a gutter without hitting any pins.

ETIQUETTE

Bowling, like other sports, has its code of etiquette. All bowlers should be familiar with it. A bowling instructor should discuss and stress the following rules of etiquette.

1. Consideration should be given to the other bowlers at all times.
2. Persons should refrain from speaking to a bowler once she has assumed her stance.
3. A player should be able to identify her own ball quickly.
4. A player should know when it is her turn to bowl and be ready to do so immediately.
5. A player should not take the approach simultaneously with a bowler on an adjacent alley.
6. When two people are ready to bowl at the same time, the bowler on the right has the right of way.
7. A player should use her own ball for both the first and second deliveries.
8. A player should stand off the approach while waiting for her ball to be returned.
9. If the ball belongs to the bowling establishment, the player should return it to the storage rack when she has finished bowling.
10. Every player should know the rules of bowling, should learn to score, and should share the responsibility of scoring.

CLASS ORGANIZATION

The majority of schools do not have their own bowling facilities. However, a suitable arrangement can usually be made with the proprietor of a local bowling establishment for the school classes to use his alleys. Morning and afternoon hours are likely to provide little business for public alleys, and, therefore, they are available for school use. Most bowling proprietors are sufficiently foresighted to recognize the value of an arrangement with the school for the use of alleys at these times. Not only will students frequent his establishment for extracurricular recreation, but they often become such bowling enthusiasts that they promote the organization of school leagues. The fees for school use are generally quite reasonable, and public alleys can usually accommodate larger classes than most school bowling facilities.

When alleys are not available for regular class meetings, the fundamentals of bowling can be introduced in the gymnasium. Plastic bowling balls and pins can be used on wooden floors, and alleys can be marked on the floor with chalk or masking tape. Softballs and Indian clubs are also commonly used for learning and practicing the fundamentals of bowling. If regular balls and pins are available, matting should be placed on the area marked for the alley. Pin setters should be instructed to stop the ball with their feet unless side boards and a backstop are set up around the pit area.

Ideally, a class hour should allow enough time for each student to bowl a complete game. Forty-five minutes is ample for a class period if the facilities permit only four bowlers to an alley. At least one hour is desirable for those classes that must allot time for getting to and from a public bowling establishment. The time is, of course, dependent upon the distance of the alley from the school.

Students seem to gain more, and certainly instruction is more ideal, when students of the same ability can be placed in one class. This situation is more likely to be possible in a college program than in a school program. When it is not possible to segregate the students as to ability, they can be organized into appropriate groups within the class. Those who have bowled very little or not at all should be in the beginning group. Those who have had beginning bowling instruction or have had bowling experience and usually score 100 or over should be in the intermediate group. Those who have had intermediate bowling instruction or scored extremely high in beginning bowling or have had a great deal of bowling experience and usually score 135 or over should be in the advanced group. With this type of class arrangement it is possible for the instructor to teach or to review a technique with one group while the other groups practice skills appropriate for their specific levels of ability. The instructor can then give corrections and suggestions to aid those with the same level of ability.

SAMPLE LESSONS FOR BEGINNING BOWLERS

It is extremely important that a great deal of time be given to developing the fundamentals pertinent to bowling, since success in bowling demands great consistency. Therefore, the rate at which the skills of bowling are taught should depend on the rate of learning of the students in the class. The following lessons are presented merely as a suggested progression, as some classes may progress more quickly than this outline indicates and others may need more time to develop some skills.

LESSON I

A. Acquaint students with equipment, costume and facilities.

1. Discuss proper costume.
2. Explain the importance of proper shoes.
3. Explain ball selection. Have each student choose an appropriate ball. Check each student's grip and the weight of her ball.

B. Demonstrate and discuss the four-step approach.

C. Have each student go to an alley or assign each one to an alley.

D. With all students on the alley approaches, teach and practice the fourth step (slide) and the arm swing without a ball. Stress the importance of body position and the direction of arm swing.

LESSON II

A. Discuss the history and growth of bowling.

B. Explain the various parts of the alley.

C. Review ball selection.

D. Review and practice the fourth step (slide) and the arm swing without a ball.
E. Teach the footwork of a four-step approach, emphasizing the fundamentals.

LESSON III

A. Review and practice the fourth step (slide) and arm swing without a ball.
B. Review the footwork of a four-step approach.
C. Add the arm swing coordination of a straight ball without a ball, emphasizing the fundamentals.
D. Demonstrate the four-step approach and delivery of a straight ball, emphasizing the starting position.
E. Explain the hand position for a straight ball, and the point of aim for a strike ball.
F. Practice swinging the ball, emphazing the hand position, the use of gravity, and the direction of the swing.
G. Have students take turns rolling the ball, using the four-step approach with a straight ball delivery. If possible, have only the one-three-five pins standing or the one-two-five pins for left-handed bowlers).
H. Introduce pertinent points of etiquette.

LESSON IV

A. Demonstrate the path a straight ball is to take by extending a string from the foul line to the pocket area, emphasizing its path across the appropriate point of aim.
B. Review and practice the coordination of the four-step approach without the ball with continual emphasis on the fundamentals.
C. Review swinging the ball.
D. Practice rolling a straight ball at the one-three-five pins, using the four-step approach and a spot point of aim.

LESSON V

A. Practice rolling a straight ball at the one-three-five pins, using a four-step approach and a spot point of aim.
B. Practice rolling a straight ball at all ten pins, using a four-step approach and a spot point of aim (each student rolling one ball each turn).

LESSON VI

A. Discuss the second ball.
1. Cross-alley theory.
2. Pin and ball deflection.
3. Standing positions and points of aim.
B. Practice bowling at all ten pins, converting the remaining pins with the second ball.

LESSON VII

A. Review the various factors concerning the second ball.
B. Explain scoring.
C. Bowl, keeping score.

LESSON VIII

A. Review scoring.
B. Discuss further points of etiquette.
C. Explain bowling terminology.
D. Bowl, keeping score.

Subsequent lessons should include adequate practice time and individual assistance from the instructor. When it is felt that a review of specifics would be helpful for the entire class, time should be taken for a class discussion. Film strips and motion pictures demonstrating the fundamentals might be shown during one or two class periods. If time allows, an informal tournament may be enjoyed.

SAMPLE LESSONS FOR INTERMEDIATE AND ADVANCED BOWLERS

In an intermediate or advanced bowling class it will be necessary to review the fundamentals and the material presented to beginning bowlers. The amount of time spent on review will vary from class to class and will depend upon the ability of the students in each class. Therefore, the following outline is presented in the form of a progression rather than by lessons.

A. Explain equipment, costume, and facilities.

B. Have students bowl in order to check individual bowling ability.

C. Review, allowing adequate time for practice:

1. The four-step approach, emphasizing the fundamentals.

2. The straight ball, the hand position for it, and the path the ball is to take.

3. The spot point of aim for a strike ball.

4. Factors concerning the second ball.

a. Cross-alley theory.

b. Pin and ball deflection.

c. Standing positions and points of aim.

5. Scoring.

6. Etiquette, terminology, and history.

D. Teach the hook ball, emphasizing the fundamentals and stressing how it differs from the straight ball. Explain its advantages and disadvantages.

E. Allow adequate time for practicing the hook ball.

F. Explain the curve ball and the back-up ball.

G. Explain handicapping and general bowling league organization.

H. When time permits, conduct a class tournament on a league basis.

BOWLING TERMS

Alley Bed. The portion of the alley between the foul line and pin deck.

Approach. The portion of the alley extending fifteen feet behind the foul line.

Baby Split. The 2-7 pins or the 3-10 pins.

Back-up. A ball rolled with left to right spin, which causes it to fade to the right as it rolls down the alley.

Bed Posts. The 7-10 pins.

Big Four. The 4-6-7-10 pins.

Blow (Error). All ten pins are not knocked down after two balls have been bowled (unless a split is involved).

Brooklyn (Jersey). The ball hits to the left of the head pin.

Bucket. The 2-4-5-8 pins or the 3-4-6-9 pins.

Cherry (Chop). Knocking down one pin of a cluster of pins with the second ball.

Curve. A ball rolled with right to left spin, which travels in a wide arc from right to left.

Double. Two successive strikes.

Dutch 200. Strikes and spares are made alternately throughout the game.

Foul. Part of the body touches the alley beyond the foul line.

Foul Line. A line dividing the approach and the alley bed.

Frame. One tenth of a game.

Full Hit. Hitting the center of a pin.

Game. Ten frames.

Gutter Ball. The first ball rolls into either gutter without hitting any pins.

Gutters (Channels). Areas running parallel to each side of the alley bed.

Head Pin. The 1 pin.

Hook. A ball rolled with right to left spin, which starts down the alley in a straight line and then curves sharply into the pins.

Kegler. A bowler.

Key Pin (King Pin). The 5 pin.

Lane. Alley.

Leave. Pins left standing after rolling the first ball.

Line. A game.

Loft. The ball, released from a high position, falls hard onto the alley.

Mark. A strike or a spare.

Perfect Game. An all-strike game (twelve strikes), resulting in a score of 300.

Pin Deck. Area on which the pins are set.

Pit. Cushioned area behind the pin deck.

Pocket. Area between the 1 and 3 pins.

Series. Three games.

Sleeper (Tandem). A pin left standing directly behind another.

Span. Distance between the thumb hole and finger holes.

Spare. All ten pins knocked down with two balls.

Split (Railroad). Pins in front of and in between remaining pins have been knocked down (only when the head pin is not standing).

Spot. A target on the alley bed.

Straight Ball. A ball that travels down the alley in a straight diagonal line.

Strike. All ten pins knocked down with the first ball of a frame.

Strike Out. Three strikes in the tenth frame.

Tap. An apparently good hit that leaves one pin standing.

Thin Hit. The ball hits the side of a pin.

Timber. When a poor hit knocks down more pins than it reasonably should have.

Turkey. Three successive strikes.

Washout. Normally a split, but the head pin is left standing.

Suggestions for Further Reading

American Bowling Congress: *Bowler's Manual.* Milwaukee, Wisconsin, American Bowling Congress, 1950.

Bowling-Fencing-Golf Guide. Washington, D.C., Division for Girls and Women's Sports, American Association for Health, Physical Education, and Recreation. Published biennially.

Broer, Marion R.: *Efficiency of Human Movement.* Philadelphia, W. B. Saunders Company, 1960.

Day, Ned: *How to Bowl Better.* Greenwich, Connecticut, Fawcett Publications, Inc., 1957.

Kidwell, Kathro and Paul Smith, Jr.: *Bowling Analyzed.* Dubuque, Iowa, William C. Brown Company, Inc., 1960.

McKee, Mary Ellen: "The Mechanics of Bowling." *Bowling-Fencing-Golf Guide,* June 1956—June 1958. Washington, D.C., Division for Girls and Women's Sports, American Association for Health, Physical Education, and Recreation, 1956, pp. 13–58.

McMahon, Junie and Murray Goodman: *Modern Bowling Techniques.* New York, The Ronald Press, 1958.

Miller, Donna Mae and Katherine L. Ley: *Individual and Team Sports for Women.* Englewood Cliffs, N. J., Prentice-Hall, Inc., 1955.

Raymer, Milton: *Curriculum for the Teaching of Class Room Bowling.* Chicago, American Junior Bowling Congress, 1958.

Vannier, Maryhelen and Hally Beth Poindexter: *Individual and Team Sports for Girls and Women.* Philadelphia, W. B. Saunders Company, 1960.

Wilman, Joe: *Better Bowling.* New York, A. S. Barnes & Company, 1953.

5

FENCING

5

FENCING

Marion R. Broer

Fencing is one of the oldest known sports and at present is enjoying a recurrence of popularity. This sport sprang from the duel and originally all swords were cutting and thrusting weapons used entirely for offense, the body being protected by armor.

Paradoxically enough, the development of the defense with the sword was a result of the invention of gunpowder. When it was possible to shoot through the armor the swordsman found he was better off to shed this type of protection and make his sword assume a defensive as well as an offensive role.

When the duel was banned in Spain in the fifteenth century, fencing was born as a scientific art. The earliest teachers of swordplay were jugglers and sword dancers who traveled with fairs from town to town. Swordplay as something approaching a system seems to have begun in the early part of the sixteenth century, and about the middle of the seventeenth the style of fencing gradually began to take shape along the present lines.

Three schools of fencing developed and have lasted through the ages—the French, Italian, and Spanish schools. Today these schools differ little except in so far as the peculiarities of the different types of weapon demand.

Fencing began to appear in this hemisphere in the late nineteenth century. It is now organized nationally by the Amateur Fencers' League of America, which sponsors sectional tournaments classified for fencers of different degrees of skill.

Through this organization, and through fencing clubs in many cities, anyone interested can continue fencing long after school and college years.

As a form of exercise fencing owes apologies to no sport. The muscles must be trained through continual, persistent practice to respond instantaneously to the rapid-fire commands of the brain. A fencer must be agile, nimble, and intelligent, and must have strength coupled with mental and nervous control. She must adapt herself to her opponent, have a constantly alert mind, and analyze with great speed. A fine correlation of mind and body is necessary for success. The hand develops a delicate sense of touch and controlled precision, the eyes acquire keenness, and the muscles are schooled to instantaneous reaction to the brain. The fencer develops stamina as a result of regular, methodical practice. Perseverance is another quality necessary in a fencer; hand in hand with it go patience and courage.

Fencing can provide a great deal of exercise in a short period of time. It can be carried on in any relatively small area, no especially constructed court or field being necessary.

There is much to recommend fencing, and its present popularity among students of high school and college age demands that it be given its well-deserved place in the physical education program. This means that the physical educator must know how to organize groups so that each individual will receive as much instruction and practice as possible during the short physical education periods.

EQUIPMENT

Foils, masks, and some type of protection for the body should be furnished by the school. Many beginners hesitate to buy their own equipment until they have learned something about the sport, even if they are financially able. If possible, enough equipment for 20 to 25 fencers should be provided. This will take care of a class that can be handled easily by one instructor.

A large gymnasium is not so desirable for fencing instruction as a smaller room, but will serve the purpose. Very little space is needed for keeping the equipment. If there is no equipment room, it can be neatly arranged in one corner of the gymnasium.

I. FOILS

A. Description. French demountable foils with belt guards are recommended. The foil is made up of the blade and the handle (Figure 5.1). The blade is flexible at the point and strong near the handle. The tongue (tang) is that part of the blade that extends up into the handle. The handle consists of the guard, which protects the hand, the grip, and the pommel, which serves to hold the blade to the handle and also gives the foil weight and balance. The center of balance should be just outside the guard. A blade that is too flexible is not practical for teaching beginners. It is excellent, however, for trained fencers. Rubber tips can be purchased, but tipping the foil with adhesive tape takes very little time, is usually more satisfactory for class use, and is less expensive. A few extra blades should always be kept on hand.

B. Method of Storing.

1. A board about 12″ wide and long enough to take the required number of foils (allow 5″ for 3 foils and add 3″ to 4″ for the end of the rack) can easily be made into a rack. Inch wide slits should be cut approximately 10″ deep at intervals of 4″. This rack can be placed on the wall 4′ or more from the floor. Three foils can be placed in each slit so that the bell guard rests on the top of the board and the blade points toward the floor. A rack such as this would have to be 4′ long to hold 25–27 foils (Figure 5.2).

2. If it is desirable to lock up the equipment when it is not in use, a longer and narrower rack, holding only one foil in each slit, can be made. A second board

FIGURE 5.1 *The foil.*

with holes for the handles of the foils can be hinged to one end of the rack so that it will drop over the top of the bell guards and padlock at the other end. This type of rack would have to be 5″ wide and 11′ long to hold 25 foils. The inch wide slits would be cut about 4″ deep at intervals of 4″.

3. To keep the foils in the best condition, provide a rack as described above and at the proper distance down the wall build out a board on which are clips to hold the tips of the foils in place. The long and shallow rack holding one foil in each slit would have to be used.

II. MASKS

A. Description and Use. Black masks of medium weight are the most practical. To avoid the development of a fear of being touched by the opponent's blade, start classes wearing masks at all times that two students practice together. Also, if masks are worn through preliminary technique practice, the students will become so accustomed to them that they will not feel hindered by the masks when they reach the more advanced bouting stage.

B. Method of Storing.

1. A mask rack, placed on the wall near the foil rack, can be made by bracing a rod about 1″ in diameter 2″ from the wall. The masks can be hung on the rod by the back spring. A pole 15′ long will hold 25 masks.

2. Masks also can be kept in a

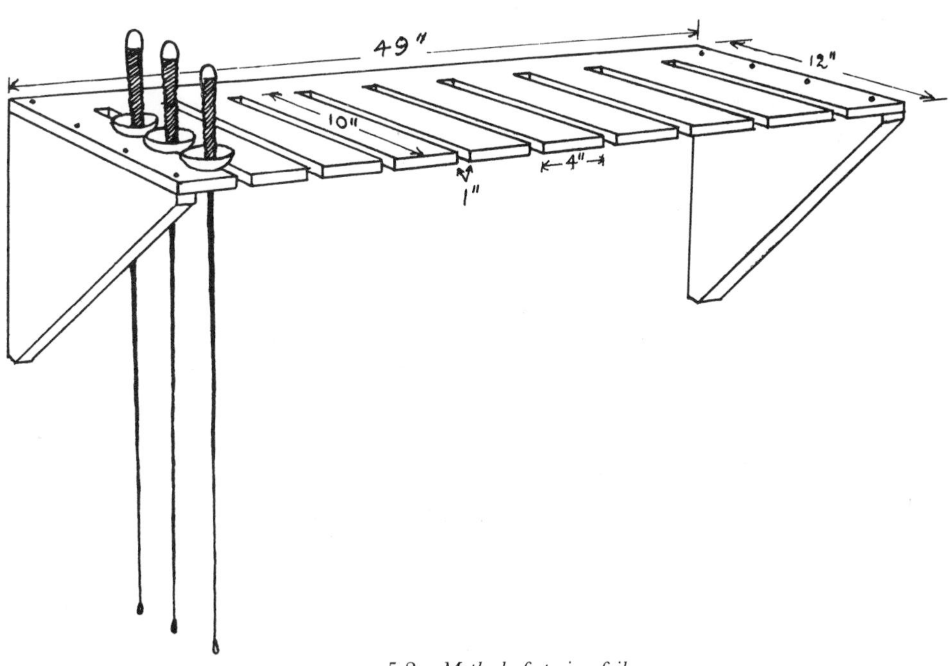

FIGURE 5.2 *Method of storing foils.*

wooden box with a hinged top that may or may not have a padlock, depending upon the situation. Two or three masks can be placed together, one inside the other, to conserve space. They are often kept in the same box as the jackets, but a great deal of time can be saved in putting equipment away, either by providing separate boxes, or by having a partition to divide the box into definite spaces for masks and jackets. A box approximately 2′ × 2′ and 2½′ deep will hold 25 masks (figure a space 12″ × 12″ × 8″ for 3 masks), and one 3′ long, 2½′ wide and 2½′ deep will take both masks and jackets. The partition should be about 15″ from one end.

III. JACKETS OR PLASTRONS

A. Types and Uses. Some protection should always be worn on the body in fencing class. The fencing jacket, which covers the entire target and the arms, is desirable whenever the situation makes this purchase possible. Because of the cost, however, many schools are able to afford only half jackets, which cover the front, back, and right side of the body and the right arm, or plastrons that protect only the front of the body. The half jackets may be turned inside out for left-handed fencers, and are preferable to the plastrons.

B. Method of Storing. A box or cabinet can be placed on the floor near the foil rack. A large wooden box with a hinged top, with or without a padlock, is satisfactory. A box 28″ × 15″ and 30″ deep will hold 25 to 30 jackets. If it is desirable to keep masks and jackets together, refer to the section on the storing of masks.

IV. GLOVES

The glove is not absolutely necessary. It is the least important part of the fencing equipment and may be omitted if no funds are available. Students will often furnish their own gloves. Old pigskin gloves serve the purpose.

V. EQUIPMENT FOR PRACTICING THE LUNGE

A. Mats. The same mats that are used for tumbling, apparatus, or corrective exercises can be hung on the wall for lunging practice. If there are no facilities for hanging them, students can work in pairs, and while one practices the other can stand beside the mat, which is placed on end on the floor, and support it by leaning against it with one shoulder. At the same time that she is supporting the mat, the student can watch her partner for corrections in form.

Some gymnasia are built with posts or with uneven walls with corners that are padded for safety in team games. These paddings can be used to good advantage in fencing practice.

B. Targets. Targets on the wall may stimulate interest. Hearts cut out of thick sponge rubber mats with smaller hearts painted on them are attractive, are easily made, and are an incentive to practice. These should be at least 12″ × 10″.

VI. COSTUME

All fencers should be required to wear tennis shoes and a gymnasium suit or fencing costume, as absolute freedom of movement is essential.

THE TARGET AND LINES OF ENGAGEMENT

I. DEFINITIONS

A. Target. The target extends from the top of the collar to the groin lines (in back, down to a horizontal line passing through the top of the hip bones), exclusive of the arms (Figure 5.3). The seam of the jacket is judged as the line of attachment of arm and shoulder.

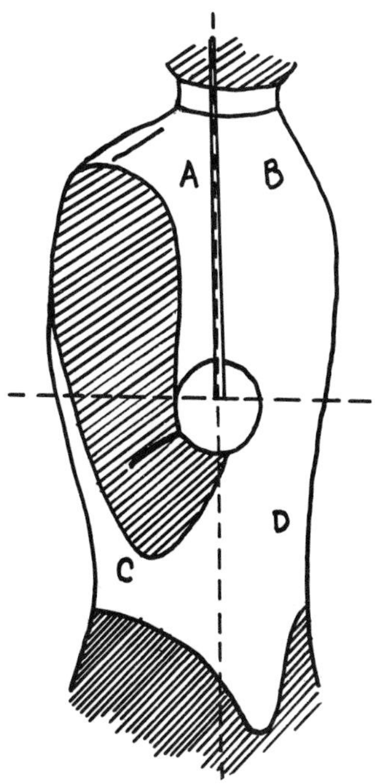

FIGURE 5.3 *The target.*

B. Lines of Engagement. A horizontal and a vertical line through the center of the bell guard of the foil divide the target into four parts for the different attacks and defenses. These sections of the target are named as follows:

1. *High Outside:* that part of the target seen to the left of the opponent's blade, higher than the guard of the foil. This section of the target is guarded by the parries of 6 and 3 (Fig. 5.3, *A*).[1]

2. *High Inside:* that part seen to the right of the opponent's blade, higher than the guard. This section is guarded by the parries of 4 or 1 (Fig. 5.3, *B*).[1]

3. *Low Outside:* that part seen to the left of the opponent's blade, lower than the guard. This section is guarded by the parries of 2 or 8 (Fig. 5.3, *C*).[1]

4. *Low Inside:* that part seen to the right of the opponent's blade, lower than guarded by the parries of 7 or 5 (Fig. 5.3, *C*).[1]

C. Position of Engagement. When two blades are crossed and are in contact, they are said to be engaged. When engaging for bouting, both fencers take the guard position (see p. 126) with their heels on the same line. They should be close enough so that each can reach her opponent with a lunge when the right arm is extended. The foils should be crossed at the weak part of the blades, approximately 7 to 8 inches from the tips. If the foils are crossed on the right, the fencers are said to be engaged on the inside. If the foils are crossed on the left, the fencers are said to be engaged on the outside.

II. TEACHING

A. Presentation.

1. Demonstrate by engaging with one of the students. Cross the blades on the right (inside) and on the left (outside).

2. Divide the class into pairs and have them take the attention position (see p. 125) approximately 10 feet apart, holding their masks in their left arms. Have them take positions on lines marked on the gymnasium floor.

3. Have the students salute their opponents (see p. 125).

4. Tell them to put on their masks.

5. Next have them go into the guard position with their blades crossed to the right, or on the inside.

6. Tell them to change the engagement so that their blades cross to the left, or on the outside.

B. Place in Progression. The target and the lines and position of engagement should not be explained until the fundamental techniques such as the grip, the guard position, the advance and retreat, and the lunge have been learned. They must, however, be explained before any of the offensive or defensive tactics can be presented, since these necessitate practice with an opponent.

[1] The parries are described on pages 138 to 143.

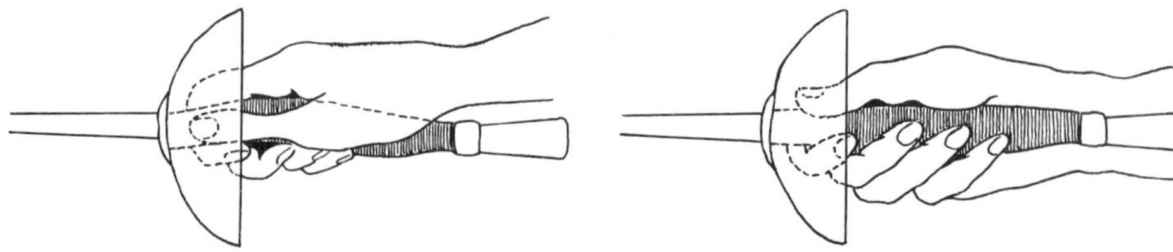

FIGURE 5.4 *The grip. Left, from above; right, from the side.*

TECHNIQUES [2]

I. THE GRIP

A. Definition. Method of holding the foil. The foil is held securely between the thumb and forefinger. The other three fingers are important in the control of the foil. They move it about the fulcrum formed by the secure grip of the thumb and forefinger. The thumb and forefinger can move the tip of the foil up and down, but the fingers control the movement of the foil from side to side.

B. Execution.

1. The grip of the foil is curved slightly and should be grasped so that the convexity of the curve fits into the hand at the base of the thumb.
2. The grip of the foil should rest between the first and second joints of the index finger.
3. The thumb should be extended on the top of the grip just back from the guard.
4. The thumb and forefinger should be on the broadest sides of the grip, which correspond to the broadest sides of the blade.
5. The other fingers curve around the grip naturally for control. The tips of the fingers should be on the concavity (inward curve) of the grip. This is extremely important, for if the fingers wrap around the grip, control of the foil will be lost.
6. The wrist should be straight.
7. The pommel rests against the center of the wrist.
8. If the foil is held correctly, there will be a straight line from the elbow to the tip of the foil.

C. Teaching.

1. Organization of Class. Have the class in a semicircle around the instructor.

2. Presentation.

a. Have each student hold a foil in the left hand and turn it until the convexity (outward curve) of the grip is toward the right.

b. Tell them to place this outward curve against the heel of the thumb of the right hand.

c. Have them extend the thumb along the top of the handle so that the tip of the thumb is just back from the guard of the foil.

d. Then tell them to close the fingers of the right hand around the handle and put the tips against the concavity (inward curve) of the grip of the foil.

e. Check each student.

f. Have each student put the tip of the foil on the floor, holding it so that the thumb is forward, and exert just enough pressure to cause the blade to bend slightly. Point out the fact that if the foil is held correctly the bend in the blade will be forward. This means that with pressure on the tip of the foil when the foil is horizontal, the bend will be up. Demonstrate this by putting the tip of the foil against the wall.

g. Have the class practice taking the grip several times, each time checking to see that the foil bends properly.

[2] The techniques are not discussed in the order in which they would be presented to a class. For this progression see page 145. All techniques are described for right-handed fencers.

3. Faults in the Grip.

a. The foil may be held upside down. Point out the shape of the grip of the foil.

b. The foil may be held sideways. Here again the shape of the grip must be emphasized. Also this can be checked by demonstrating that the blade will bend to the side instead of up when held in this manner.

c. The foil is often held too tightly. Point out the necessity for slight movements of the fingers and thumb, which are impossible if the grip is squeezed. The grip should be firm but not rigid. Have the students try to make little movements with the tip of the foil by the use of fingers and thumb, or even the thumb and forefinger alone. It may help to have them hold their right wrists with their left hands while practicing these movements.

d. A tight grip may be caused by a student's wrapping the fingers too far around the handle. In this position the fingers cannot manipulate the foil tip. Have the student check to see that her finger tips are on the concavity of the curve of the grip.

e. Long fingernails interfere with the placement of the fingertips along the inner curve of the grip of the foil. If students wish to fence with any success, they must compromise on fingernail length. Long fingernails may also cut the pad at the base of the thumb when the fingers are wrapped too far around the foil.

4. Progression. A correct grip is fundamental to the proper execution of all techniques and must be mastered before any other technique is presented.

II. THE SALUTE

A. Definition. The salute is the method of acknowledging the opponent and judges. It is given before crossing blades in a lesson or bout and again at its completion.

B. Execution.

1. Position of Attention, or Initial Position.

a. The body is in profile with the right shoulder toward the opponent.

b. The body should be erect but not stiff.

c. The feet are at right angles, heels together, with the right foot in line with the right foot of the opponent, and toes pointing toward the opponent. This right-angle position of the feet is important for all fencing techniques and should be emphasized from the first. The position of the left foot is important in maintaining stability by enlarging the base in the forward-backward plane. The right foot must be turned in the direction of the opponent since this is the direction of movement. If the toes are not toward the opponent, force will be exerted against the side of the ankle and knee on every lunge and injury will be likely to result.

d. The right arm, holding the foil, is extended so that the foil and arm form a straight line that points diagonally to the floor. The thumb is upward and the tip of the foil is about 6 inches from the floor. To keep the foil tip off the floor the arm must be held somewhat away from the body (Figure 5.5).

e. The left arm is extended slightly away from the left side of the body to balance the right arm, or it may hold the mask at the left hip.

f. The head is turned toward the opponent.

2. Salute.

a. The foil is raised level with the shoulder and pointed directly toward the opponent or toward whoever is being saluted. The arm and foil form a straight horizontal line. The back of the wrist is toward the floor (Figure 5.5, *1*).

b. The right arm is bent so that the foil is pointed up and the foil and forearm form a line perpendicular to the floor. The hand is level with the chin and the fingers are toward the face (Figure 5.5, *2*).

c. The right hand is then *snapped* to the original position of attention (Figure 5.5, *3*).

C. Teaching.

1. Organization of Class.

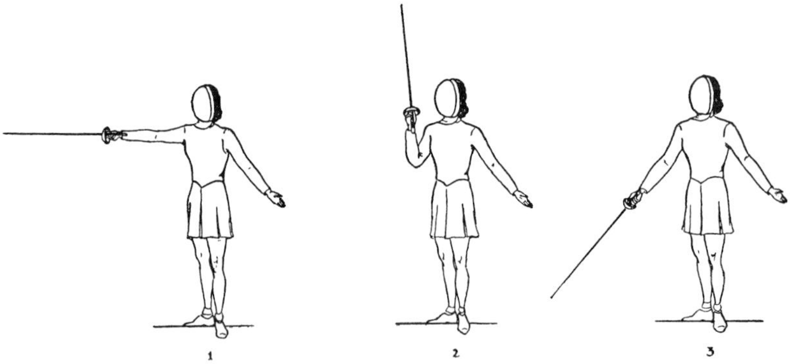

FIGURE 5.5 *The salute.*

a. Have the class in two or three lines facing the instructor.

b. The students should be far enough apart so they will not touch each other when the right hand, holding the foil, is extended to the right at shoulder height.

c. Make use of actual lines drawn on the gymnasium floor for various games, as it is much easier to learn the foot position if there is an actual line by which to guide.

2. Presentation.

a. Have the class take each of the following four positions on count and hold them while the instructor checks: (*1*) Attention. (*2*) Foil lifted to horizontal. (*3*) Foil lifted to chin. (*4*) Attention.

b. Repeat with the counts speeded up.

c. Give command for attention and one signal for the salute.

3. Progression. The salute gives the position from which the fencers come on guard, and therefore should be taught immediately after the grip is learned.

III. ON GUARD

A. Definition. The "on guard" position is that position from which all offensive and defensive tactics are started (Figure 5.6).

B. Execution.

1. The feet are approximately hip width apart. This gives a wide base for easy balance without introducing diagonal forces against the floor.

2. The weight is evenly distributed.

3. The left toe points straight ahead, and the right foot is at right angles to the left foot and on a line with the left heel.

4. The knees are bent so that they are directly over the toes. This position is important to prevent strain of the knee joints.

5. The body remains upright.

6. The left arm is bent at the elbow so that the upper arm is horizontal and the forearm perpendicular to the floor. The hand is relaxed toward the head.

7. The right elbow is bent so that the foil and forearm, remaining in an unbroken line, point to the opponent's right

FIGURE 5.6 *On guard position.*

eye. The elbow is about 6 inches from the hip.

C. **Teaching.**

1. Organization of Class. The class organization is the same as for teaching the salute.

2. Presentation. Teach from the position of Attention.

a. Have the class go through the following steps on single commands so that the instructor can check at each stage:

(1) Swing the blade to the left across the body until it is horizontal to the floor, and put the left fingers under the tip of the blade. Both arms are straight but easy.

(2) Raise the foil above the head, keeping it horizontal to the floor.

(3) Keeping the left arm in this position, release the tip of the foil and relax the hand toward the head. This puts the left hand and arm in their proper on guard position.

(4) Drop the right elbow until it is out from the right hip, and the foil, making a straight line with the forearm, is pointing to a spot that would be the height of an opponent's eye.

(5) Move the right foot forward along the line of the left heel until each foot is directly below the hip on that side, and bend the knees, keeping the body erect. If the weight is kept on the outside of the feet, the knees will bend over the toes.

b. Have the class go through the movements smoothly and quickly on the single command "On guard!"

3. Faults in Guard Position.

a. Turning (rotating) the body toward the opponent is probably the most common fault. Explain and demonstrate that when the body is turned toward the opponent, it is more open to attack, but when in profile less target is presented to the opponent and it is much more easily guarded.

b. A student may allow the right knee to drop in, which gives a very weak position both of the knee and foot. Have her check the position of this knee by running the foil down to the floor along the inside of the knee. If the knee is in a good position, with the foil vertical, the tip should be along the instep of the foot.

c. A student may transfer most of the weight to the right foot. This means the body is off balance and makes lunging or advancing and retreating practically impossible. This can be checked by having the student pick up the right foot and stamp on command.

d. The foil arm may be dropped too low. Demonstrate how much of the target is thus left unguarded.

e. The body may be bent forward from the hips so that the hips are out instead of under. Since the base is small in this direction (only the length of the left foot) this makes the body position very unstable. Give practice in bending the knees and moving the right foot without the arms, concentrating on keeping the hips under the shoulders.

4. Progression. A well-balanced, well-guarded position is absolutely essential to the proper execution of all offensive and defensive tactics and should be thoroughly taught before anything other than grip and salute are presented.

IV. THE CALL (APPEL)

A. **Definition.** The Call is the method of calling your adversary's attention to your desire to stop the bout.

B. **Execution.** The right foot is quickly stamped twice.

C. **Teaching.** Since this is a useful device for checking on the balance in the guard position, it can be presented at this time.

V. ADVANCE AND RETREAT

A. **Use.**

1. Advance. The fencer advances to get, or to keep, within attacking distance of her opponent.

2. Retreat. The retreat is used to get out of reach of the opponent or to adjust the distance before attacking an opponent who has got too close.

B. Execution.

1. Advance.

a. This is executed in the "on guard" position.

b. The fencer steps forward with the right foot, lifting the toes first (Figure 5.7, *1*). As in walking, she lands first on the heel and then the force of the impact moves across the foot to the toes. The right foot must start the advance, to maintain the wide base for stability. If the left foot were moved first the base would be decreased and balance would be more difficult to maintain.

c. The left foot must follow immediately (Figure 5.7, *2*).

d. At the end of each complete step, the distance between the feet should be the same as in the original guard position, and the body should remain in a perfect guard position.

e. The feet barely leave the floor and the heels stay in line. However, there should be no sliding.

f. The advance should be short and cautious, because a counter attack is appropriate when an opponent is advancing.

2. Retreat.

a. This is the reverse of the advance.

b. The left foot is placed back first, again to maintain a wide base.

c. It is followed for the same distance by the right.

3. Jump Advance.

a. The right foot leaves the strip first and is immediately followed by the left.

b. Both feet land simultaneously, flat on their soles and in the correct guard position about 1 foot ahead on the strip.

c. The feet should just skim the strip.

d. The legs should at no time be extended. They bend more on landing, to reduce the jar.

4. Jump Back.

a. Both feet leave the floor simultaneously.

b. The right foot lands slightly before the left.

c. The guard position should be maintained.

C. Teaching.

1. Organization of Class.

a. Have the class in two or three lines facing the instructor.

b. Have them take positions on actual painted lines running lengthwise of the gymnasium.

c. The student nearest the right should be at least 10 feet from the right wall to allow distance to advance.

d. If the class is large or if there are no lengthwise lines other than the basketball court, it may be more satisfactory to have the class on the lines all around the gymnasium, facing the instructor in the center of the floor.

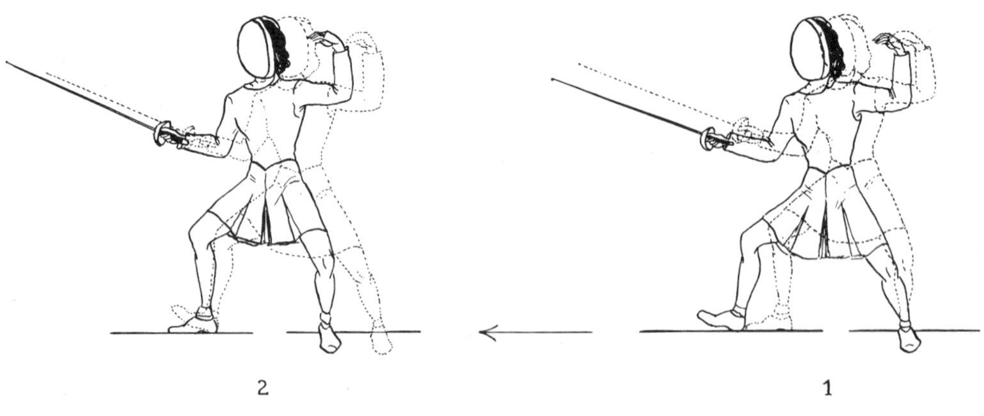

FIGURE 5.7 *The advance.*

2. Presentation.

a. Explain and demonstrate advancing.

b. In the guard position, have the class advance slowly on count. Count for the moving of each foot separately. Have the class advance a long distance to get the feeling of the sequence of movement. Gradually speed up the commands.

c. Have the class advance a complete step (move both feet) on a single command. Start the counting slowly and gradually speed it up.

d. Explain and demonstrate retreating.

e. Go through the same procedure as for advancing.

f. Change from advance to retreat counting for each step. "Advance 1, 2, 3; Retreat 1, 2; Advance 1, 2; Retreat 1, 2, 3;" and so forth. When this stage is reached, do not give more than three or four steps in one direction, as more are seldom needed in an actual bout. Start counting slowly and gradually speed up the commands.

g. Next give commands to advance or retreat without counting individual steps, and have the class continue in one direction until the reverse command is given.

h. To develop speed in changing direction, have the class advance one step and immediately retreat. The backward step should be executed by moving the left foot back immediately after it touches the floor on the advance. Next practice the reverse. That is, retreat one step and then advance.

i. As soon as the position of engagement has been learned, give practice in advancing and retreating with an opponent. Tell No. 1's to advance on the instructor's command. No. 2's must retreat in response to their opponents' advance. The distance of the retreat is dependent upon the distance of each opponent's advance.

3. Faults in Advance and Retreat.

a. The most common fault is that of bringing the feet together, thus reducing the size of the base and the stability of the body. To demonstrate the instability of this position, have students attempt to execute some maneuvers from a position with the feet together.

b. The feet may lose their right-angle relationship, thus throwing the body out of line and out of balance. Working on painted lines helps to avoid this.

c. The outer border of the left foot may be allowed to leave the floor if too long a step is taken. This spoils body balance.

d. The feet may not be advanced along the straight line. Stop often and check the foot position.

e. Various parts of the body may lose the proper guard position. Again stop the footwork practice often in order to check the guard position.

f. The feet may be dragged or scuffed on the floor. Go back to slow counting for the movement of each foot.

g. Watch to see that the knees do not become straight during this practice.

4. Progression.

The advance and retreat should be taken up as soon as the guard position is mastered. They should be practiced carefully and persistently until they are performed smoothly, quickly, and automatically.

A short drill in footwork should be included as warm up at the beginning of each class hour. As the following offensive techniques are taken up, add advancing and retreating practice to each as soon as the execution in the static position is learned.

The jump is a more advanced technique and should not be taught until the class has become proficient in the fundamental positions.

VI. LUNGE

A. Definition. The lunge is the method used to reach an opponent with the tip of the foil to make a touch. It is always executed from the guard position (Figure 5.8).

B. Execution.

FIGURE 5.8 *The lunge.*

1. The right arm is extended at shoulder height without locking the elbow or hunching the shoulder. The tip of the foil should be slightly lower than the hand. This movement must precede the movement of the foot.

2. The left leg is snapped straight and the right foot is lifted and moved forward along the line of the left heel. The body is kept low.

3. The right-angle relationship of the feet in the guard position is maintained.

4. The right knee is perpendicularly above the instep to prevent strain on the knee.

5. The left foot remains flat on the floor. If the body weight is allowed to move so far over the right foot that the left foot is rolled to the inside, recovery is very slow.

6. The body remains erect. In this position some of the weight remains on the left foot.

7. The left arm is fully extended, and is dropped back parallel to the left leg. The palm of the left hand faces up and the hand is in line with the arm. This is the position that results when the hand and arm are in the correct on guard position and the elbow and wrist are straightened. This movement of the arm adds force to the lunge and balances the extension of the right arm. It puts the left arm into position to aid the recovery by helping to lift the weight of the body.

When perfected, the lunge should be one smooth, coordinated movement from the initial extension of the right arm until the blade bends on the target.

C. Recovery from the Lunge.

1. The weight is thrown to the left foot, and the left knee is bent as the right knee is partially extended, to push the body weight back toward the left.

2. The left leg pulls and the right pushes the body back into position.

3. The right foot is lifted and placed, heel first, in its original guard position, with the knee bent.

4. The left arm is *forcefully* lifted to its on guard position. This lift of the left arm is very important in bringing the body back to position, in that it helps to lift the body weight, making it easier for the right foot to be raised from the floor.

5. The right arm is drawn back to the original guard position.

D. Teaching.

1. Organization of Class.

a. For the first practice, to get the feeling of the position, the class can be lined up in two or three lines facing the instructor. It is well to have this preliminary practice on lines that are marked on the floor. The class may be all around the gymnasium, using the basketball court lines with the instructor in the center of the room.

b. If the class is large and the instructor desires to have the students in one line, have them take their positions in profile to the instructor. In this organization it would not be possible to use the lines painted on the floor.

c. If there are enough mats to hang on the wall so that there will be space for all to practice at once, have students spread out around the gymnasium, two or three in front of each mat, depending on the size of the mats.

d. If the mats are small and there is not enough mat space for all to practice at once, divide into pairs and have one watch and check her partner as she practices. Have them change on a signal from the instructor.

2. Presentation.

a. Explain and demonstrate the technique. It is well to explain here that the straightening of the arm gives the right of way to attack when bouting, and, therefore, the thrusting of the arm *preliminary* to the moving of the right foot is extremely important.

b. Have the class practice thrusting and recovering. Count for each movement.

c. Have the class practice thrust, lunge, recover. Count for each movement. Start counting slowly, have the students hold each position for checking before taking the next. Gradually increase the speed of the commands.

d. Send the class to targets on the wall and have them take the guard position close enough to the mat so that the foil will be slightly bent when the right arm is extended. Have them practice the thrust on count to get the feeling of a touch. Check to see that the foil bends upward. The wall can be used only if mats or sponge rubber targets are available to absorb some of the force of the attack. The hard wall without padding will cause foils to break. If no mats are available, have one student stand facing her partner, who can practice thrusting against her jacket. Students take turns practicing and acting as targets for their partners. Students need to learn early that a touch does not hurt. Therefore, some practice should be done with the partner not defending herself so that she can overcome the tendency to draw her body away from the attack from fear of a touch.

e. Have the students move out from the wall to within easy lunging distance. Practice on count:

(*1*) thrust — (hold) — lunge — (hold) — recover. Check positions.

(*2*) thrust, lunge—(hold) — recover.

(*3*) thrust, lunge, recover.

Finally give simply the command to lunge and tell the students to recover immediately. Remind them that the hand should always have a fractional start on the foot even in the swiftest attack.

f. Combine practice in advancing and lunging.

(*1*) Start the students about 10 to 12 feet from the wall and have them advance and lunge against the targets on the wall.

(*2*) During floor work drill, give commands to advance and retreat, telling the class to continue in one direction until the reverse command is given and occasionally call for a lunge when the students are advancing.

3. Faults in Lunge.

a. If students are not preceding the lunge with the thrust, go back to the practice of thrusting and lunging on command.

b. If the right foot is lifted too high, the lunge will be slow and the body will be lifted, and thus the tip of the foil carried out of line. If the right foot is dragged or slid along the floor, the whole movement will be slow because of the friction of the foot against the floor. It may help to perfect the foot movements to give some practice in lunging without having the arms in the guard position. Have the students concentrate on the position of the feet and on barely lifting the right foot from the floor, carrying it forward quickly to a point where it can easily hold the weight.

c. Often too much weight is taken on the right foot, making the recovery slow. This can be detected easily because the left foot will be rolled over on the inner border. It may be due to taking too long a lunge step or bending the body in the direction of the target. Both of these faults are easily corrected by moving the student nearer the target. Have students concentrate on keeping their bodies erect. If a student persists in this fault, it may be the result of a lack of kinesthetic perception of the body position during the lunge. If the instructor stands in the on guard position, very close behind the student, grasps both of the students wrists and actually lunges with her, forcing her into a well balanced position, she can frequently give the student a feeling for the correct position.

d. The right-angle position of the feet may be lost in performing the lunge. This means that the right foot is placed forward with the outside border instead of the toes toward the target, and since the weight is moving in that direction force will be exerted against the side of the ankle and knee and injury may result. Balance is also less stable. Mark a line for the student on the floor with chalk if there is no painted line where she is practicing.

e. In concentrating on foot position and the thrust of the right arm, the extension of the left arm is often forgotten. Explain to the class the value of this movement because of the leverage action and balance. The lift of the left arm helps to make the recovery much easier. Have the class practice lunging, emphasizing a strong lift of the left arm when recovering.

f. When attacking after an advance, the student often attempts to reach her opponent by bending her body instead of lunging with her foot. She simply stops the foot movement of advancing and reaches with arm and body. This places her in a very unstable position and makes recovery slow and precarious. Explain and demonstrate the lack of stability of this position of reaching so far beyond the base, and have the class practice advancing and lunging on command with an immediate recovery.

4. Progression.

Since all attacks are made with a lunge, it is important that this be learned as soon as the guard position has been perfected.

VII. ATTACKS

A. Simple Attacks. These are attacks made without any preceding feints, or threatening motions, against the opponent's blade.

1. The Direct Thrust.

a. Execution. This attack is executed by extending the right arm in the line of engagement, with or without a lunge, according to the distance between opponents. The hand is slightly higher than the shoulder, and when the point of the foil contacts the target, the hand should be lifted slightly to prevent the point from slipping. A direct thrust can be made from an engagement or with the blades not touching. This should be done with speed.

b. Teaching. Divide the class into pairs. Have the pairs line up in two or three lines the length of the gymnasium and engage their opponents in high inside. Designate all students facing one wall the No. 1's and all those facing the other wall the No. 2's.

NOTE: This organization is used in teaching all the following techniques.

c. Presentation. Have No. 1's lunge on command three or four times, each time making a touch in high inside (see p. 123). Have them hold the lunge position and check to see that the blade is bent up. This practice will show them in the beginning that a touch does not hurt the opponent and will help to prevent half-hearted attacks that might otherwise develop from a fear of hurting the opponent. This also shows the students the need for defensive tactics.

After they have made one or two good touches, have the class recover immediately without waiting for a command. If they establish the habit of holding the lunge position, it will be difficult to teach a fast recovery.

(*2*) With both fencers in the on guard position, No. 1's may practice the cut-over, thrust, and lunge, while No. 2's parry. Count slowly, and gradually speed up the commands. Change roles of attacker and defender often.

Engaged on the inside—cut-over, thrust, and attack high outside.

Engaged on the inside—cut-over, thrust high outside, and attack low outside.

Engaged on the outside—cut-over, thrust, and attack high inside.

Engaged on the outside—cut-over, thrust high inside, and attack low inside.

(*3*) Practice the cut-over followed by the disengage. Be sure that the fencers get a good strong thrust after the cut-over, before the disengage.

(*a*) Combined with the single disengage:

Engaged on the inside—cut-over to outside—thrust—disengage and attack high inside.

Engaged on the inside—cut-over to outside—thrust—disengage and attack low inside.

Engaged on the outside—cut-over to inside—thrust—disengage and attack high outside.

Engaged on the outside—cut-over to inside—thrust—disengage and attack low outside.

NOTE: The cut-over can be used *following* the disengage if the opponent drops her foil on the parry.

(*b*) Combined with the double disengage:

Engaged on the inside—cut-over to outside—thrust—disengage to high inside—disengage to high outside—attack high or low outside.

Engaged on the outside—cut-over to inside—thrust—disengage to high outside—disengage to high inside—attack high or low inside.

d. FAULTS IN CUT-OVER.

(*1*) Over-use of the forearm takes the point of the foil too far out of line. To correct this go back to practicing the cut-over and thrust only.

(*2*) Using only the thumb and forefinger makes the grip so loose that control is almost entirely lost and a beat (see Beat) by the opponent may knock the foil from the fencer's hand. Slow practice emphasizing the use of fingers and wrist is necessary.

e. PROGRESSION.

The cut-over attack can be put into the progression after the beat has been learned. Since the students have already learned one method of changing the line of engagement (the disengage), it is better to teach the beat, which is an entirely different type of attack before the cut-over.

B. COMPOUND ATTACKS.

1. Attacks on the Blade. This type of attack can be performed directly or with a change in the line of engagement. It should always start from a position very near or in contact with the opponent's blade, to avoid the possibility of missing it.

a. BEAT. The beat is a quick, sharp blow of the middle of the blade on the middle or weak part of the opponent's blade for the purpose of opening a way for the lunge attack that immediately follows. The beat has three objectives:

1. Opening the line.
2. As a feint before an attack.
3. As an invitation to the opponent's attack.

(*1*) EXECUTION. It is executed entirely by the fingers. To beat when engaged on the inside, the blade is moved *slightly* to the right by the thumb and forefinger. The grip of the last three fingers is relaxed but a light contact with the foil is maintained. The fingers are then snapped toward the palm and the foil moves sharply from right to left, and contacts the opponent's blade with a sharp blow. In executing a beat the foil should be stopped in line so that the hand is in its normal guard position ready to go through with an attack. The beat from the outside engagement is not effective since it must be a wrist action rather than a finger action, which makes it slower, and relatively weaker.

(*2*) DEFENSE. Let the fingers relax as the opponent's blade hits. Then contract the fingers quickly, bringing the blade back into line or into the parry. If resistance is offered to the opponent's beat, the whole arm will be hit out of line and then recovery is much slower.

(*3*) TEACHING.

(*a*) Explain and demonstrate the technique.

(*b*) Have the students practice beating back and forth. This is good practice in using the fingers and also helps to strengthen the fingers and thumb. Have one beat and hold, then the opponent beat and hold, and so forth.

(*c*) Continue the same practice adding a thrust immediately after the beat. Recover the arm to the guard position before the opponent does a return beat.

(*d*) No. 1's beat, thrust, and attack in high inside. No. 2's parry 4 (see p. 139). Change attacker and defender.

(*e*) No. 1's beat, thrust, and attack in low inside. No. 2's parry 7 (see p. 141). Change attacker and defender.

NOTE: The beat from the engagement on the outside is not strong and is used only as a surprise attack when the opponent is tiring.

(*f*) Combine the beat with a disengage. Engaged on the inside—beat, thrust high inside, and as the opponent recovers disengage to high outside and attack either high or low outside.

(*g*) Combine the beat with the double disengage. Engaged on the inside—beat, thrust high inside, disengage to the outside, disengage to the inside, and attack high or low.

(*4*) FAULTS IN BEAT.

(*a*) A wide backswing makes the beat so slow that the opponent may attack while the fencer is preparing to beat. Actually, the force needed to deflect the opponent's blade can be produced with a very small backswing.

(*b*) Making the movement with the whole arm carries the blade very wide and makes recovery very slow. Go back to the finger exercise of beating back and forth.

(*c*) Following the opponent's blade out of line after the beat instead of stopping the tip of the foil at the midline makes the attack slow. The tip must be stopped immediately on contact with the opponent's blade so that it remains in line for the attack. Again, use the beating exercise emphasizing the control of the blade after the opponent's blade has been hit.

(*d*) Dropping the right arm leaves the target open for attack. Give slow practice on count.

(*5*) PROGRESSION. The beat should be taught as soon as the four parries and disengage have been learned.

b. THE PRESS (OR PRESSURE).

(*1*) USE. This tactic has the same purposes as the beat. It is particularly useful when the opponent's grip is weak or when she is tiring. As with the beat, it is not good from an engagement on the outside except as a surprise attack or when the opponent is very tired.

(*2*) EXECUTION. The press is made by pressing on the opponent's blade with the arm in the normal guard position.

(*3*) TEACHING.

(*a*) Possibilities for practice:

Engage on the inside—press, thrust, and attack in high or low inside.

Engage on the inside—press, thrust high inside, disengage and attack high or low outside.

(*b*) Possibilities of combinations:

1. With single disengage.
2. With double or triple disengage.
3. With the cut-over occasionally, if the opponent comes back with the foil low.
4. With the counter (see p. 143). Example, counter 1-2-3-press-lunge.

(*4*) PROGRESSION. This is an advanced technique and should not be taken up until after the ripostes and counters have been learned.

c. PRESSURE GUIDE. This is a sudden forward and downward pressure on the blade of the opponent. It is carried through until the strong part of the opponent's blade is reached. For teaching possibilities see the discussion above on the Press. This also is an advanced technique and should not be taught to beginning or intermediate fencers.

d. Glide. This is an attack made by gliding the blade along the opponent's blade until the thrust is completed. It should be taught to advanced fencers only. The best defense is not to allow the opponent to glide. The minute a fencer feels her opponent's foil slipping down hers, she should either attack or counter immediately to do something to stop her.

2. Taking the Blade. This is an action upon the opponent's blade in order to ward off the point and at the same time control it. It is preferably used against a straight arm. The strong part of the blade is against the opponent's weak part. It should be done with a controlled resistance to the opponent's blade, so that the point is not carried out of line. The fencer should complete the movement before delivering an attack. The blade is taken in three ways:

a. Opposition. This is a progressive opposition, without too much exaggeration, in the line of engagement, prolonged up to the attack.

b. Bind. This carries the opponent's blade from the high to the low line or vice versa, making a semicircle with the point and carrying the blade to the opposite line. The fencer contacts the weak part of her opponent's blade with the strong section of her own. The arm should be almost extended at the start and must extend completely straight forward during the bind. Contact of the blades must be maintained until the touch is made.

The bind is used against an opponent who holds her foil too tightly. When the opponent starts a bind, the best thing to do is to relax the foil and come through for an attack. The best procedure is to push hard against her foil, then suddenly relax and come through

c. Envelopment. This is made up of two binds, so that the blades end in the original line of engagement. The points make complete circles.

NOTE: These attacks are all for the very advanced fencer and should not be taught to those in the intermediate stage.

3. Counter Attacks. Counter attacks are useful in two types of situations: 1. When the opponent attacks slowly or with a bent arm. In this case a precautionary beat may be necessary. 2. When the opponent attacks with a wide movement of her blade. The counter attack should be a fast straight thrust into the most exposed line of the opponent's target. If the wide movement accompanies a slow action a disengage attack may be necessary.

The action of a counter attack should always be simple—a straight thrust, a beat thrust, or a disengage thrust. The counter attacks are not preceded by parries and so must be very carefully timed, and should be taught only to very advanced fencers.

a. Time Thrust. The time thrust is a simple attack made so as to touch the opponent when she is making an attack and at the same time to close the line that she intends to come through. This is best used against an opponent who is advancing.

b. Stop Thrust. The stop thrust is made upon the opponent's preparation to attack. It should be made at the moment that the opponent's right foot is lifted to make the lunge. Since it stops an offensive action at its inception, it is called a "stop thrust." It is best used against a fencer who feints wide, bringing the point out of line.

C. Secondary Attacks.

1. Definition. A secondary attack is one made immediately after the first, whether in the same line or not.

2. Use. Its object is to profit by the shock produced by the first attack on an opponent. It may be made up of any of the preceding simple attacks. Many combinations are possible. A secondary attack may be executed in two ways:

a. Lunge and stay, and if the opponent does not riposte (follow her parry with an attack) make a secondary attack.

b. Lunge and stay, and when the opponent ripostes, parry and immediately make a secondary attack.

3. Types.

a. REDOUBLE. The redouble is a renewal of attack by changing the line of attack with a disengage, or cut-over if the opponent holds her parry.

b. REPLACEMENT (REMISE). The replacement is a second attack made in the same line as the original attack. No attempt is made to find the opponent's blade after the preliminary attack.

c. REPRISE. The reprise is an attack made on the lunge in the same line as the preliminary attack after having found the opponent's blade by a parry.

4. Practice.

a. Students engage on the inside.

No. 1's attack high inside and stay in the lunge position.

No. 2's parry 4 without riposting (see Parries; and Riposte, p. 144).

No. 1's disengage and attack high outside.

No. 2's parry 6.

b. Students engage on the inside.

No. 1's attack high inside and stay in the lunge position.

No. 2's parry 4 and riposte high inside.

No. 1's parry 4 and make a secondary attack in low inside.

No. 2's parry 7.

c. The above practices can be given in all lines.

5. Progression. Since a secondary attack is made in the lunge position, the opponent is given an excellent opportunity to make a touch by simply extending her arm. This type of attack should be used with judgment and very sparingly, and should be taught only to advanced fencers.

VIII. DEFENSE: PARRIES AND RETURNS

A. PARRIES. These are defensive movements of the blade by which the attacking blade is diverted from the target and a touch is avoided. It is possible to avoid a

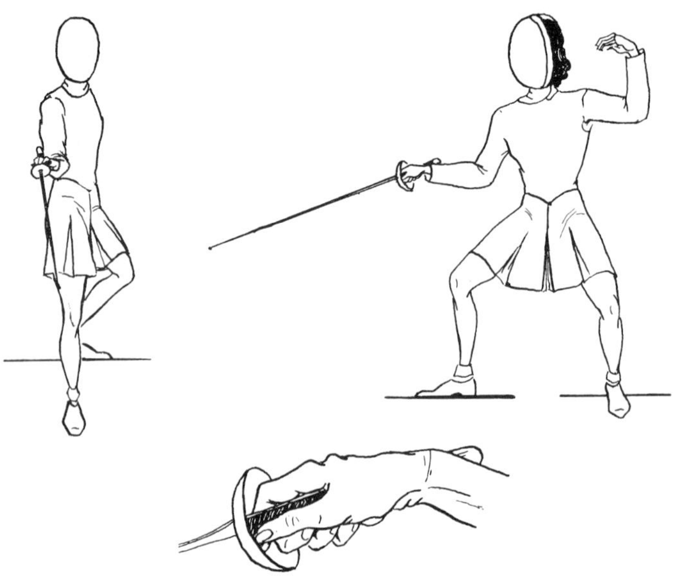

FIGURE 5.9 *The second parry (2).*

touch by retreating, but this will not be included in this discussion of parries.

1. Simple Parries. There are two types of simple parries, both of which deflect the opponent's blade from the target without changing the line. In the *opposition parry* pressure is maintained against the opponent's blade until the return. The *beat parry* is a sharp light tap against the opponent's blade, with an immediate return to position. All parries should be executed by the fingers and wrist with just enough movement of the foil to catch the opponent's blade and prevent her coming through on the target. In making a parry, the middle part of the blade should contact the opponent's blade, never the weak tip.

a. FIRST. The first parry defends the inside high line.

(*1*) EXECUTION.

(*a*) The forearm is almost horizontal, with the elbow to the right.

(*b*) The hand is pronated so that the thumb is down and the fingers toward the opponent.

(*c*) The blade points to the adversary's toe.

(*2*) TEACHING. Since this parry moves the point of the foil so far out of line, making recovery slow, and leaves much of the target unprotected, it is seldom used and will not be included in the teaching progression.

b. SECOND. The second parry defends the outside low line (Figure 5.9).

(*1*) EXECUTION.

a. The point of the foil describes a semicircle counterclockwise.

(*b*) At the end of the parry the hand is in pronation.

(*c*) The foil points to the opponent's knee.

(*2*) TEACHING.

(*a*) Fencers engage on the outside.

No. 1's attack in low outside.

No. 2's parry 2.

Change attacker and defender.

Give a command for the thrust and lunge—hold—check the parry—give a command for recovery. Tell No. 2's to parry immediately on the opponents' lunge.

Give a signal to start the action, which then is carried through to the recovery of both the attacker and defender with no further commands.

(*b*) For further information on progression and practice, see the discussion of teaching the direct thrust (pp. 132–133).

(*3*) PROGRESSION.

The second parry should be taught after the direct attacks and disengages in high inside and outside, and the fourth and sixth parries have been learned. This parry is stronger than 8, which defends the same line.

c. THIRD. The third parry defends the outside high line.

(*1*) EXECUTION.

(*a*) The hand is pronated and the foil is moved to the right.

(*b*) The tip of the foil is kept higher than the hand.

(*2*) TEACHING.

Since this is the more awkward, the sixth parry, which defends the same line, is preferred.

d. FOURTH. The fourth parry defends the inside high line (Figure 5.10).

(*1*) EXECUTION.

(*a*) The hand is in "normal" position.

(*b*) The blade and hand are moved to the left at breast height just enough to protect the inside high line of the target.

This parry can also be accomplished by moving only the blade toward the left, executing a *small* sharp beat against the opponent's foil. Recovery is faster because the arm remains stationary. This is a wrist action. Some students are more successful with the first method, others with the beat parry. It is advisable to suggest that they experiment with both, choose that which is most successful, and concentrate on it in practice.

(*2*) TEACHING. The presentation is the same as that for the second parry.

Fencers engage on the inside. No. 1's attack in high inside.

No. 2's parry 4.

Change attacker and defender.

(*3*) PROGRESSION. This is the simplest parry and should be taught as soon as the lunge has been perfected. It is the strongest parry covering this line.

e. FIFTH. The fifth parry defends the inside low line:

(*1*) EXECUTION.

(*a*) The hand slightly in pronation, is moved to the left.

(*b*) The hand is dropped lower than the elbow.

(*c*) The point of the foil is kept higher than the hand.

(*2*) TEACHING. Since the hand is low, making recovery difficult and leaving more of the target exposed, the seventh parry is recommended to cover this line.

f. SIXTH. The sixth parry defends the outside high line (Figure 5.11).

(*1*) EXECUTION.

(*a*) The blade and the hand are moved to the right in supination. They are moved only far enough to protect the body and the arm.

This parry can also be accomplished by a small sharp beat which moves the blade to the right but leaves the arm in the on guard position. Again it is suggested that the students experiment with the two methods and make a choice depending upon individual preference.

(*b*) The hand is higher than the elbow, as it is in the on guard position.

(*c*) The point of the foil remains at the height of the on guard position.

(*2*) TEACHING. The presentation is the same as that for the second parry.

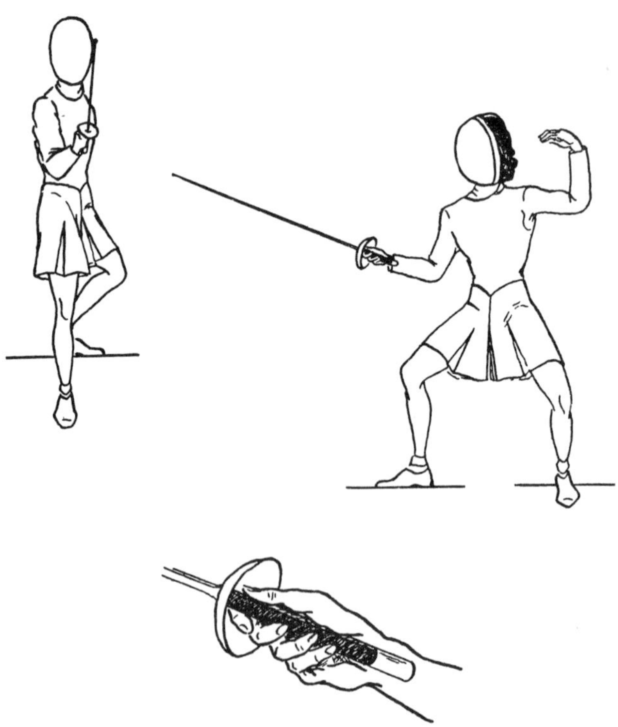

FIGURE 5.10 *The fourth parry (4).*

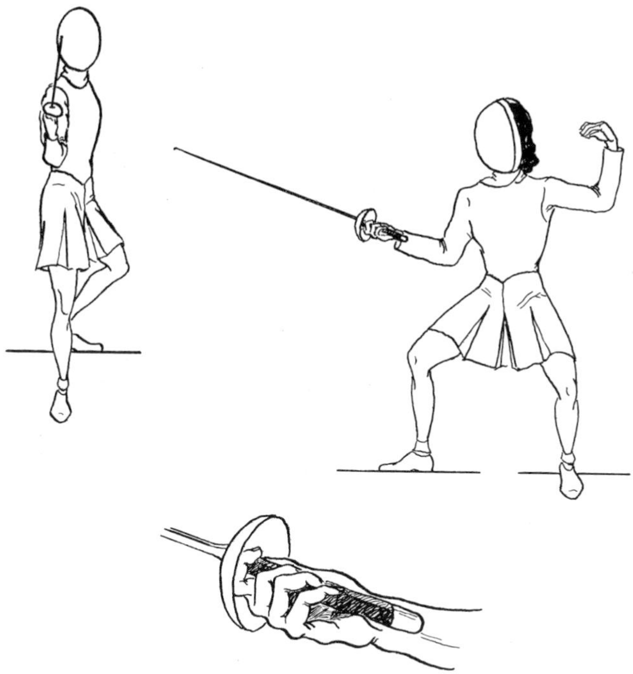

FIGURE 5.11 *The sixth parry (6).*

Fencers engage on the outside. No. 1's attack in high outside.

No. 2's parry 6.

Change attacker and defender.

(*3*) PROGRESSION.

This parry is preferred to the third parry, which defends the same line, and should be taught after the fourth parry has been learned.

g. SEVENTH. The seventh parry defends the inside low line (Figure 5.12).

(*1*) EXECUTION.

(*a*) The tip of the foil is dropped in a semicircle clockwise.

(*b*) The foil points to the opponent's knee.

(*c*) The hand is in supination.

(*d*) Recovery to the on guard position may be accomplished in two ways. The direction of the tip of the foil can be reversed as soon as the opponent's foil has been deflected, or the fencer can continue to move the tip of the foil in a clockwise direction, completing the circle. This last method moves the opponent's blade out away from the target, lifts it, and finally throws it to the outside. The fencers are engaged on the outside at the completion of this parry when the full circle is used.

(*2*) TEACHING. The presentation is the same as that for the second parry.

Fencers engage on the inside. No. 1's attack low inside.

No. 2's parry 7.

Change attacker and defender.

(*3*) PROGRESSION.

This parry is preferred to the fifth parry, which defends the same line and should be taught after the second parry. The instructor may prefer to teach this parry before the second parry.

h. EIGHTH. The eighth parry defends the outside low line.

(*1*) EXECUTION.

(*a*) The hand is moved to the right in supination.

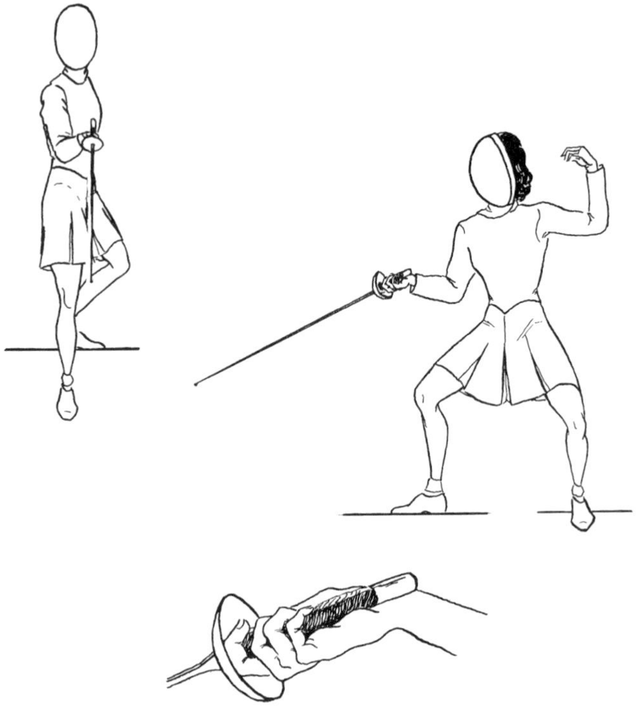

FIGURE 5.12 *The seventh parry (7).*

(*b*) The tip of the foil is dropped to point to the opponent's knee.

(*2*) TEACHING.

This is not as strong a position as that of the second parry, which defends the same line, and therefore need not be thoroughly taught.

i. GENERAL FAULTS IN PARRIES.

(*1*) If, when the opponent's blade is contacted, the student holds the parry position instead of recovering immediately to the on guard position, the opponent can easily disengage and attack in another area. To demonstrate this to the student who does not recover following a parry, engage with her, attack in the high inside, and when she fails to recover, disengage and attack either in high or low outside. This will point up, as words cannot, the importance of a fast recovery. From the very beginning a fast recovery from a parry must be stressed.

(*2*) If the parry is made by a wide movement of the arm instead of just the wrist and fingers, recovery will be slow and too much of the target will be left unguarded. Have the students practice parrying a direct thrust so that judgment of the attack is not necessary and full attention can be given to the execution of the parry.

(*3*) Dropping the hand low leaves a great deal of the target unguarded and also makes recovery slow. Engage with the student, attack in low inside, and when she drops her hand low come up and lunge in high outside. Use this only to cure her of dropping her hand. It will demonstrate how it leaves the target open. Students can be of great help to each other. Suggest that they be constantly aware of their partners' hand positions and that they remind each other to keep the hand up, opposite the center of the target area.

(*4*) Frequently, when the complete circle is used in executing the seventh parry, the student crosses the opponent's blade before dropping the tip of her blade. In other words, she moves her tip in a counterclockwise direction. This results in her contacting the opponent's blade on the left and moving it to the right *across* the low line of her own target. Thus it is easy for the opponent to come through for a touch in the low outside area. The student should be cautioned *first* to drop the tip of her foil and then to move it to the left (clockwise). This action causes her blade to contact the opponent's on the right and thus it is moved outside the target area before it is lifted, and by the time the blade moves across the body it is too high for a successful attack. This can be clearly demonstrated by having a student take the lunge position with the tip of her foil attacking the low inside area and hold this position while you slowly move your foil in a counterclockwise direction, pointing out the fact that it forces her foil across your target area.

2. Counter Parries. These differ from simple parries in that not only is the blade deviated, but also the line of attack is changed.

a. EXECUTION. In making a counter the point of the foil describes a small circle around the opponent's foil. Only the fingers are used, the hand remaining in position. The counter parries are named in relation to the line in which they are executed. In the high line the circle is started under the opponent's blade, and in the low line, over the opponent's blade. The counter parries are not as fast as the opposition and the beat parries but they are more difficult to deceive.

Example. Two fencers are engaged on the inside. The attacker disengages to the outside. The defender, to execute a counter parry, describes a small circle around the opponent's blade by going under and around, contacting the blade and deflecting it outside the limit of the target line on the inside.

b. TEACHING.

(*1*) Teach the movement of the tip of the foil around the opponent's foil. With the fencers engaged on the inside, have No. 1's disengage from inside to outside.

No. 2's follow their opponents' foils around to complete the circle.

Repeat this several times in succession from the inside engagement and then from the outside. Count for each counter parry. Start slowly, and gradually speed up the commands. Have each student touch her opponent's foil on every counter to make sure she keeps her foil close to her opponent's.

(*2*) Combine the attack with this same practice.

(*a*) Students engage on the inside:

Count 1—No. 1's disengage to the outside.

No. 2's follow No. 1's blades around (end engaged on the inside).

Count 2—repeat.

Count 3—repeat.

Count 4—repeat.

Count 5—repeat and after the counter have No. 1's attack in high inside and No. 2's parry. Change attacker and defender.

(*b*) Engage on the outside and repeat the practice ending with an attack in high outside.

(*c*) Engage on the inside and repeat the practice ending with an attack in low inside.

NOTE: The low outside attack is not usually successful as the attacker does not often get free enough to attack in that line.

In counting for the practices it is well to change the number of counters preceding the attack each time. Always start the practices with slow counting, which is gradually speeded up.

c. FAULTS IN COUNTER PARRIES. The main fault in the execution of the counter is the use of the arm instead of the wrist and fingers. This makes the foil movement large and leaves too much target exposed. It may help to have the instructor go around the class and hold each student's arm just above the wrist until she gets a feeling for making the movement with the wrist and fingers only.

Also, the student can hold her own right wrist with her left hand.

d. PROGRESSION.

The counter is a fairly advanced tactic and should not be taken up until all the elementary attacks, the simple parries, and ripostes have been learned. It would probably come into the intermediate progression sometime after the middle of the season.

B. RETURNS.

1. Definition. A riposte is the *return* thrust that is delivered after a parry. It is a reply to an unsuccessful attack. The more accurate the parry, the safer the riposte.

2. Execution. A riposte may be made with or without a lunge. The arm should be extended to reach the target.

3. Types.

a. DIRECT. A direct or simple riposte is a straight attack, delivered immediately after the parry in the same line.

b. COMPOUND. A compound riposte is any return that consists of more than one movement; that is, a feint, one or more disengages, or a cut-over.

c. DELAYED. A delayed riposte is so named because it does not immediately follow the parry, but allows sufficient delay to break the speed of the play. It deceives an initial counter parry, or waits for an opposing reaction in a line other than the direct line.

d. COUNTER. When a riposte is parried and followed by a responding riposte, the latter is called a "counter riposte."

4. Teaching.

a. SIMPLE PRACTICES. Start the practices by specifying the line for the riposte. Later allow the defender to choose any of the ripostes that are possible following the original attack.

(*1*) Students engage on the inside.

No. 1's attack high inside.

No. 2's parry 4 and riposte high inside, low inside, or disengage to low outside.

(*2*) Students engage on the outside.

No. 1's attack high outside

No. 2's parry 6 and riposte low outside. This is the only riposte that does not expose too much of the body from this position.

(*3*) Students engage on the inside.

No. 1's attack low inside.

No. 2's parry 7 and riposte low inside or disengage to high or low outside. If using the circular parry, riposte high or low outside or disengage to high or low inside.

(*4*) Students engage on the outside.

No. 1's attack low outside.

No. 2's parry 2 and riposte low outside, high outside, or high inside, coming up and over their opponents' foils.

b. COMBINATION PRACTICES. These are examples of counter ripostes.

(*1*) Students engage on the outside.

No. 1's attack high outside.

No. 2's parry 6 and riposte low outside.

No. 1's parry 2, disengage, and riposte low inside.

No. 2's parry 7 and riposte low inside. If the circular parry is used this will require a disengage.

No. 1's parry 7.

(*2*) Students engage on the inside.

No. 1's attack high inside.

No. 2's parry 4 and riposte high inside.

No. 1's parry 4 and riposte low inside.

No. 2's parry 7 and riposte high outside. If a circular parry is *not* used this will require a disengage.

No. 1's parry 6.

(*3*) Students engage on the outside.

No. 1's attack low outside.

No. 2's parry 2 and riposte high outside.

No. 1's parry 6 and riposte low outside.

No. 2's parry 2 and start to riposte high, but as opponent comes up to parry drop to low outside.

No. 1's parry 2.

NOTE: In all these practices the original attacker and defender should be shifted after two or three attacks.

5. Faults in Ripostes.

a. Using the riposte too often.

b. Riposte before completing the parry.

6. Progression. Ripostes should not be taught too early in the progression, as the fencer must have sufficient judgment to know when to use them. If beginners are taught ripostes too soon, they will use them after every attack. This is poor, since many touches will be lost to a quick opponent. Also, the surprise value of the attack is lost. Students should be taught to use the riposte when the opponent is slow in recovering from the lunge. Do not teach it until the four main parries (2, 7, 4, and 6) have become automatic.

SIZE OF CLASSES

Classes of 20 or less are ideal. However, it is possible for one instructor to handle fencing classes up to 40 if the situation demands larger classes. When this is necessary, money for equipment is likely to be limited. If so, a class of 40 can be taught with 25 foils and masks. This allows a foil and mask for each two students with a few extras in case of breakage. Since it is impossible to have a class practice continuously, the class can be divided into groups of four students, with two working and two coaching. After a short practice period they can rotate so that the other two have equal practice time. The preliminary footwork drill can still be done by all regardless of whether each student has a foil and mask. Each student must have some type of body protection (jacket, half jacket, or plastron) since a great deal of time would be lost in rotating if jackets had to be changed. However, masks and foils can be shared with little loss of time. Although this situation is far from ideal, it has been found to be workable, and even though students do not progress as far in a term as can be expected in smaller classes, the loss is not great. The students who are coaching can learn a great deal if they work conscientiously with the others in their group. It is helpful if the instructor emphasizes specific points to be observed during each practice period.

If it is possible to have equipment for 30, the students can be divided into groups of three instead of four. This situation gives more practice time to each student. Whenever possible there should be equipment for every student in the class.

GENERAL PROGRESSION

1. Description of equipment.
2. Grip of the foil.
3. Salute.
4. On guard position.
5. Call (Appel).
6. Advance and retreat.
7. Lunge.
8. Advance and retreat combined with the lunge.
9. Explanation of:
   a. the target and its divisions.
   b. the lines of engagement.
   c. the position of engagement.
10. Lunge for a touch (with no defense by opponent) in each of the four divisions of the target.
11. Direct attack in high inside and fourth parry.
12. Direct attack in high outside and sixth parry.
13. Disengage in the high line and fourth and sixth parries.
*14. Direct attack in low outside and second parry.
15. Disengage from inside to low outside and second parry.
*16. Direct attack in low inside and seventh parry.

* Whether the second or seventh parry should be taught first is a question. Students appear to have difficulty with whichever one is taught last. Therefore, each instructor should experiment to determine the sequence that seems to give the best results. Whichever is taught first, it is suggested that as soon as the first is understood, the other be presented, and practice of these parries be alternated, so that the two are learned simultaneously.

17. Disengage from outside to low inside and seventh parry.

18. All four direct attacks and parries.

19. All four disengages and parries.

20. Short period of bouting, using direct and single disengage attacks only. The instructor designates the original attacker and defender, and calls for their reversal after a couple of minutes of play.

Score: 1 point for a successful attack.
1 point for a successful parry.

21. Beat.

22. Beat combined with disengage.

23. Short period of bouting, using all tactics learned to this point, and conducted as in 20.

24. Cut-over.

25. Cut-over combined with disengage.

26. Short period of bouting as above.

27. Riposte.

28. Short period of bouting, conducted as in 20.

Score: 1 point for successful attack.
1 point for successful parry.
1 point for successful riposte.
1 point for successful parry of the riposte.

29. Counter.

30. Short period of regular bouting. (From this time on a part of each period should be given to bouting.)

31. Press.

32. Press combined with other attacks.

Very advanced fencers only:

33. Glide.

34. Bind.

35. Secondary attacks.

36. Stop thrust.

37. Time thrust.

SAMPLE LESSON PLANS [3]

I. BEGINNERS: PLAN FOR FIRST LESSON

1. Explanation of Equipment.
2. Grip of the Foil.
3. Position of Attention: Students in three or four lines the length of the gymnasium, standing, facing the instructor, on lines painted on the floor.
4. Salute:
   a. on count.
   b. on a single command.
5. On Guard Position:
   a. on count.
   b. on a single command.
6. Advance: Advance 10 to 15 steps to get the sequence of movement
   a. count for the movement of each foot (2 counts for a complete step).
   b. 1 count for a complete step:
      (*1*) slowly.
      (*2*) gradually speeded up.
7. Retreat (as above).
8. Advance and Retreat:
   a. 1 count for each step:
      (*1*) slowly.
      (*2*) gradually speeded up.
   b. Command to start the advance or retreat and students continue in that direction until given the command to change.

NOTE: Only three or four steps should be allowed in one direction before giving the command to change.

9. Lunge:
   a. Practice in lines.
   b. Practice against soft targets on the wall.
      (*1*) thrust.
      (*2*) thrust and lunge.
10. Advance and Lunge: Students in three or four lines as at the beginning of the lesson.

II. GENERAL LESSON PLAN

1. Floor work on individual techniques. After the beginning stage is passed, this preliminary warm-up practice may be performed with the fencers in pairs engaged as for a bout. Number the fencers facing one direction No. 1's, and those facing the opposite direction No. 2's. Explain that the commands will apply to

[3] Length of lesson: 35 minutes.

No. 1's and that if they are commanded to advance, No. 2's will retreat and vice versa.

2. Review of old material: (*a*) Questions and discussion. (*b*) Practice on instructor's commands.

3. Explanation and demonstration of new material.

4. Practice of new material on instructor's commands.

5. Short bout period, using all techniques learned to this point: (*a*) Beginners and Intermediates. Instructor designates attacker and defender, changing after four or five attacks. *Score:* 1 point for a successful attack, 1 point for a successful parry. (*b*) Advanced: regular bout.

6. Floor work.

III. LESSON PLANS: BEGINNERS *

Lesson 1. Equipment; grip; attention position; salute; on guard position; advance; retreat; lunge; advance and lunge.

Lesson 2. Review: grip; salute; advance; retreat; lunge against mat. Take up: target; lines of engagement; position of engagement; lunge in all lines to make a touch against opponent's target (this is done with no defense by the opponent—to give the feeling for actually going through for a touch); direct attack in high inside and fourth parry; direct attack in high outside and sixth parry.

Lesson 3. Review: salute; lunge against a mat; advance and lunge; retreat; direct attack in high lines and fourth and sixth parries. Take up: advance and retreat with the fencers in bout position, No. 1's attack in high inside, No. 2's parry 4 and reverse; same with attack in high outside and sixth parry.

Lesson 4. Review: salute; lunge; attacks and parries in high lines. Take up: disengage in the high lines with the proper parries.

Lesson 5. Review: salute; direct attack in high lines with the fourth and sixth parries; disengage in the high lines with the fourth and sixth parries. Take up: attack in low outside and the second parry; attack in low inside and the seventh parry; advance and retreat with opponent, attack in line called by instructor, proper parry.

Lesson 6. Review: all four direct attacks and parries (4, 6, 2, 7); disengage in high lines. Take up: disengage in low lines with parries.

Lesson 7. Review: 4 parries; disengage in all lines. Take up: double disengage in high lines; advance and retreat with No. 1's attacking in stated line and No. 2's using the corresponding parry.

Lesson 8. Review: the four direct attacks and correct parries; single disengage; double disengage in the high lines. Take up: double disengage in the low lines. Short bout using all the techniques learned to this point. (See General Progression 20, p. 146.)

Lesson 9. Review: the four direct attacks and parries; disengage in all lines; double disengage in all lines. Take up: beat; beat combined with the disengage. Short bout as above.

Lesson 10. Review: parries; disengage; beat. Explain and demonstrate the other four parries (1, 3, 5, 8) and explain why they are rarely used. Short bout as above.

Lesson 11. Review: disengage with all four parries (4, 6, 2, 7); beat; advance and retreat with above attacks. Take up: cut-over. Short bout as above.

Lesson 12. Review: disengage with all four parries; beat; cut-over. Take up: riposte. Short bout, giving additional points for successful ripostes. (See General Progression 28, p. 146.)

Lesson 13. Review: beat; cut-over; parries; ripostes. Take up: cut-over combined with disengage. Short bout as above.

Lesson 14. Review: beat; cut-over; riposte. Take up: beat combined with cut-over; beat and cut-over combined with ripostes. Explain the fencing strip and fundamental rules which have not been brought out as techniques were taken up. Short bout using rules.

* Plans are based on a class that meets twice a week for eight weeks.

Lesson 15. Review: combined attacks of beat and disengage; cut-over and disengage. Take up: counter. Bout.

Lesson 16. Review: all attacks taken up. Bout.

INTEREST MOTIVATION

I. FENCING CLUB

An organization for more advanced fencers stimulates interest in the sport. A student manager and an instructor of fencing usually collaborate on making plans for the club. To be a member, a student should show interest and enthusiasm and demonstrate fair ability, but she need not be a top performer. Some type of tryout is necessary for the selection of the club's membership. It is well to hold tryouts at the beginning and again toward the close of the fencing season. The latter tryouts will take care of those who have become interested and more proficient during the season and will insure a nucleus for the club the following year.

Tryouts should be attended by the instructor who is adviser for the club and a few of the more experienced members, and should in general consist of floor work for judging form and speed of reaction, and bouting with the experienced fencers.

If such an organization is to be successful, there should be a regularly scheduled weekly meeting in which attendance is required. Any student missing three such meetings should be automatically dropped. Floor work, practice exercises, and bouting constitute an evening's program. In a woman's school an occasional tea following the practice period may add to the general interest and serve as a get-together for the planning of future meetings.

In some schools, granting the privilege to club members to assist in regular fencing classes has proved very satisfactory. Opportunity to sign for coaching classes can be given during the club hour. Students should understand that if they wish to coach they must be responsible for reporting to the class early to allow time for the instructor to explain and demonstrate the day's order.

II. EXHIBITIONS

By Visits of Noted Fencers. During the season the fencing club, if there is such an organization in the school, or the department of physical education, could stimulate a great deal of interest by sponsoring a demonstration by some outstanding fencers. This exhibition should be open to all interested persons.

By Fencing Club Members. If there is a fencing club it is well to have the members plan and put on an exhibition for outsiders.

III. CLASS TEAMS

Four-fencer class teams add to the students' enthusiasm for fencing. These teams can be picked at regular tryouts scheduled near the end of the fencing season, or by ladder tournaments run in each class during the season. If the latter method is used, the top eight at the time for team trials would be the logical potentialities, and could fence in a round-robin tournament. The best four would make the class team. The announcement of the interclass round-robin should be posted in conspicuous places so that any interested student may attend.

IV. ADDITIONAL TOURNAMENTS

1. *In Fencing Classes.* Ladder tournaments can be carried on in each class hour. The match between the first two on the ladder would make an excellent event for the final meeting of each class.

2. *College Open Championship.* The tournament for the selection of the champion of the school or college should preferably be a round robin. If there is no time for this, a double elimination (or elimination-consolation) tournament may be substituted.

3. *In Fencing Club.* A ladder tournament can be posted for the club early

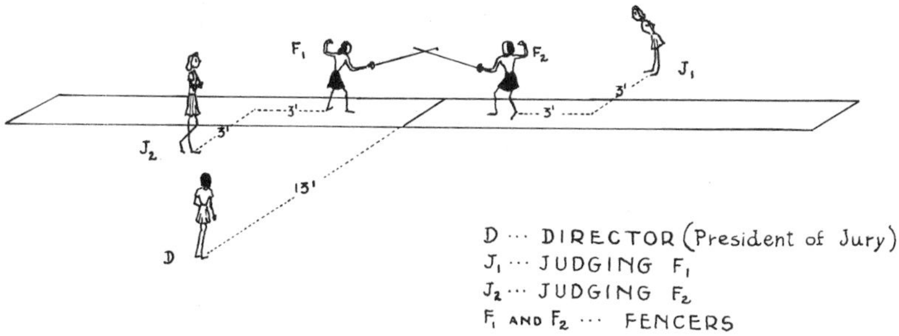

FIGURE 5.13 *Diagram showing placement of officials for fencing bout.*

in the season. The last part of each weekly meeting could be given over to challenge bouts for this tournament. Each bout should have two judges, for which the students themselves can arrange.

A round-robin tournament among the club members might possibly be arranged, depending on the size of the club.

OFFICIATING

As fencing is a sport in which one cannot participate without the assistance of officials, a short discussion of officials' duties is included.[4]

The officials necessary to carry on a bout are a President and two Judges. Four judges are preferred for any match (Figure 5.13).

PLACEMENT OF OFFICIALS ON THE FLOOR

Director or President. The President stands between the two fencers approximately 13 feet from the strip.

Judges. The Judges stand at least 3 feet behind and to the side of the opponent of the fencer that each is watching.

DUTIES OF THE OFFICIALS

Director or President. The President is in full charge of the conduct of the bout. Having ascertained that the fencers are ready, she starts the bout with the command "Play." She may halt the bout at any time with the command "Halt." The President's attention is concentrated on the phrases[5] of the bout, but she may also decide upon the materiality of touches. When any Judge signifies that she has seen a foul or a touch, the President stops the bout, confers with the Judges, and decides whether or not a touch should be awarded.

Judges. It is the duty of each Judge to engage the attention of the President when she thinks she has seen a touch or a foul. This may be done verbally or by some gesture of the hand. When questioned by the President as to the materiality of the touch the Judge may reply:

"yes"—if she has a definite opinion that a touch landed on any valid target.

"yes, but invalid," or "off target"—if she has a definite opinion that a touch landed on any parts other than the valid target.

"no"—if she has a definite opinion that there was no touch (off target or good).

"abstain"—if she has no definite opinion.

[4] For details, see *Fencing Rules,* Amateur Fencers League of America, p. 16.

[5] A *phrase* is a period in a bout during which there is no cessation of play. The term generally is used to describe a continuous sequence and alternation of play. It frequently includes an attack and one or more parries and ripostes. It comes to an end when the continuous action is interrupted even for a brief moment.

Value of Judgments.

President—1½ votes.

Judges—1 vote each.

When the fencing class has acquired enough technique to enjoy a short interval of bouting at the end of the lesson, divide the class into groups of five (two fencers, one President, two Judges). By rotating the students all can have practice in officiating as well as bouting.

NOTES ON FENCING RULES[6]

TARGET

The target for women is the body from the top of the collar to the lines from the hip bones to the groin in front and to a horizontal line across the top of the hip bones on the back and sides, and excludes the arms.[7] The sleeve seam is usually used as the boundary between the body (fair territory) and the arm (foul territory).

OFFICIAL FENCING STRIP

The width of the official strip is 2 m. (6′ 6¾″) and its length is 12.2 m. (40′) with an additional 5′ end zone at each end. The playing strip is marked with five lines across its width:

a. The center line.

b. Two "on guard" lines drawn at a distance of 2 m. (6′ 6¾″) from the center line.

c. Two "warning" lines drawn at a distance of 1 m. (3′ 3⅜″) from either end of the official strip.

BOUT

The number of touches for a women's bout is 4. The time limit is 8 minutes. If at the end of this time neither contestant has scored 4 touches, the difference between 4 and the score of the contestant who leads is added to the score of each fencer.

Example: Actual score at end of 8 minutes is 3 (fencer A) to 1 (fencer B). Fencer A is declared the winner by a score of 4 to 2. If at the end of the time limit neither contestant has scored the number of touches for a bout and the fencers are tied, the score is brought to 3 all, and the fencers compete for a single decisive touch without limit of time.

HIT OFF TARGET

A point-on hit off target invalidates an immediately following hit on the target either by the fencer making the off-target hit or by her opponent, but it does not invalidate a hit in the succeeding phrase.

VALID HITS

To be valid, a hit must be point-on and on the target. A point-on hit elsewhere (see preceding paragraph) or a hit with the side of the blade (a slap) counts nothing. A point-on hit is indicated by an upward bend of the blade or a bend away from the body of the fencer hit. A touch on the head, arms, hand, and so forth, may be judged valid whenever the fencer, either intentionally or as a result of an abnormal position (due to crouching, ducking, or some such movement) substitutes a normally invalid area for a part of the valid target.

RIGHT OF WAY

The right of way is with the attack until the attack has been parried. If the lunge is made with a straight arm, the fencer attacked must meet the blade of the attacker with her parry before she may riposte. If she does not, and the attack lands, the point shall be awarded the attacker even though the two hits are simultaneous. Only if the time thrust is clearly ahead (an almost impossible occurrence) shall the hit be awarded the fencer attacked.

[6] *Fencing Rules.* Amateur Fencers League of America, 1957.

[7] This is a change since the latest rules were published in 1957.

NOTE: An attack with the sword arm bent establishes no right of way. That is, it places the defender under no obligation to parry and the question becomes purely a matter of time. Many judges go even further and simply throw out a bent arm attack even if it lands ahead of the stop-thrust. This practice is probably preferable with beginners, but an advanced fencer should be able to defend herself by stop-thrusting without assistance from the rules. The presumption, however, should be against the bent-arm attack. That is, unless a bent-arm attack is clearly ahead, it should not be allowed.

Once an attack has been parried, the right of way shifts to the defender. When the defender's riposte has been parried, the right of way shifts back to the attacker, and so forth. That is, if the attack is parried and the defender ripostes immediately, her point shall be considered good as against that of the attacker, even though the hits are simultaneous, if the attacker does not parry her riposte.

NOTE: A parry does not establish a right of way unless it is immediately followed by a riposte. If the defender parries and does not immediately extend her arm, the attacker is under no obligation to withdraw or to await her counter attack, but may continue her own attack. The outcome of such a continuation depends solely on time. The fencer who lands first gets the point.

One cannot benefit from the right of way unless her attack or riposte lands point-on. If it lands point-on in fair territory, she shall be awarded the point. If it lands point-on off target, it shall invalidate an immediately following hit by her opponent. If it is a slap or a pass (a thrust that misses the opponent entirely) and her opponent lands, her opponent shall be awarded the point, since it is not necessary to parry an attack that is wide and will not land even if it is not parried.

OFF THE STRIP END

In foil fencing, when the retreating fencer crosses the warning line the President must stop the bout and warn the fencer. She is put back on guard with her rear foot at the warning line and if she then crosses the end of the strip with both feet, she is penalized one touch.

OFF THE STRIP SIDES

When a retreating fencer steps off the side of the strip with both feet she is put back on guard in the center of the width of the strip 3′ 3⅜″ closer to the end of the strip than the point where she stepped off. Only if this penalty puts the fencer beyond the end of the strip *after* she has been warned, is she penalized a touch.

VISUAL AIDS

A silent film, *Techniques of Foil Fencing,* was made in 1942. This film analyzes fencing techniques at various speeds of the camera with many close-ups. It takes ten minutes to run and can be purchased for $20.00 or rented for $1.00. It is distributed by the University of California, Extension Division, Department of Visual Instruction, Berkeley 4, California.

Another silent film, also called *Techniques of Foil Fencing,* was made in 1954 and is distributed by the University of California at Los Angeles, Extension Division, Educational Sales Department, Los Angeles 24, California. This is a ten-minute film that rents for $1.00 and sells for $35.00. It analyzes fencing techniques, using various speeds, and includes demonstrations of bouting.

Suggestions for Further Reading

Angell, Tommy F.: "Officiating for the Beginner." *Bowling-Fencing-Golf Guide,* Washington, D. C., American Association for Health, Physical Education, and Recreation, 1956–58, pp. 88–91.

Arnett, Katherine: "Suggestions for Group Instruction in Beginning Fencing." *Individual Sports Guide,* Washington, D. C., American Association for Health, Physical Education, and Recreation, 1952–54, pp. 93–96.

Barbasetti, Luigi: *The Art of the Foil.* New York, E. P. Dutton and Co., Inc., 1932.

Cass, Eleanor Baldwin: *The Book of Fencing.* Boston, Lothrop, Lee and Shepard Co., 1930.

Castello, Julio Martinez: *The Theory and Practice of Fencing.* New York, Charles Scribner's Sons, 1933.

Deladrier, Clovis: *Modern Fencing.* Annapolis, Maryland, United States Naval Institute, 1948.

Friedrich, Herta: "Exercises in Footwork for Beginners." *Bowling-Fencing-Golf Guide,* Washington, D. C., American Association for Health, Physical Education, and Recreation, 1956–58, pp. 78–80.

Hett, G. V.: *Fencing.* London, Sir Isaac Pitman and Sons, Ltd., 1939.

Lindsey, Ruth: "Teaching Devices." *Bowling-Fencing-Golf Guide,* Washington, D. C. American Association for Health, Physical Education, and Recreation, 1958–60, pp. 72–73.

Michigan University Intramural Sports Department, James, A. A.; Johnstone, John; Mitchell, E. D.; Riskey, Earl N.; Webster, R. W.: *Sports for Recreation and How to Play Them.* New York, A. S. Barnes & Co., 1938.

Nadi, Aldo: *On Fencing.* New York, G. P. Putnam's Sons, 1943.

Sandoz, William: "Philosophy of a Fencing Master." *Journal of Health and Physical Education,* 6:3:20, March, 1935.

Schutz, Helen Joan: "Construction of an Achievement Scale in Fencing for Women." Master's Thesis, University of Washington, 1940.

Spears, Betty: "Teaching Bouting Through Lead-up Games." *Bowling-Fencing-Golf Guide,* Washington, D. C., American Association for Health, Physical Education and Recreation, 1958–60, pp. 84–85.

Stewart, Helen: "Good Posture and Fencing." *Bowling-Fencing-Golf Guide,* Washington D. C., American Association for Health, Physical Education and Recreation, 1960–62, pp. 81–83.

Vince, Joseph: *Fundamentals of Foil Fencing.* New York, Joseph Vince, 1937.

———: *Fencing.* New York, A. S. Barnes & Co., 1940.

Fencing Rules. New York, Amateur Fencers League of America, 1957.

6

GOLF

6

GOLF

Marion R. Broer

The game of golf is one of the oldest of modern sports. Historians do not agree on its origin. There seems to be a question as to whether it originated in Scotland or on the ice in Holland.

One story has it that a Scotch shepherd accidentally hit a round stone with his staff, knocking it into a hole. This gave him the idea for a game that would be interesting for one person to play alone and would help to pass the time while he was herding his sheep. Whatever its origin may have been, the game had become so popular in Scotland by 1457 that the king, becoming alarmed, put restrictions on its practice to force the youth of Scotland to archery.

The Dutch did play a game called "Kolf" on the ice and used clubs similar to those used later in Scotland. However, the game, as we know it today, undoubtedly came from Scotland, where a much more advanced form was played than that which originated on the ice in Holland.

Some authorities state that Robert Lockhart brought the equipment from Scotland and introduced John Reid to the game. Reid and four others formed the first golf club in the United States in 1888. Others state that Alexander Findlay of Pennsylvania, having played in Scotland, brought the game to this country in 1887.

While golf can lay claim to most of the benefits derived from other sports, it has many merits that are unique. Few sports offer the long lasting carry-over value of golf, a game that can be enjoyed well past middle life. There is a great social value in the game, for it enables one to make contacts with individuals of congenial interests. The leisurely pace of the game allows time to admire the beautiful natural surroundings and promotes a comradeship not possible in faster sports. Unlike many games in which real enjoyment of the players is dependent upon being well-matched in skill, a wide variation of skill does not spoil the enjoyment of either player, nor does it ruin the chances for keen competition. Golf provides a healthy form of exercise for all levels of physical ability, and it is enjoyed equally by all ages and both sexes.

For many years golf was considered a sport in which only the more privileged financially could participate, and consequently only the wealthier private schools provided a place for it in their physical education programs. However, this situation has altered with the lower price of equipment, with the many public courses now open, and with the many private clubs offering low rates to students.

In short, golf is a game well within the means of most, played in beautiful surroundings and in the company of congenial friends, and can be enjoyed by *all* practically throughout life. The advent of the golf cart has extended the "golfing years" of many.

Recognizing the values of the game and in answer to the clamoring of students for instruction, most physical educators have now included golf in their programs. The teaching of golf is no longer primarily the teaching of individuals but has become largely a matter of group instruction.

COSTUME

Golf requires no special expensive costume. Flat heeled shoes are essential to avoid cutting up the fairways and greens as well as for the player's better balance. Cleats on these shoes give the golfer a firmer base on which to swing. Any sport costume that gives freedom of the legs and even more particularly of the arms and shoulder girdle is acceptable.

EQUIPMENT

I. CLUBS

Golf is one sport in which the manufacturer of the equipment has adjusted the vertical angle of the striking surface. For most shots, all the player must do is to decide at what angle she wishes to project the ball and then choose the proper club and use it in its natural position. Besides supplying the golfer with adjusted angles of striking surfaces, the manufacturer has also varied the length of the clubs. Thus it is possible to reduce the length of the swing as well as to adjust the angle of the striking surface simply by choosing the proper club.

A. Names and Uses.

1. Woods.

#1—driver—approximately 230 yds.: tee-off.

*#2—brassie—approximately 220 yds.: tee-off; long fairway shot, good lie.

#3—spoon—approximately 210 yds.: tee-off on short holes; fairway, good lie.

#4—approximately 200 yds.: tee-off on short holes; fairway, good lie.

2. Irons.

a. Distance

#1—approximately 180 yds.: not practical for most women.

*#2—approximately 170 yds.: fairway long shots, poor lie; fairway long iron shots; low rough.

#3—approximately 160 yds.:

b. Pitch and run; approach of medium distance

#4—approximately 150 yds.: often used by women for tee shots on very short holes; long approach club; short roll-up approaches; more distance and less loft than #5.

*#5—approximately 140 yds. or less: most popular approach club; rough and bad lies where distance

is greater than can be obtained from lofted clubs; occasionally tee shots on very short holes.

#6—approximately 130 yds.: bad rough—greater distance than niblick.

c. Hazards; bad rough; short approaches; high pitch shots

*#7—approximately 120 yds.

#8—approximately 110 yds.

#9—approximately 100 yds.

Wedge—approximately 50 yds. in to the green.

d. On green

*#10—putter

NOTE: Asterisk * designates clubs essential for minimum set.

B. Method of Supplying.

Students sometimes supply their own clubs, although many colleges buy enough equipment to supply the classes. Many professionals will ransack their own stock of used clubs or campaign among members of the club to get used clubs and turn them over to schools.

II. BALLS

A. Types of Balls.

1. Practice Balls. Practice balls are designed to have a shorter flight than regulation balls.

a. Paper wadded into a ball is in no way dangerous and gives something to hit.

b. Plastic balls may be secured at any sporting goods store. These balls are inexpensive, are more satisfying to hit than are the paper balls, and have a truer flight.

2. Regulation Balls.

If a school furnishes the balls and wishes to buy large quantities at a low cost it is possible to purchase:

a. Used balls from local professionals.

b. Repaints from repainted-ball factories.

B. Method of Supplying.

1. The school may supply buckets or baskets of balls. This method saves class time since the balls do not have to be sorted and returned to owners. However, it is an expense to the school.

2. The school may require each student taking golf to turn in two new balls. The total collection is then used by every class, the balls being divided among the members of each class for use during the period. This method has the same time saving advantage and is not expensive to anyone.

3. The school may ask each student to furnish as many balls marked with her own initials as possible. In this case the student uses her own balls. It is well to suggest that nail polish be used to mark the balls. This is one of the most successful methods of marking and almost every girl has some type of polish.

4. The school may require each student to furnish six well-marked balls. The student uses her own balls.

III. ADDITIONAL EQUIPMENT

A. Indoor Practice. If possible have sufficient space to allow all members of the class to swing at once. If the room has to be used for other sports, the first consideration must be to have equipment that is movable.

1. General Equipment.

a. Mats.

(*1*) Tumbling mats are not good because hitting the mat with the club wears out these expensive mats very quickly.

(*2*) Coco mats are excellent.

(*3*) Small door mats from the dime store will do.

(*4*) If possible to obtain, rubber mats made of hard rubber such as is used in car tires may be used. These do not wear out. They give a hard surface for hitting through on an iron shot, but as most students do not practice more than one-half hour at a time, their wrists can stand it.

b. Platform.

(*1*) A second coco mat may be used.

(*2*) A wooden platform may be built to the same height as the mat from which the ball is hit. Cover the platform with some material (rubber if possible) so the students won't slip. If the platform is not covered with rubber, have the students wear rubber-soled shoes.

2. Special Practice Equipment.

a. DISTANCE SHOTS: FULL SWING.

(*1*) Soft practice balls.

(*2*) Regulation balls.

(*a*) A canvas sheet or curtain can be suspended from the ceiling or held up by uprights. It should extend the entire width of the room to prevent the balls hitting any breakable fixtures. The canvas should be heavy and should be hung away from the wall. It should be long enough to allow an extra fold forward on the floor to keep the balls from bouncing when they fall to the floor. A curtain made of loose, overlapping canvas strips is more satisfactory than one stretched in one piece, as it absorbs the force and thus reduces the rebound. Cut the canvas into pieces about 3 yards wide. Join the strips together just at the top so that they overlap and string them on ropes so that they may be pulled into place or out of the way at the side of the room. Targets painted on the canvas stimulate the students' interest.[1] The Peoria Central High School made use of the canvas that was used around the football field during games.

(*b*) Driving cages have the advantage of being safer. If they are in a place where they can be left permanently they can be used outside of class hours.

1. Safety measures:

a. The side curtains should be deep enough to take all balls that are hit.

b. The backstop should be resilient and hang far enough from the wall to prevent rebounding.

c. All curtains must hang with sufficient looseness to absorb the force of the ball and prevent rebounding.

2. Suggestions:

a. Place the cages side by side to save in-between canvas.

b. If at all possible have at least one cage.

c. Try to have temporary cages if permanent ones are impossible.

d. High parallel bars or jumping standards may be used as braces over which felt or canvas is loosely draped to mark off individual cages against a canvas drop.

e. The manual training departments of many high schools will construct frames. These can be padded and covered with netting, and pushed into position in front of a canvas drop.

b. APPROACH SHOTS.

(*1*) A canvas drop with ample sized pockets into which students can pitch balls can be hung against the wall. The bottom should be extended forward so that the curtain slopes at approximately a 45 degree angle. A sheet of medium weight canvas, 8 to 10 feet square, with four or five holes cut in it and pockets of any light material of a different color sewed around these holes, is satisfactory.[2]

(*2*) Students can chip to tumbling mats placed against the wall or hung on the wall. Targets can be drawn on the mats with chalk. The short chip shot is the only shot that is safe in this situation.

(*3*) Students can hold hula hoops for their partners to chip through.[3] Only plastic balls and short chip shots should be used for this practice.

(*4*) Waste baskets can also be used for chip shot practice.

c. PUTTING.

(*1*) Regulation balls.

(*2*) Putting surfaces.

(*a*) There are many commercial devices that may be secured.

[1] Eastburn, Warrine: "Adaptation of Playing Fields and Gymnasium Equipment to the Teaching of Group Golf." *Athletic Handbook,* Spaulding's Athletic Library.

[2] Hall, Ray: "Suggestions for Equipment in School Golf Instruction." *Golf in Physical Education.*

[3] Griffin, Ellen: Material presented at the L. P. G. A. National Golf School, Ann Arbor, Michigan, Aug., 1961.

(*b*) An inch-thick padding of stiff, firmly made, brown matted cloth can be used as a base and covered with a carpet ½ inch thick.

(*c*) An inclined board covered with a thick carpet will give good practice.

(*d*) It is always possible to secure a carpet or strip of rug. This should be 12 feet or longer to allow for the practice of various length putts. A beat board slipped under the end of the carpet will give some incline.

(*3*) Cups.

(*a*) There are commercially made cups.

1. Rubber cups.

2. "Ringan Return" cups. When the ball enters this cup a bell rings and a spring returns the ball to the putter.

(*b*) A regular cup may be built in the inclined board. The hole should be toward the high end.

(*c*) Tin discs may be purchased or constructed. To construct a tin disc, cut a hole 4 inches in diameter in the tin and round the sides of the tin so that they slant to the floor, sloping off gradually. The edge of the cup should not be more than 1 inch from the floor.

(*d*) A circle may be chalked on the rug or carpet. Have the students hole out by putting into or just beyond the chalked circle.

B. Outdoor Practice. The area varies with the school. Usually the field is at least 100 yards long (the length of a regulation hockey or soccer field).

1. Equipment for Practice.

a. Distance Shots.

(*1*) If the field is too short for a full wood shot, use paper or yarn balls.

(*2*) If there is ample length, use a regulation ball. Stake off tees far enough apart so that there is no danger of students' hitting each other. Distance markers staked into the ground at various distances stimulate interest and help in grading.

b. Approach Shots.

(*1*) Approach to the green (see Putting).

(*2*) Use markers at the edge of the field to judge approaches of various distances.

(*3*) Pitch into a sand pit (see Sand Trap Shots).

(*4*) Pitch over hockey goals or archery targets.

c. Sand Trap Shots.

(*1*) Use a jumping pit filled with sand, dirt, or sawdust.

(*2*) Dig up a small plot of ground and play out of the overturned dirt.

d. Putting.

(*1*) A regular practice green is expensive and difficult to keep up.

(*2*) Commercial imitation turf material is available but involves some expense.

(*3*) Oiled sand greens can be constructed at little expense. Waste drain oil from automobiles can be secured at little or no cost. If new oil is purchased, use a light oil, as it mixes better.[4] A carpet drag will keep the green usable.

(*4*) Sawdust can be used but requires some treatment to make it pack firm as it is normally light and soft.

(*5*) A bit of smooth, closely cut lawn, not necessarily level, outlined with lime lines, can be used if nothing else is available.

2. Equipment for Practice of All Shots. Two or three practice holes may be laid out if 200 yards or more of play space are available. Lay out the holes so that they do not cross each other. Each should be far enough from the other so that all holes can be used at once. Each hole should be long enough to warrant at least two or three good shots so that a variety of clubs can be used. It is well to mark the boundary lines of the fairways so as to keep each player on the hole she is playing. Lime lines may be used to mark the greens. A cup should either be marked or sunk on the green.[5] If the green is such as to allow holing out, always use a sunken cup.

[4] Hall: *op. cit.*

[5] Eastburn: *op. cit.*

ACTION OF THE CLUB ON THE BALL

Since golf is a striking activity, the problem is to produce the desired amount of force and apply it to the ball, by means of the club head, in such a way that the desired flight results. If the student is to control the flight of the ball, she must understand the way the ball responds when struck by a club head moving into it in various ways.

A. If the ball is struck by a club head moving in the line of desired flight of the ball with its face square to this line, all forces combine to send the ball in that direction.[6]

1. If the line from the point of contact to the center of the ball is along the line of movement of the club head, no spin will result.

2. If the line of movement of the club head is through the ball below the ball's center, back spin will result. It has been pointed out that even the driver, which has the most vertical face of all the clubs (with the exception of the putter), has enough loft to contact the ball slightly below center and impart some back spin. Back spin is desirable to stabilize flight in the vertical plane and to keep the ball in the air longer. As the club loft increases, the point of contact on the ball is lower (Figure 6.1). Harvey, in an article in *Golfing* magazine, clearly explained the way spin is imparted to the ball.[7] He stated that only up to a point does the golf ball follow the general rule that the lower the ball is contacted the greater the back spin. The ball leaves the club face more quickly and flattens less as the angle of divergence between the path the club head is traveling and the line of flight of the ball increases. Therefore, with the more lofted clubs there is less flattening of the ball, less contact time and thus less back spin. He further stated that the number five iron imparts the most back spin because the angle of inclination of its face is the greatest at which there is enough flattening to permit the grooves of the club face to hold the ball from slipping. On the clubs with greater loft the grooves on the face become narrower and shallower as far as their effect on the ball is concerned and they do not hold the ball, making the contact time less, and back spin less.

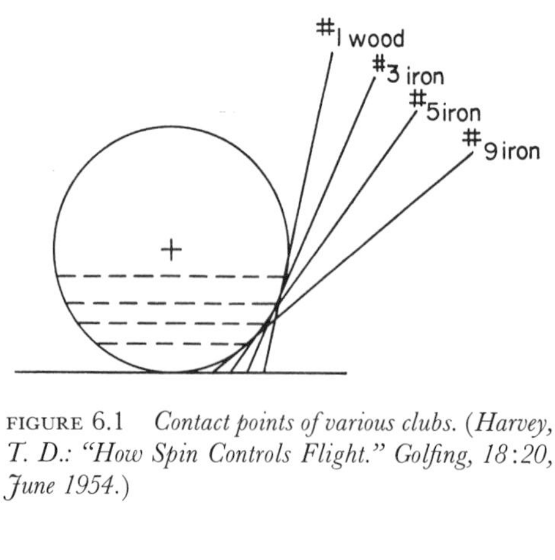

FIGURE 6.1 *Contact points of various clubs. (Harvey, T. D.: "How Spin Controls Flight." Golfing, 18:20, June 1954.)*

B. If the club is moving from the outside–in (right to left):

1. With the club face square (perpendicular) to this same direction, the ball will fly to the left but no side spin will result (Pull).

2. With the club face square to the line of desired flight, right spin will result and the ball will fly off in the desired direction, but its path of flight will curve to the right (Slice).

C. If the club is moving from inside–out (left to right):

1. With the club face square to this same direction, the ball will fly to the right with no side spin (Push).

2. With the club face square to the desired line of flight, left spin will result and the ball will fly off in the desired direction but its path will curve to the left (Hook).

[6] The reader is referred to Broer, M. R.: *Efficiency of Human Movement* for a discussion of Rebound and Spin (Chapter 8), Striking (Chapter 19), and Golf (Chapter 20).

[7] Harvey, T. D.: "How Spin Controls Flight." *Golfing, 18:* 20–23, June, 1954.

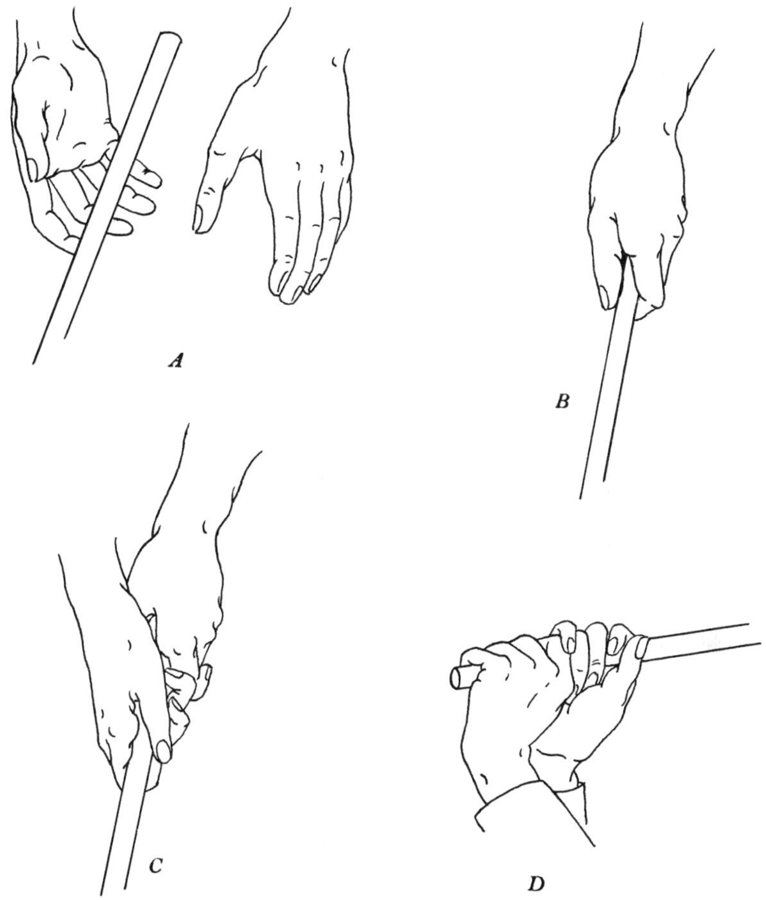

FIGURE 6.2 *The grip. A, right hand supporting the club; left ready to be placed on the club, palm down. B, left hand in place. C, the complete grip, front view. D, the complete grip showing the little finger of the right hand overlapping the first finger of the left hand.*

TECHNIQUE[8]

I. GRIP

A. Analysis.

1. Overlap. This grip is advised by most authorities because the hands act as as unit rather than applying leverage action, and the touch of the forefinger and thumb of both hands is more sensitive. This is important in sensing a feel of the club head (Figure 6.2).

a. Left Hand.

(*1*) The club rests against the middle joint of the forefinger and lies diagonally across the palm of the left hand.

(*2*) Three knuckles of this hand should be visible.

(*3*) The thumb extends diagonally across the shaft and nestles snugly in the palm of the right hand.

b. Right Hand.

(*1*) The club rests against the middle joint of the forefinger.

(*2*) The hand is placed on the

[8] Directions are given for right-handed golfers, and should be reversed for left-handed persons.

club so that, if opened, the palm would face squarely toward the objective.

(*3*) The thumb extends diagonally across the shaft.

(*4*) The pad of the thumb rests on the left thumb.

(*5*) The little finger is placed on top of or between the first and second fingers of the left hand.

c. In General.

(*1*) The grip should be secure but not squeezed.

(*2*) The club is held mainly by the fingers.

2. Interlock. This grip is the same as the above except that the little finger of the right hand *interlocks* with the forefinger of the left. This grip is not highly recommended, for it eliminates the sensitive touch of the forefinger and thumb of the left hand and tends to overpower the left hand with the right.

B. Method of Presentation.

1. Explanation.
2. Demonstration.
} of both overlap and interlock to see which is best adapted to each pupil.

3. Practice.

a. Organization of Class. Have the class stand in a semicircle around the instructor so that the instructor's eye can quickly reach all, in order to check every pupil at each step.

b. Common Progression.

(*1*) Have the pupil hold the end of the shaft with the right hand and place the club on the ground so that it is soled.[9] Then ask her to place her left hand on the end of the shaft so that three knuckles are visible. The instructor should check to see that the knuckles are visible.

(*2*) Have the pupil place the right hand on the club. The instructor checks.

(*3*) Have the pupil take her hands completely off the club and then retake the grip several times. Each time the instructor checks.

c. Suggested Simple, Effective Way to Teach Beginners.[10]

(*1*) Place a club on the ground and ask the student to pick it up using only her left hand. She will always put the hand on the club in the proper position.

(*2*) Draw the student's attention to the position of the back of the left hand.

(*3*) Explain the reasons for turning the left hand over:

(*a*) The left hand must deliver a kind of backhand blow to the ball.

(*b*) When the left thumb is on the right side of the shaft, it will not interfere with the cocking of the wrists at the top of the backswing.

(*4*) Help the student swing her club using the left hand only, until a full swing is attained. (In class, divide into two's and have partners assist each other.)

(*5*) The right-hand position is then explained and both hands are placed on the shaft.

d. Hand Dominance. In a Golf Clinic at the National Convention of the American Association for Health, Physical Education and Recreation in Cincinnati (April, 1962), Les Bolstad, golf coach at the University of Minnesota, suggested that hand dominance and eye dominance must be considered. He suggested that the dominant hand should be placed on the club first. In other words, the right handed and right eyed person should place her right hand on the club first, and as the stance is taken, the club is swung up toward the hole and the left hand is placed on the club. The club is then placed behind the ball.

C. Faults in Grip.

1. An all-palm grip loses control of the club in the upper part of the swing.

2. An all-finger grip defeats the mobility of the wrists.

3. Squeezing tightens the muscles in the forearm. Tell the student to grip with the right hand no tighter than when holding a pen to write.

[9] See Golf Terms, p. 183.

[10] Thompson, Ben: "A High School Golf Program." *Scholastic Coach,* December, 1939, p. 16. Also, Thompson, Ben: *How to Play Golf,* p. 2.

4. Right or left hand too far under or around shaft:

a. If the left thumb is down the top of the shaft, it interferes with the cocking of the wrists.

b. If the left hand is not far enough around, the face of club is not kept in position to hit the ball squarely and straight ahead.

c. If the right knuckle is under the shaft instead of at the side, there is a loss of power and control.

d. If the hands are turned too far over to the right, the club face will be closed when the hands swing naturally and the ball will be "smothered." If the hands are too far over to the left, the club will be open and the tendency is to "push the shot."[11]

D. Progression. The only preliminary to the teaching of the grip would be a short explanation of the object of the game, the lay-out of the course, safety measures, minimum equipment necessary for an individual, the names of the parts of the club, and a feeling for the swinging action. The grip is the basis of the swing and must be mastered before proceeding.

II. STANCE

A. Analysis. "Stance" is the position the player takes to make a stroke.

1. General Position.

a. The stance should be comfortable with the knees easy and the weight about evenly divided between the two feet.

b. The weight should be back toward the heels rather than on the toes to counterbalance the tendency of the force of the swing in front of the body to pull the body off balance forward.

c. If the toes are turned out slightly, balance is improved and the pivot in both directions is facilitated.

d. The width of the stance depends upon the amount of force desired. The longer the desired shot, the wider (up to the width of the hips) the stance. The wider stance allows for freer transference of weight without imperiling balance. However, when the feet are placed farther apart than the width of the hips a horizontal component of force is introduced and as this becomes greater the counter pressure of the ground against the feet is lessened. Too wide a stance also limits body rotation. In general, the feet are placed about the width of the hips apart for distance shots, and the width of the stance becomes narrower for shorter shots.

e. The club should be placed behind the ball with the face pointing squarely toward the point of aim (club face perpendicular to the line of flight of the ball) and then the stance taken.

f. When the club is soled, the length of the club and arm will give the proper distance to stand from the ball.

2. Types of Stance.

a. "Square" or "Parallel."

(*1*) explanation. The feet are placed evenly so that a line through the toes is parallel to the line of flight of the ball (Figure 6.3).

(*2*) use. This is the most commonly used stance. It is always used for distance shots unless a curve in the line of flight of the ball is desired. It is the best stance to teach beginners for all shots because with this stance the path of the club head more naturally parallels the line of the intended flight of the ball.

b. "Open."

(*1*) explanation. The left foot is withdrawn away from the line of flight of the ball. This turns the body slightly toward the direction of play (Figure 6.3).

(*2*) use. This is often used in iron play, particularly the shorter iron shots for which less force and greater accuracy are desired. It restricts body rotation on the backswing but allows the club to follow through farther along the line of the intended flight of the ball. It tends to lead to hitting across the back of the ball from the outside in, thus resulting in a slice.

[11] Fraley, Oscar: *Golf in Action,* p. 15.

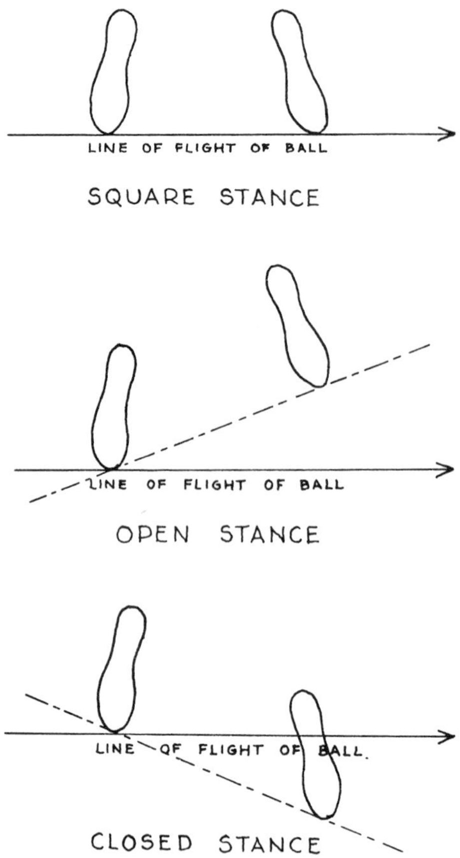

FIGURE 6.3 *Types of stance.*

c. "CLOSED."

(*1*) EXPLANATION. The right foot is withdrawn away from the line of flight of the ball. This closes the body from the direction of play (Figure 6.3).

(*2*) USE. This stance allows for free rotation on the backswing but limits rotation on the follow-through. It tends to lead to hitting across the back of the ball from the inside out, thus resulting in a hook.

3. Position of Ball.

a. GENERAL PRINCIPLES. The position of the ball varies with the distance desired for the shot. The position of the ball determines the point in the arc of the swing at which the ball is contacted, which in turn determines the direction the club is traveling at contact. Therefore, the position of the ball together with the length of the club and angle of club face determine the force applied to the ball, the angle of flight and the resultant spin. Spin is an extremely important consideration in both distance of flight and roll. When the ball is hit at the center of the arc of the swing with the club in its natural position, it is hit a horizontal blow that results in some back spin, because the ball is contacted below center. The amount of spin depends on how much below center the ball is contacted, the length of time the grooves of the club keep the ball in contact, and the amount the ball is flattened. When the ball is played back of the center of the stance, it is hit before the center of the arc is reached and is, therefore, hit a downward blow since the club is still moving downward, and greater back spin results.

Spin also affects distance, in that it is an important factor in the roll of the ball after it lands. The more back spin the less roll, since the force of the spin against the ground is opposite to the direction of movement of the ball. Therefore, for distance shots, only enough back spin to stabilize the flight and keep the ball in the air a little longer is desirable. The back spin should be minimized, as it is when clubs with a more vertical face are used and the ball is hit a horizontal blow, so that when the ball lands the forward force can easily overcome the back spin force, reversing the spin and allowing the ball to roll forward. A great deal of back spin is desirable on approach shots to the green in which little or no roll is desired. Therefore, the ball is played farther back, so that it can be hit a downward blow.

b. PLACEMENT OF BALL FOR VARIOUS CLUBS. Since the weight has shifted to the left foot by contact, the center of the arc of the swing is approximately opposite the left heel. Therefore, the ball is placed:

(*1*) Woods:

#1—approximately off the left heel.
#2—slightly back of above.
#3—slightly back of position for #2.
#4—slightly back of position for #3.

(*2*) Irons:

#2 and #3—just ahead of the middle of the stance.

#4, 5 and 6—approximately at the center of the stance.

#7, 8 and 9—behind the center of the stance; may be placed as far back as opposite the right heel for a maximum downward blow.

B. Faults in Stance.

1. Leaning too far forward causes the weight to be primarily on the toes. This may be caused by standing too far from the ball. To demonstrate the importance of weight placement to body balance during the swing, have the student stand upright with her feet together and weight back on the heels. Ask her to pivot her body fully. She will find that she is well-balanced throughout the pivot. Then tell her to place her weight on her toes and repeat. Body balance now will be very difficult if not impossible to maintain.[12] When the swing is added balance will become even more precarious if the weight is on the toes. The weight of the club and the force of the swing are in front of the body; therefore, the body weight must be kept back to counterbalance these forces.

2. Using an open stance restricts the pivot and hinders a full backswing. To make this obvious to the student, ask her to stand with her feet in an open stance and take as long a backswing as possible. Then ask her to adjust her feet to a square stance and note how this frees the body, allowing more rotation to the right and increasing the backswing. When the backswing is restricted, loss of force results, as there is less time to work up momentum. Since an open stance frees the follow through, it may be desirable for a short shot in which accuracy is of great importance. Using a closed stance also restricts the pivot, but this time on the follow through. It is often difficult for a student to tell whether or not her feet are parallel. To demonstrate this, place a club on the ground so that it touches the toes of both feet. It will then be easy for the student to see that this line is not parallel to the desired flight of the ball.

3. Placing the feet too far apart introduces a horizontal component in the force of the feet against the ground and may cause slipping of the feet. This also restricts the pivot.

4. Keeping the legs stiff also restricts the pivot.

C. Progression. The teaching of the stance should follow the teaching of a feeling for the swinging action. The relation of the ball to the feet for various strokes should be taken up after each swing is mastered without a ball.

III. THE FULL SWING

The force applied to the ball is dependent upon the speed of movement of the club head at impact and the accuracy of the contact. To assure a clean hit, the body and club must, at impact, be in the same position relative to the ball as when the ball was addressed (assuming that the ball is addressed with the club soled behind the ball with the club face perpendicular to the desired line of flight of the ball). The action is that of centrifugal force, applied from a solidly grounded triangular foundation, the three points of which are the two feet and the head.[13]

A. Analysis.

1. Backswing.

a. The weight shifts onto the right foot and the hips rotate toward the right around the spine as an axis. This puts the body into position to use the strong trunk muscles as well as the arm and shoulder girdle muscles in the swing.

b. As the hips turn, the left knee relaxes and bends in. The right leg straightens since it becomes the support for the body weight. A relaxed left side and shoulder make proper turning possible.

c. The club head is pushed straight back away from the ball and at the beginning of the backswing the club

[12] Thompson: "A High School Golf Program."

[13] *Golf Lessons.* The National Golf Foundation, Lesson 9.

head is kept low. The farther the club head travels in line with the path of desired flight of the ball, the flatter the arc and the greater the chance for accuracy in contact and the more horizontal the blow (Figure 6.4).

d. At the top of the backswing the club is approximately:

wood—parallel to the ground.

iron—varies for different length clubs: #5 about 45° angle; #7 and # 8 about 90° angle.

FIGURE 6.4 *A, wooden club, the full swing, side view. B, wooden club, the full swing, front view. C, #5 iron, the full swing. D, short iron, the full swing.*

The exact length of the backswing cannot be stated. The longer the backswing the more time there is to work up momentum, and, therefore, the more force there is available. Since the backswing is lengthened by trunk rotation, a longer backswing brings the strong muscles of the trunk into the movement. However, any lengthening of the backswing *beyond* the point at which the individual can control the club head and bring it into line at the point of impact, will result in loss of force applied to the ball. When the backswing is so long that the club head drops below the horizontal, it requires considerable strength to raise it *against* the force of gravity and bring it through fast enough so that it does not lag behind the hands at impact. Therefore, in teaching, it is wise to suggest that the backswing should not allow the club head to drop below the horizontal. A weak student may need to curtail the backswing more than this in order to bring the club head into line at impact.

2. Downswing.

Actually there is no stopping of movement in the swing, since the body action that initiates the downswing begins as the club is coming to a stop on the backswing.

a. The downswing begins with a rhythmic rotation of the body to the left (an unwinding around a vertical axis through the body).

b. The left leg straightens as it takes the weight, producing a solid wall (left side) against which to hit.

c. The right side and shoulder are relaxed to allow them to follow the swing.

d. The wrists uncock toward the end of the swing to add to the speed of the club head at the moment of impact. Since the club is long, the distal end must move through a considerable distance while the hands move through a short distance, and therefore, a great deal of speed is added to the club head. If the wrists are uncocked too soon the extra spurt of speed will be spent before the ball is contacted; if too late, the hands will be ahead of the club head at the moment of impact and the club will strike the ball with an open face (at an angle with the heel ahead of the toe). Most authorities agree that there is no uncocking of the wrists until the hands have come down to about waist height. The action of the wrists will take place more or less automatically if the student is not tense. Concentration on "cocking and uncocking" of the wrists is likely to lead to overswinging on the backswing and to bringing the club head through ahead of the hands on the forward swing. Les Bolstad (golf coach at the University of Minnesota) suggests that the hands guide and move forward *with* the club rather than being used as in a "hitting action."

e. The swing should sweep through smoothly without any sudden acceleration.

3. Follow-Through.

a. The club head follows out behind the ball in the line of flight as far as the arms will permit before it is allowed to sweep around and complete the arc of the swing.

b. The body completes its pivot with the right side relaxed.

c. The eyes are kept down on the spot behind the ball until *well after* the ball has been hit.

B. Faults in the Full Swing.

1. Making a "false pivot" or bending the knees straight forward over the feet instead of relaxing them toward the opposite knee causes the hips to stay square and makes any turning of the body impossible (Figure 6.5). It also causes the weight to be on the left foot during the backswing and right foot during the forward swing, thus pulling the body weight out of the stroke instead of putting it into the shot. A suggested exercise for practicing the pivot follows (Figure 6.6): (*a*) Hold a club across the back of the shoulders. (*b*) Shift the weight to the right heel. (*c*) With the eyes on the ball, or a spot on the ground out from the point halfway between the left heel and the center of the stance, twist the body to the right until the end of the club points to the ball. (*d*) Shift the weight to the left

FIGURE 6.5 *Full wood swing showing a false pivot.*

FIGURE 6.6 *Exercise for practicing the pivot.*

heel and twist the body to the left until the other end of the club points to the ball.

2. Allowing the head to move with the body is a very common fault. To teach students to move the body independent of the head, the same exercise as noted for pivot practice can be used. Divide the class so that each student has a partner. While one student practices the pivot, her partner immobilizes her head by placing a hand securely on each side of it. As the student gets a feeling for keeping the head still as the body moves, her partner gradually lessens the pressure until she is able to withdraw her hands altogether, and the student practicing is able unaided to accomplish a full pivot with practically no movement of the head.

Have the students face their shadows and practice the above exercise keeping eyes on the shadows of their heads. They will find it easy to see any movement of the head. When the students are able to keep the heads motionless during this practice, have them try swinging the club while watching their shadows.

3. Starting the stroke by lifting the club head abruptly with the hands instead of bringing it back low along the ground does away with the pivot, and the result is a lifting of the body and head. Usually the right hand is at fault. Keep the grip of this hand as light as when gripping a pen in writing.

4. Rotating or pronating the left hand as the club is started back puts the face out of position for a square hit.

5. Hitting too soon or trying to hit too hard is caused by throwing the club with the hands from the top of the swing. This brings the club down too fast for the club head to keep pace. The head of the club does not strike the ball squarely. Have the student swing to music.

6. Omitting the weight shift or merely whirling the body around suddenly leaving most of the weight on the right foot changes the arc of the swing. Practice the pivot exercise emphasizing the shift of weight to the left heel *at the beginning* of the downswing.

7. Attempting too fast a backswing frequently pulls the student off balance, because this backswing is difficult to stop. The speed of the backswing differs with the individual. Middlecoff suggests that it should be roughly a third of the downswing speed.[14] It should be a smooth, unhurried action.

8. Attempting sudden acceleration at the instant of the impact detracts from

[14] Middlecoff, Cary: *Master Guide to Golf,* p. 19.

both accuracy and power. Have the student practice continual rhythmic swinging.

9. A tensing of the body from attempting to put too much force into impact causes inability of the right side to follow around. Usually this is accompanied by a bending of the arms, and therefore the ball is topped. To overcome general tenseness, have the students swing continuously in rhythm. Music may be a great aid.

10. Lifting the head before impact causes the ball to be hit above the center, or "topped." This is usually due to the golfer's desire to see where the ball is going. Have the student count 3 slowly, after impact, before looking up to see the results of her shot.

11. Playing the ball too far forward may cause a topped shot. Move the ball back toward the center of the stance.

12. Loosening the grip at the top of the backswing may mean an altered grip at the time of impact and any type of shot can result. Tell a student with this tendency to squeeze the club at the top of the backswing.

13. Shanking or hitting the ball on the neck of the club, where it joins the shaft, causes the ball to fly off at unpredictable angles. The main cause of this is the use of a club that is too short, which results in pressing to attempt to get maximum distance from the club. The correction lies in choosing a longer club when in doubt and swinging freely.[15]

14. The tendency to push or pull against the club instead of swinging causes many different shots. To show the student the difference between leverage and a swinging action, the following is suggested:[16]

a. Have the student swing something with a flexible shaft, like a length of cord or a large handkerchief with a small weight attached to the end. Have her whirl it around her hand in a circle noting how little strength and movement of the hand it takes to produce this smooth whirling motion. Then have the student push or pull on the end of the cord and note how this interrupts the smooth swing of the weight. This will show the student the irregular path produced by leverage as opposed to the smooth path of a swinging motion.

b. Have the student hold the handkerchief and the club together and swing so that their movements are synchronized.

c. Omit the handkerchief.

C. Teaching. The full swing should be taught as soon as the students have learned the grip. Give the students as *few* essential points to think about as possible. The most important single factor in a good golf stroke is relaxation. A swinging action of the club head is possible only in the absence of all tenseness.

The student of golf has been told to "keep the eye on the ball," "keep the chin pointed at the ball," "keep the left heel down," "keep the left arm straight," "keep the right arm close to the side," and "let the left knee bend toward the right," and so forth. She has been given so many directives that an attempt to give attention to all of them frequently leads to tension, which interferes with the smooth sequence of the movement so necessary to force and accuracy. None of these directives is, *of itself,* important. They are only devices that various individuals have found helpful in assuring that the body and club position will be the same at impact as at address, so that the club head will hit the ball squarely in the direction of desired flight. Perhaps it is because so many individuals have written about golf and all have their own devices for correcting their individual errors that this sport has become so enmeshed in detail—detail that often hinders rather than aids learning because it produces tension. Bobby Jones states that a great measure of the golfer's "discomfiture is derived from his conscious efforts to follow prescribed routine, to look and move like someone else, or as he has been told."[17]

[15] Fraley: *op. cit.,* p. 72.

[16] Hicks, Betty: *Fundamentals of Golf,* pp. 5, 6. Morrison, Alex J.: *Better Golf Without Practice,* p. 32.

[17] Jones, Robert Tyre (Bobby): *Golf is My Game,* p. 25.

The golf stroke involves movements of many parts of the body, but these will be taken care of if the player controls a few essentials. Any attempt on the part of an individual learning golf to analyze every sequence of the swing and every movement of each segment of the body can result only in confusion, and confusion will cause tenseness. All the student need think about is to take the club head back easily and swing out *through* the ball on a line with the green.

1. Progression.

a. Explain the swinging action. First demonstrate this with something heavy on the end of a piece of string or a large handkerchief. Betty Hicks suggests holding the club between the thumb and forefinger and letting it swing, emphasizing feeling the swing of the head at the end of the shaft. She then has her students turn the club over and hold it by the head to demonstrate the difference in the feeling of the weight, and the swing, with and without the club head. Next demonstrate an easy swing of the club. (The grip must be taken up at this point.)

b. Give the students clubs and let them swing back and forth. Many will unconsciously transfer weight, pivot, and so forth correctly. Many teachers believe in starting beginners with a #5 iron, others with a #2 iron, and some with a #2 wood. The shorter shaft of the #5 makes it easier to control and therefore it may be preferable. The important thing is to start with a full swing. Music is a great aid in developing an easy rhythmical swing. Either use a victrola, if one is available, or have the class sing a well known waltz.

c. When the students have a feeling for the swinging action, the stance can be introduced.

d. Give the group a few general suggestions:

(*1*) Avoid hurrying or trying to swing hard. (Emphasize relaxation.)

(*2*) Explain the head position. Telling the students either to keep their eyes on the balls or to point their chins at a spot behind the balls may help students keep a steady position. Emphasize the importance of maintaining this position at all times throughout the swing. An accurate contact with the ball will result only if the body parts are in the same relative position at impact as when the stance was taken. Since the head is the most important *single* factor in assuring a return to this stance, control of its position is essential to a good hit.

(*3*) Let the club head follow down the fairway along the line of the flight of the ball as far as it is possible to reach before allowing it to come up and around.

e. Have the group swing, and give individuals suggestions. The student who transfers her weight and pivots naturally need not be troubled with thinking about these things and can concentrate on the one or two principles which will help her. It may be a general aid to have the class swing several times with the left hands only and then place the right hands lightly on the clubs.

f. When the group as a whole has developed an easy, relaxed, and rhythmical swing, give them soft balls. Explain that the ball is being added simply to check on accuracy of impact, not to see how hard they can hit. This is a good point at which to explain how important accuracy is. Since the ball is so small and the club head that must contact it is also small, the possible margin of error, if *any* contact is to result, is very slight. Unless the ball is hit in the center (in line with the center of gravity) most of the force of the club head will not be imparted to the ball.

g. Finally, have the students hit regulation balls.

2. Methods of Practice.

a. Swinging Without Ball. If the indoor space available is large enough so that the entire class can swing at once, and if there are two coco mats or one coco mat and a wooden platform (or even just one coco mat) to a student, the situation is ideal. With this situation have the class take their positions in two or three lines the length of the gymnasium. The number of lines depends on the length of the room and the number in the class. Have them stand so that they are all facing one end of the gymnasium. This makes it easier for the instructor to talk to the class and to demonstrate general faults and corrections.

If the space is not large enough for all to swing at once or if the equipment is limited, divide the class into two's (or three's if necessary) and have them take turns. While one student swings, her partner can watch and criticize. Rotate on the instructor's signal.

b. Swinging with a Plastic Ball. When not limited in space or equipment, divide the class into two lines the length of the gymnasium. Have the students stand about 20 feet from the wall and practice hitting balls toward the walls. Warn them to be careful not to get in the way of the club of any other student.

If the space or equipment is limited, divide the class into groups as for swinging. One student of each group may be given the responsibility of retrieving the balls.

Soft balls also may be used outdoors if the field is too short for a full wood shot with a regulation ball.

c. Swinging with a Regulation Ball.

(*1*) indoors. Practice with a hard ball indoors is only possible with a canvas back-drop or driving cage. If only one or two cages are available have the rest of the class practice with soft balls and then rotate so that each individual has an opportunity to hit several regulation balls in a cage.

(*2*) outdoors.

(*a*) If the outdoor facilities include a field 150 yards long:

1. Line up the class across one end of the field and have them hit out all the balls the length of the field.

2. On a signal from the instructor, the class walks forward in a line extending the width of the field.

3. Every student is instructed to pick up all balls in her path and carry them to the far end of the field.

4. If the students are playing their own balls, have them pile all the balls that are not their own near the center and each student can sort out her own.

5. If the school furnishes the balls, any student with more balls than she hit out gives the extras to the instructor.

6. If she has less than she hit out, the student reports to the instructor, who redistributes the balls.

7. If balls are missing after redistribution, the entire class can go back on the field until the correct number are found.

8. The class then hits the balls back the length of the field.

(*b*) If the field is too short for a full wood, either a shorter club or a soft ball must be substituted. The club chosen will depend on the length of the field and the ability of the group.

IV. THE SHORT GAME

The short game consists of nothing more than a sound golf stroke, the length of which is varied according to the distance required. Accuracy, not distance, is the essential of all iron play, and therefore, a shorter backswing is used. While authorities vary greatly as to the exact stance, they all agree that the stroke should be a smooth swing with no jabbing motion. In general the stance is slightly narrower and the ball is a little nearer because of the shorter shaft of the club. This causes the swing to be more upright and gives less distance but more accuracy. Many authorities teach an open stance, which allows a freer follow-through for greater accuracy in making short approaches. There is a very common misconception that if a lofted shot is desired, the player must, by her swing, aid the club in elevating the ball. This misconception causes the player to try to strike the ball upward, and as a result the ball is not hit squarely; it is usually hit above its center of gravity, and therefore is hit downward rather than upward. The pupil must be made to understand that the ball will rebound perpendicular to the face of the club;[18] in order to elevate the ball she must choose a club with an open face and then hit the ball squarely, allowing the club to do the work of lifting. If a sharp loft is desired, a club with a very open face is chosen and the ball is given back spin by being hit on the downward swing. This can be accomplished by playing the ball toward the right heel and playing the usual smooth stroke to hit through the ball. A ball hit with back spin will stop dead where it lands, or run only a few feet.

A. Approach Shots.

1. Types.

a. Chip. The chip shot is a low, running shot played from the edge or immediate vicinity of the green where the ground between the ball and the green is fairly level. The ball should be played so that it will clear the fairway, land on the green and roll toward the cup. If the ball hits off the green, it may hit an uneven spot and thus be deflected. For best results the straightest faced club possible should be used that will permit landing on the putting green and stopping close to the hole. Up to about 5 feet off the green a #4 or #5 iron should be used, and if farther away a #6 or #7, unless very little or no roll is desired. The ball is placed about opposite the middle of the stance. The swinging action is the same as any swing except that both the backswing and the follow-through may be shortened, depending on the distance the ball has to travel. Fraley [19] suggests that "the chip shot is a wrist and forearm job," although Les Bolstad states that there should be no wrist action at all in the short shot. The club points toward the hole at the end of the follow-through. This may be made easier by slightly opening the stance.

b. Pitch. The pitch shot is a high shot which lands with little or no roll. Since height and back spin are desired to reduce or eliminate roll, a #7, 8, or 9 club is used and the ball is placed almost opposite the right heel so that it is struck a descending blow. For this shot the arc of the swing should be more upright. The backswing and follow-through may be shortened if the distance is short.

2. General Principles. If the ball lies a few feet off the green, play a run-up shot with an iron that has just enough loft to lift the ball over the fairway to the green. Play for a roll toward the pin. As the distance to the green becomes greater or as the hole approaches the edge of the putting surface, increase the loft of the club, move the ball toward the right foot, and continue to play the same stroke, lengthening the backswing and follow-through according to the distance. A little practice with the short lofted clubs, starting about 30 or 40 yards from the green and working back, will give the student her range for each club and the length of backswing and follow-through that is necessary for the various distances.

B. Sand Trap Shots. It is infinitely better to get out of the sand trap in one shot even though the ball travels only a short distance, than to waste several swings in attempting a long shot. While there are several methods of playing from traps, there are two that are the most fundamental.

1. The Chip Shot.

a. This is used when the ball is resting on the top of the sand and the bank in front is not too steep.

b. A #6 or #7 iron is chosen.

c. The swing is the same as for any short approach except that the club may not touch the sand in addressing the ball or during the backswing.

2. The Blast or Explosion Shot.

a. This must always be used when the ball is partly or wholly buried in the sand or when the bank in front is steep.

b. A #8 or #9 iron or wedge is chosen.

c. The feet are planted firmly in the sand to avoid slipping.

[18] Broer: *op. cit.,* pp. 206–208.
[19] Fraley: *op. cit.,* p. 59.

d. Since the sand should be hit behind the ball, the ball is played forward. The distance that the sand should be hit behind the ball depends on how far the trap is from the green. In a normal sand trap shot, aim to hit the sand about 2 inches back of the ball.

e. The most important thing is to use a full iron swing *with a full follow-through.*

C. Shots from the Rough. When playing a shot from the rough the main purpose is to get the ball out onto the fairway, and distance should be sacrificed to this end. If the club head contacts grass or weeds on the downswing before impact with the ball a very weak shot will result.

1. A club with ample loft is chosen. In the average rough a #5 iron will be sufficient.
2. The usual stance is taken.
3. An upright swing with a full follow-through is used.

D. Faults in Short Strokes.

1. Lifting the club too soon because of feeling a necessity to lift the ball by the swing instead of allowing the proper club to do the work will cause the bottom edge of the club head to contact the middle of the ball and the ball to be "topped." To demonstrate how the club lifts the ball, give the student who is attempting to "lift" the ball by her swing a lofted club and ask her to hit balls at a golf bag a few feet away. The loft of the club will cause the ball to go over the bag instead of against it.[20]

2. When the golfer tries to lift the ball into the air with body action or with a flick of the wrists, she usually fails to shift the weight to the left foot, keeping too much on the right, and the result is that the lowest point in the arc of the swing is moved back and the ball is hit above the center.

3. The tendency to take too long a swing on a short shot often leads to checking the follow-through. The student gets a feeling during the down stroke that the swing is too long and unconsciously cuts it off at impact. Have this student practice hitting balls with a very short backswing to see how far they go with very little swing if the impact is clear.

E. Teaching.

1. Progression. The short shots should not be taught until the student has developed a feeling for the full swing with the essential clubs. The sand trap shots, being the most difficult, should be taught at the end of the progression.

2. Methods of Practice.

a. Indoors. Students can get good practice by chipping balls into baskets, into pockets in a canvas drop, or into mats standing against the walls. The pitch shot can be practiced with plastic or regulation balls against a canvas drop.

b. Outdoors. Mark the field at various distances and have the student attempt to put the ball between two markers. This set-up can be used for practicing approaches of various distances. If the field is marked for hockey or soccer, the hockey striking circle or the soccer penalty area can serve as objectives for the students' approach practice. Lime lines can be used to enclose a space to serve as a green. Students can also practice pitching over stationary equipment such as hockey or soccer goals or archery targets, or into a jumping pit or sand trap. The chip and explosion sand trap shots can be practiced out of a jumping pit or overturned dirt if no sand trap is available.

V. PUTTING

In teaching putting one must include a discussion of factors that vary and therefore, must be considered on every green, as well as the method of lining up the putt, and the actual stroke itself.

A. Factors in Putting.

1. The distance of the ball from the cup.
2. The *speed* of the green:

Fast Green

dry
grass closely cropped
hard

[20] Jones, Robert T., Jr., and Harold Lowe: *Group Instruction in Golf,* p. 37.

Slow Green

wet
grass not closely cropped
top dressing

3. The contour of the green and the effect it will have on both speed and accuracy: (*a*) in putting against the slope more force is necessary; (*b*) in putting with the slope less force is necessary; (*c*) in putting across the slope the aim must be above the cup.

4. The direction in which the grass has been cut. If the blades of grass are leaning toward the ball more force will be required than if they are leaning toward the hole.[21]

B. Lining Up the Ball. To line up a putt, crouch behind the ball and look over it toward the cup. Draw an imaginary line from the cup to the ball and pick out a spot on that line which is 8 to 10 inches in front of the ball. Concentrate on that spot while addressing the ball. Putt the ball to pass over that spot. If the green is not level, the player must judge the roll of the ball according to the slope, and when crouching behind the ball, line up the ball with a spot above the cup.

C. Technique. There is probably no other phase of golf with the variation of style that is found in putting. Some golfers use a very narrow stance, some wider; some a square stance, and others point their feet toward the cup. Some players shift the grip to the reverse overlap in which the forefinger of the left hand overlaps the little finger of the right, others turn the hands on the club slightly so that the palms are facing each other, and still others putt with the same grip that is used for the full swing. Some players stand fairly upright and many use a low crouch. In spite of the wide variation, however, there are certain principles that hold:

1. The grip is fairly light. A tight grip prevents relaxation.

2. The left shoulder should be toward the cup.

3. The stance is easy and relaxed.

4. The ball is played close to the feet. This puts the head more nearly over the ball and the player can look more directly down on it and less at an angle.

5. In addressing the ball, the club head is placed behind the ball so that the face is perpendicular to the line of putt.

6. The stroke should be smooth with the backswing and follow-through equal in length. This length is dependent upon the distance to be traversed and the contour and condition of the green.

7. The club head is brought backward and forward close to the ground along the line of putt, so that all movement is in the direction of desired movement of the ball.

8. The follow-through is toward the cup.

As noted, there are many different styles of accomplishing the above principles. Only two will be suggested here: (1) With the arms free of the body and the elbows slightly bent, putt with a pendulum motion of the arms; (2) With the right forearm immobilized by resting it on the right thigh, putt with the wrists. This style necessitates a bent right knee and a low crouch.

D. Faults in Putting.

1. A jabbing stroke with no follow-through makes it impossible to judge the force that is imparted to the ball. Also, stopping the club suddenly makes it difficult to keep the face of the club perpendicular to the line of putt, and thus the accuracy of the putt is affected. This same difficulty may arise from stopping the left arm or wrist, thus blocking the stroke at the start of the follow-through. Have the students putt on a carpet with no targets marked and concentrate on a smooth stroke.

2. Pulling the club in an arc to the left on follow-through causes the ball to go to the left of the cup. One device that is successful with many students is that of pointing the left elbow toward the cup. It is impossible to move the club in an arc to the left when this is done.

3. Too often players think of accuracy

[21] Fraley: *op. cit.*, p. 100.

only in terms of direction and lose their putts because they give little thought to force. Have the students putt for a certain distance marked by a line instead of for a target.

E. Teaching.

1. Progression. Since beginners should always start putting on a level surface, it is an excellent rainy day exercise and it may be put into the golf progression at any time. Some authorities advocate that putting be taught first, since such a high percentage of the total golf score is in putts.

a. The method of lining up the ball for the putt and the principles of putting must be explained.

b. These principles may be demonstrated, bringing out the reasons for each. Then a few different styles of putting may be demonstrated.

c. The class practices.

2. Methods of Practice.

a. Indoor. The first practice in stroking the ball can be done with a 7-inch sponge rubber ball or a tennis ball. These balls roll smoothly and noiselessly on a board floor and make it possible for the entire group to practice in safety. Divide the group into twos. One player places her club head on the floor in a position so that it can be used by her partner as a goal for her putt. Have the students practice parallel to the boards so that they may have a specific line to guide the club head.[22]

Next, divide the class. While part work on putting with regulation balls on a carpet, the rest can practice any swing that is being studied at that point in the progression. Rotate the groups. It is well to have the beginners start their putting on a carpet without any particular target, trying only for a smooth stroke. When this is accomplished, mark targets on the carpet and teach the students to attempt to have the ball stop just beyond the chalked targets so that they will work on judging force as well as direction. Have them start with very short putts and progress to longer distances. The next step indoors is to use an elevated board covered with carpet if one is available.

b. Outdoor. Putting can be practiced out-of-doors on a green or, if none is available, on any very smooth, not necessarily level, plot of closely cut grass.

If the class has had preliminary work inside, they can begin immediate practice in putting for the cups or marked targets. Warn them that the grass will be slower than the carpet, and therefore, more force will have to be imparted to the ball for any given distance.

If the group has had no indoor experience in putting, the same general progression as stated above can be used; that is, putting first with no definite target, and then, when the target is added, working first on short putts and progressing to longer ones.

CONSIDERATION OF OUTSIDE FORCES AND GROUND CONTOUR

I. WIND

Since heavy gusts of wind make balance more difficult, the player must take a firm position. A slightly wider stance and less vigorous swing will increase the stability of the body.

A. When playing the ball into a cross wind it is necessary to allow for the drift of the ball due to the wind. It is wise to keep the ball lower than usual as the wind close to the ground tends to have less velocity than that higher up. Therefore, a club with less loft should be chosen.

B. In hitting into a head wind, again the ball should be played low so that it will not have to resist the force of the stronger wind higher up. Also in a low hit there is proportionately more horizontal force, which is needed to resist the force of the wind. Again a club with less

[22] Always, Leonore K.: "Making Use of an Objective Record of Putting Progress," *Official Individual Sports Guide.*

loft than would be normally used is selected.

C. When there is a strong wind at the player's back the ball should be played higher than it would normally be played in order to take advantage of the wind with higher velocity and to keep the ball in the air as long as possible so that the wind has more time to act on the ball before gravity pulls it to earth. A club with more loft than would normally be used for the distance is chosen.

II. RESISTANCE OF VARIOUS SURFACES

A. Hard ground offers little resistance to the forward roll of the ball. Since there is little or no "give" as the ball hits, most of the force of the ball hitting the ground is transferred back to the ball and the ball bounces and rolls.

B. Soft ground offers a great deal of resistance to forward roll because the ground gives with the weight of the rolling ball. When the ball lands on soft ground the ground "gives" and therefore, much of the force is absorbed and the ball bounces little if at all.

C. The longer the grass the greater the resistance to a rolling ball. A ball with a given momentum will roll farther in short grass than in long.

D. Wet grass offers more resistance to a rolling ball than does dry grass and therefore, a ball with a given momentum will roll farther on a dry surface.

III. CONTOUR OF THE GROUND

Allowance must be made for various contours of fairways and greens. Since a ball will roll down-slope because of the pull of gravity, the shot should be aimed "uphill" of the green or of the cup.

When a ball lies on a hill, the slope of the ground must be studied, and it is advisable to play for safe direction even at the sacrifice of distance. A good general rule is to allow the club head to follow the contour of the ground.

Three factors must be considered: the relation of the slope to the desired line of flight, the degree of slope, and the distance to be traversed.

IV. TYPES OF HILL LIES

A. Uphill Lie. When it is necessary to stand on a hill and play the ball uphill, a slightly closed stance is used and the ball is played from the center of the stance. The nature of the stance due to the lie of the ball is such that the player is hitting up on the ball and thus exaggerated height results. For this reason a longer club with a less open face than would be normally used for the same distance on level ground should be used. The weight will be more on the right foot as it is the downhill foot, and the left knee will be bent to compensate for the slope; therefore the arc of the backswing will be flattened. As the club head follows the slope it will be more on the inside, resulting in a "pull." Allow for this by aiming slightly to the right. After impact allow the club to follow-through up the slope of the hill. Allow the club to do the work. Do not attempt to "lift" the ball.

B. Downhill Lie. When it is necessary to stand on a hill and to hit the ball downhill, a slightly open stance is used and the ball is placed slightly nearer the right foot. The right knee will be bent and the weight will be on the left or downhill foot thus limiting the pivot of the left side. Since there is more weight than usual on the left foot at impact and the arc of the swing is downward, the ball will travel abnormally low. Therefore, a club with a more lofted face than would normally be used for the same distance on level ground should be chosen. The backswing must be more upright because of the slope. There is a tendency to slice. Allow for this by playing a little to the left. Be careful to allow the club head to follow-through along the slope and not to try to lift the ball.

C. Sidehill Lies.

1. Ball Below the Feet. When playing across the slope, if the ball is below the feet, the weight is naturally forward on the toes. Therefore, take a stance that gives the best balance. Stand closer to the ball than usual and play the ball off the center of the stance. Grip the club as far up on the shaft as possible since the distance from the shoulder to the club head is longer than usual. It may help to use a longer club than would be chosen for the same distance on level ground. The tendency is to slice since the body pivot is cut down, so allow for this by aiming to the left.

2. Ball Above the Feet. If the ball is above the feet, the distance from the shoulder to the club head is shorter than usual; therefore, a shorter club should be chosen or the club should be gripped well down the shaft. Play the ball nearer the right foot and slightly open the stance. Play a flat swing, shorter than usual, and keep the hands low. Since the tendency here is to pull, aim to the right.

FAULTS IN THE DIRECTION OF THE FLIGHT OF THE BALL

I. SLICING

A. Definition. A "slice" is a curve in the flight of the ball to the right of the intended flight. A slice results from hitting the ball when the head of the club is facing to the right of the direction it is following, or from hitting from the outside in, or from drawing the club across the back of the ball from the right to the left, thus imparting clockwise spin.

B. Causes.

1. The player, trying to avoid a slice, attempts to yank the shot to the left. This pulls the club head across the ball and imparts spin, which causes a slice.

2. An incorrect grip makes it impossible for the club head to meet the ball squarely. The right hand may be too far under or the left hand not enough on top of the club. Dante and Elliott[23] advocate gripping the club so that only two knuckles of the left hand are visible from above. This places the back of the left hand toward the objective.

3. Too open a stance cuts down the pivot of the body during the backswing.

4. Too wide a stance may cause a player to slice. The feet should be approximately hip width apart.

5. The right hand lifting the club at too sharp an angle also retards the complete pivoting of the left side.

6. Uncocking the wrists too soon creates a tendency to throw the club head forward away from the body on the downswing. This causes the club to cut diagonally across the ball from the outside in. It also puts the right hand in control. Lack of proper control by the *left* hand causes the club to be drawn sharply in toward the left side at impact.

7. Pulling in the arms as the ball is struck gives a clockwise spin to the ball.

8. Lifting the head and not watching the ball because of anticipating the shot may result in any type of shot but is one of the main causes of slicing.

C. Correction. First check the grip, stance, and placement of the ball. If everything is correct, ask the student to swing several times.

Determine whether the wrists are turning as the club head is taken back. If the wrists are "rolled" the face of the club will be angled and the wrists will have to be "rolled back" exactly the same amount if the ball is to be hit squarely. It is the failure of the student to return to the square face position at impact that causes many slices. If the face is opened and closed during the swing, the chances of its being square when it meets the ball are less than if it is kept square throughout the swing. Dante and Elliott[24] advocate teaching students to keep the club head face square throughout the swing by not allowing the wrists to roll.

If the student is pulling the club head back with the right hand, emphasize the use of the left arm in pushing the club back. Have the student take several easy

[23] Dante, Joe, and Elliot, Len: *Stop That Slice,* p. 7.

[24] *Ibid.,* p. 4.

swings with only the left hand on the club and then put the right hand on very lightly (have the right just "ride along").

If, on the downswing, the student is throwing the club head away from the body, have her place a handkerchief or piece of paper between the right upper arm and the thorax. Ask her to attempt to hold the handkerchief while swinging, until the ball has been struck. This will keep the right arm close on the downswing and prevent hitting from the outside. Another method of accomplishing the same thing is to place a piece of paper or cardboard on the ground behind the ball and have the student swing inside of this marker to hit the ball. Or, one can place a marker out from the right toe and tell the student to swing many times at this marker, following through as far out to the right as possible. Then have her swing with the ball placed properly, still concentrating on swinging down through this marker.

If the difficulty is in the follow-through, ask the student to try to throw the club down the fairway as far as possible before allowing it to come up to finish the arc of the swing. This often overcomes the tendency to pull the club in and up at impact. It is sometimes necessary to put a marker on the ground forward and to the right and tell the student to aim for this marker after impact.

II. PUSHING—"QUICK SLICE"

A. Definition. The ball goes off at a sharp angle to the right. This results not from spin but from the club's moving from the inside out with the club face square to this same direction.

B. Causes.

1. The chief cause is the bending of the left arm allowing the elbow to go outward, thus opening the face of the club.
2. If the body is brought around too far ahead of the hands, the face of the club will be open at impact. This is usually caused by the player being overanxious to hit the ball.

C. Correction. Coach the student to keep the left arm straight throughout backswing and downswing and to swing easily.

III. HOOKING

A. Definition. A "hook" is a curve in the flight of the ball to the left of the intended flight. A hook results from hitting when the club head is facing to the left of the direction of swing, or from hitting from the inside out, imparting counterclockwise spin to the ball.

B. Causes.

1. Gripping the club with the right hand too far around the club.
2. Closing the stance and thus limiting the pivot on the follow-through and causing the backswing to be flatter than usual.
3. Overworking the right hand.
4. Punching at the ball.

C. Correction. First check the grip, the stance, and the position of the ball and then check the swing. Coach the student to try for a relaxed swing. Use the exercise of swinging with the left arm alone and then placing the right on lightly.

IV. PULLING

A. Definition. The ball goes directly to the left. This again is not a matter of spin but results from the club's moving from outside in with the face of the club square to this direction.

B. Causes.

1. The face of the club may be closed too much at "address."
2. The wrists may roll at impact and close the face of the club.
3. If the right elbow is too far out from the body on the downswing, the club head may be thrown out and the face turned toward the left at impact.
4. The right shoulder may be higher than the left at impact.

NOTE: If the club hits the ball squarely as it is traveling from right to left, it will send it off sharply left. If the club head is pulled across the *back of the ball* from right to left, spin will be imparted and the result will be a slice.

C. Correction. If the right elbow is out from the body, use a handkerchief or paper under the right arm as suggested to help cure a "slice." If the fault comes from rolling the wrists, have the student swing several times stopping the follow-through when the club is at its farthest point along the desired flight of the ball so that she can check the face of the club and work to have the face up at this point in the swing.

INTENTIONAL CHANGES IN THE FLIGHT OF THE BALL

I. DIRECTION

Many times on the course it is desirable to hit a ball so that there will be a curve in its flight. Most golf courses have one or more dog leg holes, making a curve to the right or left distinctly advantageous.

A. Intentional Slice.[25]

1. Use an open stance.
2. Play the ball opposite the center of the stance.
3. Take the club head back outside the intended line of flight of the ball. Push away from the body on the downswing.
4. The hands and club should be quite high at the top of the backswing.
5. Pull down and across the ball (from the outside in) toward the left foot.
6. Keep the face of the club slightly open at all times. Be careful that the club head does not turn over at any time during the downswing or follow-through.
7. Use a good follow-through.

B. Intentional Hook.[26]

1. Use a closed stance.
2. Play the ball nearly opposite the right foot.
3. Pivot the right hip away from the ball, bringing the club head sharply around as it is brought back. This results in a flat swing.
4. Swing the club head away from the body allowing the wrists and club head to roll at the moment of impact.

It is possible to regulate the amount of the hook by the degree to which the stance is closed and the swing flattened.

II. HEIGHT

Just as it may at times be advantageous to curve the flight of the ball, it may be necessary to loft the ball more than normal or to play to keep it particularly low. Long distance may be desired, and therefore the usual pitch shot that gives very little distance and no roll is not desirable, and still there may be a tall tree directly in the path of the line of flight of the ball to the green. If the tree branches do not grow too low it may be more practical to play a low shot under the branches. A low flying ball is also good when there is a high wind.

A. Hitting the Ball High.[27]

1. Play the ball approximately off the left heel.
2. Keep the weight more on the right foot than on the left so that the ball will be caught on the upswing.
3. Hit with the hands slightly behind the club head. Uncock the wrists a little earlier than usual. This also causes the ball to be caught on the upswing.

B. Hitting the Ball Low.[28]

1. Play the ball opposite the right foot.
2. The hands should be unusually far ahead of the club head on impact.
3. The stance should be slightly open.
4. The weight should be kept firmly on the left foot throughout the swing.
5. Avoid any turning of the club head at the time of impact.
6. Shorten the swing.

[25] Nelson, Byron: *Winning Golf,* p. 180.
[26] *Ibid.,* p. 182.
[27] *Ibid.,* p. 172.
[28] *Ibid.,* p. 176.

ORGANIZATION OF GOLF CLASSES

I. CLASSIFICATION OF PLAYERS

Players should be classified according to previous golf experience into beginning, intermediate, and advanced groups. If the teaching situation allows students with some experience to play a round or more before registration, it would be well to classify on the basis of scores for nine or eighteen holes on a given course. Although one or two rounds is not a truly reliable criterion of a student's ability, it would, in most cases, tend to be more reliable than the student's own judgment of her ability. This would probably be possible only for fall registration in the greater part of the country, as most golf courses are not open for play at the season when schools register for spring physical education classes.

II. NUMBER REGISTERED IN A SECTION

The number of students registered in a section depends on the facilities available indoors and outdoors and the degree of skill of the group. A beginning group should be kept smaller than a section of students who have had some previous golf experience. If only one instructor is available, fifteen to eighteen should be the absolute maximum number in any section. Ten to twelve beginners and twelve to fifteen intermediates is ideal, but in few situations can classes be kept as small as this. In many schools offering a major course in physical education, students who have previously had a theory course in the sport coach under an instructor. In this situation a few more students may be taught successfully.

CLASS SAFETY PRECAUTIONS

1. Never swing near another student. Always check to see that there is plenty of space before swinging a club.

2. Avoid walking close to anyone swinging a club.

3. All students stay behind the line until all have finished hitting the balls out and the instructor gives the signal to collect the balls.

4. Care of the hands: (*a*) Advise use of a glove for the left hand, to avoid blisters. (*b*) Advise against rings. (*c*) Advise the student to stop swinging if the hands begin to become sore.

SAMPLE LESSON PLANS

I. First Lesson. The first golf lesson with beginners should be indoors where it is easy to talk to students.

A. Announcements pertinent to a particular teaching situation such as place and time of meeting, and so forth.

B. Costume for golf class.

C. Short history.

D. Object of the game.

E. Layout of the course.

F. Clubs and their uses, and clubs required for class work.

G. The names of various parts of the club.

H. Safety precautions.

II. Sample Plan. A sample plan is given here for a class that is working indoors on a *full swing.*

A. Have all students swing without any balls for a few minutes.

B. Discuss and demonstrate putting.

C. Practice: If cages are available divide the class and have one-third putt, one-third swing at plastic balls, and one-third hit hard balls in cages. If necessary, assign two or three students to a cage and have each hit six balls before changing. Have the groups rotate on signal. Rotate from putting to swinging at plastic balls, to hitting in cages, to putting.

If no cages are available, have one-third of the class putting, one-third swinging without a ball, one-third swinging with plastic balls, and rotate as above.

D. Include a short discussion or lecture.

III. Sample Plan. A sample plan is

given here for a class working indoors on *approach shots.*

A. Short oral quiz on previous lecture material such as golf terms or etiquette. Occasionally a very short written quiz will help to stimulate interest.

B. Practice:

1. All students practice swinging without balls.

2. Divide class for special practice. While one-third of the class putts, have a group work on approach shots at a canvas, or mats, and another group hit with a full swing in cages if they are available. If there are no cages one group can work on the full swing with plastic balls. Rotate from putting, to approaching, to the full swing, to putting (Figure 6.7).

C. New lecture material.

RAINY DAY MATERIAL

Although an outdoor game, golf offers many possibilities for interesting indoor lessons both in lecture material and practice.

I. LECTURE AND DISCUSSION MATERIAL

1. History of the Game
2. Golf Etiquette
3. Golf Terms
4. Fundamental Rules
5. Difficult and Unusual Lies
6. Competitive Play

II. PRACTICE MATERIAL

A. **Full Swing.** This may be practiced by swinging without a ball, hitting plastic balls, and hitting hard balls in golf cages or into properly constructed canvas drops.

B. **Approaching.** Practice swinging without a ball and hitting regulation balls into a canvas drop with pockets. The short chip shot can be practiced into tumbling mats placed against the wall, through hula-hoops, or into wastebaskets.

C. **Putting.** Good practice may be obtained on a carpet or putting boards.

D. **Contests.**

1. Putting.
2. Approaching.
   a. Backdrop with pockets.
   b. Baskets.

INTEREST MOTIVATION

Class teams, picked toward the end of the season, will do much to stimulate interest in golf. Also a tournament for the selection of the school champion creates enthusiasm for the sport. From the results of this tournament an honorary varsity can be chosen.

In co-educational schools mixed tournaments have been run very successfully. The two-ball foursome, in which the boy and girl hit the ball alternately, has proved very satisfactory.

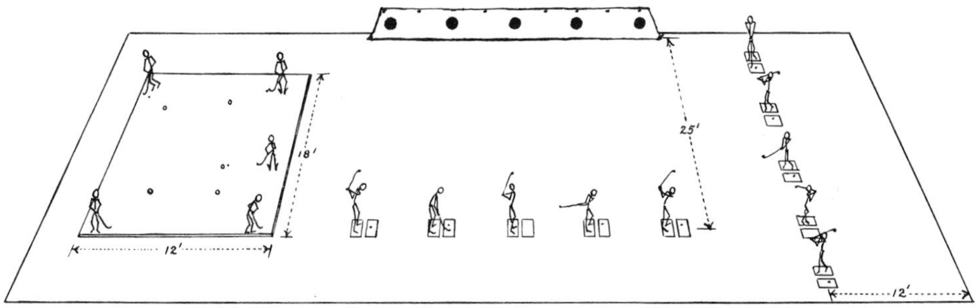

FIGURE 6.7 *Diagram of an indoor golf class.*

SUGGESTED PROGRESSION FOR A TERM OF ABOUT 6 WEEKS

Class Meeting 3 Times a Week for 40 Minutes

I. Beginners	II. Intermediates	III. Advanced
A. Object of game, layout of course *B.* Clubs: names of parts and general uses *C.* Grip *D.* Stance *E.* Full Swing #5 iron (3 lessons)[29] #2 iron (3 lessons) wood (5 lessons)—preferably #2 or 3 With each club go through: 1. Specific uses for club 2. Swing without ball 3. Position of ball 4. Swing with soft ball 5. Swing with hard ball *F.* Chip shot (2 lessons) *G.* Putting (3 lessons) *H.* Lecture and discussion of mechanical principles, rules, etiquette, and so forth	Review (10 lessons)	Review (4–5 lessons) Intentional changes in the flight of the ball (2 lessons)
	(*I*) #7 iron (2 lessons) (*J*) Short approach (2 lessons) (*K*) Sand trap shots (2 lessons)	
	(*L*) Play on course (2 lessons)	Play on course (11–12 lessons)

[29] The number of lessons is approximate and is given only as a general guide. The speed of progression necessarily depends on the size and ability of the group. Few lessons would be spent entirely on one club. A part of each would be allotted to the review of clubs previously studied. The object of the game, the rules, course etiquette, and so forth, would be worked into the lessons at convenient points in the progression.

GOLF ETIQUETTE

I. ON THE TEE

1. Observe the tee markers. Always tee the ball behind them. These are frequently moved to give the grass a chance to grow again.

2. The player with the "honor"[30] drives first.

3. Never talk or move around when another player is driving.

4. Never swing a club where you can be seen or heard by the player driving.

5. The best place to stand is diagonally in front and to the right of the player.

6. Wait until the players ahead have played their second shots *and* are out of your driving range before teeing off.

[30] See Golf Terms, p. 183.

II. ON THE FAIRWAY

1. The player who is "away"[31] plays first.
2. Never stand in the line of a player's shot.
3. Be still while a player is taking a shot.
4. If a ball is lost, or if you are playing more slowly than those behind you, signal the players behind to go through. Then wait until they are out of range before playing again.
5. Wait until the preceding players are *off* the green before making an approach shot.
6. Replace, and press down with your foot, all divots.
7. Call "Fore!" if your ball is likely to go near any other player.

III. IN A SAND TRAP

1. Leave your bag at the edge of the trap.
2. Enter and leave the trap at the point nearest your ball.
3. Smooth over foot marks and club marks with your club when you leave the trap.

IV. ON THE GREEN

1. Leave your bag at the edge of the green.
2. While holding the flag in the cup, stand quietly and to one side of the cup so that your shadow does not fall across the line of putt.
3. Place the flag at the edge of the green when it has been removed from the cup.
4. The player "away" putts first.
5. Keep your body and your shadow out of the line of any player's putt.
6. Do not move or talk while players are putting.
7. Avoid stepping on the turf at the edge of the cup.
8. Replace the flag in the cup immediately after holing out.
9. Leave the green immediately after holing out. Record the score after you have left the green.

V. IN GENERAL

1. Only flat-heeled shoes should be worn on a course. These make possible a better stance. High heels damage the course.
2. If for any reason you are playing slowly, motion the players behind you to go through. Wait until they are out of your range before taking another shot.

GOLF TERMS[32]

Address the Ball. Get into position to play the ball.

Approach Shot. Any shot made with the intention of landing on the green.

Away. The ball farthest from the hole.

Bent. A grass commonly used in the United States on putting greens.

Birdie. One below par.

Bisque. A handicap consisting of strokes to be taken at the choice of the player.

Bulge. The convexity of the face of a golf club.

Bunker. An obstacle placed on the fairway—may be a hummock of soil planted with grass, or a sand trap.

Bye. The holes remaining to be played to determine the winner of the match.

Caddie. A person who carries the golfer's clubs and who can give her advice in regard to the course.

Casual Water. Water which accumulates on a course after a storm, not always present—not part of a hazard.

Cleek. A narrow iron-headed club of little loft.

Closed Stance. The left foot slightly in advance of the right—the player tends to face slightly away from the line of flight of the ball.

Club. The implement with which the ball is struck.

Course. The area within which play is permitted.

[31] See Golf Terms.

[32] For detailed list of terms, see Herndon, Charles: *Golf Made Easy,* p. 185.

Cup. The hole sunk in the green into which the ball must be played in order to terminate play on that hole.

Dead. A ball is said to be "dead" when it lies so near the hole that the putt is a dead certainty. A ball is also said to "fall dead" when it does not run after alighting.

Divot. A piece of turf removed by the club in making a shot.

Dog Leg. A sharp bend in the fairway.

Dormie. One side is said to be "dormie" when it is as many holes ahead as there remain holes to play.

Down. The number of holes or strokes a player is behind an opponent.

Drop the Ball. The player stands facing the hole and drops the ball over her shoulder.

Eagle. Two below par.

Face. The striking surface of the club.

Fairway. The well-kept turf between the tee and the green—usually bounded by rough.

Flag. Marks the spot on the green where the cup is located.

Flight. Division of players according to ability for tournaments; also, the path of the ball in the air.

Fore. The warning cry on the golf course.

Four-ball Match. Two players play their better ball against the better ball of their opponents.

Foursome. Two players playing one ball on each side; partners alternate hitting the ball.

Green. The plot of closely cut grass which surrounds the cup—may be level or sloping.

Grip. That part of the club which is grasped and the grasp itself.

Half-shot. A stroke that is less than a full swing.

Halved. Each side makes the same score on a hole.

Hanging Lie. The ball lies on a downward slope.

Hazard. Any obstacle that interferes with the free flight or roll of the ball (natural: trees, natural water, rocks, and so forth; made hazards: bunkers, sand traps, and so forth).

Head of the Club. The heavy part of the club, used for striking the ball.

Heel of the Club. The part of the club head below the point where the shaft and the head meet.

Hole. One unit of the course including the playing tee, fairway, hazards, green, and cup.

Holing Out. Sinking the ball in the cup.

Honor. The privilege of playing first, acquired by winning the preceding hole.

Hook. The flight of the ball curves to the left.

Impact. The contact of the club with the ball.

Irons. A graded series of metal-headed clubs.

Lie. The position of the ball with reference to the ground.

Like. A player is playing "the like" when she makes an equal number of strokes to that just played by her opponent.

Links. The golf course.

Loft. To elevate the ball; also, the angle of pitch of the face of the club.

Loose Impediment. Any obstruction not fixed or growing.

Match. The game itself.

Match Play. Competition by holes; the player winning the most holes wins the match.

Medalist. The low score player in a medal tournament.

Medal Play. Competition by total scores for all holes; the player with the lowest total score wins the match.

Nassau. A system of scoring awarding one point for the winning of each "nine" and an additional point for the match.

Neck. The point at which the shaft joins the head of the club.

Odd. A player is playing "odd" when on a given hole she is making a stroke one more in number than that last played by her opponent.

Open Stance. The left foot is drawn back so the player tends to face somewhat in the direction of the flight of the ball.

Out-of-bounds. The area outside the proper course, from which balls may not be played.

Par. Perfect score for a hole; an arbitrary standard of excellence based on length of hole.

Penalty Stroke. A stroke added to the score of a hole under certain rules.

Playing Through. At the invitation of the group ahead, players behind may pass them and continue play.

Press. An error in stroke caused by trying to hit the ball too hard; an attempt to hit beyond one's normal power.

Pull. A shot which goes to the left without curving.

Push. A shot which goes to the right without curving.

Putt. A stroke taken with the putter in which the ball is rolled along the green.

Rough. The unkept territory surrounding the fairway or green.

Sand Trap. A patch of ground from which the top soil has been removed and sand substituted.

Set. A full complement of clubs.

Shaft. The handle of the club.

Shanking. Hitting the ball with the neck of the club.

Single. One player plays against another.

Slice. The flight of the ball curves to the right.

Sole of the Club. The surface upon which the club rests when addressing the ball. The club is said to be "soled" when this surface is flat on the ground.

Square Stance. An imaginary line from the toe of one shoe to the toe of the other shoe is parallel to the line of flight of the ball.

Stance. The position of the player's feet when addressing the ball.

Stroke. The act of hitting the ball.

Stymie. One ball lies directly in the line of putt of another.

Tee. 1. A small wooden elevation for the ball.
2. The ground from which the ball is put in play—markers on the tee indicate the point behind which the ball is to be played off.

Three-ball Match. Three players each playing her own ball.

Threesome. A match of three players in which two partners play one ball against the ball of the other player.

Toe of the Club. The part of the head opposite the heel; front portion of the club head.

Top. To strike a ball above the center.

Upright. A club is said to be "upright" when the angle between its face and shaft is less than ordinarily obtuse.

Water Hole. A large water hazard which lies between the tee and the green.

Winter Rules. The privilege of improving the lie of the ball on the fairway; used seasonally under local rules.

Woods. A graded series of clubs with wooden heads.

A FEW OF THE MOST IMPORTANT RULES OF GOLF[33]

HONOR: RULE 12

The option of taking the honor at the first teeing ground shall, if necessary, be decided by lot. The side that wins the hole shall take the honor at the next teeing ground. If a hole has been halved, the side which had the honor at the previous teeing ground shall retain it.

LOST, OUT OF BOUNDS, AND UNPLAYABLE BALLS: RULE 29

1. Lost or Out of Bounds. If a ball is lost or out of bounds, the player shall play the next stroke as nearly as possible at the spot from which the ball was played, adding a penalty stroke to the score for the hole. If the original stroke was played from the teeing ground, a ball may be teed anywhere within the teeing ground; if from the fairway, rough or hazard, it shall be dropped; and if on the putting green, it shall be placed.

2. Unplayable. If the player deem her ball to be unplayable (except in water or casual water) she shall either play the ball as above or drop a ball, under penalty of one stroke, either within two club-lengths of the point where the ball lay, but not nearer the hole, or behind the point where the ball lay, keeping that point between herself and the hole. If the ball lay in a bunker, it must be dropped in the bunker.

HOW TO DROP A BALL: RULE 22

1. The player shall face the hole, stand erect, and drop the ball behind her over her shoulder. If dropped in any other way, a penalty of one stroke is incurred.

2. If, in dropping, the ball touch the player, she shall incur no penalty; or, if it roll into a hazard or out of bounds, she may re-drop without penalty.

3. If in dropping, the ball rolls nearer the hole, it must be redropped. If, because of a hill, it is impossible to prevent its rolling nearer the hole, it must be placed without penalty.

MOVING OR BENDING FIXED OR GROWING OBJECTS: RULE 17

Before playing a player shall not improve her lie by bending or breaking

[33] For the complete official wording see *The Rules of Golf,* United States Golf Association.

anything fixed or growing, except as may occur:

1. In the course of fairly taking her stance in addressing the ball.

2. in making her backward and forward swing.

REMOVAL OF LOOSE IMPEDIMENTS: RULE 18

1. Except when both the impediment and the ball lie in or touch a hazard, any loose impediment may be removed without penalty.

2. If the ball move after any loose impediment has been touched, the penalty shall be one stroke.

PLAY IN HAZARDS: RULE 33

1. When a ball lies in or touches a hazard, the club shall not touch the ground, nor shall anything be touched or moved before the player strikes the ball. (See exception in official rules.)

2. If a ball be completely covered by sand, fallen leaves, or other cover, only so much thereof may be removed as will enable the player to see the top of the ball.

BALL IN WATER HAZARD

1. Rule 33. If a ball lies or is lost in a water hazard, the player may drop a ball, under penalty of one stroke, either behind the water hazard or as near as possible to the spot from which the original ball was played.

2. Rule 32. If a ball lies or is lost in casual water, the player may drop a ball without penalty as near as possible to the spot where the ball lay but not nearer the hole.

PUTTING: RULE 35

1. The line of putt must not be touched, except in placing the club immediately in front of the ball in addressing it.

2. Moving opponent's ball.

a. If the player's ball knock the opponent's ball into the hole, the opponent shall be deemed to have holed out at her last stroke.

b. If the player's ball move the opponent's ball the opponent may, if she choose, place the ball as near as possible to the spot from which it was moved, but this must be done before another stroke is played by either side.

Suggestions for Further Reading

Alway, Leonore, K.: "Indoor Group Golf Instruction." *Journal of Health and Physical Education, 9:* 1, January, 1938.

Armour, Tommy: *How to Play Your Best Golf All the Time.* New York, Simon and Schuster, 1953.

Berg, Pattie, and Otis Dypwich: *Golf.* New York, A. S. Barnes & Co., 1941.

Broer, Marion R.: *Efficiency of Human Movement.* Philadelphia, W. B. Saunders Company, 1960.

Brown, Innis and Grantland Rice: *How to play Golf;* and Bobby Jones: *How I Play Golf.* Spalding's Athletic Library, No. 224. New York, American Sports Publishing Co., 1940.

Bruce, Ben and Evelyn Davies: *Beginning Golf.* Belmont, California, Wadsworth Publishing Co., Inc., 1962.

Dante, Joe and Len Elliot: *Stop That Slice.* New York, McGraw-Hill Book Co., 1953.

Division for Girls and Women's Sports: *Bowling-Fencing-Golf Guide.* Washington, D. C., American Association for Health, Physical Education, and Recreation. Published biennially.

Eastburn, Warrine: "Adaptation of Playing Fields and Gymnasium Equipment to the Teaching of Group Golf." *Athletic Handbook,* Spalding's Athletic Library. New York, American Sports Publishing Co., 1936.

Forrest, James: *Golf Made Easy.* New York, E. P. Dutton and Co., 1934.

Fraley, Oscar: *Golf in Action.* New York, A. A. Wyn, Inc., 1952.

Guldahl, Ralph: *Groove Your Golf.* Indianapolis, Bookwalter-Ball-Greathouse Printing Co., 1939.

Harris, Mark G.: *New Angles on Putting and Approaching.* Chicago, Reilly and Lee Co., 1940.

Hartwig, Marie: "An Experimental Study of Fundamental Coaching Factors Influencing the Learning of a Golf Swing." Master's Thesis, University of Michigan, 1938.

Herndon, Charles: *Golf Made Easy.* Los Angeles, Parker, Stone and Baird Co., 1930.

Hicks, Betty: *Fundamentals of Golf.* Chicago, J. A. Dubow Mfg. Co., 1948.

Hogan, Ben: *Power Golf.* New York, A. S. Barnes & Co., 1953. New York, Pocket Books, Inc., 1953.

Jones, Ernest, and Innis Brown: *Swinging Into Golf.* Revised ed. New York, Robert M. McBride and Co., 1946.

Jones, Robert T.: *How to Run a Golf Tournament.* The American Golf Institute, 19 Beekman Street, New York.

Jones, Robert Tyre (Bobby): *Golf is My Game.* Garden City, New York, Doubleday and Company, Inc., 1959.

Jones, Robert T., Jr.: *Rights and Wrongs of Golf.* A. G. Spalding and Bros., 1935.

Jones, Robert T., Jr., and Howard E. Lowe: *Group Instruction in Golf.* New York, American Sports Publishing Co., 1939.

Kreatz, Reuben: *Golf in 10 Lessons, with the Rules of Golf and 200 Golf Tips.* San Bernardino, California, Golf Publications Co., 1938.

Lindblad, Virginia: "A Guide for Group Instruction in Golf." Master's Thesis, University of Wisconsin, 1943.

Mangrum, Lloyd: *Golf, a New Approach.* New York, McGraw-Hill Book Co., 1949.

Martin, Harry Brownlow: *What's Wrong with Your Golf.* New York, Dodd, Mead and Co., 1930.

———: *Fifty Years of American Golf.* New York, Dodd, Mead and Co., 1936.

Metz, Dick: *The Secret to Par Golf.* New York, The Macmillan Co., 1940.

Middlecoff, Cary: *Master Guide to Golf.* Englewood Cliffs, New Jersey, Prentice-Hall, Inc., 1960.

Morrison, Alex J.: *A New Way to Better Golf.* New York, Simon and Schuster, 1935.

———: *Better Golf Without Practice.* New York, Simon and Schuster, 1940.

National Golf Foundation: *Golf in Physical Education.* Chicago, 1941.

———: *Golf Lessons; The Fundamentals as Taught by the Foremost Professional Instructors.* Chicago, 1952.

Nelson, Byron: *Winning Golf.* New York, A. S. Barnes & Co., 1946.

Novak, Joe: *How to Put Power and Direction in Your Golf.* New York, Prentice-Hall, Inc., 1954.

———: *Par Golf in 8 Steps.* New York, Prentice-Hall, Inc., 1950.

Runyan, Paul: "Magic Eye Golf." *Golf,* National Golf Review, Inc., *4*:22, Nov., 1940.

Schleman, Helen B. and Virginia Hayes: *Group Golf Instruction.* New York, A. S. Barnes and Co., 1934.

Snead, Sam: *A Quick Way to Better Golf.* New York, The Sun Dial Press, 1938.

———: *How to Hit a Golf Ball from Any Sort of Lie.* Garden City, N. Y., Blue Ribbon Books, 1950.

———: *How to Play Golf and Professional Tips on Improving Your Score.* New York, Garden City Publishing Co., 1946.

———: *Natural Golf.* New York, A. S. Barnes and Co., 1953.

———: *Sam Snead on Golf.* Englewood Cliffs, New Jersey, Prentice-Hall, Inc., 1961.

Stanley Louis T.: *How to Be a Better Woman Golfer,* New York, Thomas Y. Crowell Co., 1952.

Stein, Jennette A. and Emma F. Waterman: *Golf for Beginning Players.* Columbus, Ohio, Heer Printing Co., 1938.

Thompson, Ben: *How to Play Golf.* New York, Prentice-Hall, Inc., 1939.

———: "A High School Golf Program." *Scholastic Coach,* 250 East 43rd Street, New York, *9*:21, Nov., 1939; *9*:16, Dec., 1939; *9*:5, Jan., 1940; *9*:18, Feb., 1940; *9*:10 Mar., 1940.

———: "Putting, Golf's Simplest Swing." *Scholastic Coach, 9*:22, April, 1940.

———: "Slicing and Pulling." *Golf,* National Golf Review, Inc., *4*:15, Nov., 1940.

Woodfin, Gene: "The Teaching of Motor Skill." Master's Thesis, University of Wisconsin, 1946.

TESTS

Autrey, Elizabeth P.: "A Battery of Tests for Measuring Playing Ability in Golf." Master's Thesis, University of Wisconsin, 1937.

Coffey, Margaret: "Achievement Tests in Golf." Master's Thesis, University of Iowa, 1946.

Glassow, Ruth B. and Marion R. Broer: *Measuring Achievement in Physical Education.* Philadelphia, W. B. Saunders Company, 1938.

Lumpkin, Margaret: "Evaluation of a Putting Test in Golf." Unpublished Study for Master's Degree, Wellesley College, 1940.

Waglow, I. F. and C. H. Rehling: "A Golf Knowledge Test." *Research Quarterly, 24*:463–470, Dec. 1953.

Watts, Harriet; "The Construction and Evaluation of a Target for Testing the Approach Shot in Golf." Master's Thesis, University of Wisconsin, 1942.

Wright, Dorothy L.: "Measures for Evaluating Some of the Skills Used in Playing Golf." Master's Thesis, University of California, 1942.

FILMS

Bernhard, Frederica and Elizabeth H. Flory: *Educational Films in Sports.* The American Film Center, Inc., 1946. (Write: Educational Film Library Association, Inc., 45 Rockefeller Plaza, New York 20, New York.)

Professional Golfers' Association of America, Film Library, Broadway and Main Street, Dunedin, Florida.

Sports, Physical Education and Recreation Film Guide, Business Screen Magazine in cooperation with the Athletic Institute, Vol. 1, No. 1, May, 1947. (Write: Film Guide Department, The Athletic Institute, Merchandise Mart, Room 805, Chicago 54, Illinois.)

RULES

The Rules of Golf. United States Golf Association, 1961 Edition.

7

RIDING

7

RIDING

by Jean Campbell Tugman

The late General Harry S. Chamberlain, a member of the United States Equestrian Team, once said that "no one ever learns all there is to know about either horses or riding." All students of the sport gradually discover how true this statement is. The more one learns, the more one finds there is to know.

Some may ride for recreation or sport—for such pleasures as trail riding, hacking, showing, and hunting; others pursue the art of riding much further, finding a lifetime of pleasure in their advanced work with the horse. Both categories of horsemanship require the same basic instruction, but the purely recreational rider probably will study only until she feels safe on horseback and is experienced enough to enjoy riding. It is the job of the riding instructor to help her students achieve these goals. The finer points of the art of riding require the guidance of a "master of equitation," but a beginning program that is educationally sound will prepare the student for continuing her instruction with a "master."

This important elementary education should lead the student through logical progressions designed to provide her with the kinesthetic experience that will make her "seasoned" and capable. Besides the hours in the saddle—for which there is no substitute—there should be reading of pertinent riding literature, discussion of theory and performance, and opportunities to see riding films, especially those in slow motion that show clearly the actions of the horse.

This chapter has been designed to help the accomplished horsewoman teach both beginning and more advanced levels of riding skill and to establish a sound background from which pupils can develop their sport into an art. Discussions of facilities, equipment, costume, terminology, and planning the program are included. Sample lesson plans are given for beginning and advanced riding; suggested indoor programs are offered, and extracurricular activities discussed. References on many phases of riding are given. The teacher of equitation should read as many of these as possible.

FACILITIES FOR THE RIDING PROGRAM

The physical arrangements provided for the riding program determine, at least in part, the kind of program that may be offered. Some facilities are essential; others just desirable. These may be listed as follows:

ESSENTIAL FOR RIDING CLASSES

Outdoor Ring

Fence high enough to discourage the horse from jumping out—about five feet.

Good drainage.

Soft, not heavy footing (sand not advisable).

Oval, round, or rectangular shape. The latter is preferred, with the length twice the width.

If ring is extremely large, some means of barricading a smaller area for beginning classes.

Means for harrowing the surface.

Means for laying the dust, either by sprinkling or oiling.

ESSENTIAL FOR JUMPING CLASSES

Portable Jumps

Several sets of standards with rails to be set at varying heights.

Enough rails for a variety of jumps and cavaletti.

DESIRABLE FOR RIDING CLASSES

Trails or Paths

Easily accessible without crossing heavy traffic.

Good footing.

Through woods or fields or both, with a minimum of pavement.

Indoor Ring

Extremely desirable for winter classes.

Good footing. Tanbark is best; otherwise a mixture of washed sand, loam and shavings.

Knee boards that slant toward wall; about 18 inches out at base.

Well lighted and ventilated; enough heat to keep temperature above freezing.

Entrances on two sides; double doors at one end.

DESIRABLE FOR JUMPING AND RIDING

Field

Gives horses a chance to work outside of enclosure but on level ground.

Affords site for dressage arena.

Solid Jumps or Hunt Course

Solid jumps that can be kept in place.

Space for horses to jump and move on.

Possibilities for setting up stadium jumping courses without enclosures.

EQUIPMENT

A riding instructor must know how to care for the horse and his tack, and her students must learn enough basic knowledge to enable them to take care of their own horses.

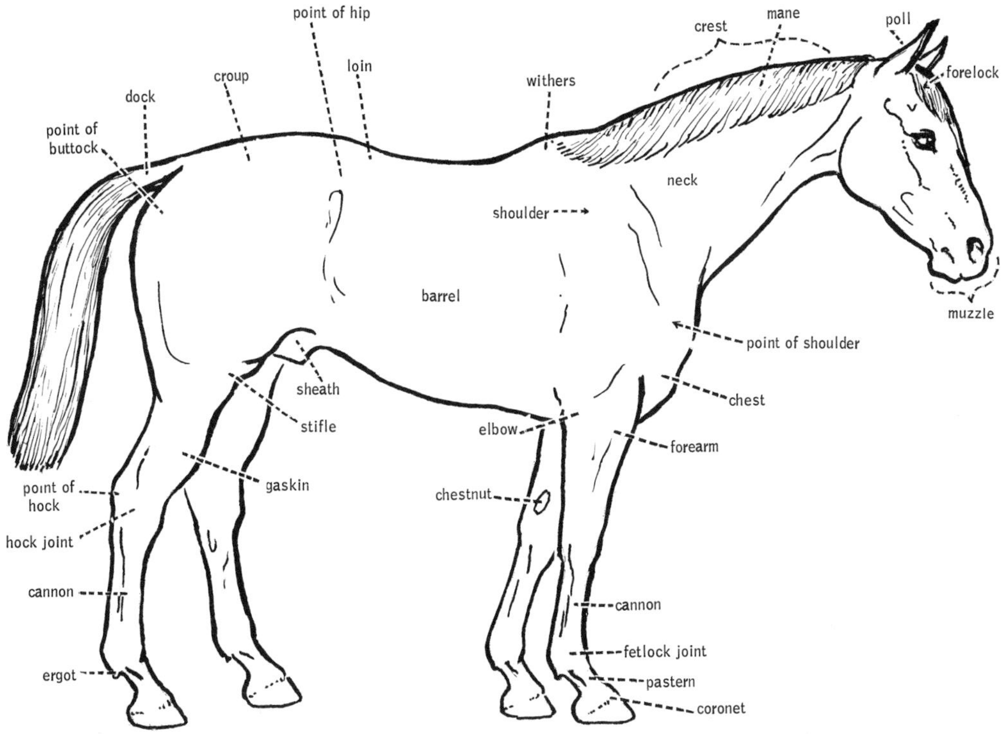

FIGURE 7.1 *Parts of horse.*

I. THE HORSE

A. The Parts of the Horse. The parts of the horse are shown in Figure 7.1. In all discussions of the animal, the instructor should use the appropriate terminology.

B. The Care of the Horse. The health of the horse is the responsibility of the stable manager. The instructor, however, should watch the horses at work and should check their feet, their general condition, and their energy.

1. Grooming. Grooming is necessary to maintain the health of the horse, to keep him clean, and to stimulate circulation of the blood. The tools used in grooming are illustrated in Figure 7.2; their uses are listed below:

Tool	*Use*
Rubber curry comb	to curry horse; remove dirt
Metal curry comb	to clean brushes
Dandy brush	to remove dirt and to lay hairs
Body brush	to remove surface dust; brush mane
Water brush	to clean mane and tail
Sponge	to clean eyes, muzzle, and dock
Hoof pick	to clean hooves
Mane comb	to clean and pull mane
Stable rag	to give final polish
Scraper	to scrape after bath

The proper procedure for grooming is as follows:

a. Select a well lighted place.

b. Collect tools, and cross-tie the horse. Begin all grooming processes at the head and work toward the tail.

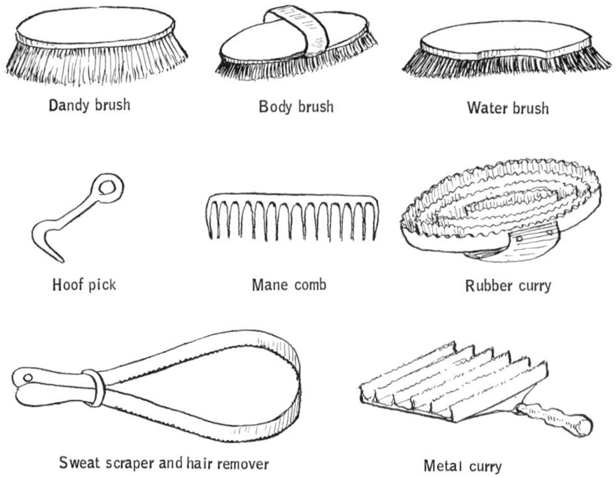

FIGURE 7.2 *Tools for grooming.*

c. Curry the horse, using a circular motion. Begin at the neck; do not curry the face, or the legs below the knee. Keep curry clean.

d. Use dandy brush with short, quick strokes, following grain of hairs. Be especially careful in areas where dirt collects (under girth, between forelegs). Keep brush clean with metal curry.

e. Use body brush. Swift, light strokes are best.

f. Sponge eyes, muzzle, and dock.

g. Brush mane and tail with water brush.

h. Use pick to clean bedding and manure from each hoof. Once a week, clean hooves with water brush and disinfectant.

i. If mane is heavy and long, pluck with mane comb. Do not cut!

j. Use stable rag to give coat its final luster. (Remember that a summer coat will shine much more than a heavy winter coat.)

k. In warm weather, if horse is sweated, wash entire body with warm water and a body brace. Scrape all excess water off, and lead horse until coat is dry.

Every horse should be groomed at least once a day. Regrooming after work is completed is very desirable. If it is not possible to perform a complete regrooming, always check the hooves for stones that may be lodged in the shoes.

2. Feeding and Watering. DAILY SCHEDULE. A definite routine of times for feeding must be followed; promiscuous feeding often causes the horse to lose weight. He should be fed hay and grain at least twice a day; water is given later. In warm weather, water should be given late in the evening, as well as after feeding.

AMOUNTS FED. The amount of food given should be in proportion to the amount of work done. Grain should be increased as work increases. Older horses, because of their poorer digestion, need an extra amount. It is better to give the larger of the two daily feedings in the evening, so that it may be digested overnight. Remember that overfeeding is more dangerous than underfeeding, and that each horse should be fed only enough to keep him in good flesh and energetic. For easy work, give five to eight quarts of grain daily; for heavy work, nine to twelve quarts. About fourteen pounds of hay is enough. If there is no bran in the feed, add a handful; if there is no salt lick, add one teaspoon of salt to the daily diet. The horse should be given as much water as he will drink.

CAUTIONS. Never feed the horse when he is hot. Never water a horse when he is hot, except for a mouthful at a time when he is being led to cool out. Never work a horse sooner than one hour after feeding.

3. Shoeing. The horse must be reshod as soon as the shoes show signs of wearing out or loosening, when the feet overgrow the shoes, or when the feet "forge." Shoes that are not too thin may be reset after the hoof has been trimmed. The average horse needs to be shod every six weeks, some require it every four weeks.

4. Conditioning. Horses that have "let down" while out at pasture should be reconditioned gradually. The time required to restore fitness varies with each horse, but hard work should never be begun suddenly. A horse should be worked at least two weeks to "leg" him up before jumping.

II. THE TACK

The parts of the saddle and bridle are shown in Figures 7.4 through 7.6.

1. Care of the Tack. In some ways, leather is like a living substance, for it has pores that must be allowed to breathe. Cleaning is advisable after each use.

a. Using a minimum amount of water, wash the leather to remove dirt and sweat.

b. Apply a small amount of saddle soap or lexol with a sponge that is almost dry. Go over the entire surface, and wipe off any excess soap.

c. Wash metal parts with water. If the metal is raw or stainless steel (not plated), clean with metal polish or steel wool.

d. If tack is especially dry, oil with neat's-foot oil.

e. Store clean tack on proper racks (Figure 7.3).

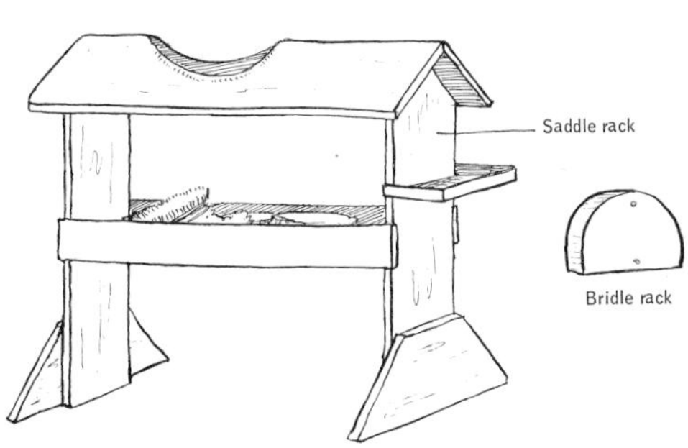

FIGURE 7.3 *Storage rack.*

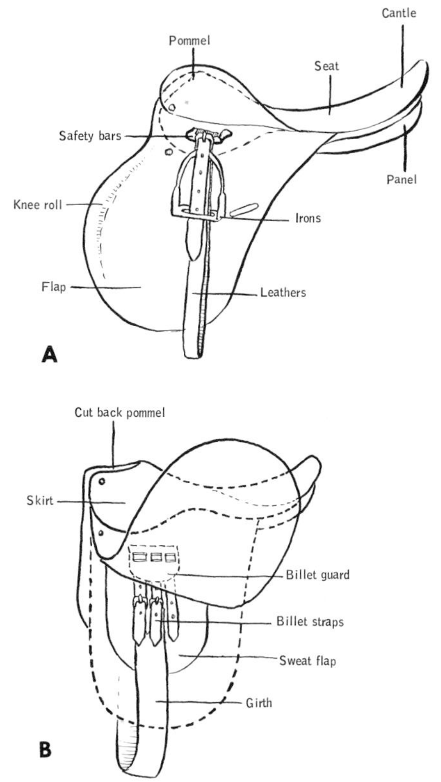

FIGURE 7.4 *A, Forward seat saddle. B, Show saddle (flat).*

f. Check stitching frequently. Repairs should be made promptly, to avoid major work later.

2. Saddles. Figure 7.4 illustrates the two saddles used most frequently in English riding: the forward seat saddle and the show saddle. A western saddle is illustrated in Figure 7.5. The cut of the saddle determines the rider's position, because the buttocks rest in the lowest part of the saddle. A poorly constructed saddle puts the rider's buttocks in the wrong position, making competent riding difficult.

3. Bridles. Three English bridles are shown in Figure 7.6: the snaffle, the pelham, and the full bridle. The choice of bridle for a particular horse depends on his "way of going." The snaffle is the mildest bridle, and the one with which

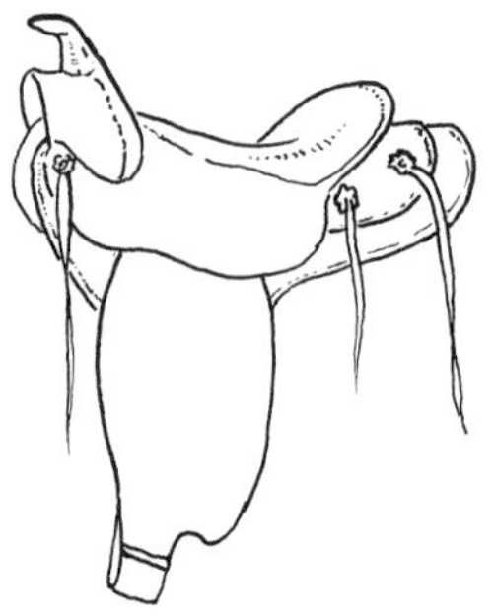

FIGURE 7.5 *Western saddle.*

many horses work well. Some horses, however, respond better to the two-bit actions of the pelham or the full bridle. It is desirable that students have experience with both single and double reins.

4. Martingales. Some horses toss their heads and may go quieter with a martingale. The three varieties are shown in Figure 7.7: standard, running, and Irish. Whenever possible, a horse should be schooled to accept the bit quietly; but in some situations this is impossible, and a mechanical device must be relied on.

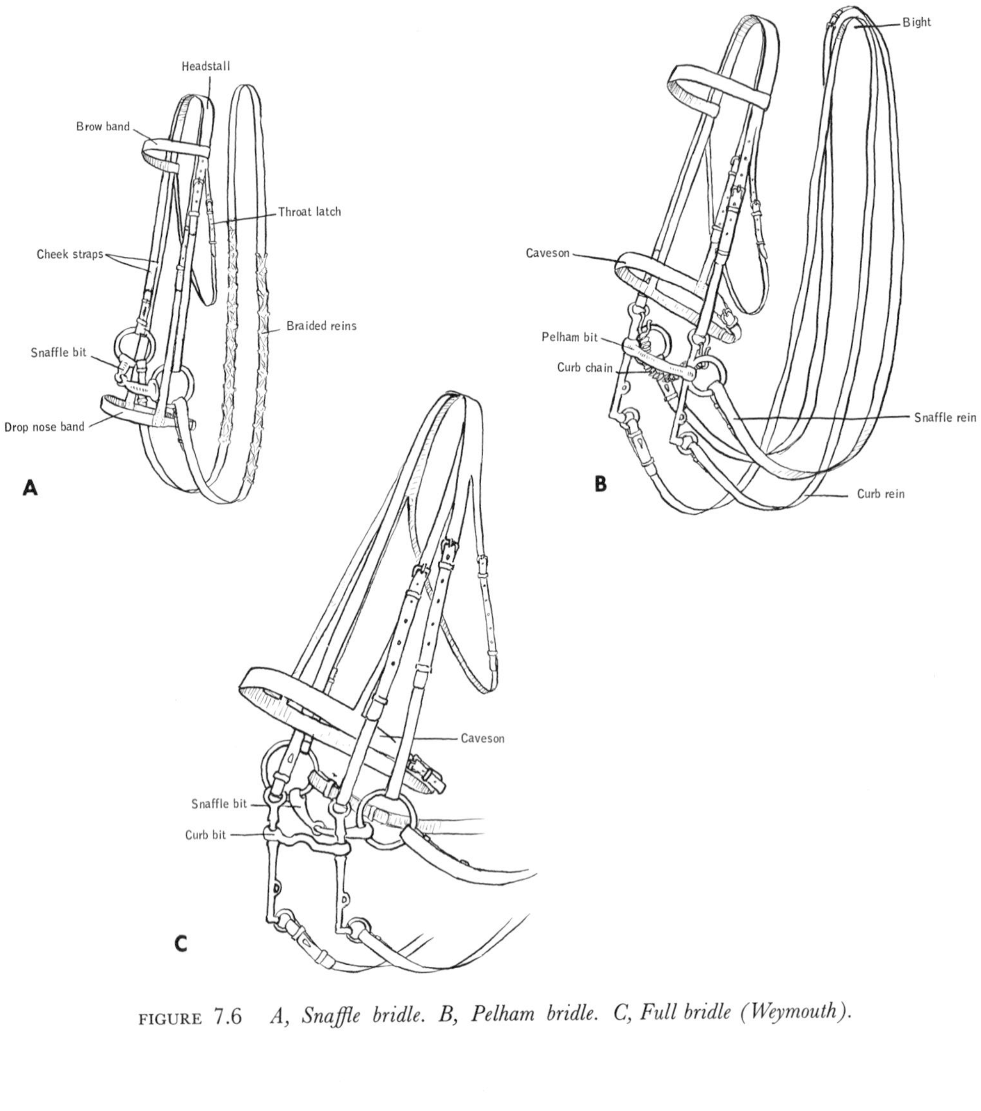

FIGURE 7.6 *A, Snaffle bridle. B, Pelham bridle. C, Full bridle (Weymouth).*

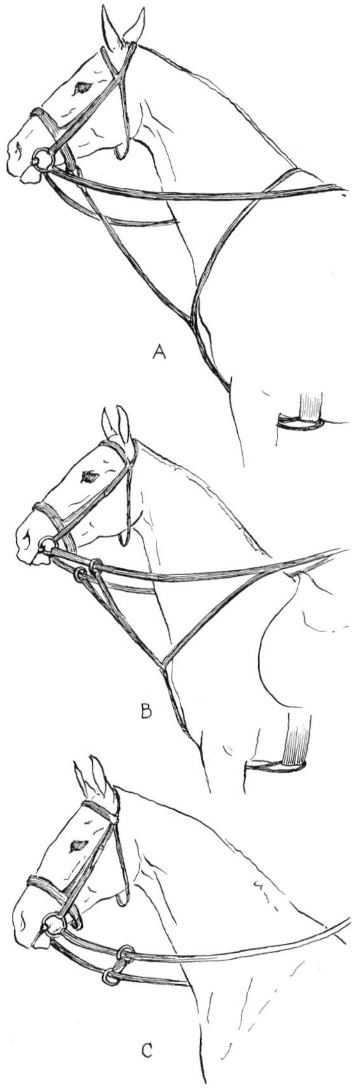

FIGURE 7.7 *A, Standing martingale. B, Running martingale. C, Irish martingale.*

COSTUME

The rider's costume is important too. If she is properly attired, it will be easier for her to maintain a good position, and she will be more comfortable.

1. Boots. High boots protect the rider's feet and legs. If necessary, the leather soles can slip out of the irons. The friction of the leather against the saddle also is desirable. Boots should extend to a point just below the knee and should fit snugly and comfortably. A short, loose boot may get caught on the saddle flap.

2. Breeches. Breeches should be comfortable and snug; if they are cut too low in the crotch, they will push the rider back in the saddle.

3. Jodhpurs. Jodhpurs, if fit well, follow the contours of the lower legs, extending to the ankles. They, too, should

FIGURE 7.8 *Hunt rider.*

FIGURE 7.9 *Saddle rider.*

not hamper movement nor be cut too low in the crotch. If they are loose at the knees, the wrinkles in the cloth may irritate the rider's skin. Jodhpurs are kept in place by straps under the boots.

4. Jodhpur Boots. These boots end just above the ankle, protecting only the feet.

5. Informal Attire. If breeches and boots are too expensive, khaki pants may be worn; but their loose legs afford little protection. The legs are more comfortable if high boots are worn under the pants. The following should be avoided always: slacks, nylon underwear, tennis shoes, crepe-soled shoes.

6. Formal Attire. The hunt rider wears high boots, breeches, stock shirt, stock, vest, jacket, a hard hat or derby (if she is over 18), gloves, and riding appointments (see Figure 7.8). The saddle seat rider wears jodhpur boots, jodhpurs, a long-cut coat, shirt, tie, and a soft derby, as illustrated in Figure 7.9.

7. Jacket. The jacket is designed to give a graceful line of movement. It should fit well, allowing full movement of the shoulders.

8. Hard Hats or Derbies. Hard hats are desirable for all riding, and should be required for jumping. They must be fastened; otherwise they are valueless. Soft hats offer no protection.

9. Gloves. Gloves are necessary in cold weather, but if they are too bulky they inhibit the rider's "feel" with the reins.

RIDING TERMS

Like all sports, riding has its own special language, which must be learned and understood.* In some respects, it is an international language, for riders all over the world use many of the same words and phrases.

Aids. Means by which rider commands and controls horse. *Natural aids:* legs, seat, weight, hands. *Artificial aids:* crop, spur, voice.

Appointments. Special equipment requirements for certain riding events; e.g., hunt whip, breastplate.

Backing. Movement of horse in backward direction with two-beat diagonal motion: right hind and left fore; left hind and right fore.

Balance. State of equilibrium in which body is controlled with minimum of muscular tension. 1. Rider: position that insures ability to adjust to motion of horse. 2. Horse: maintenance of self-carriage and ability to adjust center of gravity to accomplish different movements.

*Terminology given in previous sections is not repeated here.

Balk. Refusal of horse to move.

Base of support. Foundation of rider's position; composed of foot, ankle, and lower leg.

Between legs and hands. Use of legs to drive horse into hand rein contact.

Bore on the bit. Horse leans on bit, taking support from rider's hands.

Brace the back. Muscular contraction to make rider's upper body erect and influence her center of gravity; combined with tilt of pelvis, braced back constitutes weight influence used on horse (Müseler's *Riding Logic*).

Break. Change from one gait to another; initiated by rider or horse.

Buck. Action of horse lowering head and neck and snapping spine in upward direction; action pushes rider upward and away from saddle.

Cadence. Correct mechanical motion of gaits, implying proper rhythm and carriage; e.g., 1, 2, 1, 2 at the trot.

Canter. Three-beat gait, resulting in rocking motion in which one side of horse's body leads. Left lead: right hind; left hind and right fore; left fore. Also, a slow gallop.

Canter—change of lead. Change of lead from one side to the other; e.g., from right lead to left lead.

Canter—cross canter. Incorrect motion of canter; one entire side does not lead; e.g., right in forehand, left in hindquarters.

Cavaletti. Series of level or raised (4″–8″) poles spaced so that horse steps once between each pole. Used as gymnastic exercise for horse. (see Figure 28).

Center of gravity. Point around which a mass in space is in equilibrium.

Circular path. Round path described by horse in bending spine to keep hindquarters in line with forehand.

Close the legs. To establish contact, not grip, between inside upper calf and saddle.

Collection. State in which horse in motion is supple and light; horse is on bit, flexed at poll, and elevated in forehand as result of lowered croup.

Conformation. Build of horse.

Control. Positive influence of rider over motion of horse.

Diagonal (Posting). Rider rises at trot as one diagonal pair of legs moves, and sits in saddle as other pair moves.

Diagonal change of hand. Execution of path diagonally across ring, resulting in change of direction, track, or hand.

Dressage. Any schooling horse receives; advanced schooling given horse. (Extremely advanced movements are termed *haute école.*)

Equitation. Use of horse; combined abilities of position and control needed by rider to perform with horse.

Extension. A state of motion in which horse has long, elastic, even strides, gains ground, but is in less state of collection.

Feel. Sensation received by parts of rider's body in physical contact with horse's body or tack. Ability to sense movement and preparatory motions of horse.

Feel good. Colloquialism used to describe condition of horse after too much food and rest and not enough work.

Flank. Drill term; all horses turn together on a given signal.

Flexion. Suppleness and correct muscular tension of horse. 1. *Direct flexion at poll:* relaxation at poll, resulting in vertical face line, relaxation at jaw, lowering of croup. 2. *Lateral flexion:* ability to bend at ribs and loins, allowing horse to circle efficiently.

Give horse his head. To allow looser rein and less pressure on bit, giving more freedom to horse's head and neck.

Green horse. Unschooled or untrained horse.

Gymnastic exercises. 1. *Rider:* flexibility exercises to make rider limber and supple on horse, e.g., airplane; 2. *Horse:* flexibility exercises to improve suppleness and movement efficiency, e.g., cavaletti.

Hack. To ride for pleasure only; term originated to describe trail or cross country riding.

Halt. To stop horse; when correctly executed, horse should stop on hindquarters, all feet evenly placed and parallel, flexed at poll as result of acceptance of bit, and ready to move in any direction.

Hand. 1. Use of fingers and wrists to control forehand of horse and to establish contact through reins to bit and horse's mouth. 2. Measurement of horse's height. 3. Direction or track on which horse is moving.

Hang. To bore on bit, presenting a dead weight against rider's hands.

Haute école. Very advanced schooling of horse.

Hot horse. Excitable horse, usually thoroughbred, with abundant energy and great sensitiveness.

Hunt. To ride to hounds, chasing fox or other game.

Impulsion. Efficient, energetic thrust that propels horse actively, fluidly, and with suppleness.

Independence of aids. Ability of rider to use each part of her body separately and in coordination to control horse; e.g., to use legs to move horse, without moving buttocks.

In hand. 1. To work horse from ground. 2. To have horse under control and ready to respond.

Inside. When working in ring, the side of horse and rider nearest center of ring. (*Outside* means toward rail.)

Jump. Action of horse in vaulting an obstacle. There are four phases: approach, take-off, suspension, and landing.

Kick. 1. *Horse:* striking out with one or both hind legs at another horse or in resistance to rider's leg. 2. *Rider:* forceful reprimand made by legs to punish horse.

Lameness. Unsound, uneven movement by horse, resulting from injury or illness.

Legs. Rider: a. Lower legs form base of support for rider's position by proper placement against horse. b. Use of inside upper calf to influence horse is referred to as *leg aid.* Pressure is made by tap or squeeze, with intermittent applications timed with movement of horse and applied in varying degrees of intensity, depending on reaction from horse.

Longe. To exercise or school horse in a circular path at end of a long line.

Mechanics. Analyzed motion of each movement and gait.

Mount. 1. To get up on horse. 2. The horse.

Near. Left side of horse. (The *off* side is the right.)

Off the bit. No contact between rider's hands and horse's mouth. 1. Evasion by horse of pressure on bit. 2. Long reins or release of pressure by rider to remove contact.

On the bit. Acceptance of pressure of rider's hands by horse moving forward into bit contact; manifested by relaxation of lower jaw and a soft chewing, resulting in flexion at poll.

Overmount. A horse too difficult for a given rider to handle.

Pace. Horse's speed and rate of movement.

Post. Alternate rising and sitting of rider at the trot; accomplished by allowing body to move in response to thrust from one of horse's hind legs.

Rate. To set horse's speed and length of stride by shortening or lengthening distance of leg movements.

Rear. A vice, usually learned as a defense, in which horse stands on his hind legs, lifting his forehand off ground.

Resistance. 1. Tension or rigidity in any part of body preventing efficient movement. 2. Mental diversions causing lack of concentration.

Ring. Enclosed area for riding.

Ring figures. Manuevers executed by rider and horse, e.g., circles, figure 8, serpentine.

Rhythm. Beat with which horse moves in each gait; e.g., steady 1, 2, 1, 2, at the trot.

School. 1. Horses rented for riding education. 2. To educate a horse. 3. The ring.

Seat. 1. Style of riding: as, forward seat, stock seat. 2. The rider's pelvis, buttocks, and thighs, which make up her contact with saddle.

Self-carriage. Ability of horse to balance properly without support from rider's hands.

Shy. To move suddenly because of fright.

Squeeze. Use of legs to increase pressure against horse.

Stale. Horse that has become "sick" of routine.

Start the horse. To move horse from stationary position.

Straight line. Movement by horse resulting in only two sets of hoof prints, e.g., left hind leg in line with left foreleg.

Stride. Distance from one hoof print to the next.

String. Group of horses owned by one person.

Suppleness. Correct flexibility and lack of stiffness and resistance in movements of both horse and rider.

Tact. Quality of gentleness and empathy between rider and horse.

Take. To increase amount of pressure on reins, thereby restraining horse.

Tandem. Control of two horses by one rider; the front (lead) horse is driven, the back (wheel) horse ridden.

Tilt the pelvis. To move or rotate pelvis on the hips and spine in order to place weight more toward front or rear of saddle. To *decrease* the pelvis means to rotate so that end of spine comes closer to saddle (backward); to *increase* means to rotate so that weight comes more over the crotch (forward).

Trot. Two-beat diagonal action of horse that is very balanced, e.g., left fore and right hind, then right fore and left hind.

Turn. 1. Change of direction in motion, e.g., circle. 2. Change of direction around a stationary part, e.g., on the forehand.

Undermount. A horse too easy for a given rider to control.

Unsound. Abnormal, lame, or uneven movement or physique. An unsound horse should not be ridden if motion inflicts pain.

Volte. Circle of designated width, performed at walk, trot, and canter.

Walk. Four-beat gait in which horse moves left hind, right fore, right hind, left fore; therefore, sequence is first diagonal, then lateral.

Way of going. Manner in which horse moves at all gaits.

Wheel. In drill, to move in a group abreast around circular path.

PLANNING THE CLASSES

A. Riding Program. The riding program arranged by a camp, school, or club depends on the abilities of the students, the horses, and the teacher. For example, riders with a lower level of skill need to be taught fundamentals and should not attempt competition. Advanced riders need to be challenged and tested. The level of ability of the horses is also extremely important, and to teach even the fundamentals on horses not schooled to the aids is very difficult. Advanced work is impossible without sufficiently schooled horses. Finally, an instructor can teach only subject matter that is familiar to her. She should not attempt to teach material over which she has no command.

B. Class Size. The smaller the class, the more individual attention may be given to each pupil, and less confusion and fewer control problems occur. Horses must have room to move safely, and it must be possible to observe the riders. Beginning classes should never exceed six pupils, unless the instructor has adequate assistance. Intermediate classes are taught most easily if there are no more than ten in the group; any number over 14 should be restricted to the advanced level, where all students have control over their horses.

It is beneficial for pupils to ride at least twice a week, but, of course, every day is still better. The average lesson lasts 50 to 60 minutes, but should be shorter for adult beginners or for very young children.

C. Ability Groups. It is desirable to have the students divided into classes according to their levels of skill. Preferably these should be beginning, low intermediate, intermediate, high intermediate, and advanced. When only four or five horses are available, however, some will be too excitable for beginners and intermediates; and, in order to keep all the horses working, an advanced rider may have to be scheduled with the less experienced students. This rider should not always be the same person, or her chance to work at her own level of ability will be sacrificed. The rate of progress is a very individual matter; some move ahead rather rapidly, while others take a long time even to learn the proper position. In a class situation the needs of the group at large must be met, with as much individual attention as possible given to each pupil.

D. Mounts. The horses themselves are very important considerations, for something different is learned from each mount. Students, as they progress, should be exposed to the variety of problems presented by horses, e.g., reluctance to move, over-energetic movement, or playfulness. Usually each string includes some very honest animals on which the instructor would like to mount every beginner. Since this is not possible, one student should be mounted on the desirable horse one day; and a different student, the next day. Careful selection of mounts is essential, and the student's progress will be hastened if her special problems and the horse's merits are appropriately matched.

E. Variety of Experiences. Ring riding is the core of riding education. Instruction may be given the entire time, because the teacher can watch the students continually. Some trail work should be included however, for a horse's way of going is very different in a ring and in an open area. Cross country control is a necessary part of the rider's education.

As in all sports, more variety may be offered on the advanced level. Once competent to handle the horse, students may pursue other phases of riding, such as jumping, dressage, hunting, and showing. The instructor is challenged to keep the intermediate group interested until they have the ability to take part in the more exciting aspects of riding. Ideas for all levels of competition are given on page 231. This extracurricular program must meet the special needs of its participants.

F. Conduct of Class. Unlike teachers of other sports, the riding instructor must consider the "wills" and ideas of horses, which vary from day to day and from rider to rider. Many times the reactions of the mounts will cause changes in lesson plans. Flexibility is essential.

1. Preliminary Considerations. Three basic conditions determine the conduct of the class.

a. Condition of Mounts. If horses are "feeling good," they must be worked down before any instruction can be given. This may take one or more class periods. If, on the other hand, the horses are tired, their work should be slower and easier, with a minimum amount of movement at faster gaits.

b. Temperature. In hot weather, horses become heated easily, and therefore should not work for long periods at faster gaits. In cold weather, the reverse is true, and they can work longer without becoming warm.

c. Allotted Time. Most classes must be finished at a certain time, and the horses must be cool at that time; therefore, instruction and riding at fast gaits must stop early enough to allow the horses to cool out. Theoretical instruction or slow work may continue until the class is dismissed.

2. Warm Up. This is standard procedure for any sports class, and the horses, like the students, need to be "readied" for concentration and work.

a. Advanced students know how to warm horses up. Intermediates should be guided during warm up, so that no student's safety is jeopardized. Beginners need no warm up period.

b. The amount of warm up is decided by how good the horses feel, whether they have been worked previously that day, and what material is to be given in the lesson.

c. If the lesson is to be at the trot, not much warm up is necessary. If the lesson work is at the canter, more warm up is necessary when the horses are "feeling good"; not much is required if they are relaxed at the start. If they are especially tired, the lesson should be changed to slower, easier work.

3. Review. Although the very nature of riding implies continued review—the elements of position and control are the basis of everything—the lessons should emphasize review of the material given in the immediately previous lesson.

a. The review may be incorporated in the warm up, if the material is at all applicable.

b. If this is impossible, a brief review always should be given before new material is presented.

4. Formation for Explanations. All students must be in a position to hear explanations, and the horses must be kept in hand to prevent accidents.

a. If the explanation is at all long and involved, have the riders line up or group together and halt. Keep kickers apart from the rest of the group, and separate all horses by a safe distance.

b. Vary the place in the ring where horses line up. They tend to become very spot conscious, and like to be able to stand still while people talk, especially in the middle of the ring.

c. If the explanation is brief, the students may continue to ride in a small circle around the instructor.

d. If the weather is windy, the students should be halted downwind so that the wind is at the instructor's back.

e. If the sun is low, have the rider's turn their backs to the sun so that they may see the demonstrations.

5. Presentation. Techniques must be presented in a lucid, accurate manner and in sufficient detail, appropriate to the level of skill of the pupils.

a. Beginning riders need only the simplest explanations, with very little detail and analysis. Intermediate pupils can absorb more detailed explanations—advanced students even more. So much is involved in the subtleties of advanced skill that riders at lower levels become confused if presented with theory before they have had any chance for the appropriate kinesthetic experiences.

b. Arrange a good demonstration, either by the instructor or a competent pupil. This is essential with beginners and intermediates, and desirable with advanced pupils.

c. Repetition of techniques is necessary at each level, but, as students progress, the presentation should become more technical and the expected performance more accurate. The position for basic riding does not change, but constant reminders are essential. The factors of control vary a great deal, becoming much more demanding at higher skill levels.

6. Clarification. To be absorbed, material must be presented clearly.

a. Be sure there is an opportunity for students to ask questions.

b. If questions are not forthcoming, ask some, to be certain that the material has been understood.

c. Questions on review material as well as on new material give the instructor an indication of how well the work has been retained.

7. Formation for Practice. To improve, students must have adequate opportunities to practice their skills.

a. On the beginning and intermediate levels, individual practice can be very difficult. Therefore, have group practice of the walk and trot, so that no horses are standing still. The canter, however, is practiced most easily by a few at a time, or singly.

b. Formations for a few to practice at a time may be set up in either of two ways: the performers on the rail, with the rest of the class walking inside in the opposite direction; the performers inside, with the others walking outside on the opposite hand. In this manner no horses are motionless, and herdbound tendencies are avoided.

c. Some horses work well going from the front to the rear of the line, but many tend to rush when they sight the others. The instructor must know how the horses respond to this formation before trying it with beginning riders.

d. Advanced classes may utilize a stationary group formation with the performer moving away from the group. With some horses this type of performance is extremely difficult; with others, not so hard. When it is attempted and found not to be successful, the instructor should get on the horse and do the figure successfully; otherwise, the horse becomes more difficult the next time. If it is inadvisable to dismount the pupil at that moment, the schooling should take place immediately after class.

e. An equal amount of work must be done in both directions; this way, the riders and horses do not become "one-sided."

8. Corrections and Admonitions. The teacher must offer suggestions and corrections regularly if the experience is to be educational.

a. For all practices and movements give a preparatory command that allows the students to "ready" the horse.

b. When practice is first begun, take a look at the group as a whole and give general corrections that apply to the majority; then give individual corrections and suggestions.

c. Correct in a positive way: "Keep your leg back," rather than, "don't let your leg slip forward."

d. Try to help the students understand what the horse may tell them about errors; e.g., if he tosses his head, the rider's hands are heavy; if he switches his tail, the rider's legs are swinging.

9. Giving Assistance. Help from the instructor in controlling the horse is essential to beginners and to low intermediates. On all levels, students need assistance from the teacher to make the experience a positive one.

a. At the beginning of the class

give crops to the riders who need them.

b. In classes of beginning and low intermediate riders use your voice as a teaching aid; e.g., a sharp command to move at a trot, a quiet soothing one for a walk.

c. Horses that are compatible can work together in a small group. Some will only follow, and need a good leader; others get excited in company and work easier alone or in the lead.

d. If a horse has a favorite canter direction, send the intermediate riders out to canter on the easy lead; have the advanced riders work the horse on the difficult lead. In this way, the horse is not allowed to refuse to take a lead he may not want.

10. Safety. Safety must be a primary consideration. The conduct of any class must follow safe, common sense rules.

a. Avoid taking risks. If there is any doubt about the safety of a procedure, do not attempt it. Follow the hunch, for it is usually there for a reason. Do not be overcautious, however, or the pupils will never become confident.

b. When falls occur—and they will—stay calm, or your pupils may develop a fear of falling. *Be sure* that the student is not hurt before you remount her. If it is at all possible, put the rider up again, even if only for a short time. Not riding immediately after a fall often leads to fear.

c. Know first aid, and its principles when a serious accident occurs. Teach your riders the basic principles of first aid: they will not always be under your wing.

11. Cool Out. The well-being of the horse is at all times a critical consideration. Proper cooling out should be as great a concern to the pupils as to the teacher.

In extremely warm weather, have the pupils dismount, loosen the girths, and walk the horses in hand. This helps them cool faster. If the horse's back is wet and the wind is at all brisk, leave the saddle on with the girth loose. If the weather is really pleasant, remove the saddle and sponge the horse before leading him.

SUGGESTED LESSON PROGRAMS

This section presents a series of suggested lesson programs in outline form. The programs cover eight weeks of outdoor instruction at the rate of two lessons a week. The lesson plan for each level of group ability is presented first in brief form and then in expanded form.

I. BEGINNING CLASS

A. First Week

Acquaint the pupils with the horse.
Teach the preliminaries to riding.
Present the basic riding position.
Stop the horse; start the horse.
Keep the horse walking on.
Turn right and turn left.
Sit a slow trot.
Exercises.

B. Second Week

Review all of the first week, giving less assistance.
Sit the trot, with and without the irons.
Practice picking up and dropping the irons.
Practice self-check on position; emphasis on base of support (legs).

C. Third Week

Review the second week.
Emphasize keeping the horse at a good walk and keeping position in line.
Present posting.
Practice posting.

D. Fourth Week

Practice walk, sitting trot, posting trot.
Explain more about aids to control a horse; introduce the use of the buttocks as an aid; bracing the back.
Circle at the walk.

E. Fifth Week

Explain the mechanics of the trot; posting on diagonals.
Exercise: scissors.
Practice moving from sitting trot to posting and back to sitting.

F. Sixth Week

Review fifth week as warm up exercise.
Explain more about hands as an aid.
Circle at the slow sitting trot.
Emphasize ring etiquette.

G. Seventh Week

Ride on trail to experience longer, steady trot. (Requires enough capable assistants to help the beginners and keep the riders safe. Do not go through heavy woods.)

H. Eighth Week

Review all previous lessons.
Check on each rider's position.
Introduce canter on quiet, steady horse to pupils ready for that gait—no analysis, just the motion experience.

II. BEGINNING CLASS: DETAILED OUTLINE

A. First Week

1. Acquaint Pupils with the Horse.

a. Instruction.

1. Characteristics:
Basically timid.
Gregarious with other horses.
Amenable to gentle handling.
Easily startled.
Patient and good natured.
Response similar to that of pet dog: respects and responds well to discipline correctly administered.
Senses apprehension in people.

2. Strength:
Strong enough to carry people easily.
Stronger than rider, so rider out-finesses rather than pitting strength against strength. If he pulls his head down to eat grass, the rider pulls up on one rein rather than both—thus turning and lifting his head.
The mouth is tender but cannot be hurt by the beginner's "take" on the reins.

3. Appeal:
No two horses are alike.
Rewarding response to calmness, patience, and tact.

b. Presentation.

Bring the horse out of the barn, and let the riders look at him while you explain the animal's traits and characteristics.
Move around the animal, showing that he is used to being handled and is not afraid of people.
Have students feel his coat and stroke his neck.

c. Cautions.

Do not let the riders move suddenly.
Use a horse that is quiet and patient.
Do not let students walk behind the hind legs, but always in front of the horse.
Some horses are fed from the hands frequently, which makes them nippy.

2. Preliminaries to Riding. There are several basic procedures that the rider must learn in order to handle the horse and to get ready to ride. These are routine for the horse and must be done in a manner consonant with the animal's comfort and the rider's safety. All of these should be demonstrated by the instructor.

To approach and lead the horse.

a. Instruction for approaching.

Talk to the horse, warning him of your approach.
Place your right hand on his rump, and say "get over."
Walk straight to his head.

b. Instruction for leading.

Lead from the horse's left.
Hold the reins in the right hand, about four inches from the bit, keeping the elbow straight to maintain sufficient distance from the horse's feet.
Look straight ahead, not back at the horse.
If the horse does not follow, turn his head slightly to one side and he will be forced to move.
To stop, "take" slightly on the rein and say "halt."

c. Cautions.

Contact on the rein should be comfortable, not a vise-like grip.

Have the rider lead the horse around a bit so that they will get better acquainted before mounting.

To adjust tack and estimate length of stirrup.

a. Instruction.

Adjust (tighten the girth).

Slip left arm through reins to hold horse.

Tighten the girth by raising the buckle on the billet straps. No more than three fingers should fit between girth and horse.

Stirrup length.

Keep left arm through reins and face the saddle.

Take the iron in the left hand and place the fingers of the right hand on the stirrup bar; step back, extending the right arm.

The iron should fit under the right arm pit. If too short, the leather should be lengthened; if extremely long, shortened.

Make the same adjustment of the right stirrup.

b. Cautions.

Contact must be kept with the reins while the adjustments are made.

Some horses resent the tightening of the girth and try to "blow up" to prevent it. If the rider starts to tighten, then pauses, and then tightens again, tightening may be easier.

Girths are never made extremely tight in the barn, and therefore must be adjusted before mounting. Setting an approximately correct length of stirrup makes mounting easier; also, less adjustment is necessary after mounting.

To mount the horse.

a. Instruction.

Stand on the left side, close to the horse, facing the hindquarters.

Pick up the reins in the left hand (see Figure 7.13, page 208), then place the hand on the horse's withers.

Keep the reins short enough to prevent the horse from moving forward.

Hold the stirrup iron in the right hand and place the left foot in it, pushing the toe down. (See Figure 7.10.)

Place the left knee as close to the saddle as possible.

Move the right hand to the cantle of the saddle.

Spring from the right foot, extending the left knee.

Straighten the elbows as soon as possible so that the body weight is supported over the left leg and both arms.

Move the right hand to the pommel of the saddle, and swing the right leg with the knee straight over the back of the horse, not touching his body.

Gently lower the weight into the saddle.

b. Cautions.

If the rider jabs the horse with her left toe while mounting, have her place the left toe against the girth.

Be sure that the rider stands as close as possible to the horse when starting.

The elbows must straighten as the body rises; otherwise the upper body collapses over the horse.

The right knee must not bend as it is swung over the horse's back, or the rider's leg will kick the horse.

The entire process must not be hurried, and the rider's weight must be controlled throughout.

To readjust stirrup when mounted.

a. Instruction.

Remove both feet from the stirrup irons and relax the legs, letting them hang easily.

Feel the irons against the legs; they should hit just above the rider's ankle.

Put the feet back into the irons. If adjust-

FIGURE 7.10 *Mounting horse.*

ment is necessary, leave them in the irons, but take the weight off the left iron. Turn the knee out from the saddle enough to permit opening the buckle below the bar.

If the stirrup is long, pull up on the end of the leather until the desired position is reached.

Replace the tongue in the proper hole.

If the stirrup is short, push down with the foot until the correct length is reached; replace the tongue (see Figure 7.11).

Pull down on the underside of the leather to move the buckle against the bar and under the saddle skirt.

Repeat the process with the right stirrup.

b. Cautions.

The reins must be held while the adjustment is accomplished.

Caution the rider to sit evenly in the saddle when checking the length of the stirrups.

Be sure that the feet are returned to the irons when making adjustments.

At first beginners with heavy thighs may have difficulty getting their knees out enough to remove the tongue of the buckle, and may have to make the adjustment with their feet out of the stirrups.

After the adjustments are made, have the pupils drop the irons again. Recheck the length.

To readjust girth when mounted.

a. Instruction.

Place the reins in the right hand.

FIGURE 7.11 *Adjusting stirrup.*

FIGURE 7.12 *Tightening girth.*

Keeping the left foot in the iron, lift the left leg over the front of the saddle.

Take the saddle flap in the right hand.

Place the left hand, fingers pointing down, over the billet strap, and pull upward (see Figure 7.12). Replace tongue.

Tighten all straps evenly.

Replace saddle flap and leg.

b. Cautions.

Explain that by keeping the left foot in the stirrup, the iron is out of the way and also the rider is able to return quickly to the normal position should the horse move suddenly.

The saddle flap must be placed in the right hand, not just tucked under the left leg.

If the left hand grasps the billet strap from underneath instead of from the top, the tongue cannot be replaced.

If the horse still resists tightening of the girth, the rider should walk a bit and try again.

To hold and adjust the reins.

a. Instruction for single rein.

Take the bight of the reins in the right hand and lift up, straightening the reins.

Place the left hand, thumb pointing toward the body, over the top of the reins and grasp both reins with the little finger between them (see Figure 7.13).

Release the right hand grip, and place that hand on the right rein opposite the left hand.

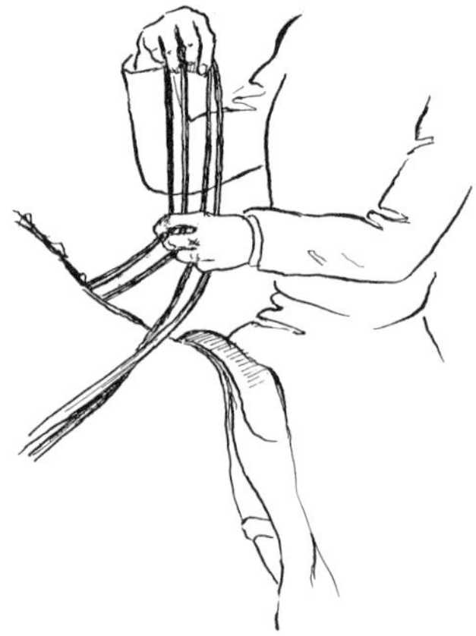

FIGURE 7.13 *Picking up reins.*

Put both thumbs on top of the reins to prevent changing the length of rein.

b. Instruction for double rein.

The process is the same, except that additional separation of the reins is necessary. The snaffle is placed outside the little finger, and the curb is placed inside the little finger. (The beginner is not expected to use double reins in the first few lessons).

c. Instruction for shortening and lengthening reins.

To shorten the reins, place the right thumb and index finger over the left rein above the left hand; then, releasing the tension of the left hand grip, slide the hand toward the horse's mouth.

Remove the right hand grip on the left rein.

Repeat the process, in reverse, to shorten the right rein.

To lengthen the reins, release the tension of the finger grip and bring the hands closer to your body.

d. Cautions.

If the beginner's horse has double reins, tie up the curb so that the beginner holds only one.

At first, beginners find it awkward to come over the top of the rein and try to pick it up from underneath. *On top* must be emphasized.

To dismount.

a. Instruction.

The process is the reverse of mounting.

Take the reins in the left hand, and place the hand on the withers of the horse.

Rise in the stirrups, and remove the right foot from the iron; swing the leg over the back of the horse, and move the right hand to the cantle of the saddle.

Support the body weight over the arms and thighs, and remove the left foot from the iron.

Drop gently to the ground, keeping the right side of the body close to the horse.

Walk forward immediately, and take the position described to lead the horse.

b. Cautions.

Keep contact with the hands while descending so that the body does not fall backward.

Emphasize "giving" in the ankles when landing.

To prepare the horse to return to stall.

a. Instruction.

Slip the left arm through the reins.

Grasp the center of the leather with the left hand, and slide the iron up the *underside* of the leather with the right hand.

When the iron is at the stirrup bar, put the leather through the iron.

Repeat the same process for the right stirrup.

Loosen the girth two notches.

b. Cautions.

The horse should never be led with the stirrups hanging. They might frighten the horse by banging against him, or they may get caught on the barn door.

3. Basic Position on the Horse. The form or position of the rider is merely a means to an end, not an end in itself, and is designed to promote efficiency and suppleness in movement. A good position makes efficient control possible. The position described here may be termed a balance or modified forward seat or style. This position is maintained without forceful grip, but by a combination of muscular control and balance. The rider's center of gravity is placed over the horse's center of gravity (see Figure 7.14).

a. Instruction.

The rider's *heels* are low, which gives the sensation of weight in the heel, not on the ball of the foot.

The *inside borders of the feet* are slightly lower than the outside, which brings the upper part of the lower legs against the saddle.

FIGURE 7.14 *Centers of gravity.*

The stirrup irons are under *the balls of the feet.*

The *feet* are almost straight ahead with the toes turned out only very slightly.

The *ankles* are relaxed.

The *lower part* of the *lower legs* is away from the horse's sides.

The inside of the *calves* is against the saddle.

The inside of the *knees* is against the saddle.

The stirrup leathers hang vertically, and the rider's heels are in line with the hips.

The inside of the *thighs* is against the saddle.

The *pelvis* rests in the deepest part of the saddle with three points of contact, two bones (ischial tuberosities) and the crotch (pubis).

The *angle* of the hips and knees is determined by the length of the stirrups. (See Figure 7.15.)

The *upper body* is held erect, but not stiff.

The *chest* and *head* are carried high, and the eyes are focused straight forward, not down.

The *upper arms* are carried close to, but not tight against, the body. The shoulders, elbows, wrists, and fingers are supple.

The *elbow* is kept at an angle of about 90 degrees.

The reins are held with the *thumb* on top and the *knuckles* facing one another, *palms* facing the body, and *wrists* slightly rounded.

The *overall appearance* is one of ease and suppleness.

FIGURE 7.15 *Short and long stirrups.*

b. Presentation.

Demonstrate while explaining each placement.

Stress the point that the rider's position resembles the construction of a building: the leg position is the foundation. If the foundation is out of line, the entire building collapses. (Demonstrate the difficulties of sitting both with legs too far forward and too far backward.)

Demonstrate the ease of rising in the stirrup irons when the base of support is placed correctly. (This is the self-check for leg position.) If the foundation is placed properly, the rider is balanced and need not hold on nor pull herself up with the reins.

c. Cautions.

Attainment of a correct position even with the horse stationary is difficult at first.

Any of the following body characteristics makes the task more difficult for the beginner:

Tight Achilles tendon—difficult to lower the heel.

Round thigh musculature—difficult to place knees against the saddle.

Generally poor posture—no kinesthetic sense of easy, light carriage.

Tenseness and rigidity—no sense of relaxed, controlled body movement.

4. Stopping and Starting the Horse. The rider next learns to maintain the proper position in motion. To allay any beginner's misgivings, she should be taught first how to stop, then how to start the horse.

To stop the horse.

a. Instruction.

This is the introduction to the use of aids in controlling the horse.

To stop the horse, the rider presses, very slightly with the top of the inside upper calf; then "takes" on the reins or increases the pressure on the bit by bending the wrists toward the body and raising the hands slightly.

This "take" is followed immediately by a return to normal, or "give."

The process is repeated until the horse responds by stopping.

The rider's seat stays in the same place in the saddle throughout.

b. Presentation.

Demonstrate stopping the horse by increased rein pressure. Reemphasize that the student won't hurt the horse by "taking" on the reins.

Explain that the gentle squeeze of the legs makes the horse understand that something is about to happen.

c. Cautions.

The squeeze of the legs is most difficult to teach the beginner, for it is a gentle movement, not a kick or a continual squeeze. If the rider raises her heels and digs them into the horse's sides, he won't stop, but will keep on going to escape the pressure.

The hands must "take" and "give." Look for white knuckles or stiff wrists that show tension in the hands. Such a hand cannot "give."

To start the horse.

a. Instruction.

Press with the legs and release enough tension on the reins to permit the horse to move forward.

If he doesn't move with a squeeze of the legs, tap with the calf and repeat until the horse responds.

Keep the seat and upper body in position.

If the horse seems "planted like a tree," turn his head to one side and repeat the aids, thereby altering his balance and forcing him to respond.

b. Presentation.

Demonstrate while explaining, exaggerating the aids the beginner will have to use.

Explain that the horse has been taught what these signals mean.

c. Cautions.

Some pupils will not want to use leg pressure for fear of hurting the horse. Assure them that he will not be hurt and that he needs pressure to understand their desires.

Beginning students must "give" more than they will as they become more experienced, to have the horse understand that forward motion is desired.

Some students lean forward when they wish the horse to move forward. This anticipation merely confuses the horse, and many times he will back up instead.

5. Keeping the Horse in Motion.

a. Instruction.

All movement must be encouraged continually by the rider; the horse is not like a machine that slips into gear and remains there. Repeated aids are necessary to keep him moving forward.

Light contact is kept on the reins, holding the horse's head straight in front of his body.

b. Presentation.

Demonstrate that stronger leg aids will be necessary to make some horses walk on; others require only light pressures.

c. Cautions.

The first coordination the beginner must learn is to use the lower leg while keeping the upper leg and the seat quiet. If the rider wiggles while the leg is used, the horse is confused.

The beginners' aids will be more exaggerated than will be necessary later on.

6. Turning the Horse to Right or Left.

a. Instruction.

The horse is *led* into a turn, *not pulled.* To turn right, the head of the horse is started to the right by increased pressure on the right rein (bringing the right wrist slightly up and toward the body), and enough "give" on the left rein to permit the head to turn right.

Simultaneously, the rider moves her left leg about one inch further back from the normal position. This encourages the horse to move his body to the right.

The amount of turn of the head and neck indicates the sharpness of the movement; e.g., a sharp turn is indicated by stronger rein, a slow gradual turn by slight pressure on the rein.

b. Presentation.

Demonstrate both the gradual turn and the sharp turn.

An analogy may be made with turning a bicycle so that the students realize that balance is involved in *riding* the horse in a turn—not *driving* him into a turn, as one would a car.

The use of the legs in the turn is very important, and later on much more emphasis will be placed on use of legs.

c. Cautions.

The increased rein pressure must not stop the forward motion, but should merely *lead* the horse in the desired direction. The legs assist in making this clear to the horse.

The correct leg position must be maintained because the leg works as an aid.

At this point the instructor should have each pupil get her own horse and attempt to perform the material that has been explained and demonstrated. This can probably take place at the second lesson of the week. If the steps have been explained carefully and slowly, there will be faster progress later on.

7. Sitting at Slow Trot. When the pupils have achieved a rudimentary idea of the preliminary exercises, the sensation of movement at the slow trot is introduced.

a. Instruction.

In preparation for the trot, the reins are shortened a little. The horse lifts his head slightly when trotting.

The rider's legs push harder and continue to act until the horse moves into the slow trot.

The rider endeavors to sit relaxed, absorbing the movement of the horse. The basic position is maintained throughout.

If the horse has a very strong trot, even at a slow speed, the beginner may have to move her upper body slightly to the rear to avoid bumping.

b. Presentation.

The instructor should demonstrate both how the relaxed body will absorb action and how the tense body will bump.

Then, with a carefully selected horse leading, all of the line should be pushed into the slow trot or jog.

If the beginners can be kept on a lead line (an assistant mounted beside each one), progress may be faster for the first few lessons.

In most situations the beginners will be alone, however, and an experienced rider should lead the line, keeping the pace slow and steady.

c. Cautions.

Any body stiffness makes sitting to the trot impossible. If the rider even tightens her knees, the buttocks become tense, and the situation is similar to attempting to sit on tennis balls!

Right at the beginning, it must be emphasized that a correct position should be held during the increased motion. If the rider pulls her heels up, the base of support is destroyed.

The legs are not used to hold the rider on the horse. The position is maintained by balance and by a minimum of muscular control—not grip.

8. Exercises on Horseback.

a. Instruction.

Rise in irons. The rider rises in the stirrups not by pulling herself forward on the reins, but by balancing over the base of support. Then she sits slowly, keeping her legs in the same position. Both the rising and sitting must be controlled movements.

Rise on knees. The rider drops stirrups and reins and brings her knees together at the front of the pommel. Then with a swing of the arms, she kneels. The hips must be brought forward over the knees, the focus of the eyes held out, not down. Then return to the saddle with control.

Drop and pick up stirrups. Without looking down at the feet, take the weight off the stirrups and remove the feet from the irons. To pick up the irons, bring the toes up and in toward the horse. Then feel for the irons and replace the feet in the stirrups. This should be practiced a great deal; first, with both stirrups at the same time, then one and the other, then at all gaits.

Lying down backwards. Let the reins slide through the fingers; then, keeping the correct leg position with the heels down, lean backward and let the head rest on the back of the horse. This stretches the thigh muscles if the rider keeps her heels down. If the heels come up there is no stretch. Then swing the trunk up, back to the erect position. Add this exercise to the rise in the irons. This entire sequence should be completed with *no change* in the leg position.

Airplane. Drop the reins, extend the arms at shoulder height. Twist the upper body and swing down, touching the right hand to the left toe. Keep the left arm extended. Then swing back to the erect position and reverse the motion. Repeat several times. Again, the legs must not move.

b. Presentation.

Exercises serve a twofold purpose: to limber the rider and to convince her that the horse will let her move about without becoming frightened.

The group should be lined up with a careful distance between the horses. Be especially careful with horses that kick.

When the students are to do exercises without reins (like the airplane), the horse should be held by an assistant.

Demonstrate and explain each exercise; then practice.

c. Cautions.

As with any exercise, the important factor is *how* it is done, not just that it *is* done. Each exercise should be practiced with mechanical correctness and with body control. Half-hearted, sloppy attempts are worthless.

The *leg position* must be maintained in all practices.

Adults learn these exercises more slowly than small children, and therefore need more patience and encouragement from the instructor.

B. Second Week

1. Self-check on Position. (See presentation of basic position.)

C. Third Week

1. Keeping Position in Line. It is essential, as soon as the beginner has some idea about controlling the horse, that she assume the responsibility for some safety factors.

a. Instruction.

A body-length distance of one horse must be kept between one horse and another at all times.

If horses are allowed to get too close, there is a chance of a fight. Conversely, if too great a distance is allowed, many horses will suddenly realize the gap and decide to catch up rapidly.

b. Presentation.

The instructor has been assuming responsibility for this precaution by telling students when to hold back and when to close up. Now the student should be told to watch this at all times and try to keep the proper distance.

c. Emphasis.

This is a safety factor for both riders and horses.

2. Posting. Posting makes a faster trot easier for both horse and rider. The rider's alternate rise and return to the saddle gives the horse's back a chance to relax, and the rider has less motion to absorb. It is a rhythmical, easy movement in which the horse establishes the cadence and lifts the rider by the impulse of his hind foot's moving forward.

a. Instruction.

To post, the rider permits herself to be lifted slightly forward and upward every time one hind leg comes forward; she returns to the saddle as the other hind leg moves forward.

The rhythm is a steady 1, 2, 1, 2.

The upper body of the rider is kept erect over the pelvis, moving only slightly forward as the speed of the trot increases.

The leg position does not change.

The hands are able to stay in the same horizontal plane because of the relaxation of the elbow joints.

b. Presentation.

Demonstrate posting, explaining that the rhythm is steady and even.

The horse should do more work than the rider; but, at first, the beginner feels as if she were doing a great deal. The rhythm will come and go when the student is first learning to post, but eventually it becomes an automatic action.

c. Cautions.

Most riders will pick up the posting rhythm easily if they have mastered the sitting trot well enough to be able to keep their position.

If they post too high or stay up too long, emphasize the count: 1, 2, or say "up, down."

Have the riders move the horses on enough to make the lifting easier. If the trot is slow there is less impulse from the horse.

Don't let the riders lean forward when starting; this becomes a difficult habit to break.

Emphasize the leg position, the steadiness of the hands, and general relaxation.

The techniques of posting recur throughout a riding career; at this point, the rhythm of the motion and maintenance of body position are the chief considerations.

D. Fourth Week

1. Aids. Aids are the instruments by which a rider makes her wishes known to the horse. Basically, the animal is pushed everywhere, never pulled. The legs tell the horse to move forward, backward, sideways, and to turn. Enough intermittent calf pressure is applied to get the desired response from the horse. The rider's position and weight are very important factors in control of the horse. First, the rider must learn to sit in the saddle with her buttocks relaxed and supple to absorb movement and to feel the action of the horse. This is termed *following the horse.* Next, the pupil learns to use the weight placement and seat to inspire the horse to move. This is termed *initiate movement* and is taught through the exercises of bracing the back and tilting the pelvis.

a. Instruction.

Bracing the back means tightening the back muscles (see Figure 7.16) all the way from the shoulders to the pelvis in a downward direction. This theory is explained very clearly in *Riding Logic* by Wilhelm Müseler. Fundamentally, the use of the back muscles helps the rider to maintain an erect upper body position, determine the placement of the center of gravity, and thereby influence the horse.

Combined with the bracing of the back is the tilt of the pelvis. When the pelvis is tilted to bring the end of the spine closer to the saddle, the weight of the rider is brought deeper into the horse. When tilted in the opposite direction the seat is brought more out of the saddle.

The combined actions of bracing the back and tilting the pelvis downward into the saddle push the horse forward and into the bit.

b. Presentation.

Present this material when the rider is not mounted.

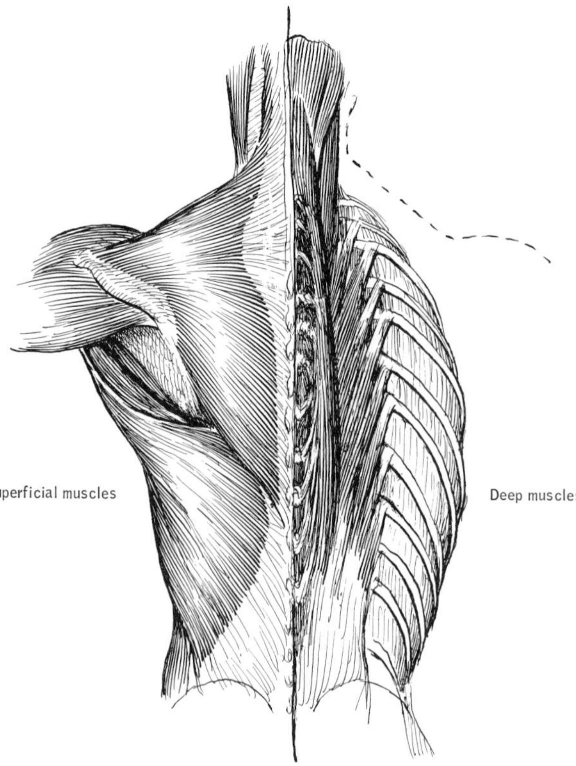

FIGURE 7.16 *Muscles of back.*

When standing, the rider makes a fist, tightening the biceps with the elbow bent. At the same time the back muscles will tighten. The rider may feel this; the teacher should place her open hands on the student's back and palpate this.
Next the rider learns to tighten the back muscles without tightening the forearms.
Tilting the pelvis may be taught first in a lying position with the knees bent, feet on the floor.
When the rider flattens the back, the pelvis rotates in the desired direction.
This rotation should be practiced next in a seated position, then in a standing position.
The combined actions should be practiced.
Finally the application is made on the horse.
The action of bracing and tilting is made, then the rider returns to normal and repeats the action.

c. *Emphasis.*

Flexibility in the pelvis and spine are essential before any positive influence may be attained.
This exercise must be practiced daily off the horse as well as on.

2. Circle at the Walk.

The circle (volte) at any gait should be a round path, where the horse bends in his spine and keeps the hindquarters following the forehand. The speed of the gait should not increase on the circle, and forward motion must continue.
The rider's outside leg is used one to two inches farther back from the normal position; the inside leg is used lightly in the normal position to keep the horse in motion. The inside rein tension is increased slightly and the outside rein tension lessened enough to permit the horse to turn.
The legs continue to act with every stride the horse takes in the circle, and the hands keep the same amount of tension throughout.

b. *Presentation.*

Demonstrate the circle, stressing the aids and round path.

The beginners circle should be larger than will be desired later on.

c. Emphasis.

The rider must understand the circular path. If she does not, have her walk it on foot first.

As in turning, too much rein pressure will halt the horse.

To start the circle, the horse must be listening to the rider, or he will refuse to leave the line.

Then at the midpoint of the circle, the horse may wish to stop in the center of the ring, so stronger aids are necessary.

Toward the end of the circle the horse may wish to cut the last part of the path. When this happens, the aids are used in opposition to prevent his turning, rather than initiate it, e.g., if the horse wishes to cut to the left, the rider uses left leg and right rein pressure.

E. Fifth Week

1. Mechanics of the Trot; Posting on Diagonals.

a. Instruction.

To post correctly with the motion of the horse, riders must understand the action of the trot. It is a two beat, diagonal gait, i.e., left fore and right hind, right fore and left hind. This causes the 1, 2, 1, 2 rhythm.

To post with a specific diagonal set of legs eases the burden for the horse in a circular path. While on the trail, the rider should alternate diagonals arbitrarily.

In a circle, the horse's inside hind leg makes a smaller circle, thereby doing less work. So the rider should give that leg the additional task of lifting her seat.

To rise with the inside hind leg, the rider will be moving also with the outside front leg, which the rider can see. To move with that leg, the rider should rise as it moves forward, or sit as it comes back and the hoof hits the ground.

If the pupil is not moving at that time, she may sit one or three beats (odd number) and then rise. If she sits two beats (even number) she will not change the diagonal.

The beginner should look at the shoulder or hoof (not lean over, but merely look down) and check her diagonal.

The diagonal is designated by the outside front shoulder action; therefore, when the rider posts with the right shoulder, she is said to be posting on the right diagonal; and with the left, on the left diagonal.

When changing hand or direction, the rider sits one beat in the center of the path and changes her diagonal.

b. Presentation.

First, the riders should watch a horse trot, and see if they are able to analyze the motion.

The motion and diagonals should be explained. Then ask if the students can see the diagonals on the demonstrator.

Students should then walk on and call out to the instructor their own horse's motion at the walk.

When mastered, the same exercise should be done at the sitting trot.

Next, the riders should post and tell the instructor if they are correct. Assistance will be necessary at first.

Frequent changes of direction should be made, so students learn to sit one beat and change the diagonals smoothly.

c. Emphasis.

Many students favor one diagonal and find it more difficult to pick up the other. Constant admonitions help correct this.

Some students see the shoulder move away, and others see the hoof hit the ground. Therefore both explanations should be given.

As soon as this is understood, the student becomes responsible for posting on the correct diagonal at all times.

Some horses also have a favorite diagonal and skip to put riders on it. Such horses must learn to lift riders with ease on both diagonals.

2. The Scissors Exercise.

a. Instruction.

Preparation:

The instructor holds the horse.

The rider drops reins and stirrups.

If the coat is buttoned, release the bottom buttons.

The rider places hands on knee, rolls and swings the legs freely forward and backward.

Increase the backward swing, clicking the heels together over the back of the horse, as the shoulders are brought down parallel to the neck of the horse.

Return to the upright position.

Exercise:

Swing backward again and at the height of the swing, place one leg under the other and roll sideways on the lower hip.

Open the legs, push up with the arms and sit up. The rider will be facing the rear of the horse.

Then the hands are placed on the hips of the horse, and the exercise repeated in the reverse direction.

b. Presentation.

Demonstrate all steps.

Do not let a beginner try the exercise on a horse that has not experienced the movement previously.

c. Emphasis.

The exercise is accomplished with a swing, not a slow crawling action.

The legs must be spread away from the horse, not hugging the saddle.

Females have to drop the shoulders lower than males, who have more shoulder strength.

The hands are the base of support and must not move until the legs are opened. If at any time the rider loses balance and the hands remain as they should, she will drop to the ground on her feet.

F. Sixth Week

1. Hands as an Aid.

a. Instruction.

The hands act in three ways: to guide the horse, to control the forehand, and to maintain speed.

The beginner at first tries only to keep the hands quiet and soft, and independent of body movement.

With more coordination, the rider learns to accept more responsibility with the hands. A light contact with the horse's mouth should be maintained at all times.

b. Presentation.

Part of the value of this presentation is to give the students different horses to ride, with various "ways of going" and different head carriages.

The horse that is slightly fussy, will show the student the need for tact and soft hand contact.

c. Emphasis.

Beginners hesitate to take contact on the horse's mouth. In the beginning, the lightest contact possible is desirable. As progression is made, more contact is desirable, provided the balance of the rider is independent of the hands.

Hands are "the last word" in control; legs and seat initiate motion, but the hands finish it, and their indications must be sensitive, soft, and accurate.

2. Ring Etiquette.

a. Instruction.

Do not pass a horse in front unless it is permitted and the rider is capable. Pass wide enough so as not to excite the front horse. Continue on far enough, so the speed of the front horse is not hampered.

If a horse gets loose, stop your horse immediately and try to stand still until the other horse is caught.

When lined up in a stationary position, keep at least six feet between all horses.

If for any reason horses get close, do not let them get their noses together. This usually ends in a misunderstanding and a fight between the two.

If you are mounted on a horse that kicks, warn others.

If your horse takes you in to another horse and you cannot stop him, apologize to the other rider so she knows that you at least know better ring manners.

b. Presentation.

As soon as riders have elementary control, explain what they should try to do.

If a situation occurs which points up a matter of ring etiquette, expose the riders to the correct procedure, even if they are not capable of putting it in practice.

c. Emphasis.

All etiquette is a matter of safety for both riders and horses.

G. Seventh Week

1. Trail Etiquette.

a. Instruction.

Obey the leader and stay behind her at all times.

Keep the proper distance between horses at all times.

Do not pass, but stay in formation.

Do not hold branches or twigs; do hold gates.
Warn people of hazards; holes, dogs, etc.
When crossing highways, stay closed up and flank across.
If there are kickers, keep them at the end.

b. Presentation.
Warn riders about trail etiquette.
Take the group out with enough assistants and with all mounted on sensible, honest horses.
Do not go in heavy woods, open fields, or very rough ground at first.
Practice what you preach.

c. Emphasis.
Insist on proper etiquette at all times.
Be sure that the leaders know what the rest of the group is doing at all times.
Keep the pace steady and warn before any changes of either faster or slower paces.
Try to make the rides enjoyable and safe.

H. Eighth Week

1. The Canter.

a. Instruction.
Put each rider who is ready, one at a time on a quiet horse that will canter by voice control.
The rider is just to experience the motion of the canter. No analysis should be given.
Tell the student to sit quietly, in the same position, and relax to let her seat rock with the motion of the horse.

b. Presentation.
Send the cantering horse out on the rail in the opposite direction from the rest of the group.
If there are two horses that work well together on a lead rein, the canter introduction is given easily.

c. Emphasis.
Stress that relaxation is necessary; the horse does the work, not the rider.
Do not send riders out to canter, unless their sense of balance is good.

III. LOW INTERMEDIATE RIDING

A. First Week

Review preliminaries to riding.
Check positions of riders.
Watch each pupil walk, sit trot, and post.
Stress position, emphasizing lower leg placement and use of legs as an aid.

B. Second Week

Review diagonals.
Work on smoother posting motion.
Circle at the sitting trot.
Demonstrate the canter; start pupils cantering on horses that are easy to control and smooth gaited.

C. Third Week

Continue canter work.
Attempt very short periods of posting without stirrups.
Work on seat, as an aid to stop, start and turn the horse.
Exercises.

D. Fourth Week

Review trail etiquette.
Ride on the trail.

E. Fifth Week

Explain the mechanics of the canter and teach leads.
Practice getting the correct leads.
Posting without stirrups.

F. Sixth Week

Emphasize hands as an aid.
Large circle (half-school or half of the ring) at the posting trot.

G. Seventh Week

Using a smooth gaited horse, give all riders the experience of riding bareback to *feel* the horse's motion.

H. Eighth Week

Ride on the trail.
Canter in the ring at the end of the ride.

Finish the lesson with individual criticisms for all.

IV. LOW INTERMEDIATE CLASS: DETAILED OUTLINE

Only new material is discussed in this section. Readers should refer to the section on Beginning Riding for material that is not clear.

A. Second Week

1. The Canter.

a. Instruction.

The seat of the rider remains in the saddle and gently rocks backward and forward to absorb the same motion of the horse. The upper body finishes the absorption by *very slight* backward and forward movement.

The weight is on the pelvis, not in the stirrups or on the thighs, and the entire body is relaxed, yet controlled.

The position is maintained by balance on the three-point contact of the sitting bones and crotch, and muscular control at the thigh, knee, and calf positions.

b. Presentation.

Demonstrate the proper movement at the canter.

Demonstrate the possible errors that result in inability to absorb the motion. (See Emphasis section.)

Finish the demonstration with the correct position.

c. Emphasis.

The most important quality for the ability to canter correctly is suppleness in the spine and pelvis.

Students must be reminded that the horse, not the rider, canters. The rider merely "uses up" the end of the motion.

Grip and tenseness cause problems: grip with the knees forces the seat muscles away from the saddle; stiffness in the spine causes a jar at each stride.

If the weight is shifted forward over the crotch and on the thighs, the body will bounce.

Some riders in efforts to absorb the motion lean backward, getting behind the movement of the horse, instead of being with the motion. If this habit becomes established, it is difficult to break.

B. Third Week

1. Posting without Stirrups.

a. Instruction.

Without the feet in the stirrups, the rider should maintain the same position she would with stirrups.

The toe is slightly higher than the heel, and the thighs, knees, and calves must have enough contact not to slide about.

The rider's pelvis will not move as far away from the saddle as it does when posting with stirrups.

b. Presentation.

This is a strenuous exercise for the less skilled rider and should *not* be continued for any long periods.

The best presentation is to let the riders individually do as many steps at a time as each is able before becoming fatigued. Then return to sitting the trot and rest and repeat.

c. Emphasis.

The value of this exercise is that the rider will not be able to post unless the legs are placed properly.

Another value is to prove to the rider she is competent without stirrups and need not panic should she lose them unintentionally.

C. Fifth Week

1. Mechanics of the Canter; Leads at the Canter.

a. Instruction.

The canter is a three-beat gait; during which one side of the horse's body appears to lead, or move in advance of the other side. If the horse is cantering with the right side "leading," he is said to be on the right lead.

The sequence is: left hind, right hind and left fore, right fore. The left lead would be the opposite sequence.

During beat 1 (left hind) the weight is toward the hindquarters; beat 2 (right hind and left fore) the weight is centered; and on beat 3 (right fore) the weight is completely on the forehand. (See Figure 7.17.)

Then a short pause occurs where the impulse of the gait brings the weight backward in preparation for the first beat of the next stride.

FIGURE 7.17 *Canter sequence.*

The combination of the sequence of leg movements and the leading of one side means that the horse's balance is more precarious at the canter than at the trot. To enable him to balance easily and efficiently, the direction of movement must coincide with the lead; i.e., if cantering to the left, the horse must be on the left lead.

To make the horse canter on the right lead, the rider strongly uses the left leg about three inches behind the girth, and and right leg lightly at the normal position. The seat is deep in the saddle, with the right side of the pelvis very slightly ahead of the left side and a bit more of the body weight on the left side of the pelvis. The upper body weight is just slightly behind the vertical to push the horse forward into the canter. The right hand is raised very slightly making the horse look where he is to go, and support on the left rein prevents his looking in too much.

If the horse takes the lead opposite from the desired one, he must be stopped and started again, not allowed to canter on the wrong lead.

The rider again may see the lead by looking at the shoulders. The leading one will move farther forward than the other shoulder.

b. Presentation.

Demonstrate the canter and see if the riders can analyze the gait before giving them the explanation.

Use a horse if possible with white markings on the legs to accentuate the motion, and with a good cadenced canter.

After the explanation has been given, demonstrate again.

c. Emphasis.

Starting the horse from the walk into the canter is easier for the beginner. They do not have the ability to make the horse understand at the trot that the canter is wished instead of a faster trot. That is a more advanced movement.

The *ever present problem* is to maintain the correct body position while the horse is in motion. If the rider's body does not remain quiet and steady, most horses will stop cantering.

D. Seventh Week

1. Ride Bareback.

a. Instruction.

The rider is mounted without a saddle. If a saddle pad with a surcingle is owned, it should be used. The saddle pad not only makes the back less slippery but protects the rider's clothing.

The position should be maintained effortlessly with the toe relaxed and legs hanging easily. The rider sits to all gaits; walk, slow trot, and canter.

b. Presentation.

Use one or two smooth-gaited, flat-backed horses; and change the riders during the period.

If too much bareback riding is done at first, the rider may become very stiff and sore.

c. Emphasis.

The most important asset to bareback riding is for the rider to feel the motion of the horse. Therefore, the rider must be relaxed in the buttock muscles to feel through them.

The position is maintained, as always, predominantly by balance. If the rider grips strongly she will find herself slipping from side to side, but if she relaxes she will move with the motion.

V. INTERMEDIATE RIDING

A. First Week

Review preliminaries; check positions.
Review ring etiquette.
Watch each pupil walk, trot, and canter.
Review proper leg position and use of legs as an aid.

B. Second Week

Concentrate on the posting motion, making it smoother and lower.
Circle at the sitting and posing trot.
Emphasize the use of seat as an aid.
Halt from the sitting trot.
Check on their knowledge about canter leads.

C. Third Week

Teach unilateral movement—turn on forehand.
Practice canter leads.
Emphasize hands as an aid, introducing more active hands.
Post and canter without stirrups.

D. Fourth Week

Review turn on the forehand.
Circles at the walk, trot, and posting trot.
Teach the forward position at the halt and walk.
Elementary drill figures.

E. Fifth Week

Teach backing.
Review trail etiquette.
Canter with and without stirrups and give individual critiques.
Drill.

F. Sixth Week

Ride on the trail, including a canter away from home.

G. Seventh Week

Review backing.
Introduce *feel* at the walk, review analysis.
Commence posting on specific diagonals on command.
Work on the forward position at the trot.

H. Eighth Week

Introduce *feel* at the trot, review analysis.
Pick up specific lead from the straight line down the center of the ring.
Review backing, turn on the forehand, and elementary drill.

VI. INTERMEDIATE RIDING: DETAILED OUTLINE

Only new material is discussed. Refer to Beginning Riding and Low Intermediate Riding sections for material that is not clear. From this point on, the comments on the manner of presentation will be omitted. It is assumed that the instructor will give explanations and demonstrations as described in the sections on Formation for Explanation and on Presentation.

A. First Week

1. Leg Aids.

a. Instruction.

The intermediate must learn more finesse with all aids, first with the legs.
Basically, there are three positions in which the leg is applied: 1) the normal position which affects the whole body; 2) one to two inches forward, the forehand, 3) and two to three inches backward, the hindquarters.
There are three applications of the legs: the tap or press to inspire movement; the sharp use, to reprimand; and the resistant pressure, to restrain unwanted movement.
The legs are used: 1) to inspire the hindquarters or motor of the horse, 2) maintain the desired motion, and 3) bend and supple the horse.
The use of leg aids must be timed in rhythm with the movement of the horse; i.e., right leg of rider applied as horse's right leg is about to move.

b. Emphasis.

The legs must not move unnecessarily, nor be so active as to immunize the horse to them.
If the horse is unresponsive, the spur should be used to act as an extension of the leg. It is applied with a prick, not a kick. Only riders whose legs are steady should be permitted to wear spurs.

B. Second Week

1. Smoother Posting.

a. Instruction.

The action of posting should be very slight and only the side of the seat that is pushed should rise if the horse's gait is smooth. It is not an even lift and cannot be absorbed as one.

The action becomes more forward and less upward and therefore the upper body is affected less.

b. Emphasis.

Do not work too hard! Nothing extra should be added by the rider. The horse initiates the motion.

2. Halt from the Sitting Trot.

a. Instruction.

The horse must come to a halt smoothly and quietly, with his weight on the hindquarters and feet evenly placed.

The rider must use legs to push him forward, keep her seat deep to coordinate his motion and then restrain him with resistive hand pressure, so he goes forward into the bit and halts accepting the pressure and flexing his jaw. (See Figure 7.18.)

The transition should be smooth, even, and without stiffness.

b. Emphasis.

The rider finds she is using the same aids to start and stop the horse. Many are confused to use their legs to push the horse into the bit rather than stopping by a pull on the reins.

The seat must not come out of the saddle, nor the upper body move forward to the hands. The seat is the center of the motion and the hands come toward the body, not vice versa.

C. Third Week

1. Turn on the Forehand.

a. Instruction.

The horse turns, almost in place, with his forelegs making a very small circle, the haunches describing a larger circle around the forehand. The movement sequence to the left is: right hind leg moves left, crossing in front of the left leg; the left steps to the side and uncrosses; the left foreleg moves slightly to the left; the right foreleg is lifted, made parallel to the left and replaced.

The forehand is held in place by even rein contact, while the right leg moves the hindquarters to the left. The left leg is used to keep the movement slow and

FIGURE 7.18 *Halt on bit.*

prevent the right foreleg from pivoting, rather than lifting and replacing.

The rider's weight should be displaced slightly to the right side to push the horse left, but also remain deep in the saddle to prevent forward or backward movement. (See Figure 7.19.)

b. Emphasis.

Get the horse in hand before starting, and keep the forehand stabilized. Otherwise the horse will move about in a small circle instead of a turn.

D. Fourth Week

1. Forward Position.

a. Instruction.

The rider's upper body inclines forward, arching the lower back, thereby taking the weight off the saddle and transferring it over the thighs, knees, and into the ankles. The hands are lowered, maintaining contact so there is a straight line from the rider's elbow to the bit.

The lower leg position does not change.

In this position motion is absorbed by the hip, knee, and ankle joints.

b. Emphasis.

Do not let the upper body collapse.

Focus up and out, not down.

Keep the hip joints partially closed so that the seat is not too far above the horse.

Keep the weight in the heels, or the upper body position will fall forward or backward.

Do not support on the neck of the horse, but keep the hands one to two inches away from the horse, keeping rein contact independent from balance.

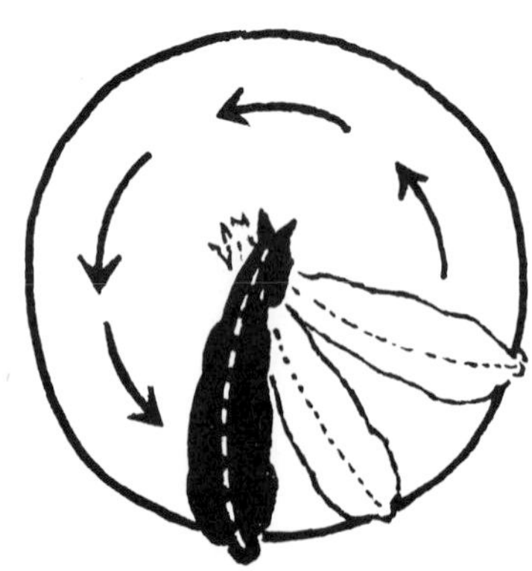

FIGURE 7.19 *Turn on forehand (to right).*

2. Halt from Posting Trot.

This is accomplished as from the sitting trot. The tempo of the trot is decreased slightly, the rider sits, and then halts.

3. Elementary Drill Figures.

a. Instruction.

To drill or ride in formation, the riders must have enough control to make their horses move, irrespective of what the preceding horse does.

The riders must know also what the figures are before trying to ride them. This means drill on foot.

Most formations are adapted from four basic patterns.

These are diagramed in Figure 7.20.

Drilling is introduced at the walk, and then ridden at the slow sitting trot.

b. Emphasis.

Ride into the corners and use all space available.

Know where you are in relation to the others, and watch each other continually.

Keep spacing for figures where horses cross in front and pass through.

Guide when moving in one line, so all horses are even and the lines straight.

E. Fifth Week

1. Backing.

a. Instruction.

Backward movement is mechanically difficult for the horse, and therefore, is an advanced movement.

The motion is two beat (as the trot) left hind and right fore, and right hind and left fore. The legs should be lifted and moved together, not dragged backward singly.

The horse backs with the body straight in one line. The back of the horse must be supple, and not hollowed.

The head must be in the proper place, not raised or lowered excessively. (See Figure 7.21, *A* and *B*.)

The rider pushes the horse forward with the legs and seat, and then restrains with the hands. The leg pressures are soft and not forceful. The intermediate actively "gives and takes" with the hands in response to the movement of the horse. Later on, the hand action becomes less active and more subtly resistive.

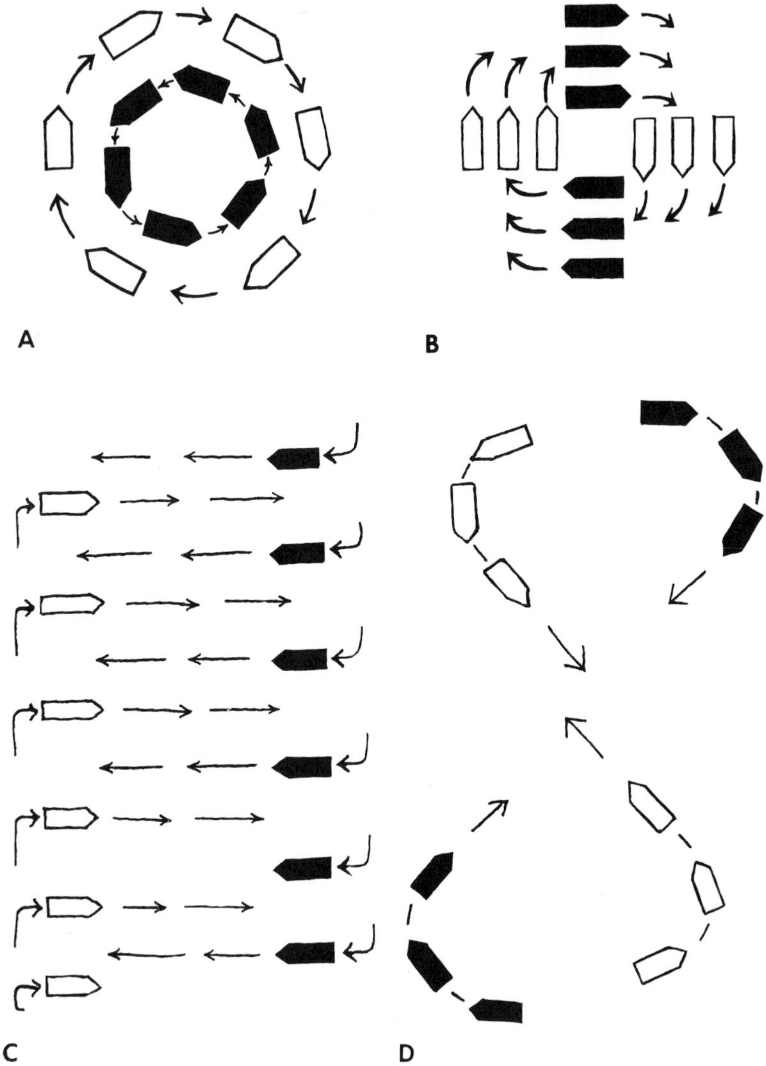

FIGURE 7.20 *Drill patterns: A, circle; B, wheel; C, flank and cross through; D, diagonal change and cross through.*

b. Emphasis.

There must be enough impulsion to get a two beat motion.

The horse must be on the bit and collected to start.

If the hindquarters move to one side, a stronger resistive leg pressure should be applied on that side as well as more rein pressure on the same side.

Corrective leg pressures must be applied only as strongly as needed, otherwise, the horse will over-correct.

The upper body remains erect or slightly forward, but never backward.

The rider must *feel* the horse's readiness to move and not try to back until he is balanced and ready.

F. Sixth Week

1. Trail Riding.

The affinity of the horses for home makes cantering in the homeward direction much more

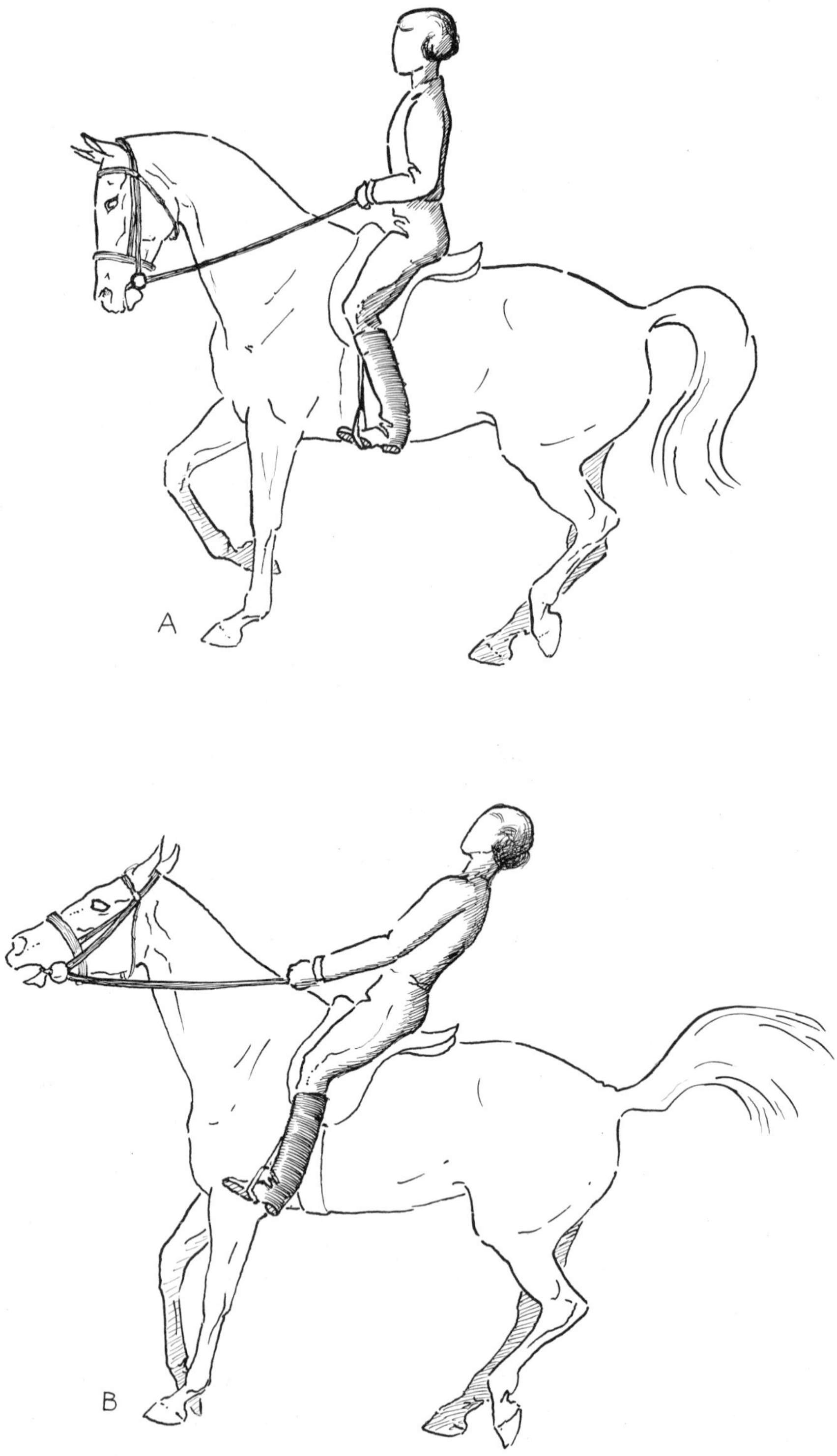

FIGURE 7.21 *A, Correct backing. B, Incorrect backing.*

difficult. Intermediates should canter on the trail only away from the stables.

G. Seventh Week

1. *Feel* at the Walk.

a. Instruction.

The rider tries to know the motion of the horse's body without looking.

At the walk, the rider should shut her eyes and try to feel the sway of the hindquarters as each hind leg comes forward. Next, the rider should feel the motion in the forelegs.

b. Emphasis.

Feel through the seat and even the general sense of balance is inhibited by tenseness.

Do not let the rider look, but make her practice *feeling*.

2. Pick Up Specific Diagonals on Command.

The rider sits the trot, watching the shoulders move away from her, and then commences to post on the diagonal requested. Both diagonals should be picked up with equal ease.

H. Eighth Week

1. *Feel* at the Trot.

a. Instruction.

The rider should try to *feel* the action of the sitting trot first.

Next, she should post and try to *feel* which hind leg is lifting her. If the left lifts her, the left side of her pelvis will be pushed higher and farther away from the saddle than the right side. Correspondingly, the right side will return to the saddle sooner, temporarily taking the body weight. Therefore, as the diagonal is named by the front shoulder, the side of the pelvis hitting the saddle sooner coincides with the posting diagonal; i.e., when the rider is lifted by the left hind leg, the right side of the seat takes the weight first, and the rider is posting on the right diagonal.

Eventually, the rider will *feel* at the sitting trot and start correctly on either diagonal with no visual assistance.

b. Emphasis.

Feel that the lift and return to the saddle are unilateral.

VII. HIGH INTERMEDIATE RIDING

A. First Week

Review position; safety and ring etiquette.
Watch each rider walk, trot, and canter.
Review leg position, stressing placement and aid.

B. Second Week

Walk, trot, and canter without stirrups.
Explain the use of the seat as an aid.
Circle at the trot and canter.
Present *feel* at the walk and trot.

C. Third Week

Emphasize the hands as aids.
Work on *feel* at the trot and halt.
Post and canter without irons.
Trot in the forward position.

D. Fourth Week

Introduce work on the bit at the walk and sitting trot.
Work on the halt from the sitting and posting trot.
Introduce *feel* at the canter.
Review turn on the forehand, and backing.

E. Fifth Week

Introduce collection and extension at the trot.
Work for subtleness of aids.
Review halts from the trot; then trot from a halt.

F. Sixth Week

Drive tandem.

G. Seventh Week

Drilling.
Canter in a forward position.
Review collection and extension at the trot.

H. Eighth Week

Individual performances of elementary ring figures.
Cavaletti: trotting in a forward position.

VIII. HIGH INTERMEDIATE RIDING: DETAILED OUTLINE

Refer to previous sections for material that is not covered here.

A. Fourth Week

1. Work on the Bit.

a. Instruction.

When the horse is on the bit, he softly chews or mouths the bit, relaxing his lower jaw and giving at the poll.

The pressure is felt from the bars of the horse's mouth to the rider's hands through the medium of the reins. (Figure 7.22 shows the relationship of the bit to the horse's skeletal system.)

The motion of chewing is active and felt through the fingers, and is not a heavy, dead, pressure. When the horse works on the bit, he salivates.

b. Emphasis.

Drive the horse forward into the bit; do not try to pull him back into it. The rider's legs instigate the pressure, and the hands receive it; not the reverse.

If the rider's hands are not sensitive, the horse will not stay on the bit, but will finds ways of getting over, behind, or above to escape the pressure.

The rider's legs must be active or the horse's forward motion is not maintained and his body becomes stiff.

2. *Feel* at the Canter.

a. Instruction.

The *feel* at the canter is again the sensation of movement underneath the rider.

The leading motion should be felt, by the slight predominance of weight on the leading side, and the unilateral movement of the hindquarters.

The beats of the canter should be felt, so that if the timing is disturbed the rider knows it immediately. Sometimes the horse cross canters, or has one lead in front and the other behind. This motion should be changed immediately.

b. Emphasis.

The prerequisite for *feel* is the ability to keep the seat close enough to the saddle to sense the motion. If the rider is tense and the seat muscles leave the saddle during the stride, it will be difficult to *feel* the canter leads.

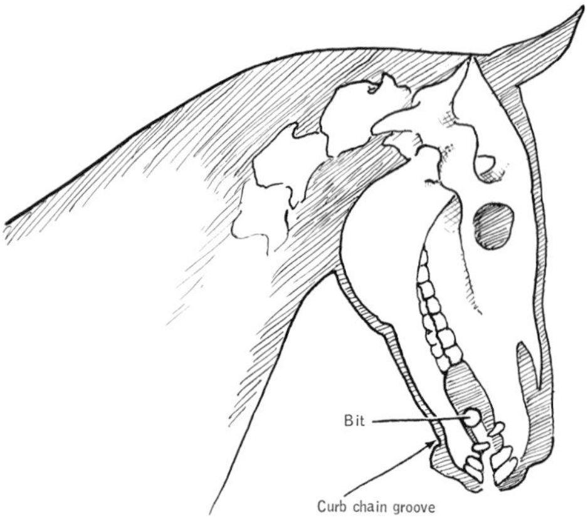

FIGURE 7.22 *Skeletal profile of horse.*

Shutting the eyes may improve the student's awareness of both her and the horse's balance.

B. Fifth Week

1. Collection and Extension at the Trot.

a. Instruction.

The terms are defined in the section on Riding Terms.

The horse when collected moves energetically with action more up and down than forward, and at the same time is relaxed. He lowers his hindquarters, and raises his forehand, flexing at the poll and bringing the face line closer to the vertical. This must not be forced or stiff, and incorrect collection is much worse than no collection.

The cadence and rhythm of the gait must not be interrupted.

The horse is driven forward by seat and legs and restrained by hands, or driven together as if from both ends of a spring.

When extended, the horse is less collected, covers more ground with each stride and slightly lowers the forehand. The speed of the gait should not increase excessively.

The horse is urged strongly with seat and legs and allowed a bit more release on the reins.

b. Emphasis.

The rider's aids must be independent and the seat deep or the horse cannot understand the commands.

In collection, the rider must not restrain the horse enough to lose forward motion, or allow stiffness in any part of the spine: back, neck, or hindquarters.

In extension, the horse must not skip or move unevenly.

The degree of collection and extension attained by riders on this skill level is very slight.

C. Sixth Week

1. Driving Tandem.

a. Instruction.

One horse is driven in front (lead horse) and another horse is ridden behind (wheel horse).

The wheel horse's reins and the left driving rein are held in the rider's left hand in the regular riding grip.

The right driving rein is held in the right hand with a driving grip; i.e., the rein is between the thumb and index finger. (See Figure 7.23.)

The lead horse is controlled by voice and by rein contact, and must be pushed up into the bit at all times.

The wheel horse is controlled predominantly by seat and legs.

The path of the wheel horse must be directly behind the lead horse. The wheel horse should initiate movement a fraction of a second before the lead horse.

Trotting is the easiest gait at which to drive tandem, then the walk and canter, and eventually the jump.

Ring figures as described for one horse may be done with the tandem team: circles, changes of direction, and actual drilling with advanced riders.

b. Emphasis.

When first starting, follow the lead horse wherever he goes, so he is never allowed to turn and face the wheel horse.

Keep the lead horse on the bit at all times.

D. Eighth Week

1. Elementary Ring Figures.

a. Instruction.

1) VOLTE—a circular path of designated diameter. (See Figure 7.24.)

FIGURE 7.23 *Driving tandem.*

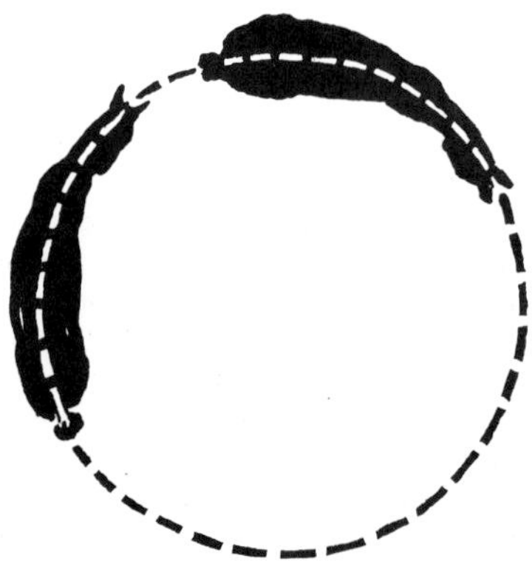

FIGURE 7.24 *Volte.*

2) DEMI-VOLTE (Half-circle)—the path is half of a volte, with a return to the track on an oblique line. It may be ridden also in reverse with the oblique line first, followed by the demi-volte path. (See Figure 7.25.)
3) "FIGURE 8"—This path is a figure of eight, or two circles, one in each direction. The circles must be round, not oval, and the horse flexed in the direction of movement. (See Figure 7.26.)

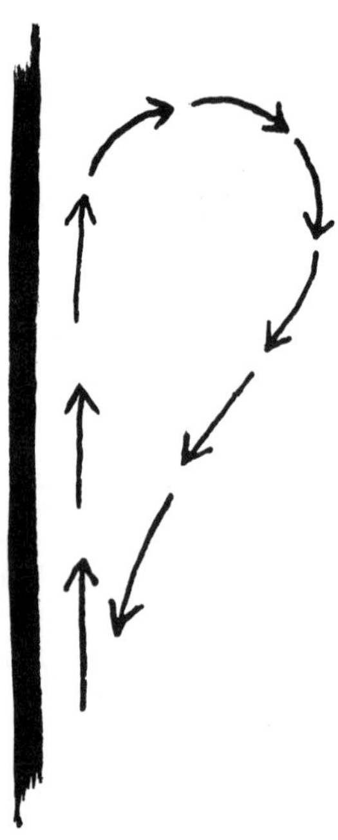

FIGURE 7.25 *Demi-volte.*

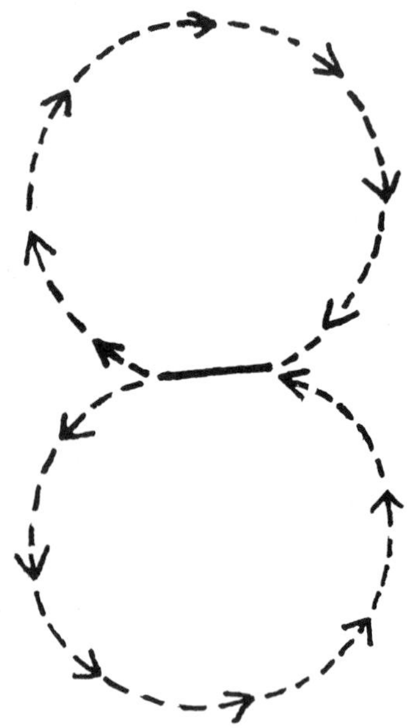

FIGURE 7.26 *Figure eight (8).*

4) THE SERPENTINE—is a series of half circles and straight paths as shown in diagram. (Figure 7.27.) The paths of both the circles and straight lines must be ridden accurately.

b. Emphasis.

Ring figures are definite patterns and must be ridden with accuracy.

High intermediates may execute these at the walk, sitting trot, and posting trot; cantering them becomes an advanced exercise.

2. CAVALETTI.

In this situation the cavaletti are used as a lead-up to jumping.

a. Instruction.

The cavaletti is defined in the section on Riding Terms.

It is illustrated with a jump at the end of the series in Figure 7.28.

The horse should maintain a good working trot without change of timing or unevenness as he moves over the poles.

The rider should remain in the forward position throughout the series, allowing the horse freedom to move over the bars.

b. Emphasis.

The rider's position must not collapse and

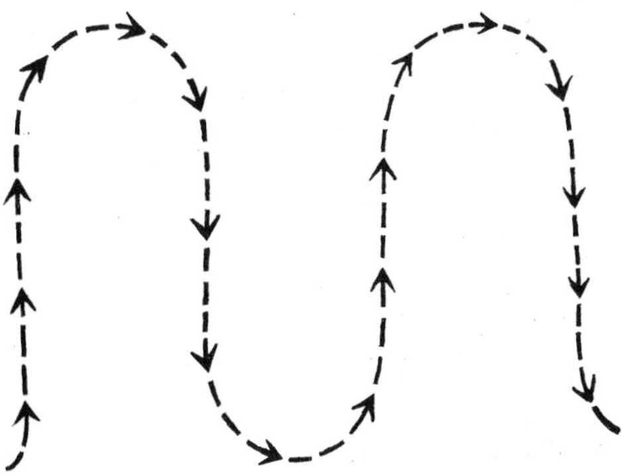

FIGURE 7.27 *Serpentine.*

the balance must be maintained without support from the reins.

IX. ADVANCED RIDING

A. First Week

Review preliminaries and stable procedures.
Check each rider's position and control at the walk, trot, and canter.
Review and emphasize the use of legs.

B. Second Week

Emphasize the use of seat as an aid.
Work on the bit at walk, trot, and canter.
Ring figures at the trot.

C. Third Week

Emphasize hand aids.
Work in a forward position at the trot and canter.
Drill and drive tandem.

D. Fourth Week

Work on collection and extension at the walk and trot.
Give individual *critiques* on aids.
Cavaletti with small jump at the end.

E. Fifth Week

Review collection and extension.
Ring figures at a canter.
Cavaletti and higher jump.

F. Sixth Week

Ride on the trail.

G. Seventh Week

Work on collection and extension at the canter.
Cavaletti and jump.

H. Eighth Week

Simple ring rides—individually performed.
Jump a simple course.

X. ADVANCED RIDING: DETAILED OUTLINE

Refer to previous section for material that is not covered here.

A. Fourth Week

1. Individual Critiques on Aids.

At this level the aids used by the rider should be known only to horse and rider, not obvious to the observer. All aids should be subtle, clear,

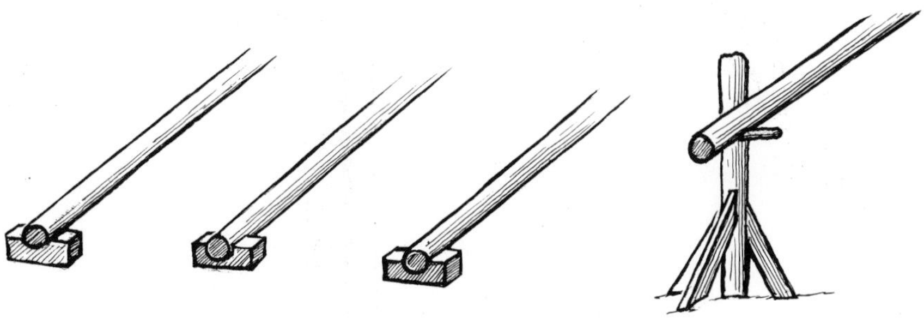

FIGURE 7.28 *Cavaletti.*

and meaningful to the horse; and should be given in the pattern of legs and seat, then hands. The rider should ride, not drive the horse. The horse should be a willing, happy performer.

B. Fifth Week

1. Cavaletti with Jump.

This develops the jump out of the cavaletti exercise. The horse continues the trot over the bars and then the jump, while the rider keeps the same position throughout. (See the illustration of good jumping form in Figure 7.29.)

C. Eighth Week

1. Simple Ring Rides.

These serve as introductions to dressage rides, and are made out of combing ring figures and transitions from one gait to another.

2. Simple Jump Course.

A simple course consists of jumps placed about the ring, so the rider must jump, then change direction and jump again. This is introductory to a stadium jumping course as illustrated in Figure 7.30.

INDOOR ACTIVITIES

Most riding facilities do not include indoor rings, so plans must be made for inclement weather. An important part of the rider's education may take place on rainy days.

Sample Plans for Eight Indoor Programs

1. Cleaning and grooming the horse.
2. Teaching the parts of the horse; finish with a quiz.
3. Discuss care of tack, cleaning tack.
4. Teaching the parts of tack, and taking apart and reassembling a saddle and bridle.
5. Discuss the theory and practice bracing the back and tilting the pelvis.
6. Lecture on the safety and trail etiquette for horse and rider.
7. Lecture on common diseases and ailments of horses and first aid treatment for horses.
8. Show film loops on stable care, shoeing, and basic theory of aids.

FIGURE 7.29 *Good jumping form.*

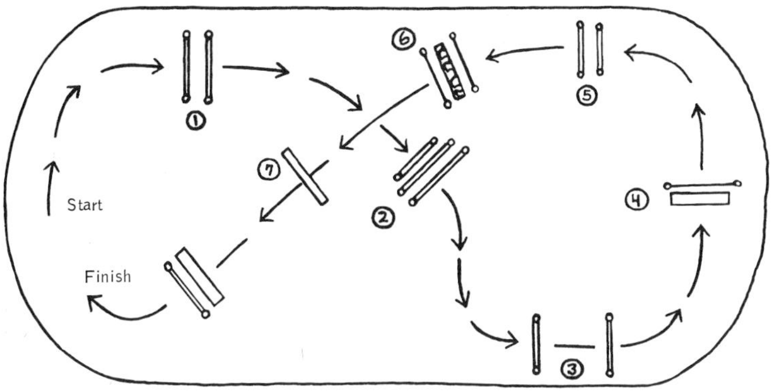

FIGURE 7.30 *Stadium jumping course.*

EXTRACURRICULAR ACTIVITIES

A good portion of riding is competitive, either between riders or on a self-challenge basis. Consequently, riders should learn the sportsmanship of competition as early as possible. Many people know how to win, but most need to learn how to win gracefully and how to lose graciously. The instructor should evaluate pupils' abilities carefully and then place them in competitions that coincide with their skill levels. Intermediates may compete in easy games on horseback (see bibliography), and in equitation. Advanced riders should be challenged within their skill levels and if possible compete in both intra-group and regular horse show competitions.

A club may be organized to sponsor lectures, movies, and guest instructors. If the nucleus of riders is large enough, a group may be set up with skill and knowledge tests for entrance requirements. This group may assist with instruction, give exhibitions, and help with trail guiding.

Suggestions for Further Reading

Anderson, C. W.: *Head Up, Heels Down.* New York, The Macmillan Company, 1944.

Ansell, M. P. (Lt. Col.): *Jumping,* London, The Naldrett Press, Ltd., 1954.

Baucher, F.: *Horsemanship, Including the Breaking and Training of Horses.* 3rd American ed. Philadelphia, Parry and McMillan, 1856.

Benoist-Gironiere, Yves: *The Conquest of the Horse,* Warford, England, Mayflower Press, 1952.

Beudant, E.: *Horse Training, Out-door and High School.* New York, Charles Scribner's Sons, 1950.

British Horse Society and the Pony Club: *Manual of Horsemanship.* London, 5th ed. 1961.

British Show Jumping Association: *Know the Game, Show Jumping.* London, Educational Productions, Ltd., 1954.

Brown, Paul: *The Horse.* New York, Charles Scribner's Sons, 1943.

Chamberlain, Harry D. (Brig. Gen.): *Riding and Schooling Horses.* Washington, D.C., Armoured Cavalry Journal, 1947.

———: *Training Hunters, Jumpers, and Hacks.* New York, D. Van Nostrand Co., Inc., 1952.

d'Endrödy, A. L. (Lt. Col.): *Give Your Horse A Chance.* London, J. A. Allen & Co., 1959.

de Sevy, L.: *Seats, Gaits, and Reactions.* Trans. by John C. Hamilton, The Cavalry School, Fort Riley, Kansas, 1946.

de Souze, Baretto: *Advanced Equitation.* New York, E. P. Dutton & Co., Inc., 1926.

———: *Principles of Equitation.* New York, E. P. Dutton & Co., Inc., 1925.
Fillis, James: *Breaking and Riding.* London, Hurst and Blackett, 1890.
Fort Riley Manuals: Cavalry School, Kansas, 1944.
Part I–Education of Rider.
Part II–Education of the Horse.
Part III–Animal Management.
Part IV–Horse Shoeing.
Part V–Horse Shows, Race Meetings, and Hunter Trials.
Hitchcock, F. C. (Capt.): *Saddle Up.* New York, Charles Scribner's Sons, 1937.
Kays, D. J.: *The Horse.* New York, A. S. Barnes & Co., 1953.
Lyon, W. E. (Lt. Col.): *Balance and the Horse.* New York, Charles Scribner's Sons, 1953.
MacGregor-Morris, Pamela: *The World's Show Jumpers.* Garden City, New York, Hanover House, 1956.
McTaggart, M. F. (Lt. Col.): *Mount and Man.* New York, Charles Scribner's Sons, 1927.
Müseler, Wilhelm: *Riding Logic.* 2nd ed. London, Meuthen & Co., Ltd., 1949.
Podhajsky, Alois: *Die Spanische Hofreitschule.* Wien, Verlag Rudolph Hans Hammer, 1954.
Santini, Piero: *Learning to Ride.* Cleveland, Ohio, The World Publishing Company, 1942.
Self, Margaret: *Fun on Horseback.* New York, A. S. Barnes & Co., 1945.
———: *Horsemanship.* New York, A. S. Barnes & Co., 1952.
Seunig, Waldemar: *Horsemanship.* Trans. by Leonard Mins. Garden City, New York, Doubleday & Company, Inc., 1960.
Simpson, George G.: *Horses.* New York, Oxford University Press, 1946.
Stanford, Leland and J. Stillman: *The Horse in Motion.* Boston, James R. Osgood & Co., 1882.
Steinkraus, William: *Riding and Jumping.* Garden City, New York, Doubleday & Company, Inc., 1961.
Talbot-Ponsonby, J. A. (Lt. Col.): *The Art of Show Jumping.* London, Naldrett Press, 1955.
Toptani, Ilias (Count): *Modern Show Jumping.* New York, A. S. Barnes & Co., 1954.
Vernon, Arthur: *The History and Romance of the Horse.* New York, Dover Publications, Inc., 1946.
Wall, John F.: *A Horseman's Handbook on Practical Breeding.* American Remount Association, Washington, D.C., 1945.
Watjen, Richard: *Dressage Riding.* London, J. A. Allen & Co., 1958.
Williams, Moyra: *Horse Psychology.* South Woodstock, Vermont, The Countryman Press, 1956.
Windisch-Graetz, Mathelide: *The Spanish Riding School.* London, Cassell & Co., Ltd., 1956.
Wright, Gordan and the United States Equestrian Team: *Horsemanship.* The Vermont Printing Company, 1958.
Wynmalen, Henry: *Dressage.* New York, A. S. Barnes & Co., 1952.
———: *Equitation.* New York, Charles Scribner's Sons, 1952.
Young, John R.: *The Schooling of the Western Horse.* 3rd ed. Norman, Oklahoma, University of Oklahoma Press, 1957.
Xenophon the Athenian: *About Horsemanship.* Trans. by Denison Hull. Private publication, 1956.

PERIODICALS AND RULE BOOKS

American Horse Shows Association Rule Book. Published annually by A. H. S. A., 40 East 54th Street, New York.
Fédération Équestre Internationale. Rules and Regulations. 10 ed. 1958.
a. Combined Training Events.
b. Dressage Competitions.
c. Jumping Competitions.
Riding Guide. Division for Girls and Women's Sports, American Association for Health, Physical Education, and Recreation. Published biennially (1962).
The Chronicle. Middleburg, Virginia. Published weekly.
Rule Book. United States Combined Training Association. 1959.

FILMS

British Horse Society and the Pony Club. Film strips and lectures. 16 Bedford Square, London, W. C. 1.
United States Equestrian Team, Inc. Gladstone, New Jersey. Olympic and Equestrian Team films available.

8

SWIMMING

8

SWIMMING

Gertrude Goss

In swimming there are two factors that must be recognized from the beginning. These are *breathing* and *relaxation*. They are of the utmost importance, because, until the swimmer has accomplished both, she will never be "at home in the water." No great distance in the water can be covered, nor can swimming be done with ease, until both have been mastered. Often the swimmer herself does not know why it is difficult for her to swim with comfort. An experienced teacher can point out the reason and soon have the swimmer at ease in the water. One of the best aids in teaching swimming is music. No matter at what level—beginning, intermediate, or advanced—through the use of music the swimmer becomes more relaxed and therefore can swim more easily and farther. Music helps the beginner overcome her fear of the water. Intermediate and advanced swimmers can increase their endurance and power by swimming longer distances under the relaxing influence of music. This aid has been successfully used at Smith College since 1925. Most of the recordings used, particularly for beginning classes, are in 3/4 or 4/4 time, because these have a regular, even beat. Later on, uneven rhythms can be introduced and swimming strokes adapted to them.

Today most of us learn to swim during our early years. This is as it should be, because then there are fewer fears to hamper the learning process. Some, however, do not have access to the water and receive their first swimming instruction in school or college. It is they who make up our beginners' classes.

TEACHING STROKES AND DIVING

I. BEGINNING INSTRUCTION

A fear of the water usually has been built up in students who reach adolescence without knowing how to swim. They lack experience in the water and perhaps have heard of frightening accidents in it. The only uses they have for water are bathing and drinking. They have always shut their eyes and held their breath whenever the water covered their faces, and have never been in water deep enough for them to get the feeling of having it support them, or when they did the water was so deep and cold that a nonswimmer has no desire even to try to swim. Along with this, these students sometimes are lacking in coordination.

Before anything else can be learned, the potential swimmer should stand in water waist high and feel it move around the body. The teacher should watch to see that the water covers the student's whole body as she moves up and down in it. The student must accustom herself to the *feel* of the water by standing and jumping up and down in it, and splashing it over her chest and face.

In order to make progress in learning, a beginner needs to have confidence in the person who is teaching her. She must know that she will not be pushed into the water or pulled under unexpectedly. There are many shallow-water games that can be played to help a beginner overcome fear and accustom her to being in the water, and at the same time to enjoy it.[1]

Suddenly she is thrust into a new experience; she *can* open her eyes under water; she *can* breathe out under water; her arms and legs *can* be controlled while in the water.

When this has been accomplished, the next step is to have the potential swimmer float *on top of* the water and let the water support her.

A. Back Float. The back float comes first because it does not require the swimmer to put her face in the water. She merely drops back with arms stretched sideways and lets the water hold her up. This should be practiced by two's, with one student standing at the head of or beside the floater to give her support *if she needs it.* The floater must keep her eyes open and be relaxed while floating.

FIGURE 8.1 *Standing from a back float.*

B. Stand from Back Float. The stand from a back float must be learned next. The arms are extended out from the sides for the back float. In standing, the arms are pulled in toward the body, then forward, and the legs are drawn upward by bending the knees, then straightened toward the bottom (Figure 8.1). The movement is done forcibly as the head is drawn forward to the chest. When this can be done, the individual can work alone without the help of another person.

If the water is shallow enough, a still easier way of allowing the water to lift the body is to have the beginner sit in the water, put her hands on the bottom behind her and move the upper body backward. As the upper body and head are moved backward the feet will rise and the whole body will be lifted by the water. When this has been accomplished, the beginner can move out into deeper water and, with a partner, drop back and float. The next step is to stand from a float, and finally to float and stand alone.

C. Breathing. Before going on to the

[1] See game books listed at end of chapter.

face float, practice in breathing should be given to the beginner. *Breath-holding* comes first. The beginner should stand in water about waist high, breathe in through the *mouth,* close the mouth, and submerge holding the breath. This should be done several times. Each time the face is put in the water the breath should be held for a longer time. The face should be put flat into the water with the beginner urged to keep her eyes open and look at the bottom of the pool.

Next, *continuous breathing* should be practiced. This can be tried on *land* first. In swimming all breathing *in* is done through the *mouth* and *out* through the mouth alone, or through the *mouth and nose.* Have the beginner take a breath through the mouth as the head is turned to one side. Turn the head forward and breathe *out* through the mouth and nose, or the mouth alone. Count 1, 2, 3, while breathing in, 4, 5, 6 while breathing out. Music helps the swimmer to relax while practicing. Strauss waltzes in particular are good to use. This should be done continuously so that the breath is not held at any point. Now have the beginner *stand in water* waist deep with the body bent forward from the waist. Breathing should be practiced in and out, putting the face in the water for exhalation, and turning the head to the side for inhalation. This must be done until the beginner feels perfectly comfortable and does not get out of breath.

Special Note to the Teacher: Some swimmers do not breathe out when their faces are in the water, although *they say* they do. Watch them. If they *are* breathing out there will be bubbles around their heads—if no bubbles, they are holding their breath. Too much cannot be said about the importance of proper breathing. It is a must. Improper breathing tires a swimmer more than anything else.

Opening the eyes under water can be practiced while breathing is being taught.

D. Face Float. The second float to be learned is the face or prone float. Once the beginner has learned to exhale under water, she can attempt this float.

Water shallow enough for the beginner to sit down in is easiest for the first trials. The beginner should roll over on the stomach, with the legs extended directly behind and weight supported on the hands. In this position a breath should be taken, and the face moved forward into the water. At the same time the arms should be extended forward, slowly, beyond the head. When this is done the body will rise toward the surface. Sometimes a push with the feet helps.

If the water is too deep to sit in, the beginners can work by two's. Standing in the water, facing each other, one beginner can bend forward at the waist, take a breath, and give a slight pushoff from the bottom, extending the arms and legs, and with the face in the water float toward the other person, who assists the floater in standing up again.

When teaching the face float in a pool, have the student stand with her back to the wall and extend both arms in front. Have her bend one leg at the knee, and place that foot against the wall. She stands on the other foot, with the knee slightly bent. Instruct her to take a breath in through her mouth, hold it, lean forward, and push off. She should hold her breath, then let it out slowly and stand before she needs another breath (Figure 8.2).

In order to *stand* from a face float, the student must press down against the water with both hands and lift her head. As this is done, she should simultaneously draw both knees toward her chest and then stand.

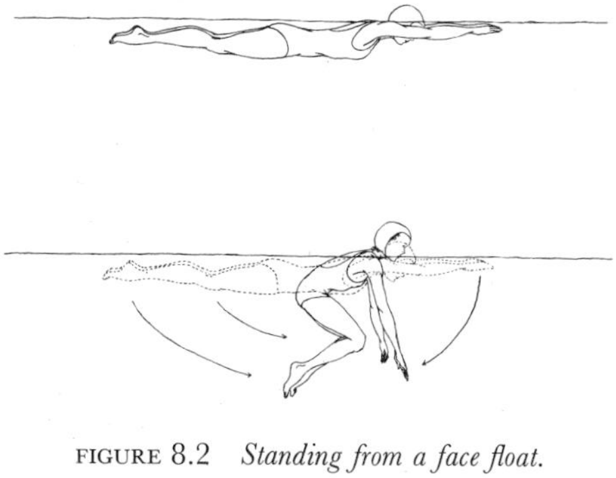

FIGURE 8.2 *Standing from a face float.*

The face float and stand must be learned before the beginner can be left to work alone. Both the floats and stands from floats should be practiced until the beginner is perfectly balanced and relaxed in the water.

E. Glide on Face and Back. The beginner has now learned that the water can support the body, particularly if the body is *relaxed.* Movement across the water involves nothing more than a push with the feet. The object of the glide should be to streamline the body so that it moves easily *across* the water, and to give the beginner the feeling of having the water support her as she moves. If she tends to roll from side to side have her spread arms and legs slightly apart. A greater distance can be aimed at with each glide.

F. Change in Body Position. Confidence and control are learned through the ability to change from face float to back float and vice versa.

1. Face to Back Turn. In the face float both arms are extended over the head. To turn onto the back, one arm remains extended, while the other arm comes down and across the body and is extended to the other side. The head is turned to the side toward which the turn is made. Both arms finish in the side horizontal position.

2. Back to Face Turn. In back floating the arms are extended sideways from the body. To turn on to the face to the left, the right arm is swung across the body as the right leg is crossed over to the left. The arms move from a side horizontal position to an extended position beyond the head.

G. Floats with Kicks.

1. Face Float with Kick. Having mastered the float and the glide, the beginner must now learn the kick. At this stage the movements of the legs are very elementary. In most floats the legs tend to sink, and an easy kicking motion will bring them nearer the surface. The start for the face float with kick is the same as the start for the glide. From the pushoff the legs are extended and an up and down movement from the hips is made. The emphasis is on the *up* kick. On the up motion only the heels should break the surface of the water. The knees and ankles should be relaxed. This kick can be practiced with hands on the bottom or with the hands bracketed on the wall before using it with the glide.

When learning this kick, many students try so hard that they become tense, and kick from the knees, bringing the entire leg out of the water. In doing this, pressure is put against the air, not the water, and there is no movement forward.

2. Back Float with Kick. The back float with kick is the same as used with the face float, up and down. Only the toes come out of the water. The body should be straight with the back of the head in the water. The teacher should see that the head is not lifted, or the chin tucked in as far as has been allowed up to this time. Students should practice this kick holding on to the side of the pool. When the kick is used on a glide, the arms should be close to the sides of the body, or extended, close together, beyond the head.

H. Floats with Arm Movements.

1. Arm Movements with Face Float. The most natural movement of the arms when first used in the face float position is the "dog paddle," or "human stroke." In this movement, first one arm is extended forward and pulled down and back toward the body, then the other. One arm is sliding forward as the other arm is pulling back. The head is held

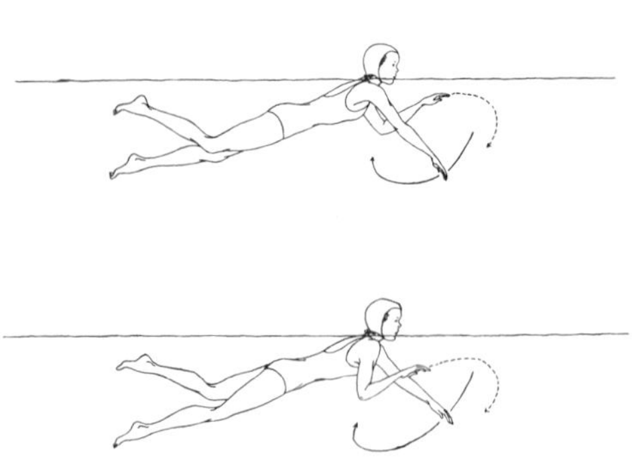

FIGURE 8.3 *The human stroke, or dog paddle.*

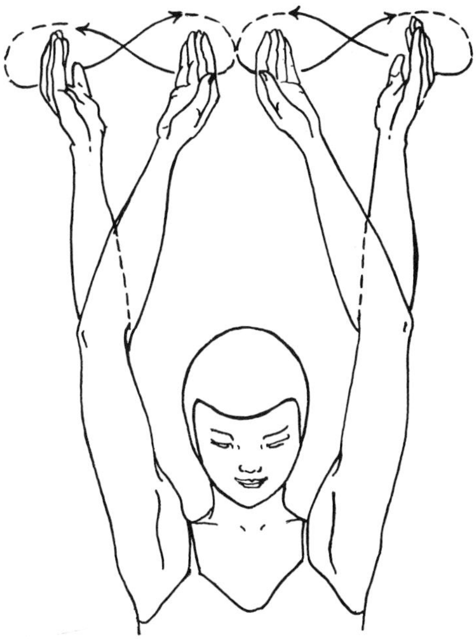

FIGURE 8.4 *Close up of arms in overhead sculling. (From Goss, G.:* Stunts and Synchronized Swimming, *1957.)*

high above the water, and there may be an easy kick of the legs while practicing. The arm motion may be practiced standing on the bottom, and then in the glide position (Figure 8.3).

Today, many teachers do not use the "dog paddle" except for instructing the very young. The out-of-water arm recovery has been found most satisfactory, right from the beginning. Of course, breathing must never be neglected. Music can be used both for relaxation and for rhythm. Count 1, 2, 3—4, 5, 6 on each arm pull.

2. Arm Movements with Back Float. The movement of the arms used at this point is called sculling (Figures 8.4 and 8.5).

a. FIRST STEP. To introduce this, the teacher can have the students stand in shallow water. They should place their hands flat on the pool deck, shoulder width apart, and from this position slide the hands out in the direction of the little fingers—palms down. Then the thumbs are turned up, which makes the palms face each other. They are then pushed or squeezed toward each other. The arms are straight except for a slightly bent elbow.

b. SECOND STEP. The students should repeat the motion while standing with arms extended along the sides of the body.

c. THIRD STEP. Finally, they should drop back and float, keeping straight and doing the same motion, which causes movement toward the head. A slight flutter kick may be done in order to keep the feet up. The students should try to hold their legs straight together and let the sculling motion alone propel them. This sculling motion is basic to all water stunts, which are such fun to do, and which every swimmer wants to learn.

I. KICKS WITH ARM AND LEG MOVEMENTS. The beginner can now practice

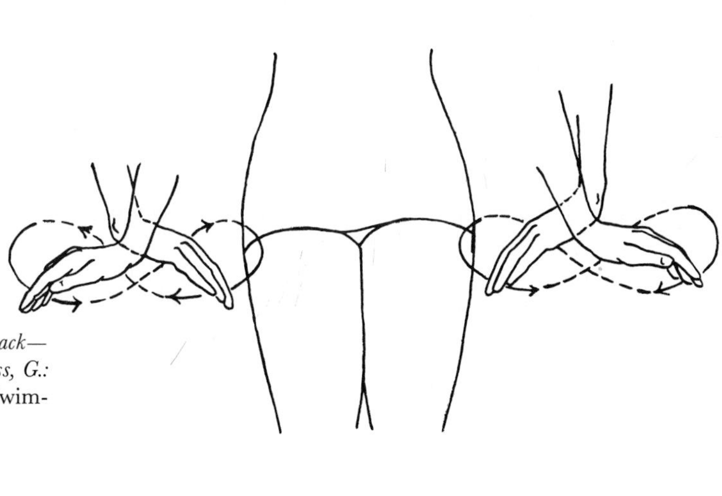

FIGURE 8.5 *Sculling on back—move toward head. (From Goss, G.:* Stunts and Synchronized Swimming, *1957.)*

both arm and leg movements in the face float and back float positions.

J. Summary of Beginning Instruction. Practice in the preceding phases of swimming should have proved to the beginner:

1. That she should have no fear of the water.
2. That the body is buoyant.
3. That the eyes can be kept open under water.
4. That she can breathe in the water, and how to do so.
5. That she can float on either back or face.
6. That she can stand after doing either float.
7. That she can turn from her back on to her face and from her face on to her back.
8. That with easy movements of the arms and legs she can move across the water.
9. The method of performing the sculling motion.

Having accomplished these things, the beginner is ready to learn the strokes in swimming.

II. THE CRAWL

The crawl is the fastest of all swimming strokes. The body lies streamlined and flat on the water. The arms pull one at a time, alternately. The legs move up and down from the hips, also alternating. The head is in line with the body throughout the stroke. In order to breathe *in,* the head is turned to the side, and a "bite of air" is taken. For efficiency there should be a minimum of body roll as the head is turned.

A. Leg Movements

1. Fundamentals.

a. The legs are straight but relaxed; the toes pointed so that the sole of the foot is against the water on the up beat.

b. As one leg is lifted, the other is dropped in the water.

c. The emphasis is on the *up* kick with very little splash, only the heels coming out of the water.

d. The kick is from 12 to 18 inches in depth.

e. The rhythm is even; when used with the arms, the six beat seems to be the best for most swimmers to learn first. That means three beats to the pull of each arm.

2. Practicing Leg Movements Only.

a. On land, lying with legs over the edge of the pool.

b. On land, lying on a stool or bench.

c. Holding on to the side of the pool or the dock. (Practice first with emphasis on the kick only, then add breathing.)

d. From face float, kicking across pool using the legs alone, holding the breath.

The student should next breathe *in* through the mouth, push off from the side or bottom of the pool and breathe *out* while doing the flutter kick. In teaching a group, have them start together and see which one can go the longest distance, or get to a given point first. Everyone loves a race.

e. With flutter boards held in extended arms using the legs alone.

In this practice the distance covered should be increased as the beginner progresses. This can also be practiced as a race. The instructor must be sure, however, that the swimmers keep their kick relaxed. When they try too hard, the tendency is for them to become tense.

3. Faults in Leg Movements.

a. Too much bend at the knees and ankles.

b. Lifting the legs *out* of water. Only the heels should break the surface.

c. Pressing down with the legs. This will stop the progress forward and, in extreme cases, unless the toes are pointed, the swimmer sometimes moves backward.

d. Rigidly lifting and lowering the legs.

e. Not keeping the legs parallel with the long axis of the body.

B. Arm Movements. There is no one way in which the arms should be recovered. The individual student should be allowed to use her own best way so long as she does not impede her progress forward. There are, however, some basic principles from which all students must start.

1. Fundamentals.

a. The arm is extended forward over the water until at full reach.

b. The hand enters the water beyond the head with the elbow slightly higher than the hand. The hand is dropped forward from the wrist and cupped. (Figure 8.6.)

c. The pull begins when the fingers of the hand enter the water.

d. On the pull the arm is bent slightly.

e. The pull continues until the arm is straight down in the water.

f. In the *bent arm* recovery the elbow is lifted out of the water first, the movement starting at the shoulder. The arm is again moved forward to the point of entry beyond the head.

g. In the *straight arm* recovery the hand goes out away from the body, with the little fingers leading. When the arm is out of the water, the hand is turned palm down and the arm moves forward until the fingers are placed in the water well in front of the shoulder. The straight arm recovery is not high, but it must clear the surface of the water.

h. The hand in front of the head does not start down until the other arm has started forward.

2. Practicing Arm Movements Only, On Land.

a. The arm movements should be explained and demonstrated.

b. As flexible shoulders are important in the crawl, the shoulder motion can be practiced first. To practice this, stand with the upper body bent forward, letting the arms hang. Lift and rotate first one shoulder and then the other. As one shoulder is raised the other is lowered. At first use just the shoulders, letting the arms continue to hang. Then gradually

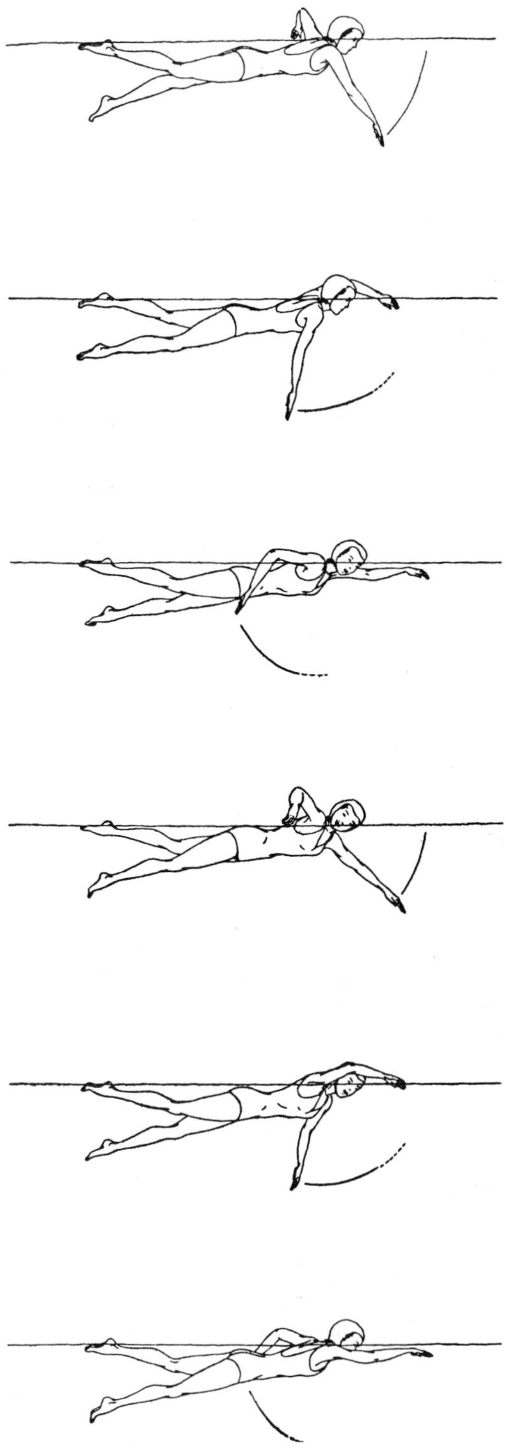

FIGURE 8.6 *Action of the arms and legs in the crawl stroke.*

lift the shoulder *and arm* with the forearm loose, until the elbow is high and there is no body rotation. The forearm and hand are then moved forward until the arm reaches straight forward. The hand is then pulled straight down under the shoulder, and the arm is ready to be lifted again. This movement is practiced on land until a certain amount of rhythm and flexibility have been acquired.

c. Breathing can be practiced on land by having the swimmer turn the head to whichever side seems more natural for inhalation. The breath is taken in as the arm on the breathing side is lifted. As the same arm moves forward the head is turned forward, and the swimmer breathes out.

3. Practicing Arm Movements Only, In Water. The swimmer can now practice the movement of the arms while standing in water between waist and shoulder depth.

a. Lean forward from the waist with one arm extended in front of the body. Continue with the breathing, practicing with the arms alone. This practice may be done standing still or walking forward as the arms pull down.

b. Repeat the same practice in the water, letting the feet come up from the bottom and flutter at will. Emphasize and encourage correct breathing at all times.

c. The arm and breathing practice can be done with the feet bracketed at the side of the pool or dock. If there is no place for bracketing the feet, the swimmer's feet may be held, low in the water, by the instructor. For group practice, divide the class in two's, and have every other swimmer practice the arm movements while the partner gives support. The partner lies flat on the deck while giving the support.

4. Faults in Arm Movements.

a. There is no power in the pull if the wrist is turned up instead of dropping forward. The pull should start with the fingertips, fingers always closed.

b. The arm is not pulled down far enough under the body, or the arm is pulled too far back.

c. The arms are not pulled down in a straight line.

d. In entering the water, the hands come across in front of the head; this stops the progress ahead and prevents a straight pull down.

e. The arms zigzag down through the water instead of pulling straight toward the hips.

C. Whole Stroke. Having practiced the leg and arm movements and breathing separately, the swimmer is ready to go on to coordinate the three. The body assumes a better balanced position when a pushoff is used to start. This pushoff can be taken from the bottom or from a wall.

Music in waltz time may be profitably used at this point.

The swimmer should be encouraged to breathe once every complete arm stroke.

D. Body Position. The swimmer should be as flat on the water as possible, her head in line with her spine. This position tends to streamline the body, so that it moves through the water with the least possible resistance.

E. Breathing. The head should be *turned* for breathing, not lifted; lifting the head tends to change the body position and lower the legs.

III. THE ELEMENTARY BACKSTROKE

A backstroke can be practiced along with the crawl. The swimmer has learned to float both on the face and the back, and should now learn strokes in both these positions. The elementary backstroke is a resting stroke, and allows the swimmer to move while in a resting position. In this stroke the back is flat on the water with the head in line with the spine and the chin tucked slightly forward. The arms and legs move entirely under water.

A. Leg Movements. The legs start straight and together, with the toes pointed. On count *one* the legs remain in this position. On count *two* the legs are drawn up toward the body with the knees spread and either the heels or the soles of the feet together. On count *three* the legs are moved sideways and together. The power of the kick is in bringing the legs *forcibly together* at the end of count three. On count *four* the legs remain straight and together.

B. Arm Movements. At the start of the stroke the arms are along the sides of the body. On count *one,* the hands are moved up along the sides of the body with the elbows back and the hands close to the body, the fingers pointing toward the feet until the hands reach the shoulders where the fingers point diagonally upward and outward. On count *two,* the arms are moved diagonally upward and outward, halfway between the side horizontal and the straight upward position. On count *three,* the arms are pulled forcibly back to the sides of the body. On count *four,* the arms are held at the sides.

The pull with the arms and the drive together with both legs come at the same time.

C. Whole Stroke.

On count *one,* the legs remain straight and together. (Figure 8.7.) The hands are moved up along the sides of the body to shoulder level. On count *two,* the legs are drawn up with the knees spread. The arms move diagonally up and outward. On count *three,* the legs are spread sideways and whipped together. The arms pull to the body, back to the starting position. On count *four,* the legs and arms are held for the glide.

D. Breathing. Regular breathing is important in the backstroke even though the face is out of the water during the entire stroke.

The breath should be taken in through the mouth during the recovery of the stroke, and let through the mouth and nose during the pull and glide.

E. Practicing Leg Movements Only.

1. On land, sit and lean the upper body back, resting on hands or elbows.
2. In water, lie on back, holding on to the side of the pool or dock.
3. Assume the floating position on the back, hold the arms straight at the sides or place the hands on the hips. A sculling motion with the hands may also be used, while practicing the leg movement.

F. Practicing Arm Movements Only.

1. Standing on land.
2. In the water, by two's having one assume the back floating position. Number two supports number one's ankles.

G. Arm and Leg Movements Together.

1. On land, stand and practice both arms and one leg. Use first one leg and then the other for this practice.
2. In water, push off on back with the arms starting at the sides and the legs straight and together; practice the whole stroke.

H. Faults in Elementary Backstroke.

1. Faults of Body Position.

a. Bringing the head too far forward, causing the legs to sink.

b. Bending forward at the waist in a near sitting position, causing too much resistance against the water.

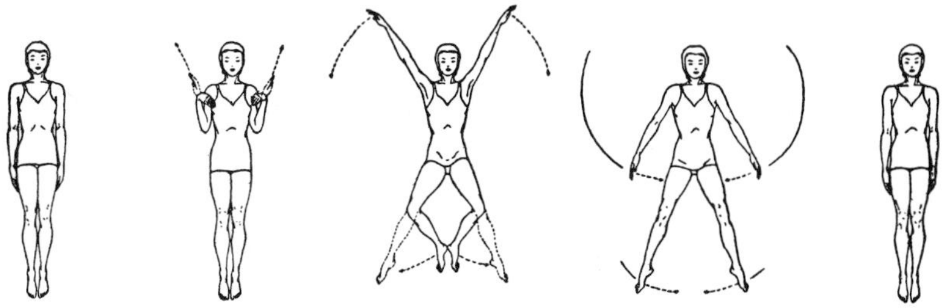

FIGURE 8.7 *The elementary backstroke.*

2. Faults of the Legs.

a. Bringing the knees up too high on the draw, causing the swimmer to curl forward.

b. Moving the legs with a jerk and *kicking* out instead of moving them out slowly.

c. Letting the legs float together instead bringing them together with force.

d. Not holding the legs straight and together at the end of the whip.

3. Faults of the Arms.

a. Not keeping the arms close to the body when the hands move up to the shoulders.

b. Not making the movement continuous until back at the starting position.

c. Not getting an even pull with both arms.

d. Bringing the arms up across the body.

e. Not pushing against the water with force on the pull to the sides.

f. Not holding the glide at the end of the pull.

g. Breaking the surface of the water at any time.

IV. THE BREAST STROKE

This stroke has gone through many changes in the last few years. The result of these changes has been to bring about a new stroke, the butterfly. This stroke having been accepted, there are now four strokes instead of three. It is mentioned at this point because it was developed from the breast stroke.

Before taking up the movements of these strokes in detail, a brief review of their development follows.

Originally the head was held high out of the water, as it still is in life saving. This position, however, is poor for racing because it makes the body ride the water at too much of an angle, increasing the resistance. Now the head is lifted *forward* during the pull of the arms, just high enough so that a breath can be taken through the mouth, and lowered during the recovery and glide of the arms for speed.

At first the "frog" kick of the legs was used. Gradually, the arm pull and the leg drive have dropped from the horizontal plane, with the knees well spread on the draw, into a plane between the horizontal and the vertical. The arms pull obliquely *downward* and *back,* and the knees *drop* (still slightly separated) so that the greatest amount of power comes from the circumduction of the leg and not from the "frog" kick action with the knees wide spread and closed together.

Next, using a *pull through* of the arms, under-water swimming of the breast stroke became very popular. This introduced the long arm pull, which gave added power to the stroke.

The real change came with the bringing of both arms out of water on the recovery part of the stroke, which was the beginning of the butterfly breast stroke (V). The arms come out of the water on their recovery, and the pull is not as long as it had been. It is shorter and more downward. This stroke was used by many men and some women in the Berlin Olympics (1936). All this time the leg kick remained the same except for the slight lowering of the knees. This new arm stroke conformed to the breast stroke rules, as they state only that "all movements of the arms must be symmetrical and simultaneous, and all recoveries must be over the water."

Many swimming authorities felt that it was not fair to allow the butterfly breast stroke to be used in the same race against the orthodox breast stroke because of the advantage gained. A swimmer was allowed to swim either method during a race, or to change from one to the other. In 1946 F.I.N.A. made a distinction between the orthodox (including the underwater style) and the latest stroke by ruling that the swimmer, on coming to the surface, must complete the race using the type he did on his first surface stroke. In the London Olympics nearly everyone chose to swim the butterfly breast stroke, and at Helsinki all were using this stroke, bringing both arms out of the water on the recovery part of the stroke.

We shall examine first the original breast stroke.

A. Leg Movements Only. At the start of the stroke the legs are straight and together, with the toes pointed. On count *one,* the legs are held in the starting position. On count *two,* the feet are drawn up, the knees bent and apart. On count *three,* the feet move apart and are "whipped" back to the starting position. On count *four,* hold and glide.

B. Arm Movements Only. Start with the arms extended forward, the hands just below the surface of the water and flat. The face is in the water. On count *one,* the palms turn outward and both arms are pulled slightly downward and sideward, almost to the side horizontal position. A breath is taken during this movement as the head is lifted forward. and upward, just high enough for the mouth to clear the top of the water.

On count *two,* the elbows are bent and the arms are brought in together under the chest, the palms down, the elbows close to the sides, the index fingers meeting. The breath is let out on counts two, three, four, and the face is lowered in the water. On count *three,* the arms slide easily forward below the surface with the palms down, to starting position. On count *four,* hold and glide.

C. Whole Stroke. The starting position is with the arms and legs extended, and straight (Figure 8.8). On count *one,* the legs remain still. The arms pull to a position just in front of the shoulders. Count *two,* the legs are drawn up. The arms are brought in under the chest. Count *three,* the legs are moved outward, then together. The arms slide forward to the starting position. Count *four,* the legs and arms are held together.

D. Breathing. The head is lifted forward on count *one,* as the swimmer breathes in through the mouth. On count *two,* the head is lowered and the swimmer breathes out through the mouth and nose or through the mouth only (either way is correct). Correct breathing should be practiced from the very beginning. It can never be stressed too much. The swimmer continues to breathe out on counts *three* and *four.*

E. Practing Leg Movements Only.

1. On Land.

a. Sit, leaning the weight back on the hands; practice movements of legs only.

b. Stand; practice movements of first one leg and then the other.

c. Lie flat on a stool; practice leg movements only.

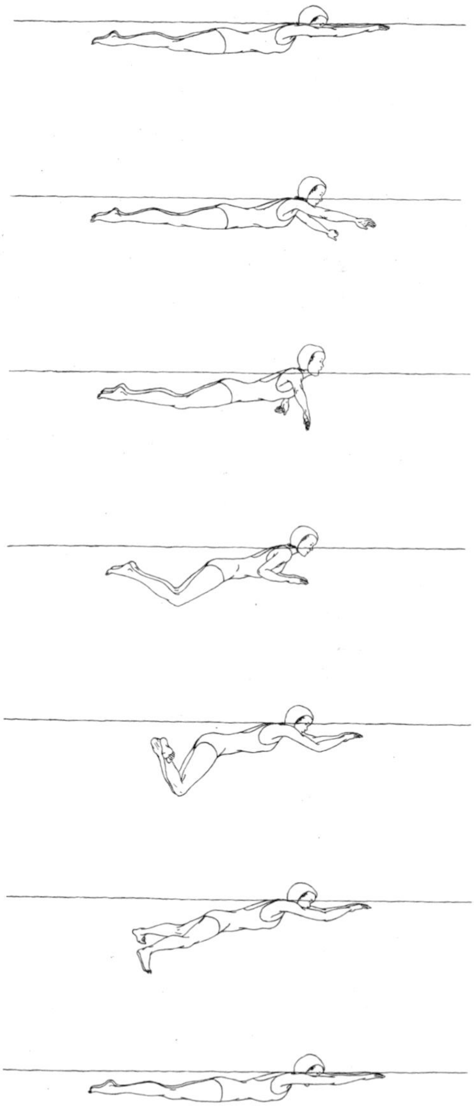

FIGURE 8.8 *The breast stroke.*

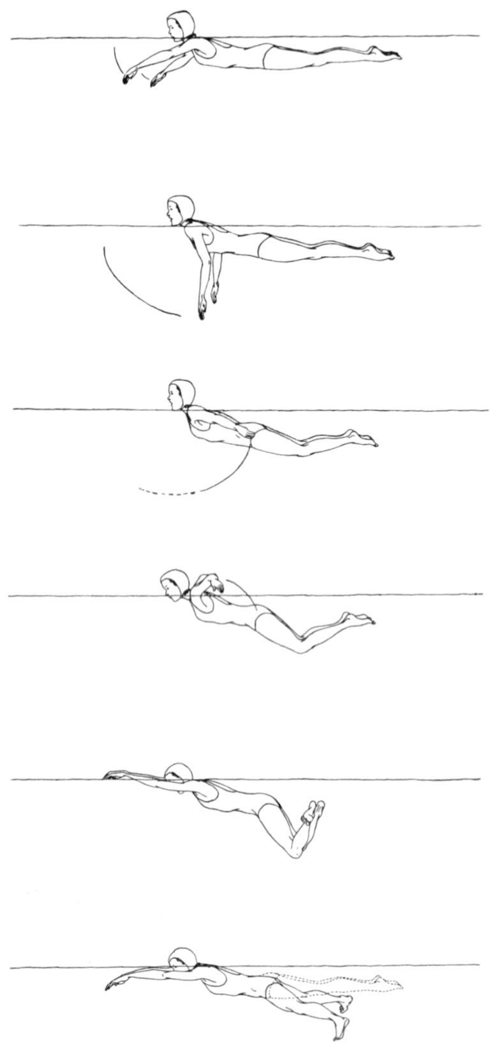

FIGURE 8.9 *The butterfly breast stroke.*

2. In Water.

a. Hold on to side of pool or dock.

b. Hold a flutter board in front of body, practice the leg movements only.

F. Practicing Arm Movements Only.

1. On Land.

a. Stand, practice arm movements only.

2. In Water.

a. Stand, bending forward so that the shoulders are submerged.

b. Push off from bottom or side and practice the arm movements only.

G. Arm and Leg Movements Together.

1. On land, sit with the arms and legs in front of the body; practice movements of both together.

2. In water, push off and practice the whole stroke.

H. Faults in Breast Stroke.

1. Breathing and Body Balance.

a. Breathing at the wrong time breaks the rhythm of the stroke, and tires the swimmer.

b. Turning the head to the side at any time is apt to make for incorrect body balance.

2. Faults of Legs.

a. Kicking the legs *out* instead of moving them out easily.

b. Starting the leg movements too soon.

c. Using a scissors instead of a breast stroke kick, namely the frog kick.

d. Not getting enough drive together.

e. Not holding a slight glide at end of each stroke.

3. Faults of Arms.

a. Pulling them too far back on count one.

b. Bringing the arms out of water.

c. Pushing the arms forward from the chest with a jerk.

d. Not getting an even pull with both hands.

V. THE BUTTERFLY BREAST STROKE

The first change in the breast stroke as a racing stroke came with bringing both arms out of the water on the recovery. The variation was called the butterfly breast stroke.

A. Leg Movements. The kick is the same as in the breast stroke (see page 244), except that the knees are dropped a little more underneath the body, and there is not such a wide spread.

B. Arm Movements. On the recovery, the arms are thrown outward and forward over the surface of the water. The elbows should be a little higher than the arms and the arms should be relaxed.

The palms are turned down. The arms are moved to a forward point beyond the head. When the hands come in contact with the water, they start a downward pull. Since the pull is straight down, it gives the body a lift forward over the water.

C. Whole Stroke. Starting with the body straight, arms and legs extended, the arms pull down, then the knees are dropped, and the legs move out and are *driven together* as the arms are lifted from the water and move back to the starting position. (Figure 8.9.)

D. Breathing. As the arms are pulled down, the breath is taken *in.* For some swimmers, it is best to breathe once every other stroke while practicing at first. In racing it is essential not to breathe so frequently.

VI. THE BUTTERFLY STROKE

The latest development is the separation of the orthodox breast stroke and the butterfly breast stroke into two separate strokes and events by F.I.N.A. and A.A.U. They were swum as such in the 1956 Olympics in Australia by the men, who have continued doing so ever since.

D.G.W.S. has just made the same change in their rules. Separating these strokes means that there are four racing strokes instead of three, and that the individual medley and the medley relays consist of four strokes. At present the F.I.N.A., A.A.U., and D.G.W.S. rules for the new butterfly stroke read:

The swimmer must remain on the surface:

a. Both arms must be brought forward together over the water and brought backward simultaneously.

b. The body must be kept perfectly on the breast, and both shoulders in line with the surface of the water.

c. All movements of the legs and feet must be executed in a simultaneous manner. Simultaneous up and down movements of the legs and feet in a vertical plane are permitted. *Scissors, frog* and *single flutter kicks* are prohibited.

d. When touching at the turn or on finishing a race, the touch shall be made simultaneously with both hands, the shoulders remaining in a horizontal position.

e. Any competitor introducing a side-stroke movement shall be disqualified.

Now that the *butterfly stroke* (Figure 8.10) has come into being and the rules read "Simultaneous up and down movements of the legs and feet in a vertical plane are permitted," a different kick is being used called the *dolphin* or *fishtail.* This kick has been experimented with since 1930. It is most simply described as a *double flutter crawl kick.* It is easier to learn, according to some coaches if the swimmer has swum only the crawl and not the breast stroke before.

A. Dolphin (Fishtail) Kick. The kick involves not just the legs alone, but a movement of the whole body in a fish-

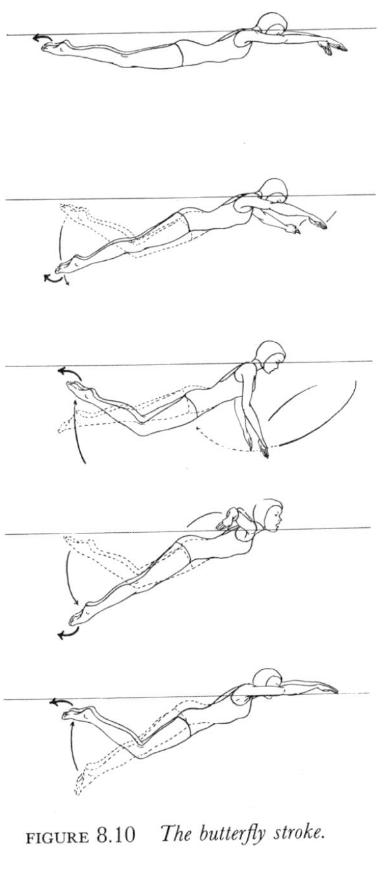

FIGURE 8.10 *The butterfly stroke.*

like action, with particular emphasis in the lower back region.

From a trailing position of the legs, the hips are lifted to start the upward movement of the legs. The knees begin to bend as they pass through the line of body progression. When the feet are just below the water, the knees are quickly straightened and the legs brought forcibly down. As in the crawl kick, the feet are relaxed and the toes are slightly turned in. In using this fishlike motion there is much less resistance to the water than when using the froglike kick with its recovery against the water. It can be practiced as follows:

1. Hold on to the side of the pool, legs together.
2. Go under water and do the dolphin kick with the arms at the sides of the body.
3. When the body or hip movement is felt, then the bend of the knees and drive at the end of the up and down strokes can be worked on.
4. After learning the above motions, stress the action of the ankles so that the feet press against the water on both up and down beats of the legs.
5. This kick can be practiced with a kick board.

B. Arm Movements. The action of the arms is the same as that described for the butterfly breast stroke. The glide can be lengthened or shortened according to the distance to be covered.

C. Timing Arm and Leg Movements. The most satisfactory rhythm used to date is two leg beats to one cycle of the arms. As the legs are the controlling part of this stroke, it will be analyzed according to their action.

The legs start straight and together except for a slight bend at the knees. The arms extended beyond the head begin the stroke.

The hands take hold of the water for the pull, the hips start upward, and the legs finish the down beat. The legs drive up while the arms are pulling. Then the legs begin the second down beat as the arms go back over the water to the extended position beyond the head.

D. Breathing. The head is lifted by the downward, backward pull of the arms. This lift of the head should be *forward,* just high enough to enable the swimmer to take in a a breath through the mouth. Lifting the head too high will lessen the swimmers forward movement.

VII. THE SIDE STROKE

The side stroke is *not* a racing stroke and most speed swimmers stay away from it, believing it to be harmful. However, there are many swimmers who do not desire speed and who find this stroke restful and powerful. It is also very important in life saving. With a knowledge of the side stroke, the single overarm and trudgeon can be learned. The side stroke may be executed on either side. The following description is for a swimmer who swims on the right side.

A. Side Balance and Glide. Before going into a discussion of the movements used in the side stroke, it is helpful for the swimmer to learn the side pushoff and balance. This position requires more control than either the face or back floats, which have already been learned.

1. Standing in shallow water, turn so that the left side is toward the edge of pool or dock.
2. Grasp the rail with the left hand and place both feet against the side of the pool, with the knees bent. The right arm is extended out across the water, the head resting on the right shoulder and turned so that the swimmer is looking *back* toward her feet.
3. Take in a breath, push off with both feet and let the body lie on the side. Slowly exhale and straighten the body. Hold the body balance on the side for as long as possible.
4. The left arm should rest on top of the left thigh, the right arm extended beyond the head. The legs should be together with the left leg on top of the right.

B. Leg Movements Only. Start on right side with legs extended together, and the toes pointed. On count *one,* draw the knees slightly upward keeping the legs together. Count *two,* separate the legs, moving the top leg forward as the under leg moves backward. Count *three,* drive the legs together back to the starting position. The drive is with the sole of the left foot and the instep of the right foot. Count *four,* hold the legs together at the end of the drive.

C. Arm Movements Only. On right side. On count *one,* the right arm pulls down in the water. Just after the start of the right arm pull, the left arm is carried across in front of the body, with the hand leading. Counts *two* and *three,* the right arm is drawn up toward the right shoulder and extended forward beneath the surface, to the starting position, as the left arm pulls down close to the body, back to the top of the left thigh. Count *four,* hold and glide at the end of the stroke.

D. Breathing. A breath is taken in during the glide, and let out slowly, during the stroke itself.

E. Whole Stroke. Count *one,* pull the right arm down three-fourths of the way to the body. Just after the right arm pull starts, the left arm is brought across the body, beyond the right shoulder. At the same time the knees are drawn slightly upward. Counts *two* and *three,* the right hand is moved up toward the right shoulder and slides forward to the starting position as the left arm pulls back to the top of the left thigh. At the same time the legs are separated and drive together. Count *four,* hold and glide.

F. Practicing Leg Movements Only.

1. On Land.

a. Lie across bench or stool.

b. Lie on edge of pool or dock, with the legs extended over edge.

2. In Water.

a. Holding on to side of the pool or dock.

b. Practice the kick only, with flutter board. To help keeping the side balance, push off from the bottom or side of the pool.

c. Without flutter board, push off, maintaining side balance, and practice the leg movements alone.

G. Practicing Arm Movements Only.

1. On Land. Stand and practice arm movements only.

2. In Water.

a. Stand with the water not quite shoulder high, the body leaning to the right.

b. Same as above but moving to the right, letting the arm movements move the body. Feet may be dragged along the bottom during this practice.

c. Push off using only the arm movements.

H. Practicing the Whole Stroke. From pushoff, practice both arm and leg movements trying to decrease the number of strokes over a given distance each time (Figure 8.11).

I. Faults in Side Stroke. Not remaining on the side throughout the stroke.

1. Faults of the Legs.

a. Using force on the separation of the legs instead of moving them easily apart.

b. Moving the upper leg *up* toward the surface of the water instead of forward.

c. Moving the under leg down in the water instead of back.

d. Letting the legs drift together, instead of using a drive.

e. Crossing the legs at the end of the drive.

f. Using a reverse scissors kick.

g. Bending the knees too much on the draw.

2. Faults of the Arms.

a. Using force during the recovery movements.

b. Swinging the left arm out, away from the body.

c. Letting the left arm go back beyond the thigh at the end of the pull.

d. Pulling the right arm down too

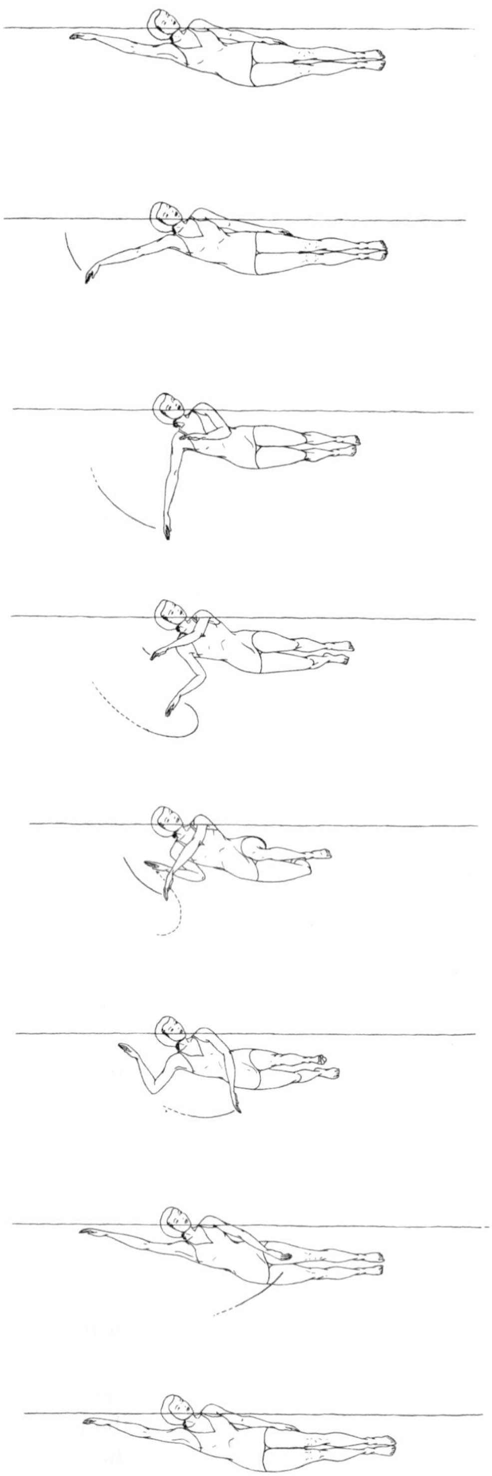

FIGURE 8.11 *The side stroke.*

far under the body, causing the swimmer to bob up and down.

e. Pushing the right arm forcibly forward from the shoulder on the recovery.

f. Bringing either hand out of the water at any time.

g. Not holding the glide at the end of each stroke.

VIII. THE SINGLE OVERARM OR SIDE OVERARM STROKE

A. Single Overarm Stroke without Roll.

1. Description. After the side stroke has been learned, it is fairly easy for the swimmer to learn the single overarm stroke. For this stroke, the body position is the same as in the side stroke and the legs continue to do the scissors kick. The arms alternate their pulls, but the top arm instead of recovering under water is lifted out of the water with the elbow bent and relaxed, and is extended to a point beyond the head. A clean entry should be made with the hand. The body remains on the side throughout the stroke.

2. Practice. The single overarm stroke may be practiced by simply continuing the side stroke and having the swimmer lift the top arm out of the water on recovery (Figure 8.12).

It is possible also to practice the arm movement on land. In water about waist deep, stand and lean to the right side, submerging the shoulders; practice the arm movements alone, recovering the top arm out of the water.

When this stroke is practiced in the water, the left arm is relaxed from the time it lifts out of the water until it enters the water with the fingers leading, at a point beyond the head.

3. Breathing. A breath is taken in during the glide and let out durng the stroke.

4. Faults in Single Overarm Stroke. The faults of the under arm and legs are the same as in the side stroke. The top arm faults will be:

FIGURE 8.12 *The single overarm or side overarm stroke.*

a. Bringing the arm too high out of the water, which tends to submerge the body.

b. Not lifting the arm high enough so that it drags through the water, causing resistance against the water.

c. Reaching too far forward with the arm, causing the body to roll onto the face, instead of staying on the side.

d. Circling the arm around the head, instead of reaching straight forward.

e. Letting the arm drop into the water on the entry instead of entering with the fingers first, and the arm following.

f. Throwing the arm forcibly forward, making the stroke jerky.

B. Single Overarm Stroke with Quarter Turn. This is not a stroke, but sometimes is an easy progression in going from the single overarm to the double overarm or trudgeon stroke. In it the reach of the top arm is well beyond the head so that in reaching forward the body is rolled over on the face, and as the arm pulls down, the body rolls back to the side. The action of the under arm and the legs is the same as in the side stroke and the single overarm.

The quarter turn can be learned by many more easily without a land drill. Try going directly from the single overarm into the quarter turn, adding the longer reach ahead and the roll of the body from the side to the front and back again.

1. Arm Movements. On count *one,* as the right arm is pulled down the left lifts out of the water and is moved as far in front of the head as possible. As the arm is reached forward, the body rolls on to the face, putting the face in the water. Counts *two* and *three,* the right hand comes up to the right shoulder and moves forward under the water as in the side stroke. The left arm is pulled down to the left side, making the body roll back to the side. On count *four,* there is a *very short* hold or glide when the stroke is finished and while the body is on the side.

2. Leg Movements. The leg action is the same as that in the side stroke except that the separation of the legs is somewhat narrower. The kick is made while the body is on the side and the legs are held together while the body is on the face.

3. Faults in the Overarm Stroke.

a. Pulling the arms down away from the body instead of straight down. The right arm tends to this more than the left.

b. Dragging the left arm through the water on the recovery instead of lifting it out of the water.

c. Bringing the left arm too high out of the water.

d. Circling the left arm around the head on the recovery instead of reaching forward.

e. Starting the leg kick when the body is on the face, instead of on the side.

IX. THE TRUDGEON OR DOUBLE OVERARM STROKE

The trudgeon is a hand-over-hand stroke plus a scissors kick with the legs. It is an excellent distance stroke and when once learned and coordinated it can be used indefinitely with very little effort. There is more roll in the trudgeon than the crawl due to the scissors kick. Having already learned the scissors for the side stroke and the single overarm is a good start toward the trudgeon. The trudgeon can also be learned with the crawl as its background.

A. Leg Movements. Grasp the side of the pool with the left hand high and the right hand low against the wall (all movements are given for a person who does the side stroke on the right side). In this manner, hold the body floating on the right side with the legs extended straight behind. On count *one,* do the scissors kick while the body is in a semi-side position. Breathe in. Counts *two* and *three,* complete the leg drive as the body rolls onto the face and hold the legs together after the drive. Breathe out.

B. Arm Movements. Stand in shallow water, bend forward submerging the shoulders. The right arm should be extended straight forward, and the left arm straight back. On count *one,* the left arm recovers forward, over the water, as the right arm is pulled down. The body roll onto the face starts as the left arm is moved forward. Counts *two* and *three,* the body rolls back to a semi-side position with the pull of the left arm and the recovery of the right arm.

C. Whole Stroke. On count *one,* breathe in from a side pushoff, with the right arm extended forward and the left arm back, the legs together. As the right arm is pulled down, the left arm recovers out of the water, reaching well forward. Do a scissors kick with the legs while on the side; roll the body onto the face as the leg drive is finished, and exhale. Counts *two* and *three,* the legs are held together. The body is on the face as the left arm is pulled down and the right arm recovers out of the water, rolling the body to the semi-side position. There is a *very slight* pause each time the body rolls back to a semi-side position.

D. Faults in Trudgeon.

1. Incorrect coordination.
2. Kicking when the legs should be holding.
3. Not making the rhythm slightly uneven.
4. Not lifting the arms high enough to clear the surface.
5. Having an unequal pull with the arms.

E. Teaching of Trudgeon. The trudgeon can be learned from two approaches. The approach used depends on the strokes already learned by the swimmer.

1. From the Side Stroke. For this no land drills are necessary.

a. Practice the single overarm.

b. Practice the single overarm with quarter turn.

c. Go directly from the single overarm into the trudgeon.

2. From the Crawl.

a. Practice the flutter kick alone; then add a major scissors kick and a slight body roll.

b. Practice the scissors kick at the side of the pool or dock.

c. Push off on face, roll the body to the left at the last half of the left arm pull. Let the legs drag, merely practicing the arm movements and body roll.

d. After practicing the roll and arm movements, add a major scissors kick to the flutter kick as soon as the body is on its side.

X. THE TRUDGEON CRAWL

For the swimmer who has learned the trudgeon or the crawl, the trudgeon crawl is a fairly simple stroke to learn. As a matter of fact many crawl swimmers are actually doing a trudgeon crawl unknowingly by employing a major scissors beat between flutters.

When learned after the trudgeon, the swimmer adds three or four flutters between the scissors kick in place of holding the legs still.

When learned after the crawl, the swimmer rolls slightly to the breathing side and makes a narrow scissors kick, then rolls back on to the face, continuing the flutter kick.

XI. THE BACKSTROKE

There are many variations in the backstroke, but in many ways it is the crawl turned over on the back. It is one of the four racing strokes, and is the fastest stroke on the back.

A. **Leg Movements.**

1. **Technique.**

a. The swing is from the hips with the legs relaxed. The toes are pointed and the pressure is on the up beat.

b. The legs are bent slightly at the knees and ankles.

c. The kick is an up and down motion about 10 to 12 inches in depth.

d. The six beat rhythm seems best for most swimmers—that is, three beats to each complete arm cycle.

2. **Practice.**

a. Sit on land, lean back on hands or bent elbows for support; lift both legs together; be sure the toes are pointed; practice six beat kick.

b. Bracketed to side of pool or dock.

c. From back pushoff, practice kick alone with arms extended straight overhead.

d. From back pushoff with arms finning or sculling along the body, practice kick only.

B. **Arm Movements.**

1. **Technique.**

a. The arms work alternately. As one arm pulls, the other arm is recovering.

b. The lift of the arms out of the water starts with the little fingers.

c. The arm is moved out away from the body so that no water splashes the face. The arm is straight, but relaxed on the recovery.

d. The hand, cupped, goes into the water when the arm is *well above* shoulder height, but not as high as in the old method, which was beyond the head.

e. The hand goes into the water with the palm dropped forward. The pull is not deep as before, but more parallel to the surface of the water, so there is little or no body roll. The pull starts with the finger tips, and is followed by a squeeze into the sides of the body.

2. **Practice.**

a. On land, standing.

b. In the water, lying on the back with the legs held by another person.

c. From back pushoff, practice the arm movements alone.

C. **Whole Stroke.** Push off on back in water and practice both arm and leg movements, making three leg kicks to each complete arm pull (Figure 8.13).

D. **Body Position.** The body should be flat on the water, to make as little resistance as possible. The head should be

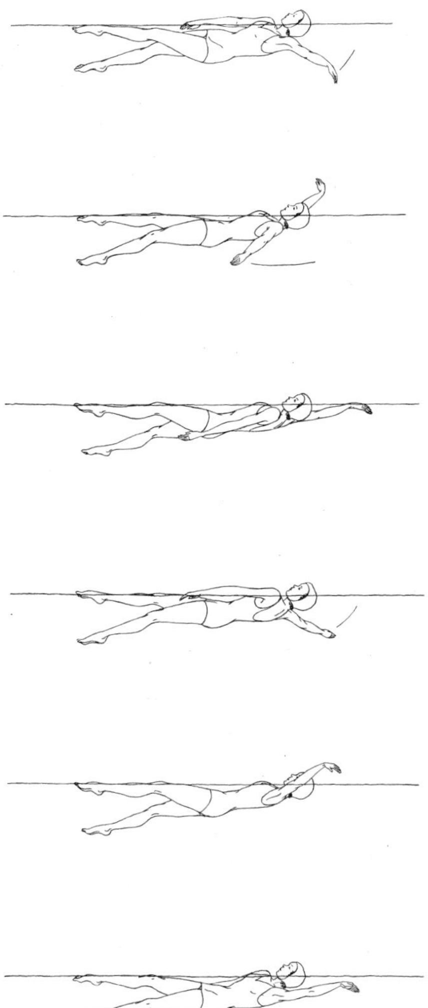

FIGURE 8.13 *The backstroke.*

well back, with the chin tucked in just enough so the swimmer is looking toward her feet, the head in line with the body. Some coaches and swimmers prefer having the head further back in the water. Today the swimmer is taught to look up toward the ceiling or the sky.

E. Breathing. The breath should be taken in once every complete arm cycle.

F. Faults in Backstroke.

1. Faults of Legs.

a. The entire motion is rigid (not relaxed).

b. Kicking from the knees instead of from the hips.

c. The toes turned up and the ankles rigid.

d. Too shallow a kick.

e. A downward pressure of the legs.

2. Faults of Arms.

a. Recovery is too rigid. The arms are bought too close to the face. The recovery should be a movement of the arms to the above-shoulder entrance.

b. Letting the elbows drag and enter the water first, instead of the finger tips.

c. Completing one complete arm cycle before the other arm starts, breaking rhythm.

XII. DIVING

Along with learning how to swim, there is considerable value in having the swimmer learn how to enter the water head first. Courage and confidence are developed increasingly as the individual goes through the learning stages and into more difficult dives. An added skill is accomplished along with freedom of movement and grace. Diving also has value as an exercise. It should be started early, while the swimmer is still a beginner.

a. Jumping into the water feet first may come before diving. Start the jump from the shallow end of the pool and work up to the deep end.

b. Before the dive is done from the side of the pool, the beginner can stand in shallow water, with the arms extended over the head and the thumbs locked together, take a breath, bend forward from the hips, and, giving a push from the bottom, dive forward under the water.

It is always a good idea to have a demonstration and explanation. The swimmer must be shown:

1. How to come to the surface by lifting the head and turning the hands upward.

2. Breath control. Take a breath, hold it while going down, and let it out on the way up.

3. Form. Keep the arms straight overhead on a line beside the ears, with the thumbs locked together. Have the fingers enter the water first and the feet last.

A. The Sitting Dive. In teaching a beginner to dive, it is best to have her start from a point as close to the water as possible. In most cases, the first dive is the sitting dive. At first, the diver simply falls into the water, glides, and comes to the surface. The start is made with the arms extended over the head, the beginner bending forward until the finger tips are in the water. Keeping the head down, the beginner drops into the water, and must be encouraged to go deep, so the entire body and legs are in the water before the turn to come up is made. If the dive is done from the side of a pool, the heels rest in the gutter, and knees are *spread.*

Breathing is most important, and the diver must be reminded to take a breath, hold it while going down, and let it out on the way up. This must be repeated over and over, until done with ease.

Assistance may be given by the instructor holding the diver's head low and giving her an easy push as she drops forward.

A sitting dive with the knees *together* is the next step.

B. The Kneeling Dive. Kneeling on one knee with the toes of the other foot over the edge of the pool or dock, the diver falls forward into the water. In practicing this dive, the beginner kneels alternately on one knee and then on the other, keeping the head between the arms.

C. The Dive From One Leg. Standing with the toes of one foot over the edge of the pool or dock and with the knee bent, the beginner reaches the other leg straight back, locks arms together over the head. The upper body bends forward over the water and the rear leg is lifted straight up. Balance is lost forward and both legs are lifted. In practicing this dive the beginner stands alternately on one foot and then on the other.

D. The Dive Forward From Both Feet. The diver should stand with the arms up over the head, the thumbs locked together. Bending forward from the waist, she should reach for the water and drop in.

E. The Standing or Dock Dive. The diver should stand *erect* at the edge of the pool, with legs together and toes not over the edge, but with the whole foot flat on the surface. The arms are extended forward at shoulder height.

Bend the knees slightly as the heels are lifted, push *up,* straightening the knees, then bow forward to the water, lowering the arms and head, with the finger tips reaching for the water.

After this dive has been practiced the diver may start with the arms at the sides and move them forward and upward over the head, as the push up is taken from the side (Figure 8.14).

1. Diving Practice.

a. Standing back from the edge, practice an easy spring jump in place. The emphasis should be on the *push up* with an easy ankle and knee action. This practice may be done first without the use of the arms; then have the arms move forward and upward as the ankles push up.

b. Stand around the diving board. Lean forward, place the hands flat on the board and practice the spring.

c. The spring jump can also be practiced by placing the hands at shoulder height on a wall and jumping up in place.

d. In recent years the trampoline or rebound tumbling has become popular. This can greatly assist a person not only in learning how to spring straight up, but allows her to practice knifes, somersaults, and twists well up in the air without the fear of landing flat on the water. There are, as in everything else, rules that must be followed. To state a few:

(*1*) Students should never use the equipment without an instructor

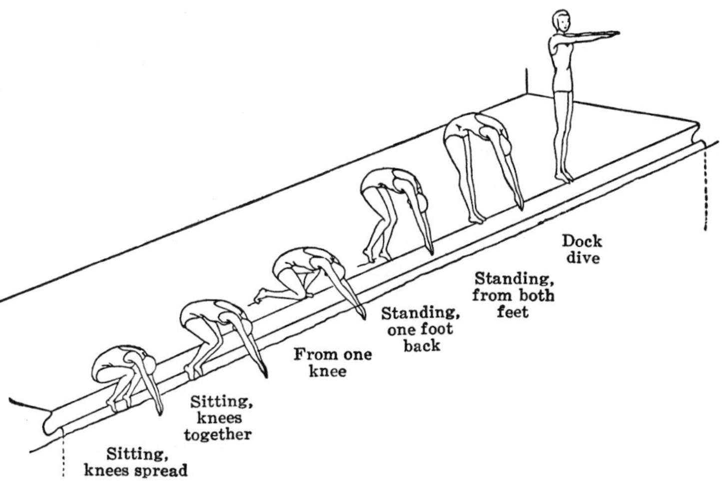

FIGURE 8.14 *Diving progression for a beginner.*

present, and someone must be stationed at both sides and at each end of the trampoline.

(*2*) Beginners should not be allowed high bouncing. Control and good form come first.

(*3*) At first they should learn simple exercises without bouncing too high.

(*4*) No horseplay should be allowed.

(*5*) Only one student at a time should use the trampoline, until they can perform with control and balance singly.

2. Faults in Diving.

a. There is a tendency to overthrow the legs. This is caused by a push back of the feet from the take-off, by putting the head down too soon or by pulling the arms down too soon and with too much force.

Corrections:

(*1*) Get an upward push, keep the legs straight and do not relax them on leaving the take off.

(*2*) Keep the arms extended over the head and do not pull them down under the body on the entry into the water.

b. Tendency to land too flat and too far out. This is caused by leaning forward on the take-off and pushing out instead of up.

Corrections:

(*1*) Continue to practice the spring jump with the emphasis on pushing *up,* with the top of the head leading.

(*2*) Practice by two's, having one kneel down facing the diver. In this position, extend one arm out over the water in front of and just below the knees of the diver. The diver pushes *up,* in order to get over the arm from the take-off.

(*3*) Practice the one-legged dive. Stand with all the weight on one foot and the knee bent, the other leg lifted straight behind. As the upper body is bent forward over the water, the rear leg is lifted straight up. Give a slight push from the take-off with one foot; both feet should meet well up in the air and enter the water together and in line with the body.

3. Technique.

a. Push *up* from the take-off and do not lean forward until *after* the push.

b. The position of the body on entry into the water should be perpendicular.

c. Go *straight down* toward the bottom before starting up.

d. The position of the head and arms govern the line of movement.

F. Springboard Diving. So far, the diving discussed has been done from a stationary take-off. Having mastered this, the diver is ready to learn how to dive from a springboard that will "give" as the diver leaves it. When used correctly, the board aids the diver greatly in gaining height. It is therefore very important for the diver to learn how to use the board. *Height* and *balance* are essential. See section on Trampoline.

1. Standing Dive.

a. Stand on the board about 4 inches from the diving end, the feet apart, jump up and down, getting the final push from the balls of both feet. On the upward lift move the arms forward and upward. The arm lift must co-ordinate with the push from the feet. The arms aid greatly the body balance. When first practicing this jump, do not strive for height. Balance must be maintained, and then the diver can strive for height.

b. After getting balance and a certain amount of height, the diver can use the same start as above, and on the lift, go straight up and enter the water feet first.

c. From the same take-off, go up and enter the water head first. This practice should continue until the diver has control, balance, and a certain amount of height—in other words, has the "feel of the board." The diver must "stay with the board" and leave the board only as the board lifts.

2. The Running Front Dive. In all running dives the required approach is at least three steps and a jump or hurdle. The diver should pace back from the end of the board the desired number of steps and hurdle to find where each dive should be started and then always start from the same place, and with the same foot. Practice in the approach can be done first away from the board, walking out the desired steps using both arms and legs. Having practiced this, she is ready for the dive.

a. Position on the Board. Step up on the board. Assume an easy, good posture. Stand with arms at the sides, head up, and chin in.

b. Approach and Takeoff. At least three steps and a hurdle are required on the approach. The steps should be taken naturally and gracefully with the arms at the sides. In taking the hurdle, the knees are lifted high and both feet come down together on the end of the board. As the board comes up, the arms are lifted forward and upward, and the final push is from the balls of the feet. The lift of the arms should start at the shoulders (Figure 8.15).

c. Position in the Air. Good form in the air is what divers strive for. The body should be stretched at full reach, the balance controlled. The head should be in line with the body, the legs together and straight, the toes pointed, and the back slightly arched.

d. Entrance into the Water. In all head-first dives, the tips of the fingers should enter the water first, the rest of the body following in a *straight line.* The entrance should be as nearly perpendicular to the water as possible. The legs should be straight and together, toes pointed.

e. Practice for Running Front Dives.

(*1*) Practice the approach and use of arms, first away from the diving board, then on the board.

(*2*) Work to get a *high hurdle,* bring the knees well up in front, and at the same time lift the arms.

(*3*) In order to get the feel of the board, practice jumping going up *with the board.*

f. Faults in Running Front Dives.

(*1*) Jacking on the dive. (Having a bend at the hips on a straight dive.)

(*2*) Going too far out and thus not entering the water in a vertical line. This is caused by leaning forward on the take-off or leaving the board too soon.

(*3*) Not lifting the arms well up on the take-off. This will cut down height and send the diver too far out.

(*4*) Over-throwing the legs. This is caused by pushing the legs back on the take-off or by relaxing the knees while in the air or by throwing the head forward when leaving the board.

3. The Swan Dive. This dive is quite similar to the running front dive and in competition the running front and swan dives are considered the same dive. The difference lies in the movement of the arms to a right-angle position while in the air. As the diver leaves the board, the arms are lifted forward and outward.

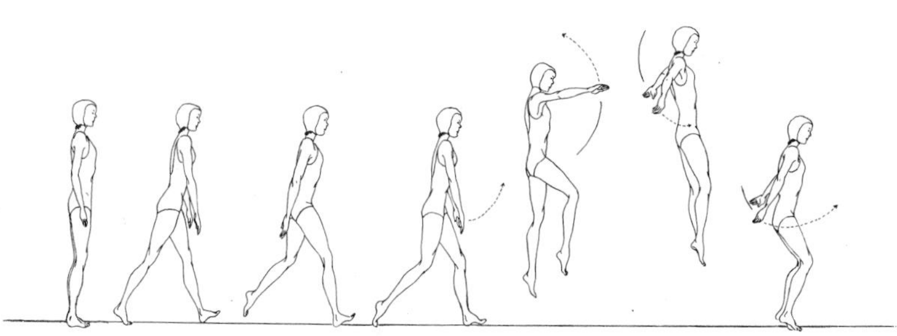

FIGURE 8.15 *The approach for running dives.*

This position is held during the rise. They are brought together just before the entrance into the water.

There is more of a lower back arch in the swan dive than in the front dive. The head is back, and the chest expanded while in the air. The take-off and entrance into the water are the same as in the running front dive. The feeling of the movement of the arms comes with practice.

a. PRACTICE ON LAND. Lying flat on the floor with arms extended forward beyond the head, move them to the side horizontal position with palms turned up or kept flat as desired. At the same time the back should be arched, the head raised, the legs should be held together in a straight line and the toes pointed, as the legs are lifted from the floor. Standing, practice the position described above, with a jump upward and forward.

b. FROM BOARD. Standing at the end of the board with the arms extended and together over the head, swing the body forward from the ankles, moving the arms to the side horizontal position. This position should be held until just before entering the water when the arms are moved back together over the head. As the body balance is lost the back should be arched and the head lifted. As the diver enters the water, the back is unarched or flattened, the head is moved forward, and the arms are brought together (Figure 8.16).

c. APPROACH. The approach is the same as in the running front dive. The body should go straight up from the board. As the diver goes up, the arms move to the side horizontal position, the lower back is arched, and the head is lifted forward. This position should be held until just before entering the water,

FIGURE 8.16 *The swan dive.*

when the arms are brought together and the head is moved slightly forward.

d. ENTRANCE. The entrance is perpendicular to the water as in the running front dive.

e. FAULTS IN SWAN DIVE.

(*1*) Same as in the running front dive.

(*2*) Taking the swan position too soon (from the board) thus cutting down the height.

(*3*) Holding the swan position too long.

(*4*) Failing to arch the body *after* the lift.

4. The Front Jackknife Dive (Running). Another type of running dive is the front jackknife. Instead of remaining straight throughout the dive, the body is jacked at the hips at the height of the dive, and the hands are brought in against the instep or toes. The knees must remain straight. This position is held until just before entering the water when the body is straightened and a straight entry is made.

a. LAND PRACTICE. Standing erect with the knees straight, bend the upper body forward and reach down with the hands until they touch the instep. The head should be held up. Practice this until it can be done easily.

To get the idea of the lift from the hips, stand erect, bend forward from the hips and swing the right leg forward, touching the instep with both hands. Return to standing position. Practice this, using first one leg and then the other.

b. FROM BOARD. The approach is the same as the running front or swan dive. From the take-off, the body should go straight up from the board. At the height of the lift, the jackknife position is taken. To assume this position, the hips are lifted, the body is bent at the hips, and the hands and insteps are brought together. The head is forward, the knees are straight. (Figure 8.17.)

Just before entering the water, the body is straightened by raising the legs from the hips. The head stays between the arms.

In learning this dive, the beginner may not at first reach the instep with the hands, but with practice, the hands will reach lower and lower. At all times it must be remembered to keep the *knees straight.*

c. FAULTS IN JACKKNIFE.

(*1*) Going out too far from the board. This is caused by going into the jackknife position too soon, which takes away from the height of the dive.

(*2*) Holding the jackknife position too long, which causes a poor entry into the water.

(*3*) Having an over-throw of the legs. This is caused by dropping the arms and ducking the head instead of bringing the feet up to meet the hands, or by a backward push with the feet when leaving the board.

(*4*) Bending the knees. Rather than bend the knees, do not go so far down with the hands unless the knees remain straight. Keeping the knees *straight* is essential for all the jackknife dives.

5. The Back Dive. This is generally the first dive a diver learns with the back to the water.

a. BEGINNING.

(*1*) The diver stands at the end of the diving board, back to the water and facing the board, with feet parallel to the diving board. The arms are lifted straight over the head, the thumbs locked together. The diver is supported at the hips. Support is given by the teacher or another diver, who knows when to let go. Keeping the head well back, the diver bends backward over the water. When the upper body is pointing downward, the support is released and the diver drops into the water.

(*2*) Without support the diver bends backward over the water and drops in.

b. WITH SPRING. The diver goes to the end of the board and, turning away from the end, practices the lift by "jumping the board."

(*1*) POSITION. The diver stands the the end of the board, with the arms raised in front to shoulder level. The

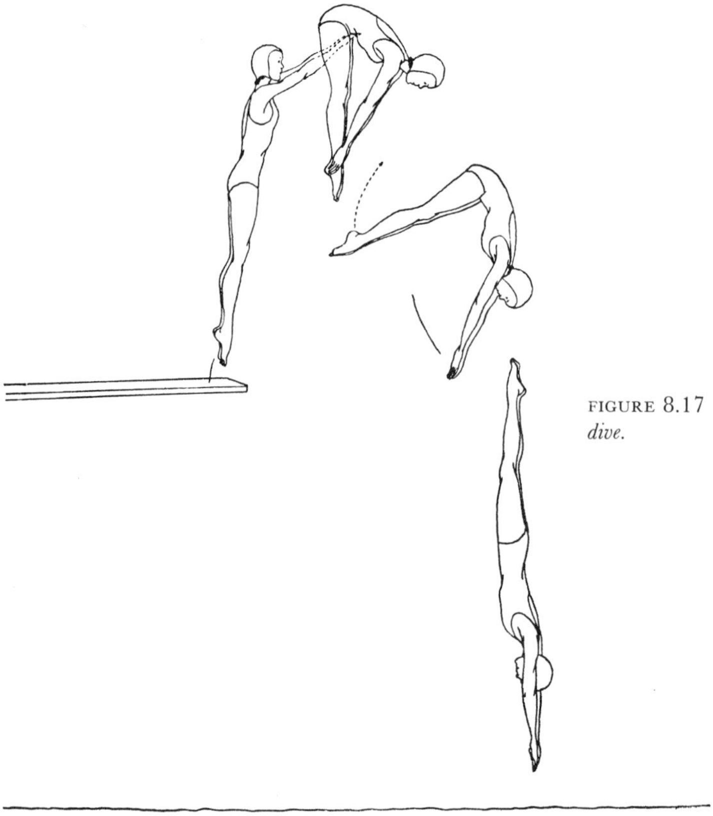

FIGURE 8.17 *The running front jackknife dive.*

heels are slightly over the end of the board with the weight on the balls of the feet. To maintain balance a high eye mark is helpful. That is, the diver focuses her eyes on a spot on the wall in front of her. The legs should be straight and the body erect.

(*2*) THE LIFT. Holding the above position, the arms are lowered to the sides and raised to the side horizontal position (slowly and in one movement). As the arms are lowered, the heels are lowered, then as the arms move forcibly forward and upward, the heels are lifted and the feet extended so that on leaving the board the movement of the arms and legs *together* lifts the body into the air. (Figure 8.18.)

(*3*) IN THE AIR. The lift is taken *with* the board and the body goes straight upward almost over the board; the arms are over the head and in line

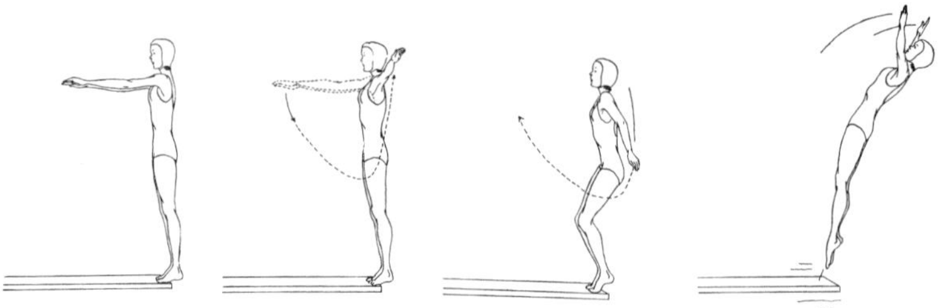

FIGURE 8.18 *The take-off on the board for the back dive.*

with the body. At the height of the dive, the head moves back, and the back is arched. The arms can be held over the head or move sideward to the swan position as the body drops backward to the water. But on the entrance the arms must be together (Figure 8.19).

(*4*) ENTRANCE. The finger tips enter the water first, the body is straight, legs together, and toes pointed.

(*5*) FAULTS IN BACK DIVE.

(*a*) An over-throw of the legs. Caused by leaning backward from the board and not getting the push up through the whole body. Relaxing the legs.

(*b*) Going out too far from the board and too nearly parallel to the top of the water.

(*c*) Turning in the dive. Caused by an uneven pushoff, or by turning the head in trying to see the water.

6. The Back Somersault Dive. The back somersault is done in any of three positions: in a tuck, pike, or layout (straight) position. For the *tuck position,* the knees are drawn close up to the body, the front of the legs grasped by the arms. The tuck should be as compact as possible. From a low board, this is the easiest position. In the *pike position,* the body is bent at the hips, legs straight, the same as in the jackknife dives. In the *layout position,* the body remains straight throughout the dive.

The backward somersault dive is first done in a tuck position.

a. ON LAND. The somersault dives are a form of tumbling, and they are learned easiest on a mat. The diver should assume a *squat position,* grasping the front of the legs and, sitting back, pull the knees up to the chin and roll over backwards. The next step is for the diver to *stand* and as the upper body is

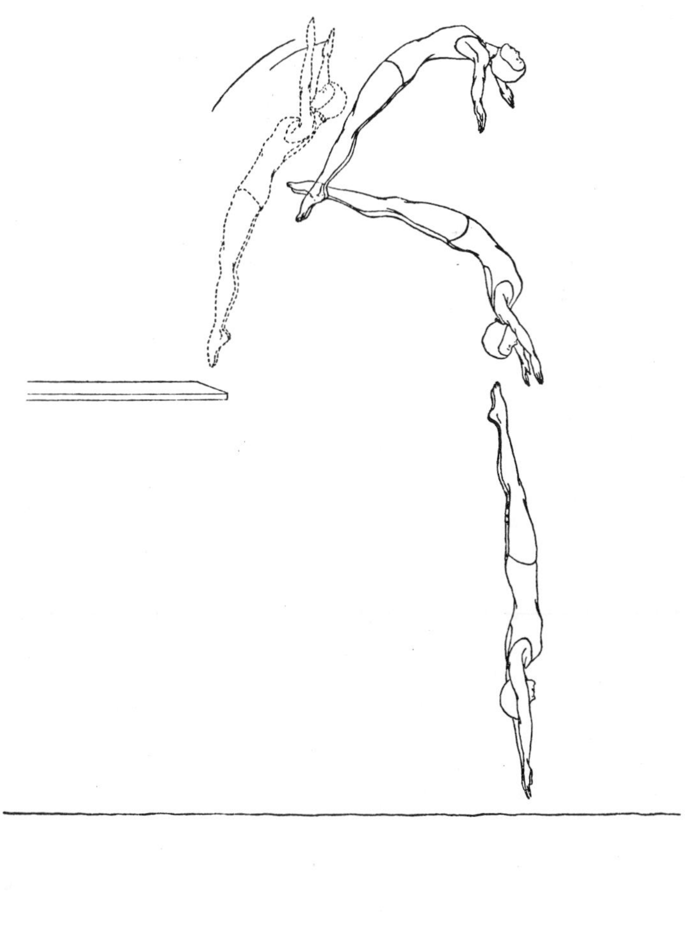

FIGURE 8.19 *The back dive.*

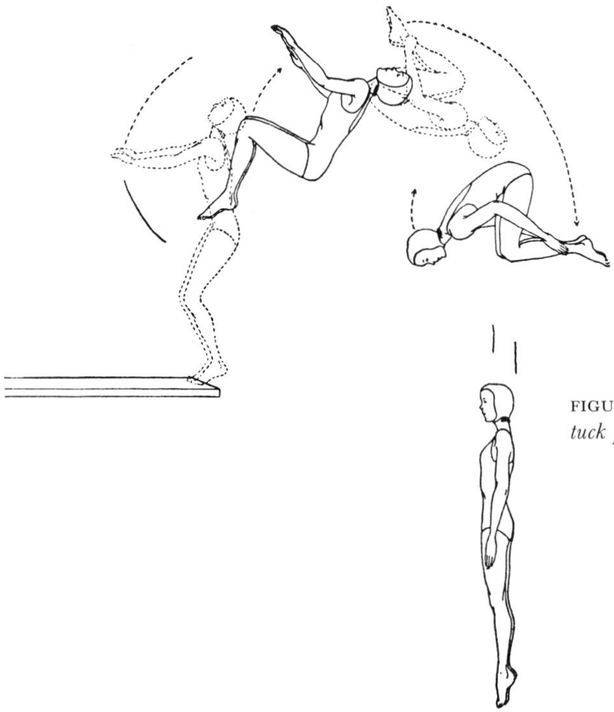

FIGURE 8.20 *The backward somersault in a tuck position.*

thrown backward, bring first one knee and then the other up to the tuck position.

b. FROM BOARD. The diver should take the same starting position as for the back dive. From this position the arms are lowered, then swung upward and back, the head moves backward at the height of the lift, and the knees are drawn close up to the body and grasped by the arms as the body moves backward. The legs are straightened for the entry and the feet enter the water first, the arms being at the side. (Figure 8.20.)

The backward somersault dive is then done in pike and layout positions.

In the beginning the diver does not try for height but rather to turn before entering the water, and to clear the diving board. Gradually, height must be attained before the entry.

In all feet-first entries, the arms are close to the sides on the entrance into the water.

c. FAULTS IN BACK SOMERSAULT DIVES.

(*1*) Not entering the water in a vertical line with the arms at the sides and the body straight.

(*2*) Not springing up from the board before starting backwards.

(*3*) Twisting on the dive.

7. The Back Jackknife Dive. The start for this dive is the same as for the back dive. Before trying the dive from a board, land practice is helpful.

a. ON LAND. The same land practice can be given as in the front jackknife, remembering there must not be a backward lean on this dive, or on any dive. In all jackknife dives the knees are kept straight throughout the dive. At the height of the dive the body is bent at the hips and the fingers touch the toes. On entering the water, the body must be straight.

b. FROM BOARD.

(*1*) Standing erect at the end of the board as for the back dive, jump *up* and *back*, entering the water feet first.

(*2*) Taking the same starting position jump up and back, lift the hips and bring the hands in front of the insteps in the pike position. The diver heads down toward the water and the legs are lifted back and up, the diver entering the water head first (Figure 8.21).

This practice continues with the diver getting more and more lift from the board, and a better held pike position before opening. A shoulder lift on the take-off will aid in getting height.

c. FAULTS IN BACK JACKKNIFE.

(*1*) Twisting on the backward jump.

(*2*) Not jumping back far enough to clear the board with the head.

(*3*) Bending the knees to get into the pike position.

8. The Running Front Dive With Half Twist. When a twist is used in diving, a turn of the entire body is made. The twist may be used in combination with jackknife dives and somersaults to make more difficult dives. The twist which is learned first is the running front dive with a half twist.

a. LAND PRACTICE. Merely to get the movement of the arms and the upper trunk, stand with the arms extended over the head. To twist to the right, lower the right arm and turn the

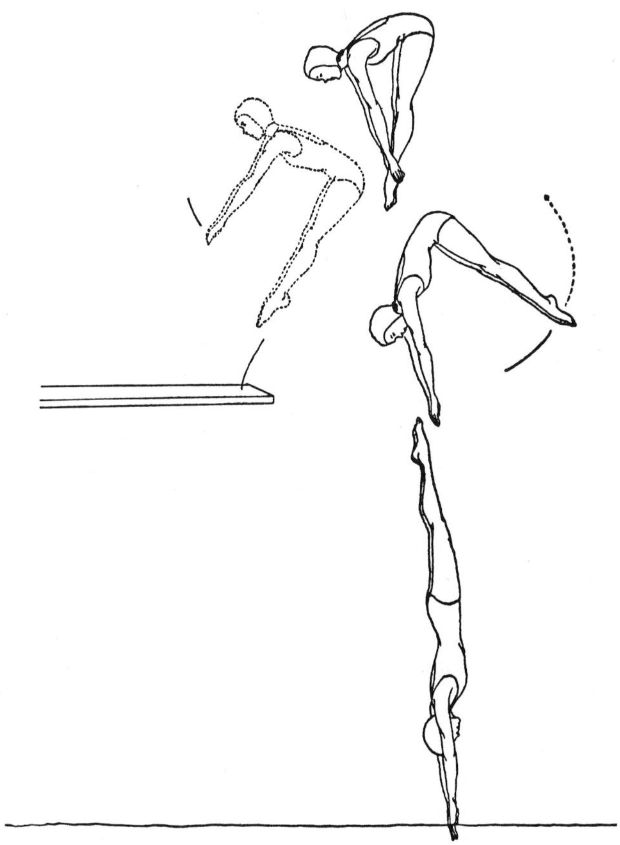

FIGURE 8.21 *The back jackknife dive.*

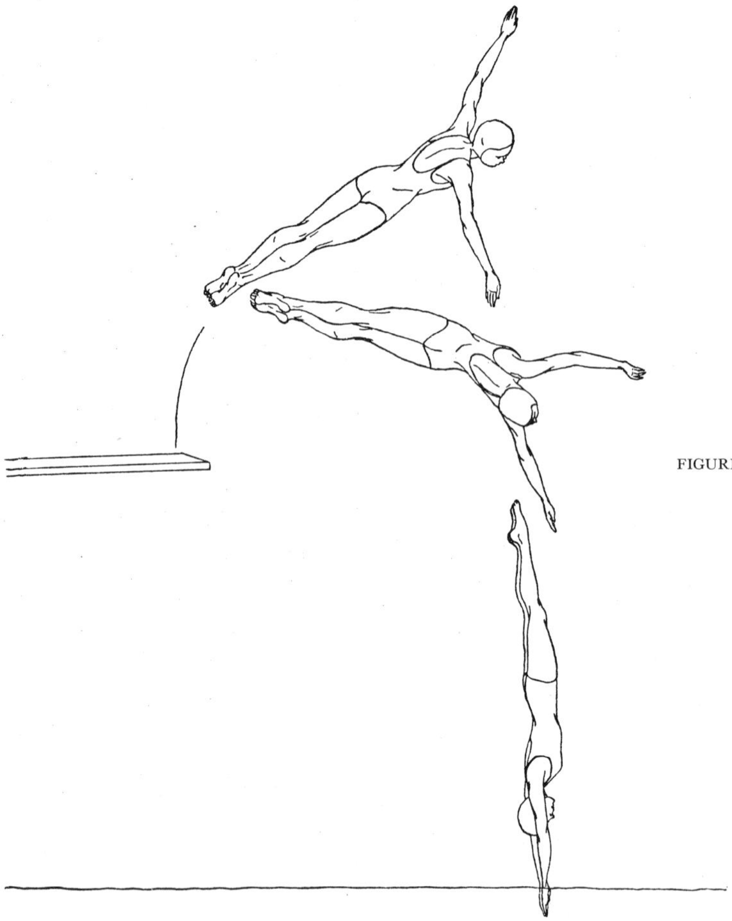

FIGURE 8.22 *The half twist dive.*

head to the right. Some prefer a *turn* of the body to the desired side, without lowering the arm. In this case the turn starts with the shoulders and a turn of the head. The entire body must turn the desired distance.

b. FROM BOARD. The approach, take-off, and the start upward from the board are the same as in the running front dive. As the height is reached the arm to the side of the turn is lowered and the head is turned to the same side. The twist is made by the entire body. The entrance is made with the body straight and facing away from the board (Figure 8.22).

c. FAULTS IN RUNNING FRONT DIVE WITH HALF TWIST.

(*1*) Lowering the head to the side instead of turning it throws the body over to the side.

(*2*) Starting the twist too soon takes away from the height and causes poor entry.

(*3*) Folding the body up for the turn instead of keeping it straight.

9. The Running Front Dive With Full Twist. In order to make a full twist, when the diver is at the height of the dive one arm is thrown across the chest forcibly, and then is extended parallel to the other arm over the head. The head is turned forcibly in the same direction as the arm. If enough force is put into the turn, the body goes completely around and enters the water as in a front dive.

10. The Jackknife Dive With Twists. The diver can now combine jackknife dives with twists. In doing so, the diver must be sure to go into the jackknife position before starting the twist. Either the running front jackknife or the back jackknife can precede the twist.

11. The Forward Somersault Dive. The forward somersault is done in one of three diving positions, the tuck, pike, or layout. (For description, see back somersault, page 261.) From a low board the somersault in the tuck position is the easiest. It can be likened to the forward roll, which practically everyone has done in a gymnastics class, or on the lawn as a small child.

a. LAND PRACTICE. On a mat, take a squat position, grasp the front of the legs with the arms, bring the chin well in and the head forward. Holding the position, roll over forward.

b. AT SIDE OF POOL OR DOCK. Taking a squat position with the knees well up in front, grasp the knees with the arms, and roll over forward into the water. Hold this position and try to land in the water as far around as possible.

c. FROM BOARD. From a running approach, push *up* from the board, tuck the chin well in, turn over once, and enter the water feet first, with the body straight and with the arms at the sides.

After learning the somersault in the tuck position, the diver can go on to the pike (Figure 8.23), and then the layout positions. The last two should not be attempted unless the diver has unlimited skill.

12. The Half Gainer Dive. The half gainer is one of the most beautiful dives to watch, and when it is well done, it appears very simple to execute. However, this is not the case as the dive involves leaving the board forward, and turning back toward the board for the entry. This makes the preliminary practice very important in order to avoid injury to the diver.

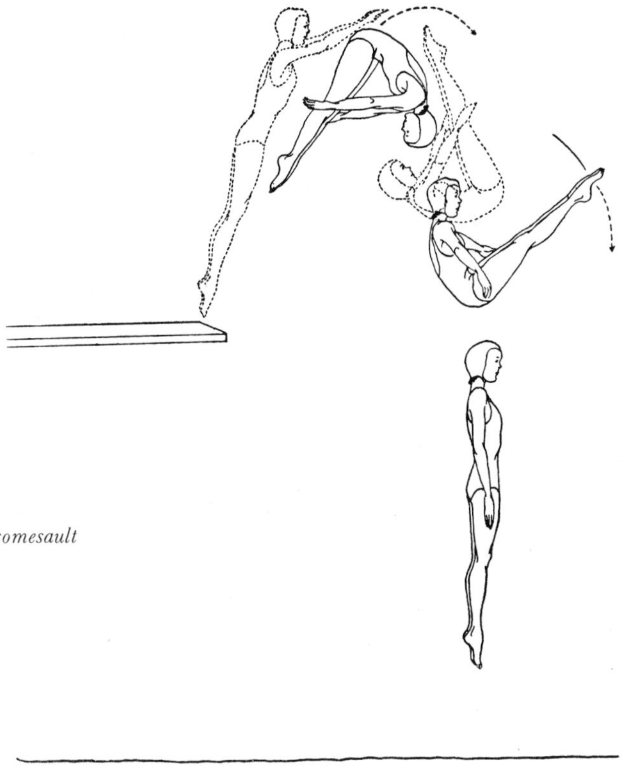

FIGURE 8.23 *The running forward somesault in pike position.*

a. Land Practice. A one foot take-off is sometimes the easiest approach to the whole dive. Therefore, starting with the weight on one foot, swing the other leg forward and upward with straight knee and at the same time bend backward from the hips and move the arms up and backward over the head. Alternate the use of the legs remembering the dive is to be done from *both feet.*

b. From Board. Standing with the weight on one foot, jump out over the water and at the same time swing the other leg forward and upward bending back from the hips and swinging the arms up and back over the head; enter the water head first.

After the one foot take-off has been accomplished, the diver goes on to the two foot take-off. (Figure 8.24.)

c. Technique.

(*1*) At first get well out from the board to avoid hitting it. Then work to *get up.*

(*2*) Move the arms and upper body back, as the legs are sent forward and upward.

(*3*) The feet should be lifted well up from the board, in order to obtain height.

(*4*) The thrust forward of the feet from the board must be done with controlled force.

XIII. STUNTS.

In writing about swimming for girls and women, one must include a discussion of water stunts. They are not new, but interest in them has grown, and is

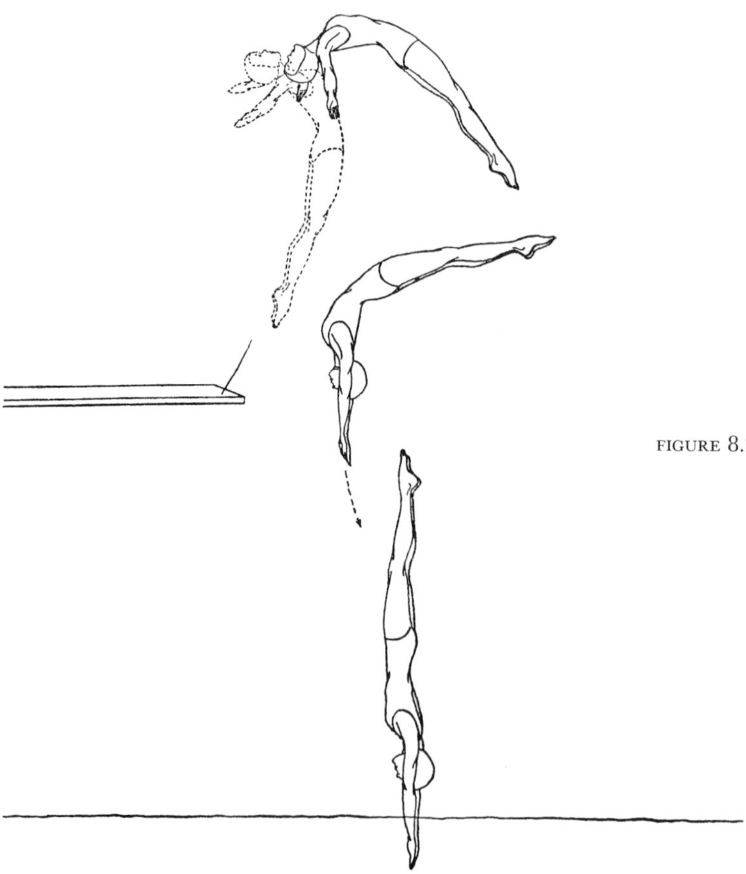

FIGURE 8.24 *The half gainer dive.*

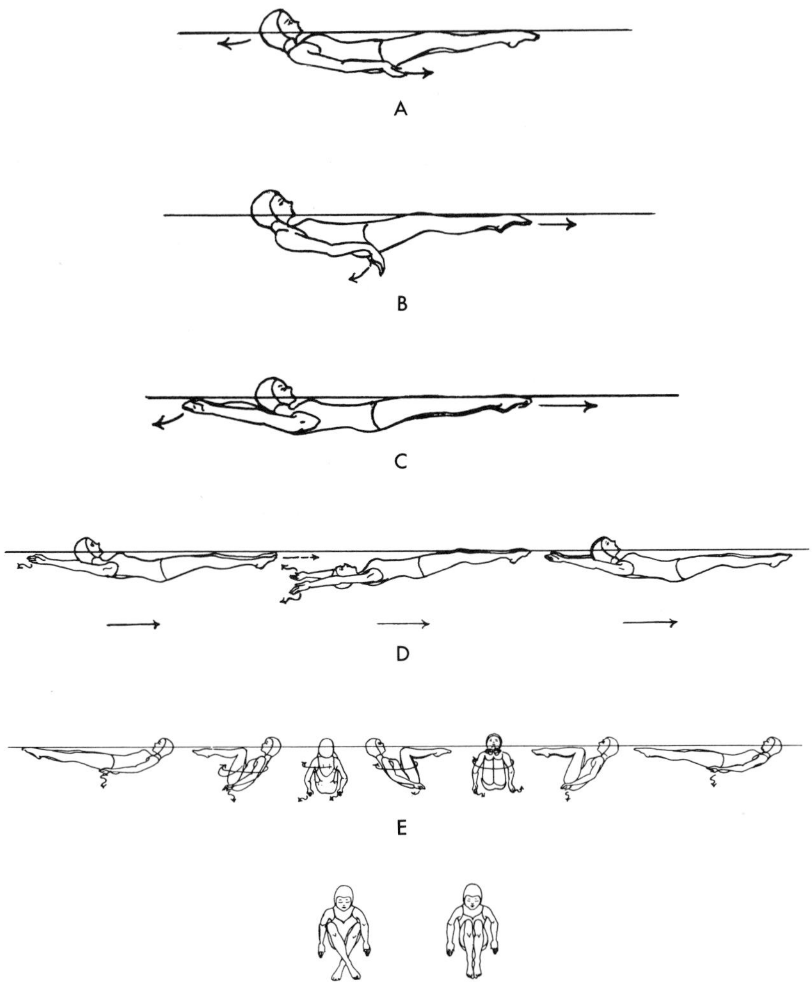

FIGURE 8.25 *A, Sculling on back—move toward head. B, Sculling on back—move toward feet. C, Sculling on back—arms overhead, move toward feet. D, Torpedo. E, Spinning top or tub. F, View from above. (From Goss, G.:* Stunts and Synchronized Swimming, *1957.)*

continuing to grow, so that wherever there is water they are being taught and practiced. Stunts are not only fun to do but they give the swimmer an added skill in the water.

1. Sculling. The movement basic to *all* water stunts is "sculling." In sculling, a figure-eight motion is made with the hands and the legs remain still. The body moves in the direction opposite to that of the pressure against the water. Study the diagrams in Figure 8.25, and then try to perform in the water the movements illustrated.

2. Back Somersault Tuck.

a. **Starting Position.** Scull in place, on the back, the arms at the sides, back of head in water, chin tucked in. Hold body parallel to the surface of the water, legs straight and together.

b. **Execution.** Draw the knees up *tight* to the body and at the same time

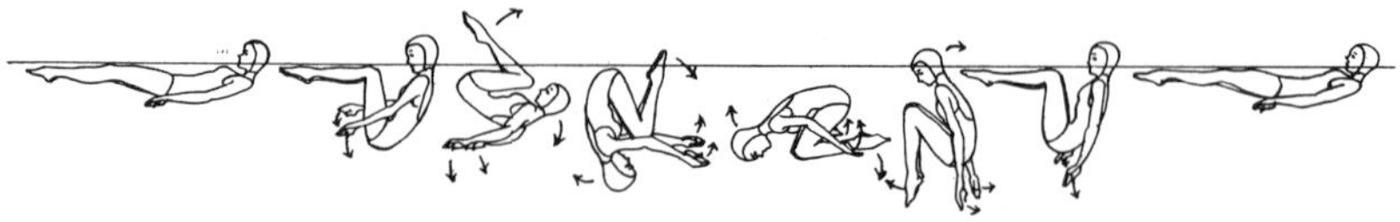

FIGURE 8.26 *Backward somesault—tuck position. (From Goss, G.:* Stunts and Synchronized Swimming, *1957.)*

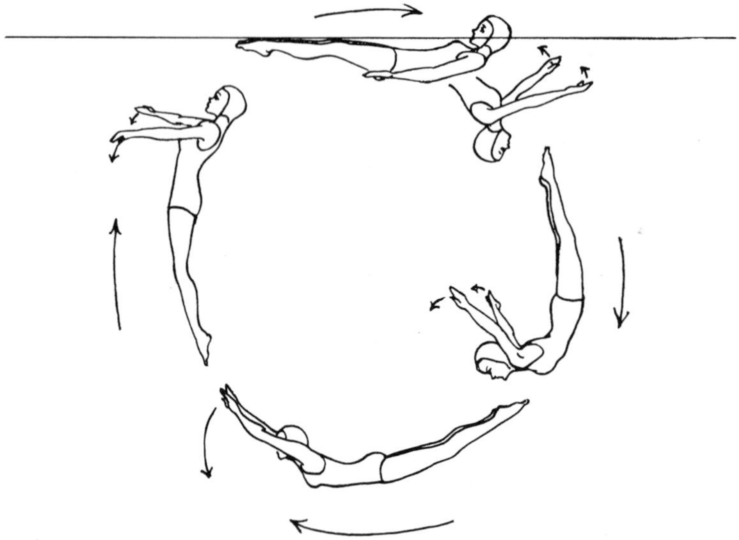

FIGURE 8.27 *Dolphin. (From Goss, G.:* Stunts and Synchronized Swimming, *1957.)*

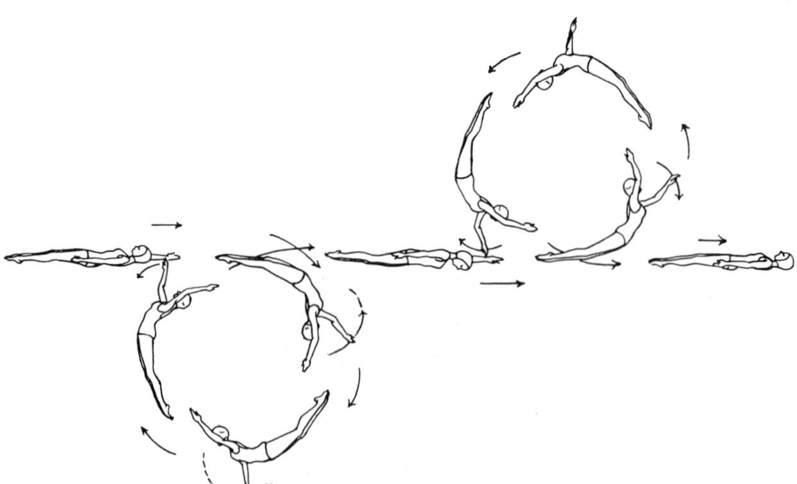

FIGURE 8.28 *The shark figure eight. (From Goss, G.:* Stunts and Synchronized Swimming, *1957.)*

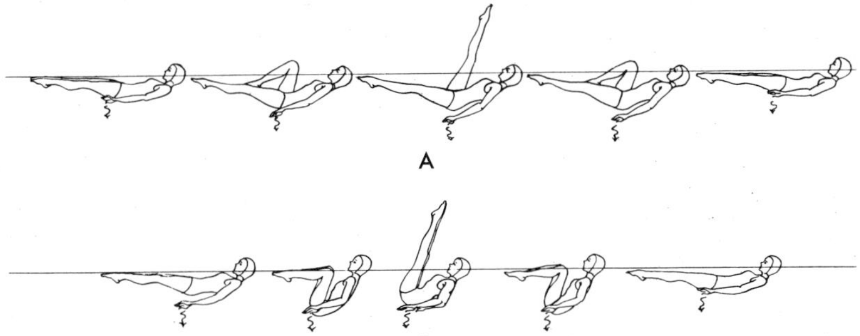

FIGURE 8.29 *A, Single ballet leg. B, Double ballet legs. (From Goss, G.:* Stunts and Synchronized Swimming, 1957.)

move the head well back, as the palms of the hands push toward the feet and then are lifted up toward the surface.

The back somersault also may be done in *pike* position, in which the bend is at the hips and the legs are held straight.

3. The Dolphin. The dolphin is a back somersault done in layout position. Make a complete circle, with the body straight, legs together, and toes pointed. Remember to go *deep* in the water. There should be no "overthrow" of the legs when the turn is made.

4. The Shark. Scull on back, then roll onto side, extending the top arm overhead and parallel to the water, elbow slightly bent. Make a *wide* sculling motion with the under arm, moving it toward the head, until a complete circle has been made. The circle is made with the entire body below the surface of the water. Only the top arm, the "fin," is kept out of the water.

5. The Shark Figure Eight. Scull in a complete circle on the right side; then roll onto the left side, changing arm positions. Continue to scull until a complete circle is made in the opposite direction.

6. Single Ballet Leg. The ballet

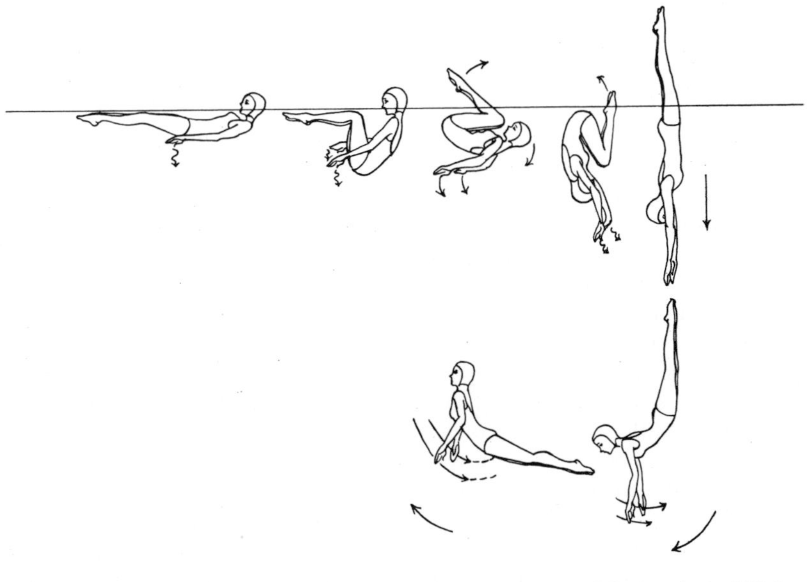

FIGURE 8.30 *Kip. (From Goss, G.:* Stunts and Synchronized Swimming, *1957.)*

FIGURE 8.31 *Catalina. (From Goss, G.:* Stunts and Synchronized Swimming, *1957.)*

leg stunts require a very strong sculling motion. Try the single ballet leg first. Keep one leg straight on the surface of the water, with toes pointed. Draw the other leg up to the chest, then extend it upward. Complete the movement by drawing the knee back to the chest and returning the leg to starting position.

7. Double Ballet Legs. This is basically the same stunt as the single ballet leg. Both legs, however, are drawn to the chest and extended in this figure.

8. The Kip.

a. **Starting Position.** Scull in place on back.

b. **Execution.** Do a half backward somersault in tuck position. When the head is down, stop; extend both legs, straightening the body at the same time. Go down, head first, in a vertical line. To come up, lift the head and turn the hands up. On reaching the surface, return to the starting position.

9. Catalina. Scull in place on back. Raise one leg to the ballet position. Then do a half-roll *away* from the raised leg. The other leg, which has been kept parallel to the surface, is then brought to the already extended ballet leg. Go down, head first. Finish the movement with the body on and parallel to the surface, the arms at the sides.

The few stunts described here give only a glimpse of what is being done today in water stunts and synchronized swimming. In order to do even the simplest stunts well, the sculling motion must be practiced daily, in all directions. Then the stunts themselves may be practiced. They are fun to do—good luck!

OUTLINE OF TEACHING PROCEDURE

The material presented in this chapter can be taught individually or in groups to swimmers. In school and college teaching most of the instruction is given in groups. If it is possible, the beginners' classes should not have more than twelve students each at any one time. The intermediate and advanced classes can have as many as thirty in a section. In order to have the swimmers in the proper groups, a swimming test should be given each student. If such a test cannot be given the teacher may find that she has sections in which there is a wide variety of abilities, making her job much more difficult and lessening the progress of each student. In some instances it is impossible for classification tests to be given, and the teacher must have a mixed group at all times.

For classified groups of students, a possible outline of work is presented here, and the teacher can keep the group working together on more or less the same strokes, dives, and stunts. In each class period part of the lesson should be given over to games and stunts. To make the lesson more interesting, it is suggested that the teacher change the order of work given to each class, and not always use the same set outline. This can be done by starting the lesson one day with games and stunts, followed by strokes and diving, and starting the next day with diving, followed by strokes and stunts, and so forth.

In each class there are always a number of "excused" swimmers. These girls can be given a reading assignment on some phase of swimming, or better still they can be given some teaching to do. It has been found that having the students do a certain amount of work in helping each other enhances their interest in swimming and makes them more intelligent concerning their own problems in the water.

I. BEGINNING PROGRAM

This group should include those students who have little or no swimming knowledge. A term of swimming is generally ten weeks. Each class meets twice a week for 30 minutes. In this time it is hoped that they learn:

1. To overcome fear of the water.
2. To relax while floating on the back, face, or side.
3. To change body positions while in the water.
4. An elementary crawl and an elementary backstroke.
5. Breathing in the water.
6. To jump and dive into water of shoulder depth, then into deep water.
7. As much of the side stroke or the breast stroke as possible.

In attempting to teach beginners, it is most important that the water be *warm:* at least 80 degrees. It is very difficult for the swimmers to be relaxed and comfortable if the water is any cooler. Ideally, a beginning swimming class should not have more than 12 members.

The following is a possible outline of work for beginners:

Lesson 1. Getting used to the water by means of simple water games. (10 minutes.)

BALL TAG. The players are scattered around the shallow end of the pool. One is "It" and has a ball. The one with the ball throws it, trying to hit one of the other players. When hit by the ball that player becomes "It."

WALKING RACE. Line all players along one side of the pool in shallow water. On a signal, they all get to the other side of the pool as fast as they can. The one getting there first is the winner.

Work on breathing. Start by having the students put their faces in the water and hold the breath. Then have them breathe in through mouth, put faces in the water, and breathe out through the mouth, or mouth and nose. (10 minutes.)

Work on back float and stand. (10 minutes.)

Lesson 2. Another game, putting their faces in the water, having first taken a breath, holding it and letting it out slowly. The winner is the student who can keep her face in the water the longest. (10 minutes.)

CAP TAG. Players scattered in shallow end of pool. One or more persons are "It." In order not to be tagged, the entire cap must be under water.

Review and continue work on breathing. Review back float and stand. (10 minutes.)

Work on face float and stand. (10 minutes.)

Lesson 3. Review as needed. (10 minutes.)

Work on change of body positions. (10 minutes.)

From a pushoff, do the face float and stand.

Do the back float and stand. (5 minutes.)

Continue breast or side stroke. (5 minutes.)

Lesson 4. Review as needed. (10 minutes.)

Use a land drill first, then in the water,

practice the elementary backstroke. (15 minutes.)

End with a water game. (5 minutes.)

Lesson 5. Practice jumping in from the side of the pool at the shallow end. (10 minutes.)

Review breathing and back and face floats. (10 minutes.)

Continue work on the elementary backstroke. (10 minutes.)

Lesson 6. Demonstrate and have practice of the elementary crawl or the "human stroke" on land, then in the water. (20 minutes.)

Jumping in shallow water. On coming to the surface, swim to the opposite side either on the back or on the face. (5 minutes.)

Continue work on breathing. (5 minutes.)

Lesson 7. Review lesson 6. Start with the "human stroke" and go on to the overarm crawl. (25 minutes.)

Play a water game. (5 minutes.)

Lesson 8. Jump in deep water. Swim to side of pool. (15 minutes.)

Review as needed. (15 minutes.)

Lesson 9. Work on parts of the crawl or the whole stroke.

Work on "sitting" and "kneeling" dives from the edge of the pool. (15 minutes.)

Lesson 10. Work on the crawl covering a longer distance, with correct breathing. (20 minutes.)

Review "sitting" and "kneeling" dive. (10 minutes.)

Lesson 11. Dive from the standing position. Dive in first standing on one foot, then from the other foot and finally from both feet. (15 minutes.)

Work on the crawl. (15 minutes.)

Lesson 12. Work on treading water and sculling. (10 minutes.)

The scissors or frog kick, depending on which stroke is being taught. On land, bracketed at side of pool, and with kick board. (15 minutes.)

Continue diving from the standing position. (5 minutes.)

Lesson 13. Demonstrate the side stroke or the breast stroke, whichever has not already been taught. (5 minutes.)

Drill on land for the arms alone. Drill standing in shallow water. Do pushoff from wall. From the pushoff, try movement of the arms alone. Add the leg kick to the arms. (20 minutes.)

Work on diving. (5 minutes.)

Lessons 14 through 20. Continue work on the side or breast stroke. Continue work on the crawl and diving. Some students learn faster than others and they should be allowed to go ahead.

II. LOW INTERMEDIATE PROGRAM

For those who are beyond the beginning stage. This group is taught:

1. The crawl, continued from the elementary stroke.
2. If the breast stroke was started in the beginning group, work on it should be continued, and the side stroke should not be introduced until the end of the series.
3. The side stroke.
4. The single overarm stroke.
5. The trudgeon or double overarm.
6. Diving.
7. Simple water stunts and games.

We assume that anyone in low intermediate swimming has overcome all fear of the water, has learned an elementary crawl, the elementary back stroke, and has started working on a side stroke or a breast stroke.

Lesson 1. In order to find out the ability of the students, have them demonstrate the material given in beginning swimming.

Lesson 2. Continue work on the crawl and the side or breast strokes.

Lesson 3. Repeat lesson 2 and add more work on diving.

Lesson 4. Start the side stroke. Diving and stunts.

Lesson 5. Repeat 4.

Lesson 6. Add work on the single overarm. Review and continue work on the crawl. Diving and stunts.

Lesson 7. Work on the single overarm with quarter turn in preparation for the trudgeon. Continue the crawl.

Lessons 8, 9, 10. Work on the trudgeon mostly, but give some part of each lesson to other strokes that have been taught, and to diving.

Lessons 11 through 20. Have the students work on swimming the strokes they have learned for greater distances, emphasizing relaxation, rhythm, and power. Give them additional work on diving and stunts.

III. HIGH INTERMEDIATE PROGRAM

1. Continue work on the crawl.
2. The backstroke.
3. The breast stroke.
4. The butterfly breast stroke, provided the breast stroke has first been learned.
5. A review of strokes already learned.
6. Diving.
7. Stunts.

In order to be classified as a high intermediate swimmer, the student should have a fair crawl, side stroke, single overarm, trudgeon, and perhaps breast stroke.

Lesson 1. A demonstration by the class of the strokes they already know how to swim, and the dives they can do.

Lesson 2. Continued practice of the crawl. Demonstration of the breast stroke to show the class the complete stroke, if this has not been done already. In any case, it can be reviewed. Land drill for the breast stroke kick. Practice of the leg movements alone bracketed at the side of the pool. Using the kick boards, practice kick across the pool.

Lesson 3. Demonstrate the backstroke. Practice leg kick alone on land. Practice leg kick alone in the water, bracketed. Practice leg kick across the pool, scull with the hands, or have them extended over the head. Practice the arm movements alone on land. Practice the arm movements alone with legs held by another student. Practice the arm movements alone across the pool. Try the whole stroke.

Lesson 4. Review practice of the leg movements alone for the breast stroke, as needed. Land drill for the arm movements. Water drill for the arm movements standing in shallow end of pool. Coordination of the whole stroke on land. Coordination of the whole stroke from pushoff in the water.

Lesson 5. Review 3 and spend half the period on diving.

Lesson 6. Demonstrate and work on the arm movements of the butterfly breast stroke. Practice the following ways: on land, standing; in shallow water, standing; and from a pushoff with the legs trailing.

Lesson 7. Work on the whole stroke (butterfly breast). Swim lengths to music, using any desired stroke.

Lessons 8, 9, 10. Work on the back and breast strokes. Diving and stunts.

Lesson 11. Demonstrate free style start and turn. Practice the start. Practice the turn. Practice the start and turn across the pool.

Lesson 12. Review lesson 11 and the crawl.

Lesson 13. Demonstrate the backstroke start and spin turn. Practice the start. Practice the turn. Practice the start and turn across pool. Diving and stunts.

Lesson 14. Review lesson 13 and work on the backstroke as needed, add the somersault turn.

Lesson 15. Demonstrate the breast stroke and the butterfly breast stroke start and turn. Practice the start. Practice the turn. Practice start and turn across the pool.

Lesson 16. Review lesson 15 and work on the breast stroke, and the butterfly breast stroke.

Lesson 17. Practice any of the strokes, starts, and turns. Swim the crawl in pairs to music.

Lesson 18. With music swim the crawl, backstroke, breast, and side strokes in pairs.

Lesson 19. Work on diving the entire

period. Any students not allowed to dive may continue to practice strokes, swimming lengths of the pool continuously.

Lesson 20. Review lesson 18 and add swimming by fours.

The Red Cross life saving and instructors' courses are also desired by many students, and should be made available to all who qualify for them. Ideally, every swimmer ought to be a Life Saver.

IV. ADVANCED PROGRAM

This group included the students who wish to make a swimming team. They are already good swimmers or divers and can be given work on conditioning and endurance as well as on starts and turns for all racing strokes. The divers learn additional springboard dives, and practice to improve the dives they know. This group works toward competition in meets, and must be given very careful training.

V. PROCEDURE WITH UNCLASSIFIED GROUPS

When the teacher has groups that have not been classified as to abilities, she must make her own classification within the group. In this way she might have, in a group of thirty, possibly five or six working on the very beginning phases, another six or eight working on the side stroke, others on the crawl, and still another group on the backstroke. These groups must each be given a certain section of the pool in which to work and the teacher must distribute her time among the groups. As a safety measure, and to help in the teaching, one of the "excused" swimmers can be put in charge of each group. In addition to practicing the strokes, the swimmers must give a part of each lesson to diving and stunts or games.

VI. STIMULATING INTEREST

Competition is a great stimulus to interest in swimming. Competitive meets between the groups and classes are an added feature.

Motion pictures are valuable in teaching students at all levels of swimming skill.

VALUES OF SWIMMING

Basic to good instruction is the careful progression in the teaching of swimming. This makes possible the benefit of the values of competitive and recreational swimming as well as water safety. Each step in the progression must be followed carefully. In the end, the student who works and who has ability will improve to the point that her swimming will be of the greatest pleasure to herself, and may be the means of saving her life or that of another person.

I. COMPETITION

It is human nature to want to measure one's abilities against another's. But competition must be organized, and governed by definite rules. The competition may be within a school or college, or it may be inter-school or inter-college, inter-club, or merely such competition as can be held between the regular sections in swimming. A popular form of competition between schools and colleges is telegraphic meets. Every swimming program should be planned to include some form of organized competition. Swimming rules for women are drawn up by a committee of the Division for Girls' and Women's Sports, and can be ordered from the Division at 1201 Sixteenth Street, N.W., Washington 6, D.C.

II. WATER SAFETY

It is important for everyone to learn how to swim. As the swimmer's ability increases it is equally important for her knowledge and practice in safety skills to develop. Every well-rounded swimming program should include instruction in life saving and water safety. The American Red Cross, and Mr. Carroll Bryant in particular, have set up outlines of instruction and practice that can be followed in school and college programs. Information regarding these courses can be secured through local Red Cross Chapters or by writing to the national headquarters in Washington, D.C.

III. RECREATIONAL SWIMMING

Recreational swimming is not new, but in the last few years much greater emphasis has been placed on it. It includes all sorts of stunt swimming and diving, special formations en masse, and games, all of which are done "for fun." The stunts are first learned and played by the student for the pure joy of the activity, and to see how many different water tricks she can learn. She can compare her skill with another's, and thus competition is introduced. In swimming meets, stunt events can be run in between the more formal events, to show the skill of the participants and to entertain the spectators.

Today, in practically all sections of the country, stunts are put on a competitive basis, and teams of stunt swimmers compete against each other. In making stunts competitive it is a great mistake to forget they are primarily done for fun. The addition of stunts and formations has already done a great deal to make meets more interesting and educational. Spectators are generally inspired to try some of the stunts themselves. Through stunts the swimmer learns how to handle the body in many different positions in the water, and in doing so gains added control and grace, which cannot be acquired through swimming strokes alone. There are stunts and skills for all types of swimmers.

IV. SWIMMING CLUBS

Swimming is a sport that appeals to a great number of students because they wish to be able to swim at home and in the summer months. Not all students wish to be able to do more than feel at ease in the water. Yet, in every school or college there is a group of students who are particularly interested in swimming. These girls can be organized into a swimming club, and be given a special name appropriate for the school and the sport. The members of the group should meet at least once a week and work out particular stunts and formations as well as increase their skill in swimming. Demonstrations by this group will arouse great interest and enthusiasm for the sport. This same group may have the special responsibility of assisting in the lifeguard duty at the pool. They are also of great value in handling large classes that contain students at many levels of ability.

V. COEDUCATIONAL RECREATION

Another aspect of swimming is the part it can play in coeducational recreation. "Mixed swimming" is popular in many schools and colleges. If dressing rooms and other arrangements can be adapted to this plan, "splash parties" for boys and girls are popular and a valuable part of the program.

Suggestions for Further Reading

Armbruster, David A., Sr., et al.: *Swimming and Diving.* 3rd ed. St. Louis, Missouri, C. V. Mosby Co., 1958.

Curtis, Katherine Whitney: *Rhythmic Swimming.* Minneapolis, Minnesota, Burgess Publishing Company, 1942.

Goss, Gertrude: *Swimming Analyzed.* 20 Chestnut Park, Melrose, Massachusetts, 1957.
———: *Stunts and Synchronized Swimming.* 20 Chestnut Park, Melrose, Massachusetts, 1957.
Gundling, Beulah and Peg Seller: *Aquatic Art.* 403 Iowa Theater Building, Cedar Rapids, Iowa, 1957.
Hobden, F. W.: *Springboard Diving.* London, William Cloes & Sons, Ltd.
Jarvis, Margaret: *Swimming for Teachers and Youth Leaders.* London, Faber and Faber, 1947.
Kiphuth, Robert J.: *Swimming.* New York, A. S. Barnes & Co. 1942.
Lukens, Paul W.: *Teaching Swimming.* Minneapolis, Minnesota, Burgess Publishing Company, 1948.
Mann, Matt and Charles Fries: *Swimming.* New York, Prentice-Hall, Inc., 1940.
Spears, Betty: *Beginning Synchronized Swimming.* 2nd ed. Minneapolis, Minnesota, Burgess Publishing Company, 1958.
Torney, John A., Jr.: *Swimming.* New York, McGraw-Hill Book Company, Inc., 1950.
Yates, Fern and Theresa W. Anderson: *Synchronized Swimming.* New York, The Ronald Press, 1951.

PERIODICALS AND AQUATIC GUIDES

Amateur Athletic Union Handbook. 233 Broadway, New York 7, New York.
American Red Cross: *Swimming and Diving* and *Life Saving and Water Safety.* Obtainable at all Red Cross Offices.
Aquatic Games, Pageants and Stunts. Beach and Pool Magazine, 425 4th Avenue, New York, 1959.
Aquatics Guide. Division for Girls and Women's Sports, A.A.H.P.R., 1201 Sixteenth Street, N.W., Washington 6, D.C. Published every two years.
Gundling, Beulah: *The Aquatic Artist.* A monthly mimeographed bulletin. Write: Henry Gundling, 403 Iowa Theater Building, Cedar Rapids, Iowa. Price $5.00 a year individual membership, $15.00 a year club membership.
Junior Swimmer—Swimming World. A monthly for competitive swimmers and divers. 12618 Killion Street, North Hollywood, California.
Manual of Canadian Synchronized Swimming. Peg Seller, 19 Bayview Avenue, Lakeside, Montreal, P.Q., Canada. Useful for familiarity with Canadian rules.
Official Synchronized Swimming Handbook. A.A.U., 233 Broadway, New York 7, New York.
Swimming Times. A monthly magazine, excellent for men and women teachers and swimmers. Price $2.50 a year, including postage. Write: Capt. B. W. Cummins, 4 Waddon Park Avenue, Croydon, England.

CHARTS

Three Water Ballet Charts. F. Coleville, G. Goss, and B. Wallace. Price $2.50 a set. Write G. Goss, 20 Chestnut Park, Melrose, Mass.

FILMS

Fundamentals of Diving. Norman Sper, 1943 North Cherokee, Hollywood, California.
Matt Mann and his Swimming Techniques. Glenview, Illinois, Coronet Productions.
Springboard Diving. Bell and Howell, Inc., 1801–1815 Larchmont Avenue, Chicago, Illinois.
Springboard Techniques. Mike Peppe, Coronet Industrial Films, 65 East South Water, Chicago, Illinois.
Swimming—The Front Crawl. Bell and Howell, Inc., 1801–1815 Larchmont Ave., Chicago, Illinois.
Swimming, Elementary, Advanced and Fundamentals of Diving. Fred Cady, Division of Audio-Visual Education, Los Angeles County Schools, 808 North Spring Street, Los Angeles, California.
Teaching Johnny to Swim. Color or black and white. American Red Cross, Washington, D.C.

SLIDES

Diving. Nine loops with one fancy dive on each. Complete with adapter and instructions. Commentary by Phil Moriarty, diving coach at Yale University. Price $15.00.
35 mm. Color slides of Beulah Gundling demonstrating 27 key positions in execution of aquatic figures. Set of 27 slides with complete notes. Price $9.00 net, payable to "Aquatic Art," 403 Iowa Theater Building, Cedar Rapids, Iowa.

9

TENNIS

9

TENNIS

Gertrude Goss

Although tennis is an individual sport, there is evidence to question that individual instruction is the ideal method for teaching it. Recent educational research indicates that, generally speaking, people learn better and more easily when taught in groups. If well organized, and not too large in numbers, the classes can be broken into squads or teams for instruction. This way the student learns and enjoys developing skills along with others. Individual instruction is not really necessary anymore, and to insist on it discourages the average physical education teacher from even trying to include tennis in her program. The teacher must allot a certain amount of time in each class period to each student, making allowances for individual build and temperament. Good form must be insisted upon at all times. But good form will be different for each player. These facts should always be taken into consideration while teaching. One has only to watch the champions play to see that each has his own particular style.

The essentials that each must have are ease of movement, which includes rhythm and balance; strength of stroke; and the ability to put the ball where it should go at the proper time, which requires footwork. Practice and unlimited patience are necessary. The player who is satisfied to push the ball back over the net with no regard for the essentials will never make a good tennis player.

In teaching it must be remembered that enjoyment of the game is important.

At the end of each class period, the student should feel that something has been learned. This will help produce enjoyment of the game and give the necessary stimulation. If the student continues practice outside the class period, it generally means that class instruction has been enjoyed, that she has gained something from the instruction, and that there is stimulation for further practice.

HISTORY

The origin of the name is quite obscure, but it would seem to come from the French "tenez," meaning "take it," "play," "ready." In a poem written by Froissart the striker calls "Recipi" (take it) after each stroke. Good authorities find an ancient derivation of the game in Egypt, Persia, and Arabia, before the time of Charlemagne. In A.D. 1300, it was known as La Baude. It was played in a crude form in the moats of castles, where Charles VIII used to watch the game. Later Henri IV and Louis XIV (who kept a regular staff to look after his court) were patrons and players of tennis.

The sixteenth and seventeenth centuries were the heyday of the game both in France and England. Henry VII played, and revoked the edicts that forbade it. There was a court at Windsor Castle in his time, and it was still in existence in 1607. Henry VIII built the court at Hampton Court Palace in 1529 and 1530, and this court is in use today. A picture of James II as a boy shows him standing on a tennis court holding a short-handled racket strung diagonally. Before a racket was used, the players used gloves for protection; then, for greater protection, cords were wrapped around the gloves. Finally, in order to obtain a longer reach, a racket was made from a combination of paddle and cords. The first balls were leather and filled with hair.

Scoring was difficult in the beginning. The points were called "chases" and were scored 1, 2, 3, 4, and so on. Fifteen "chases" gave a player one point, and each game consisted of four or five points; thus came the use of the scores "fifteen," "thirty." The term "love," which means "no score," came from "for love," which means "for nothing" or "without stakes." And so the player who has no score is said to be "love."

After the rules were simplified, tennis became more popular than ever. It spread from England and France to Bermuda, and was brought to the United States in the 1870's by Miss Mary Outerbridge.

In 1881 the United States Lawn Tennis Association was formed in Boston and New York. All the official tournaments are sponsored by the U.S.L.T.A., whether on cement, asphalt, or clay. Few tournaments in this country are played on grass; however, the National Doubles Tournament at Longwood Cricket Club in Brookline, Massachusetts, is on grass, as is the National Singles Tournament at Forest Hills, New York.

At first local tournaments were played on different court surfaces. In 1900 international competition, the Davis Cup Matches, began. These matches are for men. The cup has been won by England, France, the United States, and Australia. Women have the Wightman Cup matches, which are between England and the United States. These matches were started by Hazel Hotchkiss Wightman and are played alternately in England and in the United States. From 1939 until 1946 these matches were not played. City, state, sectional, and national tournaments on all surfaces are now widely popular, and tennis is back to its own.

CLASSIFICATION OF STUDENTS

The general classification of students for group instruction is as follows: Beginners, Intermediates, Advanced.

I. BEGINNERS

Those who have never played tennis at all join this group.

II. INTERMEDIATES

Those who have "played at" tennis but have not had much instruction and have had no tournament experience join this group. This is the most difficult group to teach since, in most cases, the students have acquired bad habits. They are the students who play "push" tennis and have no idea of footwork.

As the intermediate group is the largest and the most varied in skills, it is a great help to have two divisions, low intermediates and high intermediates.

The *low intermediate* group are those who are little better than beginners and therefore need to be drilled on the work given to beginners. Their faults must be corrected, and when they are permitted to play tennis, they must continually be encouraged to use good form.

The *high intermediate* group are not quite up to the advanced group. They need drill on footwork and anticipation. They should be given as much "playing" as possible and something very definite to better their playing ability to work on during each lesson.

III. ADVANCED

If possible it is a good idea to have tryouts for the advanced group. The instructor should accept only those who have good rhythm, balance, footwork, and power. General play and court practice can be taught to them.

If a large number of courts and enough instructors are available, instruction can be given to each group throughout the day. The students can be put where they belong according to their ability. Remember, it is the individual need that is important.

The students should be encouraged to play on the courts at any time, and during the tennis season all the courts should be in use. On rainy days all the available backboard space can be kept busy. Advanced players, as well as beginners, need backboard practice. Experience has shown that footwork and stroke delivery *sometimes* can be improved more quickly by backboard practice than on a tennis court.

If there is no available wall space inside, which is seldom today, footwork

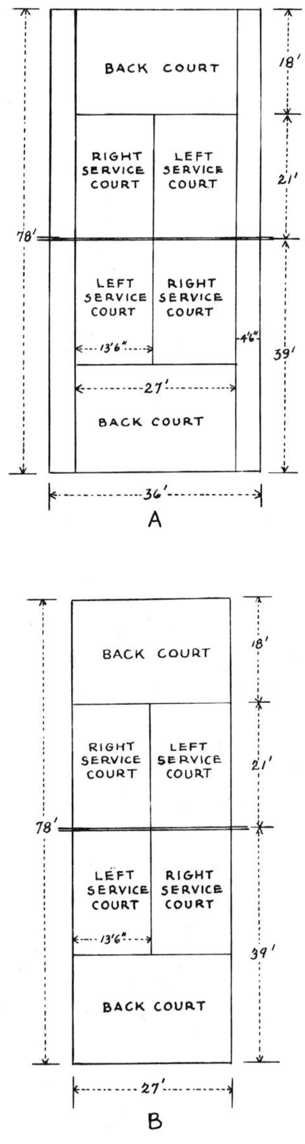

FIGURE 9.1 *A, diagram of a doubles court. B, diagram of a singles court.*

exercises can be given both with and without jump ropes. Also, the tennis Ready-Net can be set up very quickly. The Re-Bound Net, which is described on page 295, is excellent for group teaching indoors because it can be played on simultaneously from both sides.

TENNIS EQUIPMENT

Each potential tennis player should consider the matter of proper equipment for the game before going on to the courts.

I. RACKET

The better players should *choose* and *own* their own rackets. Physical Education Departments should buy some perfectly adequate, inexpensive rackets and have them available for group teaching.

There are several considerations in buying a racket. First of all, the racket must "feel" right to the individual. The handle of the racket should be small enough so that the thumb comes over the middle finger by a joint when using the Eastern forehand grip. The 4½ or 4¾ grip is right for most women. The racket should be of light to medium weight, 12½ to 13¾ ounces for a woman. The balance should be even—or slightly heavier in the head—according to personal preference. In choosing a racket the player should swing many different rackets (weights and grips) in order to find the right one. It is not always important to buy the most expensive racket.

Care of Racket. A racket should be kept in a press and a cover (with a little white talcum powder) when not in use. It should also be kept in a dry place. If the racket becomes wet, dry it immediately with a cloth.

II. BALLS

Only balls approved by the United States Lawn Tennis Association should be used for tournaments. Seconds obtained from sporting goods companies are adequate for class use. Colored balls are very helpful where lighting conditions are poor. Yellow is good indoors, and red is good for snow on all-weather courts. Dye the balls with ordinary Tintex and dry them immediately in a clothes dryer. The ball bounce is not substantially affected by dyeing. Colored balls may also be purchased. When working in squads, it is sometimes helpful to have each squad use a different-colored ball.

III. TENNIS CLOTHES

White is the accepted color for tennis clothes. Either a dress or shorts may be worn and the clothing should allow for plenty of freedom of movement. Low white tennis shoes or sneakers should be worn and white socks, either of wool, which will absorb perspiration and help prevent blisters, or of cotton. A visor or

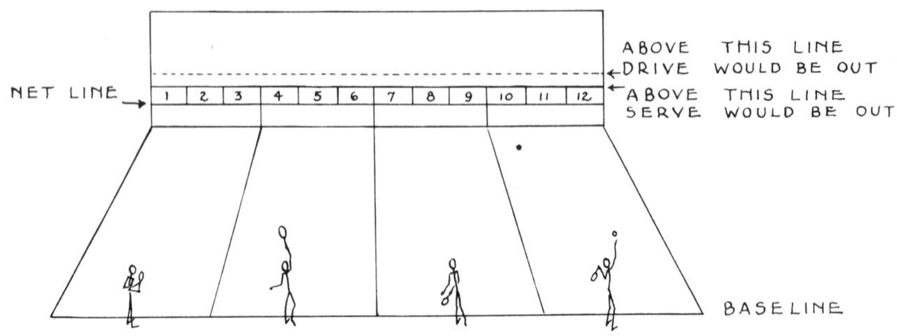

FIGURE 9.2 *Diagram showing backboard practice.*

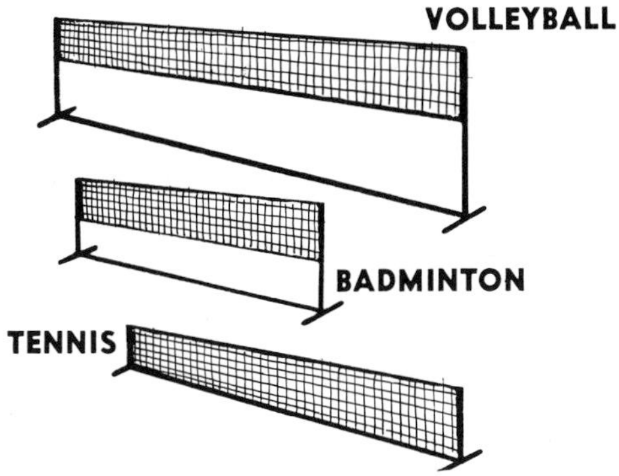

FIGURE 9.3 *The Ready-Net.*

tennis cap is very useful when playing against a bright sun.

IV. BACKBOARDS

Backboards made of beaverboard are the most satisfactory to work on, as the rebound of the ball is not so fast as from wood or cement, and it is more accurate. A line the height of a net should be drawn across the backboard. On the floor a base line should be drawn parallel to the net line at the proper distance from the net. Above the net line, squares can be marked off and numbered. The more advanced students can practice hitting certain numbers in front of them for accuracy. This is very good for practice for the serve as well as the drives. One and one-half feet above the service boxes, a line can be drawn to designate the point above which balls hit would go out of court. (Figure 9.3.)

V. THE RE-BOUND NET

The use of the Re-Bound Net is discussed in the section on backboard practice.

VI. THE READY-NET

The Ready-Net is a portable, self-standing game unit. It consists of two telescoping posts on a single 30-foot base. The net can be kept strung and always ready for use; it adjusts for tennis, volleyball, and badminton.

CONDITIONING EXERCISES FOR TENNIS

Footwork should be practiced before the strokes of tennis, as it is important, first of all, to have the body and feet in the right position. The player must learn that the feet should never rest flat on the ground. The weight should always be forward, whether standing still or moving. The knees should be relaxed or slightly bent. Even while waiting for the ball, the feet are constantly in motion. Some players skip, others hop or slide, and still others rock back and forth from one foot to the other. The object of all this movement is to keep the body in motion so that when the ball comes, it can be driven to the desired place with the impact of the whole body.

To beginners various ways can be presented for improving their footwork. This practice can be given indoors at a backboard or outdoors around the tennis court.

I. FOOTWORK

Run with the weight on the balls of the feet. The push should come from the ankles as each step is taken. The knees should be relaxed. Forward steps can be taken with slide steps at the end of a short run. Slides forward can be taken turning one shoulder or the other toward the net for forehands or backhands. These movements should first be demonstrated by the teacher, with an explanation of their importance.

1. Run in place slowly, then faster, then slowly again. Push from the balls of the feet.

2. Run for a given distance, come to a sudden stop, and lunge to the right as though reaching for a volley. Repeat to the left.

3. Run, come to a jump stop, lunge to the right, crossing over, and reach. Repeat to the left.

To show how to get from "waiting position" with body square to net into a position to return a drive with the side to the net, have the students:

1. Stand square to net, feet apart, weight on the balls of the feet. With a hop off both feet, turn the body a one-quarter turn so that the left shoulder is toward the net. Do same hop turning the right shoulder toward the net.

2. Take a few running steps forward, hop, turning left shoulder toward the net. Shift the body weight from the rear foot to the forward foot.

3. As in Number 2, take steps forward, hop, turn right shoulder toward the net.

4. Take running steps, or slide steps, diagonally forward; turn left shoulder toward net.

5. Take same slide or running steps forward, turn right shoulder toward net.

This practice may be given indoors or outdoors as desired or according to the weather. Practice in moving is first given without a racket. With the exception of the rope jumping exercise, do the same practice with the racket in hand.

II. USE OF JUMP ROPES

The use of jump ropes has been found to be excellent practice in starting and in getting the push from the balls of the feet.

1. Practice jumping from both feet, getting the push from the balls of the feet.

2. Jump first from one foot, then the other, getting the same push.

3. Jump starting from an erect position, go down to a squat position, then slowly back to a straight position.

4. With jump ropes, run forward a given distance. Then, without changing the swing of the rope or turning around, run straight back to starting position.

5. With jump ropes, run forward to the net along the side line. Then, without stopping or turning around, continue skipping diagonally backward.

STROKES

I. THE FOREHAND DRIVE

It is essential that a player should have sound ground strokes before attempting any other. Therefore, the forehand and backhand drives should be learned first. Many beginners learn the strokes quicker if started at the net with a volley, and gradually moved back in the court. The forehand drive is the stroke used to return balls that have hit the court in front and to the right of a right-handed player. This is the most important ground stroke in tennis, because more than one-half of the shots are made from the forehand. In returning such a drive, balls hit from just below waist height are the easiest. The object of the drive is to send the ball low over the net and deep to the opponent's base line.

A. The Forehand Grip. The grip used most generally is the "Eastern" or hand-shaking grip. This grip has the strength of the hand *behind* the racket (Figure 9.4).

B. Finding the Forehand Grip.

1. Hold the racket by the throat, with the left hand. Have the butt end toward the body. Grasp the end of the racket with the right hand as though "shaking hands" with it. When looking along the racket, there should be a V be-

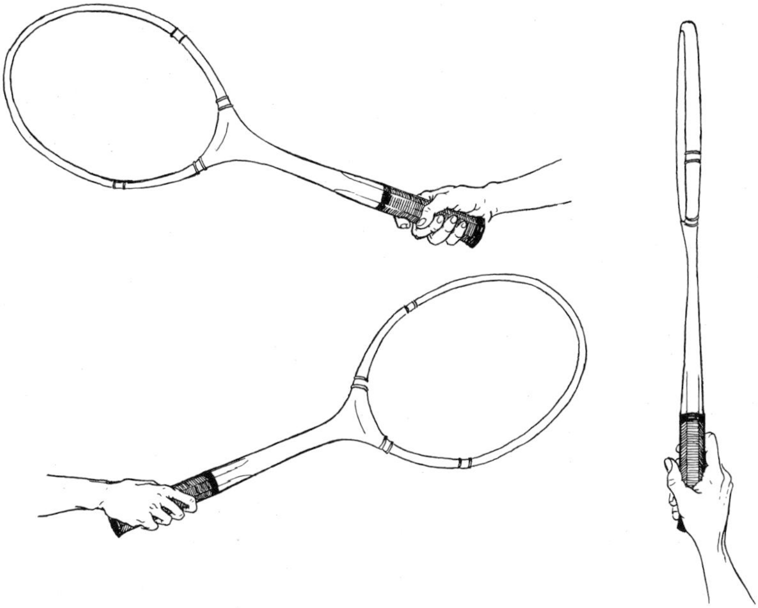

FIGURE 9.4 *Eastern forehand grip.*

tween the thumb and first finger. When holding the racket away from the body, the head of the racket should be slightly higher than the wrist. The fingers and thumb should be well around the racket and should slant toward the head of the racket.

2. Hold the racket by the handle. Place the head of the racket on the ground in front of you with the narrow edge of the frame facing upward. In this position looking down at the racket, there should be a V between the thumb and first finger. The fingers are spread and slanting toward the racket head. Pick the racket up, holding the head slightly higher than the wrist.

The grip should be accommodated to the individual and, therefore, will vary slightly with each player. At the moment of impact with the ball, the grip must be firm.

C. Body Position. In stroking a forehand drive, the body must be sideways to the net. For right-handed players, this means the left foot and shoulder must be forward. At the start of the swing, the weight is over the rear or right foot. The weight should be on the whole foot and the knees slightly bent. As the ball is met, the weight moves forward and over the ball of the forward foot so that the entire body is moving toward the net and in a line with the direction of the ball (Figure 9.5).

D. Backswing. Roughly speaking, there are two kinds of backswings: circular, and straight or horizontal. Either of these backswings is acceptable, depending on which is better for the individual. Leading players and coaches are advocates of each type.

The circular backswing has more freedom and rhythm. With beginners, however, there is sometimes a tendency to meet the ball from underneath. This causes the player to lift the ball too high in the air. To prevent this, the racket should be lined up *behind* the ball, and the drive made in a line parallel to the ground.

For many players the straight backswing is easier, in that in bringing the racket straight back it is easier to swing

FIGURE 9.5 *Forehand drive.*

forward and meet the ball from *behind.* After players have learned the straight backswing, they may change to a small or short, circular and more rhythmical backswing. The straight backswing is more efficient and more modern.

The backswing should be started before the ball bounces (that is as it leaves the opponent's racket) so as to give the player plenty of time. Some players start the backswing as the ball crosses the net toward them. When an early backswing is used there is a slight pause at the end of the backswing before the player moves the racket forward to meet the ball. As the arm is brought back, there is a slight rotation of the body away from the net.

E. Impact and Follow-through. Watching the ball closely, the player moves the body and racket forward, aiming to meet the ball with the middle of the racket strings. Some players meet the ball *after* it has started to drop from the bounce. To speed up one's game it is faster to meet the ball before the peak of the bounce. The ball should be carried forward on the racket, rather than jabbed at and let go from the racket. On the follow-through the player should reach as far forward as possible, letting the racket head do the work. There is a slight body rotation forward with the right shoulder coming forward and well around. The ball should be met slightly ahead of the forward (left) foot.

F. Essential Points in Forehand Drive.

1. Watch the ball until it comes off the racket.
2. Have the body at right angles to the net.
3. Move forward into the stroke, not only with the racket, but with the body weight.
4. Start the backswing as the ball crosses the net, or as the ball leaves the opponent's racket.
5. Keep well back from where the ball strikes the ground, to avoid rushing the shot and crowding the ball.
6. In the beginning wait for the ball to come to you. The beginner's tendency is to be on top of the ball. This causes jabbing at the ball with a cramped elbow.
7. Meet the ball from behind in order to send a low, deep drive over the net. A 6-inch net clearance is safest.
8. When meeting a low bounding ball, bend the knees to get down to it rather than drop the racket head.
9. Carry the ball forward on the strings of the racket rather than push the ball away with them.
10. Follow through as far as you can reach in the direction you want the ball to go.

II. THE BACKHAND DRIVE

The backhand drive is used to return balls that come to the left and in front of a right-handed player. Many coaches teach the backhand drive along with the forehand, as they have many points in common. The backhand should be just as easy to learn as the forehand for that reason. Unfortunately, it is the weaker stroke with most players. This often is due solely to lack of practice. It is just as important a stroke as the forehand, and woe be to the player who has a definite weakness on this side.

A. The Backhand Grip. Most women players and many men use the grip having the thumb up the back of the racket. This grip gives added support and, therefore, added control to the stroke. The straightness of the thumb will vary. But part of the thumb should be *behind* the racket. To find this grip it is necessary to shift the position of the hand on the racket. This is done most easily while the player is in the waiting position (Figure 9.6).

B. Body Position. The body position will still be at right angles to the net. Right-handed players will have the right foot forward instead of the left. As in the forehand stroke, the body moves from the rear (left) foot to the forward (right) foot. The foot position is reversed. The arm must swing across the body instead of to the side of the body. The shoulder does not get behind the drive as in the forehand, but is used more at the time of impact with the ball, and on the follow-through. As in the forehand stroke, the racket *head* should carry the fall forward (Figure 9.7).

C. Backswing. The body weight moves back over the left or rear foot. At the same time the racket is drawn well back across the body, with the arm not held rigidly, but with the hand grip firm. As the arm moves back, there is a slight body pivot to the left. The racket face should be brought back on a line with the ball.

As in the forehand drive, the racket should be brought back as the ball crosses the net, or when the ball leaves the opponent's racket.

D. Impact and Follow-through. The ball should be met about 1 foot in front of the right or forward foot, with the body weight moving forward from the rear foot. The knees should be slightly bent. The swing forward starts with a pivot from the hips. The arm moves forward with the racket well away from the body to avoid crowding the ball, which results in a cramped, jerky stroke. On the start of the swing, the arm is slightly bent, but it straightens out as the ball is

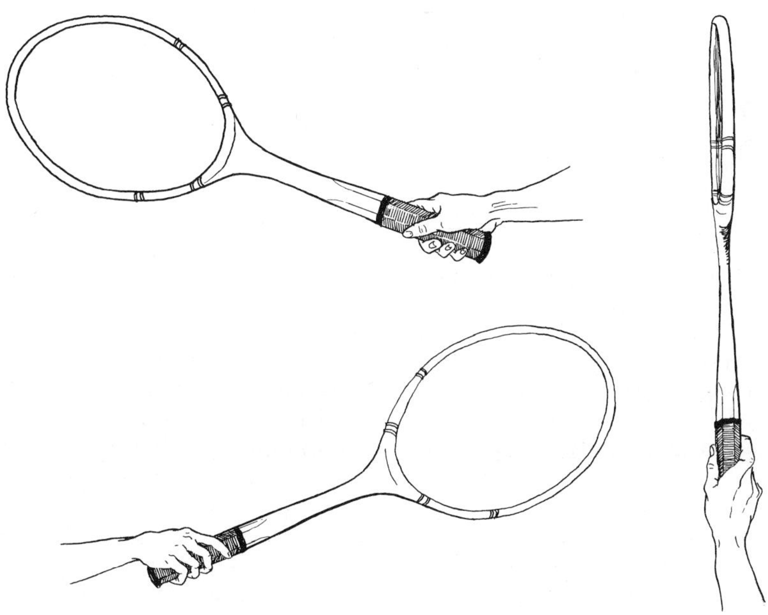

FIGURE 9.6 *Backhand grip.*

FIGURE 9.7 *Practice over the net.*

met and is straight for the follow-through. The arm swing should not stop when the racket meets the ball but should be carried forward in the direction of the flight of the ball. The racket head should be held up throughout the stroke.

E. Essential Points in Backhand Drive.

1. Watch the ball at all times.
2. Be sure to meet the ball with shoulder or side toward the net.
3. Get in position to meet the ball as soon as it leaves the opponent's racket.
4. Do not crowd the ball.
5. Have the proper grip (the best one suited to you, but be sure part of the thumb is behind the racket).
6. Let your racket head carry the ball forward.
7. Follow through after hitting the ball.
8. Keep the racket well away from the body with the head held up.
9. Do *not* run around your own backhand.

III. THE SERVE

The opening stroke of every point and every game is the service. This should be the opening for the attack. The importance of having a good serve, therefore, cannot be overestimated. A good serve must have two features, pace and direction. The ball should be placed where the receiver will have a difficult time in returning it. In order to obtain speed, the ball should be "hit down" from a high point, with the whole body weight in the swing. A tall player has an advantage over a short player in that she can hit down on the ball from a higher point. The short player should concentrate on placement and direction, which can be just as advantageous as speed.

A change in the direction of the serve can be as effective as speed. The ball should be placed so that the receiver cannot come immediately to the net. As it is tiring as well as unnecessary always to hit the ball hard, advantage can be gained through placement and a change of pace.

A. Grip for the Serve. There are two grips that may be used in learning the straight flat service. The first and simplest for most players is achieved by placing the racket on the ground and picking it up by the handle (Figure 9.9). The second grip is the same as that used for the Eastern forehand.

B. Body Position. Standing sideways to the net, the left foot is 2 or 3 inches behind the base line, the right foot is almost a foot and a half behind the left. The shoulders are turned in the direction the ball is to be sent. The balls and racket are held in front of the body. The weight should be evenly balanced on both feet.

C. Backswing. From this position

FIGURE 9.8 *Flat serve.*

the racket is swung *down,* the head of the racket pointing toward the ground, and *back* and *up* to a bent arm position behind the shoulder. At the same time the body weight is brought back over the right foot and the body rotates slightly away from the net. The motion is much the same as used in throwing a ball.

D. Impact and Follow-through. From behind the shoulder the racket is swung well *up* over the head. The ball should be met with a straight arm reach. At the height of the reach, the wrist is dropped forward; the racket head, therefore, drops slightly and leads on to the follow-through forward and across the body. The force of the body goes along with the arm swing and the weight is brought well forward on the follow-through (Figure 9.8).

This movement may or may not be continuous from start to finish. The continuity depends on the height of the toss of the ball.

E. The Toss. The ideal toss is straight up and a little to the right. It should be as high or higher than a reach with a fully extended arm, as the purpose is to meet the ball well up in the air. If the toss is too high, it necessitates a break in the arm swing and a pause behind the shoulder. This causes a loss in momentum from the beginning of the swing, and a loss of rhythm. If the toss is too low, it makes for a hurried swing and generally the ball is met too low and is netted. The swing is cramped by a low toss, and the body action is taken out of the stroke. If the toss is wide and to one side, it causes the server to swing out to the side of the body.

F. Essential Points in Service.

1. A free, well-coordinated backswing is necessary (Figure 9.10).
2. Meet the ball well overhead with a fully extended arm.
3. Practice the toss until the desired height and direction are consistently maintained.
4. Follow through forward with the racket after meeting the ball.
5. The body weight must move *with* the arm swing.

G. Practice of Service. Judy Barta

FIGURE 9.9 *Grip for flat serve.*

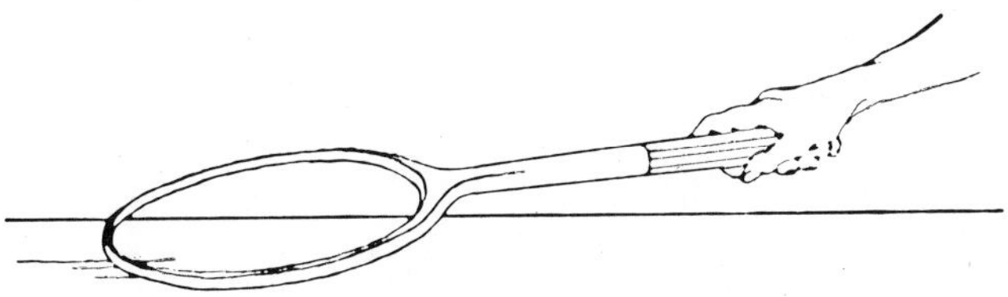

FIGURE 9.10 *Ball-Boy Server (Judy Barta).*

has produced a Ball-Boy Server for practicing the serve. It suspends the ball at any given height. The slightest hit releases the ball and sends it into the opposite court. As there is no toss, the player can concentrate on the hitting action of the swing. The server is adjustable and returns to its pre-set height after each ball is attached.

IV. THE VOLLEY

In addition to having a good drive, it is important to know how to volley. The drives are used mostly from the base line, but the volley is used closer to the net. In the drive, the ball first comes off the ground. In the volley, the ball is met *before* it touches the ground. To be able to go to the net and volley often means the end of a long rally with the point going to the better volleyer. If a volley is deep or well-angled, the opponent has little chance to return it. In drives the pace is put on the ball by the person driving, but in the volley the pace is put on the ball by the opponent. In the volley there is very little, if any, backswing.

A. Grip in the Volley. The grip for the volley may be the same as used in the forehand drive. For some players it is advisable to shorten the grip. It is best not to change the grip for the backhand volley. The racket head should be raised at a more decided angle than for the drives, probably around 45 degrees. If the racket head is allowed to drop, the power goes out of the stroke. The grip must be firm.

B. Backswing and Action. There is generally a very short backswing in volleying. While waiting to volley, stand squarely facing the net, about halfway between the service line and the net. As the ball comes, start the backswing. For a forehand volley, step forward on the left foot and, at the same time, turn the body slightly to the right side in order to move the body weight into the stroke. The ball should be met well in front of the body. Volleys that are taken shoulder high are the easiest. The movement of the swing is forward and slightly downward, according to the height of the ball and the distance from the net. When volleys are taken lower than net high, it is important to get down to them by bending the knees. At the same time the face of the racket must be opened (tilted back) in order to clear the net with the ball (Figure 9.11).

V. THE BACKHAND VOLLEY

The action in hitting a backhand volley is much the same as that in the forehand

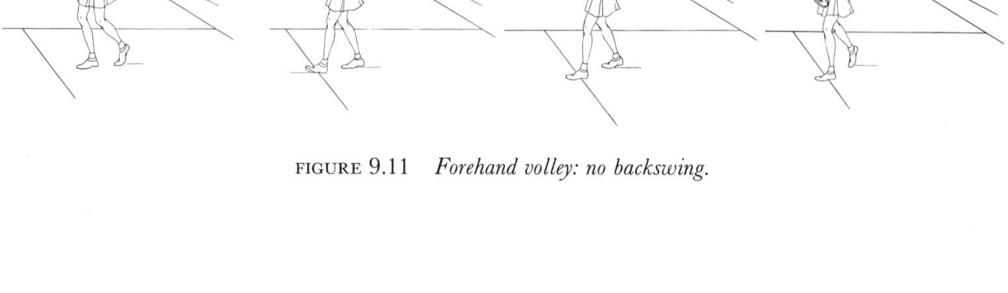

FIGURE 9.11 *Forehand volley: no backswing.*

FIGURE 9.12 *Backhand volley.*

volley. The ball is taken on the opposite side of the player. Therefore, the step is taken on the right foot instead of the left. The grip on the racket may or may not be changed. The grip must be firm, the backswing short, if any, and the left side of the player should be turned slightly to the net in order to put weight into the shot (Figure 9.12).

In volleying remember to angle the shot, or send the ball deep to the opponent's base line. When played correctly, it should be a point for the one who employs it. It is an invaluable stroke in doubles especially, and, as tennis is played today, it is being used more and more by singles players.

VI. THE LOB

The lob is a ball hit high into the air. Its use is to drive the opponent back from the net in order to get to the net yourself or, perhaps, to give yourself a short rest after being run around the court.

A. Kinds of Lobs. There are two kinds of lobs, offensive and defensive, or deep and short. The deep lob drops just inside the opponent's base line. The shorter lob is just high enough to clear the opponent's reach. Both lobs are fairly deep, but the shorter lob gives the opponent less time in returning. The best place to send a lob is into the opponent's backhand corner (Figure 9.13).

B. Technique and Timing. In the lob there is less of an impact against the ball than in the drive. Instead of a straight follow-through, there is a definite lift of the racket. The backswing is slowed and shortened. The ball is hit from *underneath* and is lifted into the air (Figure 9.14).

In doubles play the lob is one of the most effective strokes. It should be used when the opponents have come close to the net. As points are generally won by the players who are at the net, using the lob against such players is a successful way to send them back, and to give the users the important attacking position. It is invaluable against players who are good at volleying.

The lob is not used as much in singles as in doubles, perhaps because most players do not come to the net as often in singles as in doubles, and it is a useless shot against base line players. It should be used more as a surprise to the oppo-

FIGURE 9.13 *Deep (long) and short lobs.*

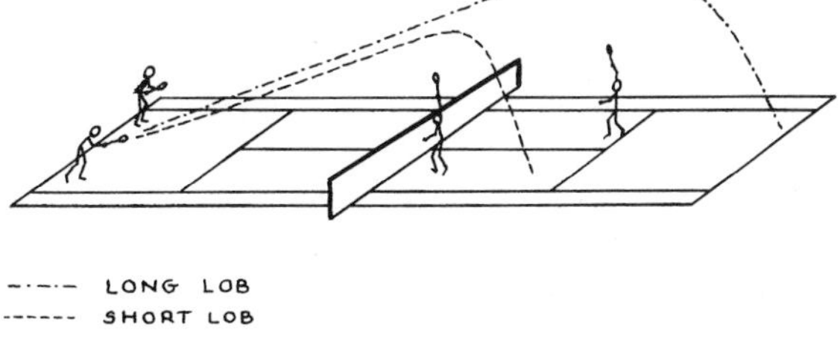

FIGURE 9.14 *Hitting a lob.*

nent as she comes to the net. It is safest to use the lob against a player whose smash is weak, or one who is weak at returning high balls.

C. The Lob as an Attack. The lob used to be thought of as a purely defensive stroke and a sign of weakness on the user's part. As tennis has developed, however, variety in strokes has become more and more necessary. Now the lob, when used correctly, can be an attacking weapon. Accuracy and timing are of the utmost importance in its use. It can be used against players who have come to the net, to drive them back, and give the users the opportunity to gain the net and the attacking position for themselves.

VII. THE CHOP

To add to the variety of strokes, a player can use the chop to good advantage. A chop alone should not be relied upon. It should be interspersed with the drive. The change in spin and speed of the ball will often throw an opponent off balance and break up her rhythm.

A. Grip in the Chop. The best grip to use is with the racket held halfway between the Eastern forehand and the backhand. This grip can be used for both the forehand and backhand chops.

B. Action. In the chop the action is actually that of "chopping" the ball. Some say to meet the ball as though one were slicing off its back cover. The swing is short in the back and forward-downward in movement. This motion cuts down the bounce of the ball making it shorter and lower. The right shoulder leans into the ball and the body weight moves from the rear foot to the forward foot. The player faces the net more squarely than in the drive. The racket head is held above the wrist (Figure 9.15).

C. Use of the Chop. The chop is used chiefly to break up the game of a player who has a stronger drive. The

FIGURE 9.15 *The chop.*

player who uses a chop can slow down the pace of a faster player. It should never take the place of the drive, but when used in conjunction with it can be very dangerous to an opponent. By itself it is seldom a winning stroke, as it is more a defensive than an offensive stroke.

VIII. THE DROP SHOT

The drop shot calls for a much lighter touch than the chop and has a shorter follow-through. It is hit, however, in much the same manner as the chop. The object in using the drop shot is to drop the ball just over the net, catching the opponent at the base line. Therefore, it is used as a change of pace, as a surprise stroke, and is particularly effective when the opponent's drives are going well and she can cover the base line from side to side.

A. Grip. The grip is the same as for the chop; namely, halfway between the Eastern forehand and backhand.

B. Action. The body should face the net more squarely than for a drive. There is very little backswing, and a light touch on the ball. The follow-through is shorter than in the chop. The face of the racket is dropped back to give back spin to the ball. The "chopping" movement is the same as for the chop.

C. Use. The drop shot is even more useful than the chop in breaking up the movement of an opponent from side to side along the base line. This is true because the drop shot should actually just "drop" over the net, and chop strokes often drop deeper on the court. Use of the drop shot should, of course, be interspersed with drives and lobs.

IX. THE OVERHEAD SMASH

The overhead smash is useful against a player who uses the lob. When placed correctly it should mean a winning point. It is hit in the same way as the serve. The smash can be used from any position on the court. There are times, particularly when the player is forced to move backward to take a lob, when the lob should hit the ground before "smashing." Usually, however, this stroke is used no further back than the middle of the court. Of course, to hit a smash, the ball must first have been lofted in the air by the opponent.

A. Grip. The same grip as for the serve should be used.

B. Action. As the ball is dropping, the player about to use the smash stands in the same relation to the ball as when catching a high fly ball. The racket is swung back as in the serve, and the ball is met well over the head, as high as possible in the air. The player often leaves the ground to reach the ball. The racket is brought forward and downward after meeting the ball. The body weight comes forward with the swing. (Figure 9.16.) If the ball is allowed to drop too low before being hit, it will be netted.

TEACHING METHODS

This concludes a brief description of the strokes most generally used in tennis. The problem now is to describe the teaching of these strokes to groups of students. It is most desirable, if possible, to teach each student separately. In school and college situations where most of the student body wishes to learn tennis, the lessons must be given in groups.

First, footwork is of the utmost importance. Ten or fifteen minutes can be devoted to conditioning exercises related to tennis, which would include footwork. Be sure to have enough jump ropes for all the students. Encourage these students to take ballet lessons. Aside from giving exercises in footwork, it is helpful to show moving pictures of leading tennis players in action. Students are great imitators, and seeing how they should move is one of the most helpful ways of starting them. The teacher should be able to demonstrate the strokes she wishes to teach. Students should be encouraged to see as

FIGURE 9.16 *Overhead smash.*

much good tennis as possible. Early in a season this is not always possible, but showing moving pictures has a very good effect, and the teacher can point out the things she is emphasizing in the class periods.

I. BACKBOARD PRACTICE

In the beginning, students make more progress and advance faster with stroke practice at a backboard than if all their work is given on a tennis court. Footwork improves and the ball always comes back to them from the board. This is important in group practice, as the teacher cannot be with every student every minute. If they are left on the courts to do stroke practice among themselves, they are unable to give each other the desired practice. The boards may be outside near the tennis courts, or in the gymnasium. The most desirable place for them is at the courts. In this case, the group can be divided, some working at the boards while others go on to practice over the nets. There is also an advantage in having a place for indoor practice, so that when the weather is rainy or cold classes can be held as usual (Figure 9.3).

A. Forehand at Backboard. The teacher should demonstrate the forehand grip and swing, first without hitting a ball, then hitting a ball at the backboard. Have the students practice the forehand swing.

For practice hitting against a backboard, have the students number off to use the available space. This space should not be crowded, and each student should be given ample time to get the feel of what she is doing.

It may be desirable in the beginning to have the class work by twos.

1. Number one stands with her side toward the net or board. Number two drops the ball in the proper place for number one. Number one drives the ball at the backboard, but does *not* return it from the board. Numbers one and two alternate in practicing.

2. Each girl tosses and hits her own ball, number one driving and number two retrieving the balls. At first, hit the ball without returning it. As soon as possible go on to the drive and the *return,* working on footwork and getting into the proper position for the return. Insist on the students moving and returning the ball after one bounce.

3. To add the element of a game, have two players drive the ball alternately at the backboard. One player drives and the other returns the drive, and so forth in alternating turns. This is similar to handball and squash. Points

courage the
as long as
tch the ball
ir side posi-
ng the ball.
ARD. The
e grip and
, have the
d grip and
on to the
nd to the
monstrate
ackhand.
ne players
th plenty

ber one
board.
e proper
practice
turning
e.
its own
balls.
return
ossible
ehand
oard.
off the
returns

game as
ing balls,
e to their

BACKHAND

o see how
ng. Return
come off the
ounce. In a
nber of good

tennis scores,
side. Have two
ing. Start with
of the players.
nake the return,
on.
D. SE... CKBOARD. Dem-
onstrate t... t out the value of
having a g... ompare with mo-

he drive from
ed by another
he ball trying
er two's base
the balls and
opposite base
tries the same
cticing. No at-
turn the drives.
f tries, see how
made (Fig...

g a ball c...
, numb...
o num...
its th...
ive ...

tion used in throwing a ball. Practice throwing balls at the backboard.

Players practice the grip and swing, without a ball. For practice with a ball:

1. Players work by twos. Number one stands behind the base line. Practice serving without returning the ball. Number two retrieves. Alternate practice. Endeavor to have the ball hit the board above the net line and below the top box line. When fairly accurate, count the number of good serves in five minutes' time. Change with partner.

2. Practice serve and follow up ball for a return after the service.

3. Serve and follow up for return and continue keeping ball going.

4. Play a game with partner. Start with service and take alternate balls on return. Score as in tennis. Have each player serve through one game.

E. THE RE-BOUND NET. In place of using a wooden backboard for indoor or outdoor practicing, purchase a Re-Bound Net. An invention of Judy Barta (tennis player and teacher; founder of the Ball Boy Company, Inc.), this net is a bounce-back net of heavy-duty nylon, positioned on a light-weight, port-

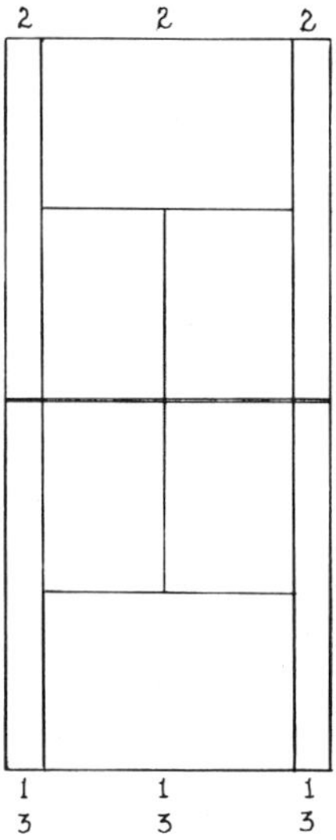

FIGURE 9.17 *Long drives over the net—base line to base line.*

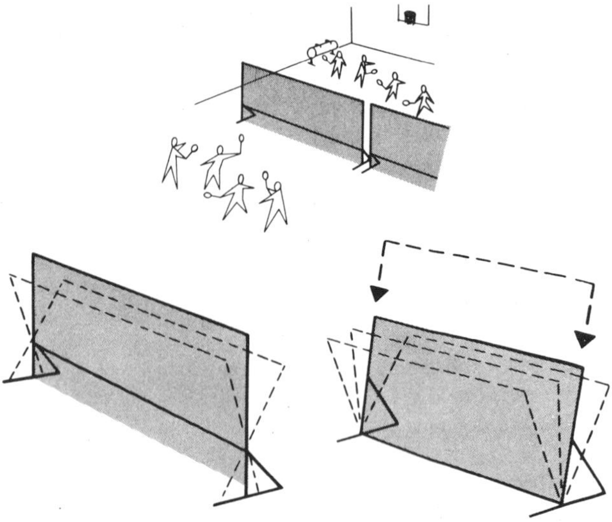

FIGURE 9.18 *Re-Bound Net (Judy Barta).*

able steel frame. The net can be played on from both sides at the same time, which is an asset where space is limited and there are numbers to be taught.

There is of course a difference in timing when stroking the ball from a net rather than off a wall. The net gives a student more time to get ready. Those of us who have taught tennis know that a wall surface returns the ball too fast to be handled correctly, if at all.

II. NET PRACTICE

A. FOREHAND OVER THE NET.

1. A demonstration of the forehand drive over the net by the teacher.

2. Students practice t
a self toss, or hit a ball toss
player. Number one hits
to drive it deep to num
line. Number two collect
drives them back to the
line. Number three then
drive. All take turns pra
tempt is made at first to re
Out of a given number o
many good drives can b
9.17).

3. To practice hittin
from a toss or a throw
tosses or throws the ball t
forehand. Number one h
ing to send a long, low dr

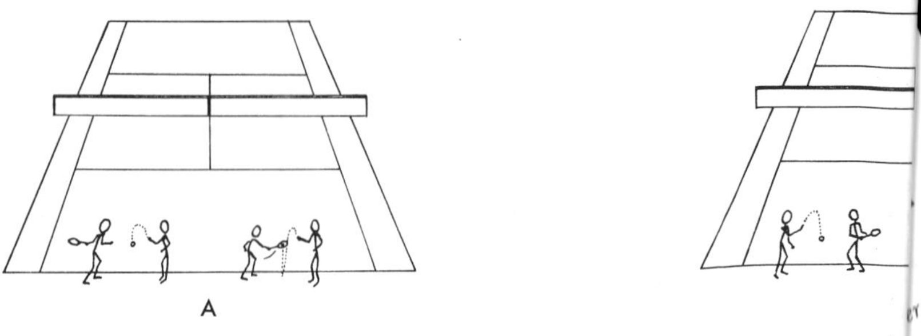

FIGURE 9.19 *A, Forehand drive from toss by another person. B, Backhand drive from* ... *erson.*

to number three's base line. All take turns with this practice, giving each the same length of time to practice the drive (Figure 9.20).

At first the throws should be to the ideal place for a return. They then should be changed so that the striker must move forward or to the right for the forehand drive.

B. The Backhand over the Net. The formations for forehand practice can be used for backhand practice in the following order:

1. Drive from self-tossed ball.
2. Drive from toss or throw by another person.
3. Backhand drive, making striker move by use of variety in throw.
4. Have the thrower mix the throws between forehand and backhand until the striker can hit from both sides. Making the striker move is most practical, as tennis is a game of continual movement and very few shots are taken while the players are standing still. The players must move, getting to the proper place to return the ball, and then stroke it back over the net. The player must also learn to take balls on both sides equally well, and so the toss to both sides is important.

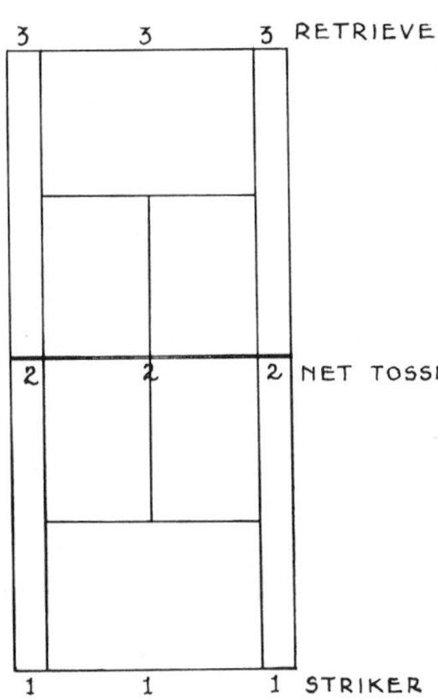

FIGURE 9.20 *Nine on a court. The person at the net throws the ball to the striker, mixing the throws for forehand and backhand drives to the opposite base line.*

FIGURE 9.21 *Ball-Boy throwing machine (Judy Barta).*

III. THE BALL-BOY MACHINE

For years many teachers have used the "human" ball throwing or hit method to teach the basic tennis strokes. Neither method has been entirely satisfactory, mainly because the throw is inaccurate. Judy Barta has developed, through careful study and research, the Ball-Boy Machine.* This machine can be adjusted to hit a ball at any pre-set speed, height, and position. It enables the student to have concentrated practice in stroking balls that come directly to her from the same place and at the same speed. These strokes can be practiced first standing still, then moving. Forehand and backhand strokes can be taken alternately. In fact, every stroke in tennis can be practiced (Figure 9.21).

IV. RALLY BY TWOS

When the players become fairly accurate at returning the ball from throws, they should be encouraged to rally over

* Obtainable from the Ball-Boy Company, Inc., 26 Wilburn Street, Bronxville, New York.

the net. The teacher should, if possible, take each member of the class separately and rally with her. Then the student must go on practicing with someone of the same, or better, ability.

One of the most difficult problems in teaching a group of beginners is to give each member of the class a chance to practice with someone who is a better player. The teacher cannot play with each member of the group all the time, but must give each student an equal amount of her time. This being the case, it is sometimes necessary to have the group work for a longer time hitting thrown balls, rather than have them work together rallying and not getting anywhere with the practice. The teacher must see this situation and be alert for any needed changes. The students can be asked to practice between class lessons with players who are *better* than they are, and who will give them the practice they need.

V. THE SERVICE OVER THE NET

It is possible to have twelve players practice the serve over the net on one court. Number ones can serve first, serving straight over instead of into the service courts on a diagonal line. Number twos retrieve the balls and serve them back to number threes, who retrieve and serve to number fours, who in turn serve. In some cases the students not serving can correct the serves of those who are serving. This often helps the students who are not serving, for, in watching others, they see what they should not do when it is their turn to serve.

If there are backboards by the tennis courts, the players can take turns serving at the boards, and serving over the net. This is an ideal situation.

If there are enough courts for the group, have them practice with four on a court and serve into the proper service court (Figure 9.22).

To the serve, practice in the return of service can be added. Number ones serve first. Number twos return. Number twos

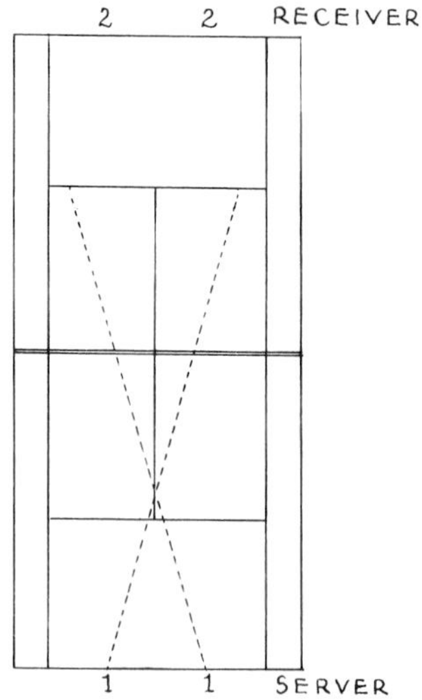

FIGURE 9.22 *Practicing the serve into the proper service court.*

serve. This practice can go on until the players are ready to play a game.

At this point the players should work on the three-stroke game—the serve, forehand drive, and the backhand drive. The emphasis should be on driving the ball correctly and keeping the rallies going. The ball must be hit properly, and bad form must be stopped in the beginning.

VI. THE VOLLEY

Having learned the drives and service, the next stroke for a player to know is the volley. Tennis has developed rapidly in the last few years, and it is necessary for players to be able to go to the net as often as possible. To do this, one must learn to volley. A player who can volley well need not have long, tiring rallies with an opponent, as the volley is often the finishing stroke that "puts the point away."

The teacher demonstrates the volley, showing body position, footwork, and stroking. Both forehand and backhand volleys should be shown. Then the group, without a ball, should go through the motions used in volleying.

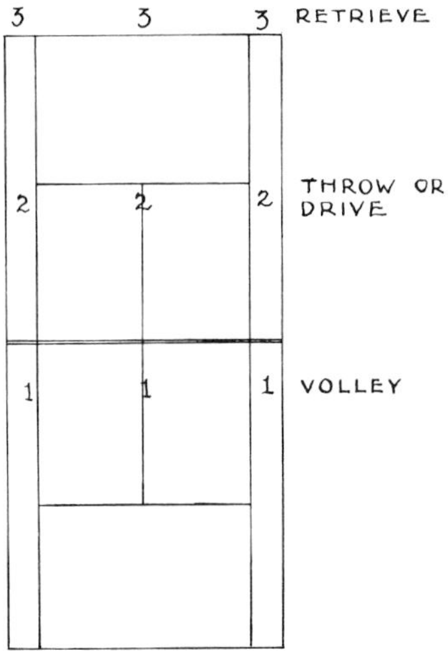

FIGURE 9.23 *Practicing the volley with nine on one court: 1, volleys; 2, throws or drives ball; 3, retrieves.*

Nine players can then be put on a court to practice the volley. Number ones volley, number twos throw, and number threes retrieve. Shoulder-high balls are the easiest to volley. In the beginning, the throws should be made on that level. Throws should be made to both sides with the volleyer taking the balls as they come. The players rotate during this practice so that each has an equal amount of time to practice (Figure 9.23).

If the players can drive the balls to each other for this practice, it is better than throwing as the pace is put on the ball by the thrower or driver.

During this practice, the teacher should move around the class so that each member gets the same amount of time receiving her drives.

It is possible to give instruction up to and including the volley to a group of beginners and intermediates during one term of eight weeks. But the players must practice outside the class period during the season.

VII. THE LOB

The teacher must first discuss and then demonstrate the lob. The stroke should be taught only to the more advanced groups, as there are other strokes that should be learned first, and to be able to lob really well requires a great deal of skill. After the demonstration by the teacher, the players can practice the lob with nine players on one court. Number twos drive the balls to number ones who lob the balls back to the opposite base line. Number threes retrieve the balls. The players must rotate so that each has an equal practice time (Figure 9.24).

In some cases in the beginning, number ones will need to practice lobbing self-tossed balls, and then go on to lobbing balls that are coming toward them from other players.

To practice the short lob, number twos move up to the net while number ones practice the lob, sending the balls just above the reach of the number twos and not deep to the base line. The threes retrieve the balls. Again the players must rotate so that each has an equal practice time (Figure 9.25).

VIII. THE CHOP

The teacher first demonstrates the chop. The players can practice the stroke

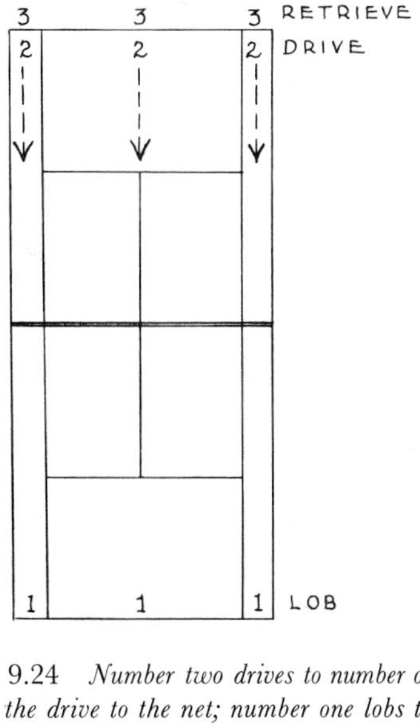

FIGURE 9.24 *Number two drives to number one and follows the drive to the net; number one lobs the ball back to number three.*

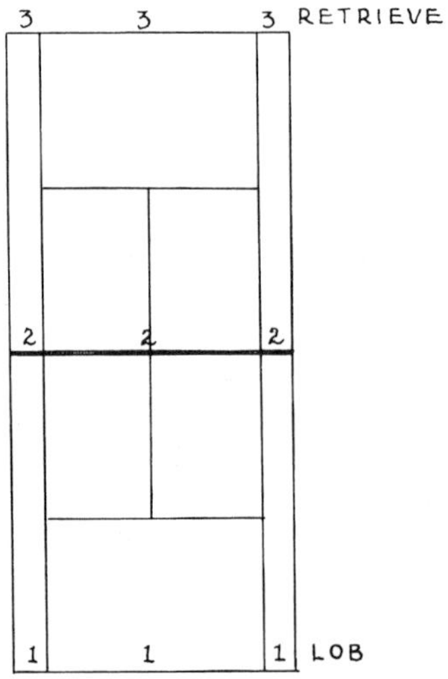

FIGURE 9.25 *Practicing the short and deep lobs over head of player at net.*

by threes, having nine players on one court. Number twos hit the balls to number ones. The ones in returning the balls use the chop. The threes retrieve the balls. In some cases ones and twos rally with each other, both players using the chop. Number threes come in for practice, while number ones retrieve, and so forth (Figure 9.26).

IX. THE DROP SHOT

The same type of practice formation can be used to practice the drop shot. The object is to "drop" the ball over the net when the opponent is expecting a drive to her base line. It is one of the most difficult shots in tennis, and also one of the most effective when used at the *right* time.

X. THE OVERHEAD SMASH

This stroke is the same as the overhead service. Instead of tossing the ball herself, the player hits a ball that has been lifted into the air toward her.

1. Number twos practice this smash, number ones having thrown the ball well up for twos to hit.
2. Number ones lob the ball while the twos use the overhead smash in returning it.
3. Number threes change places with number ones, for equal time in practice (Figure 9.27).

Along with the practice of strokes taken up separately, the players must be given time to apply the strokes while playing in a game. The players must be encouraged to think for themselves.

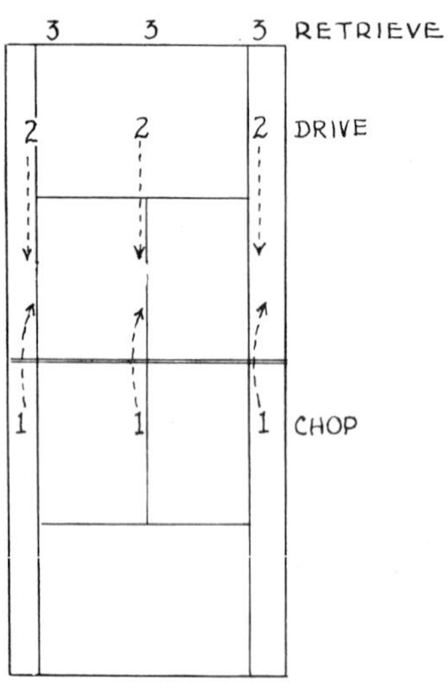

FIGURE 9.26 *Practicing the chop. Nine on one court: 1, chops; 2, drives ball to No. 1; 3, retrieves.*

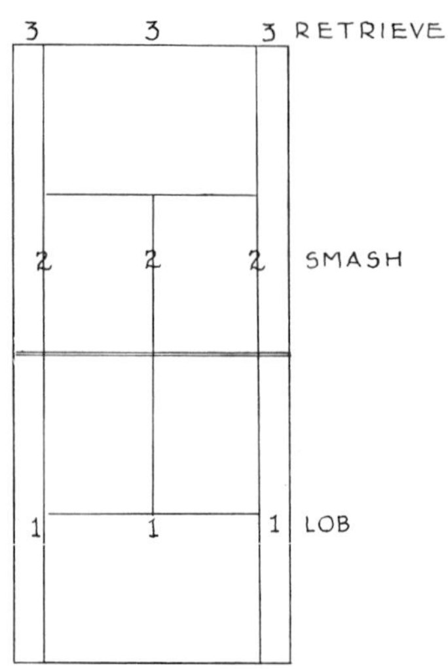

FIGURE 9.27 *Practicing the smash from a short lob. 1, lobs to No. 2; 2, overhead smash; 3, retrieves.*

Stroke practice alone will not let them do this. Therefore, in each class period time must be given over to playing. Good form in strokes must be insisted upon at all times but not a set type of play to which all must conform. So long as a player is moving easily and has strength of stroke and accuracy, she may be said to have good form.

Many players having a foundation of good strokes are beaten because they fail to think. A player must have the "will to win" or she will find herself beaten by inferior players whose strokes are poor, but who have the power of concentration and have learned to think quickly and put their thoughts into action.

LESSON PLANS

The following is a suggested outline of lessons for tennis instruction.

I. BEGINNERS

Lesson 1. Discuss importance of footwork. Give group exercises in moving, rope jumping, and running short slides sideward and forward. Discuss and demonstrate forehand grip and body movement. Practice all movements.

Lesson 2. Review lesson 1. Add hitting forehands at backboard.

Lesson 3. Review 1 and 2. Discuss and demonstrate backhands. Practice.

Lesson 4. Practice hitting forehands and backhands at backboard.

Lesson 5. Continue forehand and backhand practice. Emphasize footwork. Keep rally going off backboard.

Lesson 6. Forehands and backhands over the net. First just driving balls without return. Then from throws by threes.

Lesson 7. Review lesson 6. Add rally.

Lesson 8. Review parts of 6 and 7 as needed.

Lesson 9. Rally taking balls forehand or backhand as they come. Discuss scoring. Demonstrate scoring taking one court. Use forehand for serve. Have students score. Instructor makes corrections.

Lesson 10. Serve by demonstration first. Then have group practice at backboards or back stops.

Lesson 11. Review 9 and 10.

Lesson 12. Practice serve on court over the net. Combine serve and return practice.

Lesson 13. Review 12.

Lesson 14. Practice serve. Review forehands and backhands, rallying. Play.

Lesson 15. Play.

Many beginners will not be ready to learn to volley at this point. If not, the time is best spent devoting part of each period to *practice* on the serve, forehands and backhands, and the latter half of the period to playing the "three stroke" game. Lessons 16 through 20 could be based on this kind of practice.

Lesson 16. Demonstrate volley. Discuss its use. Practice volleys by threes, using throw.

Lesson 17. Continue practicing volley from throws or drives.

Lessons 18 through 20. Individual review as needed.

During each lesson the instructor *must* give time to each student separately, in order to correct mistakes before they become fixed habits, and to give as much encouragement as possible.

II. THE INTERMEDIATE GROUPS (LOW AND HIGH)

The majority of students who choose tennis for their activity while in college would be classified in what we call the intermediate group. As this group contains a wide range of ability, it seems best for teaching purposes to divide it into two groups, namely, *low intermediate* and *high intermediate.* The low intermediates are those who are just beyond the very beginners and who need some work on the beginners' level before going on. The high intermediate players are those who have played a weak sort of tennis with a limited variety of strokes and need considerable instruction in more strokes and practice before they can be called advanced.

The teacher must remember that at all times the student must *enjoy* playing. The learning should never become drudgery. Accomplishment gives a person great satisfaction. Lessons should be planned so that the student gets the feeling of enjoyment and accomplishment. A good test of this is when at the end of a class period students want to stay on for more practice, or you find that they are playing extra hours outside of class. Encourage them to see as much good tennis as possible, as this is a great stimulus.

A possible outline for low intermediates:

Lesson 1. Review exercises to develop footwork. Discuss forehand and backhand grips. Practice change from forehand to backhand. Practice by threes hitting forehands over the net.

Lesson 2. Review lesson 1 as needed. Practice forehands by threes with emphasis on moving before hitting the ball.

Lesson 3. Repeat discussion of backhands. Practice backhands by threes.

Lesson 4. Review 2 and 3. Practice mixing forehands and backhands. Start from the waiting position each time.

Lesson 5. Review parts of lessons 2, 3, 4 as needed.

Lesson 6. Discuss and practice the serve at backboards.

Lesson 7. Practice the serve over the net, first without the opponent's returning the serve, then with return of service.

Lesson 8. Review scoring. Then have all play "three strokes" game.

Lesson 9. Repeat lesson 8.

Lesson 10. Practice the serve. Continue playing, trying for deep base line drives.

Lesson 11. Discuss and practice the volley.

Lesson 12. Practice the volley.

Lesson 13. Discuss singles tactics. Play, working for a forcing shot in order to go to the net and finish off the point with a volley.

Lesson 14. Review lesson 13.

Lesson 15. Review lesson 13.

Lesson 16. Review practice of strokes as needed.

Lesson 17. Repeat lesson 16.

Lesson 18. Discuss doubles tactics. Play doubles.

Lesson 19. Play doubles.

Lesson 20. Play doubles.

A possible outline for high intermediates:

Lesson 1. Give exercises for footwork, including rope jumping. Have students choose opponents and play. Instructor goes to each court and makes necessary suggestions.

Lesson 2. Discuss general play with the entire group. Have them continue to play.

Lesson 3. Have them all rally, working for depth of drive. Practice the serve.

Lesson 4. Repeat lesson 3.

Lesson 5. Work on volleys the first half. Play the last half, trying for forcing shots.

Lesson 6. Repeat lesson 5.

Lesson 7. Discuss the lob. Practice the chop and short lobs.

Lesson 8. Repeat 5 and 7. Play the last half of the period, trying to use these two strokes at the right times.

Lesson 9. Continue playing.

Lesson 10. Continue playing.

Lesson 11. Discuss the drop shot. Practice the drop.

Lesson 12. Repeat lesson 11. Play the last half of the period.

Lesson 13. Discuss and play doubles.

Lesson 14. Play doubles.

Lesson 15. Play doubles.

Lesson 16. Play doubles round-robin tournament of one set each within the group.

Lesson 17. Continue round-robin.

Lesson 18. Continue round-robin.

Lesson 19. Play singles round-robin of one set.

Lesson 20. Play singles round-robin of one set.

III. THE ADVANCED GROUP

The advanced group can be a selected group. Tryouts can be held, and only those players accepted who have good footwork, rhythm, and power. They are generally found to need more playing time with emphasis on court tactics in both singles and doubles, and additional strokes to add variety to their game. They are also found to have good forehand and backhand drives, fairly good serves, and possibly a "volley" they can count on.

A possible outline for teaching this group for one season would include:

Lesson 1. Have a discussion of tennis, emphasizing the importance of footwork. Spend five to ten minutes jumping rope. Have the players rally with each other, watching stroking and footwork.

Lesson 2. The players choose opponents and play singles.

Lesson 3. Teach the volley to the group. Demonstrate and have students practice.

Lesson 4. Singles play with emphasis on getting to the net to volley.

Lesson 5. A discussion of singles play. Continue practice as needed.

Lesson 6. Demonstrate the chop, discussing its value. Practice the chop.

Lesson 7. Review practice of the chop. Play.

Lesson 8. Demonstrate the drop shot. Practice the chop and the drop shots.

Lesson 9. Play, using as much variety of strokes as possible.

Lesson 10. Discuss doubles play. Play doubles.

Lesson 11. Continue playing doubles.

Lesson 12. Demonstrate the overhead smash. Practice the smash.

Lesson 13. Review lesson 12. Doubles play.

Lesson 14. Review of strokes as needed by class individually.

Lesson 15. Continue the review of stroke practice. Play.

Lesson 16. Demonstrate and discuss the lob. Practice.

Lesson 17. Review lesson 10. Practice other strokes as needed.

Lesson 18. Practice or play as needed.

Lessons 19 and 20. Practice or play as needed.

It is most important that students should play outside the lesson period as much as possible. No one can learn to play tennis without continued practice. The above outline seems like a lot to teach a group, but the most that can be done for many students is to show them the different strokes. Those who *want* to learn will practice and apply the strokes they need to their game.

TACTICS

I. THE SINGLES GAME

The first thing which any tennis player must learn is that there are only two sections of the court in which to stay for any length of time: namely, the forecourt, well inside the service line, for an attacking game, and behind the base line for a defensive game. The ground in between is called "no man's land" and should be passed through as quickly as possible. If a player is caught in this "no man's land," her opponent will either drive deep beyond her so that she cannot get back for returns, or will drive the ball at her feet, which is an almost impossible shot to return. Therefore, learn in the beginning either to stay behind the base line or get well up to the net. When playing against a steady base line player, do not hesitate to go to the net—and keep going to the net.

A. The Serve. The ideal serve, of course, is one that is hit so hard and is so well placed that the opponent cannot reach it. As this cannot always be done, you must at least *place* your serve so that your opponent is only able to hit back a weak return. This will enable the server to go up to the net and so be the attacker. The serve should be varied, from side to side, short and deep, and straight at the receiver, so that she is unable to anticipate it. If your opponent has a weak backhand, do not always play to it, or she will move to be in a position to make the return. To keep her in the back court, have the serve drop back as deep as possible. Try to make your opponent move to meet the ball. Have a change of pace as well as a change of direction. The main point in serving is to gain an attacking position for the server and to keep the opponent wondering where the ball is coming next.

B. Return of Service. The receiver will want to place herself where she can get the ball back and place her return so that her opponent will have difficulty in returning it. The server momentarily is the attacker and what the receiver does with the ball determines whether or not the attacking position can be won by her. If the serve pulls the receiver well over to one side off the court, the server should come to the net for a volley. Should the server come up to the net too fast, she leaves her backcourt wide open for a "cross court" return. If the receiver should hit the ball hard, straight down the side line, or if the server comes well up to the net, on her serve, the receiver should lift a lob over her head or pass her down either side line. If the server is slow in coming up, a drive right at her feet is an effective shot. If the service comes to the receiver's backhand in the left service court, a cross court drive on the return is a good one. These returns are good if the server comes to the net to volley. They are for the most part "passing shots." If the server insists on staying at the base line, the problem is not how to pass her, but how to vary your returns so that she not only must run from side to side but must come up. The shot to use in this case is a chop or drop shot, as this breaks up a hard hitting-driving type of game on which a person who plays on the base line depends. Find out her weak points and play through her strength to them as much as possible and have a variety of shots that you can use and depend on.

C. General Position in Rallies. First of all, remember to keep out of "no man's land." Then, if you find yourself playing against a hard-hitting, driving game from the back court, stand 4 to 5 feet *behind* and in the middle of the base line and vary your returns so that your opponent must move not only from side to side, but up and back as well. If your opponent is not a hard hitter, stand a little *inside* the base line. Then be sure to move your weight forward into your drive and do not be caught moving backward. On your return either follow your drive directly to the net or get back quickly behind the center of your base line. If you are a good volleyer, you should endeavor to get to the net, as points are scored more quickly for you there than by prolonged base line rallies, which in the end may simply tire you out, particularly in a long, even match. Another point to remember is that if your plan of attack is not working, be quick to change to another plan. Never play the kind of game your opponent likes. There are certain fundamentals a player must never lose sight of:

1. Be Alert. Always keep moving. Be in position to move *forward.* Don't be caught moving backward. Weight must be forward. Keep the heels off the ground.

2. Watch the Ball. Follow the ball right on to the middle of your racket and off the racket. Also keep an eye on your opponent to see where she is on the court and try to anticipate the type of stroke she is using on her return to you.

3. Anticipate. When watching good players you will note that they never seem to be moving. On further observation, you realize that they have anticipated the shot to them and are already in the proper position to make the return.

II. THE DOUBLES GAME

Today in doubles it is important to have speed and be able to *get to the net before your opponents.* The doubles team that can get to the net first and has the ability to volley well is in a position to win more points. The secret of good doubles play is to have good teamwork with your partner. It is important to give information to each other, such as "mine," "yours," and "out." The partners should be equal in playing ability. A strong and weak combination is often beaten by two players who are beneath them in general playing ability but have learned to play well together. Good singles players do not always make good doubles players, as doubles is a team game and the first principle is to play well *with* your partner. It is often true that to be a good doubles team the players must also be good friends. So, in choosing a doubles partner, it is a good plan to choose someone from whom you will receive encouragement and support rather than a person you know to be a better player, but one with whom you are uncongenial.

A. Court Position. The best court formation is to keep as nearly parallel as possible. Either both players should be well up together or both should be back. In playing on a parallel line and when both are up, you must watch for returns that come between you. It is a good idea to have an understanding as to who is going to take these shots. If you are at the net, your opponents will try to pass you by sending a ball right between you, or one just inside the side lines, or they will put up a lob. For the passing strokes you must be alert, have good footwork, and have skill in volleying. For the lob you must both get back and have an understanding as to which one is to take it. Then if you can, both get to the net together. The Australian formation is a very successful one to use. In it the receivers have one player at the net as well as the side which is serving. To avoid trouble for your partner, the return of serve must be out of reach of the opposing net player.

B. Service in Doubles. The service in doubles is probably more important than the service in singles. If your service is weak and you cannot get to the net on it, your partner will have to come back with you, and your opponents in the meantime can come to the net and so gain the attacking position. A serve which is down the middle of the service court is a difficult one for the receivers to hit to the side lines and should be tried on the serve as often as possible. The server must remember that her job is to get to the net on her serve, or else she will put her side immediately on the defensive. In doubles the serve must be won by the server.

C. Receiving in Doubles. One of your opponents is already at the net and should be able to handle any shot which comes to her. The exceptions are if she has been drawn to the center of the court, in which case a drive down her alley is a good return, and so is a well-placed lob over her head. The server is often the best one to attack. If she is slow in coming up to the net, a drive at her feet is a good one. If she comes in fast, a diagonal lob will often work out well for you and confuse your opponents. Another shot that will bother her is a slow angled drop shot.

Some important things to remember in doubles are:

1. Doubles is a *team* game.
2. Have a thorough understanding with your partner.
3. Always be in a parallel position with each other.
4. Both should be able to get to the net, but should also know when to get back to the base line.
5. The serve, volley, and overhead smash are of greatest importance.
6. Most points are made by the team that is at the net.
7. The lob is used in doubles to send your opponents away from the net.
8. Decide who is to get the center ball.
9. Give information to each other, such as "mine," "yours," and "out."

TOURNAMENTS

I. COMPETITION

In tennis many kinds of tournaments are of value. These are discussed elsewhere, but there is also opportunity here for class, school or college, and interhouse or dormitory tournaments. The number of tournaments depends upon length of season and number of courts available. Ideally, there should be some competition for groups of all levels of ability—particularly for intermediate as well as advanced groups. But this takes time, and the shortness of the season limits the number of tournaments it is possible to run off. At least an all-school tournament and class competition can be arranged.

II. TENNIS CLUBS

In some institutions there is a tennis club which has special hours for practice and special competition. These students can help coach less experienced players, give demonstrations, and help officiate and act as linesmen and ball boys in important matches.

It is a great stimulus to the sport to bring in some excellent players, amateur and professional, to show the students the best in the sport. Matches in the vicinity can also be brought to the attention of the students.

III. PLAY FOR BOYS AND GIRLS

Tennis, like badminton, is a very popular sport for boys and girls together, and courts should be made available for them. This as a rule needs no planning as it is a natural weekend sport. Students are, moreover, glad to have instruction to improve their game for playing with friends both at home and at school.

MATCH ADMINISTRATION

I. SETTING UP THE COURT

One of the chief problems in running off a tennis tournament is having enough able officials on hand. The United States Lawn Tennis Association holds clinics to train school and college students in umpiring and lining. This instruction has been received very enthusiastically by players and non-players alike. After the clinic the students are given practice in umpiring and lining and those who qualify are given rating cards and may be called upon for tournament matches.

There follows a diagram of a tennis court set up with the proper officials (Figure 9.28).

A. Duties of the Umpire.

1. Rules. The umpire must have an absolute knowledge of the playing rules, tournament regulations, and their correct enforcement.[1]

2. Before the Match. Have score card and pencils. Write down names of players and learn how to pronounce them. Measure height of net. Supervise players' toss for serve or court. See that other officials are in their places. When players have finished warming up, announce the match and start the play with "Linesmen ready? Play."

3. During the Match.

a. Keep entire attention on the match.

b. After each point mark the score first—then announce it. Announce the score clearly and correctly.

c. Repeat the decision of the linesman and foot fault judge, so the players and audience can hear.

d. If the score has been given incorrectly, say "Correction" and give the right score.

e. Call "Not up" if a player does not reach the ball on the first bounce.

f. See that the gallery does not disturb the players. If it does, stop the play, and ask for the cooperation of the spectators. If necessary call a "let" and have the disturbed point played over.

g. See that the players change courts at the end of odd games.

h. In announcing the score, give the server's score first. Announce advantage by saying, "Advantage Miss Smith" —never say, "advantage striker or receiver." Announce the game score by saying, "Game Miss Smith; games are

[1] The material on officiating at a tennis match was obtained from Mr. Winslow Blanchard through an Umpires Clinic held as Smith College. Further material on officiating may be secured from the United States Lawn Tennis Association, 120 Broadway, New York.

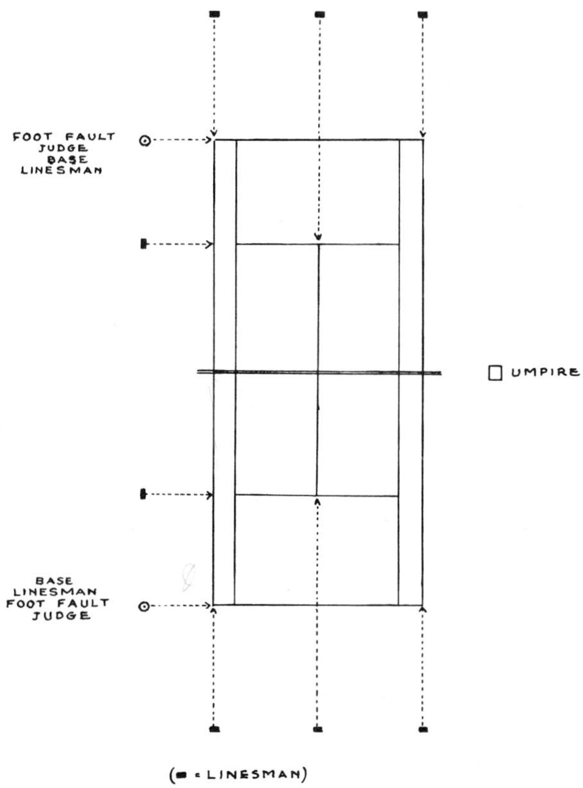

FIGURE 9.28 *Diagram showing the position of linesmen, foot fault judge, and umpire in a doubles match.*

three to one, Miss White leading, first set." Announce the set score by saying, "Game and second set Miss Smith, 7–5; sets are one all." At the end of the match say, "Game, set, and match Miss Smith, score 2–6, 6–4, 6–4."

B. Duties of Linesman.

1. Know that ball falling on any part of the line is good.

2. Only call "out" or "fault"; *never* call "good."

3. Sit *facing* the line she is to call. Must not leave without the umpire's permission or until another linesman has taken her place. During play must not smoke or move about. Should not catch or return balls for the players. This is the ball boy's job; if there are no ball boys, let the players get their own balls.

4. Give decisions instantly, loudly, and decisively. On close decisions it is permissible to wait an instant. Never call "out" until the ball has struck the ground outside the court.

5. If the linesman does not see whether the ball is good or out, she should put her hands over her eyes as a signal to the umpire that she failed to see the play. The umpire makes the decision or calls on another linesman to do so. In case no one can decide, the umpire has the point replayed.

6. If a player is standing between a linesman and the line for which she is responsible, the linesman should stand so that she is able to make a decision on her line.

7. A linesman may change her decision if she is sure she has been wrong. The umpire must then decide whether or not a "let" shall be given.

C. Duties of Foot Fault Judge.

1. A foot fault judge must know the foot fault ruling and when to enforce it.

She should do this with a clear, definite voice.

2. The foot fault judge should sit directly opposite the base line and should not converse with the base linesman.

3. It is customary to warn a player first before penalizing her, although there is nothing in the rules requiring this procedure.

TENNIS TERMS

I. THE RACKET

Racket Face. The hitting surface of the racket.
Open Face. When the hitting surface is facing upward.
Closed Face. When the hitting surface is facing downward.
Flat Face. When the racket frame is at right angles to the ground.
Handle. The wooden shaft of the racket.
Throat. The part between the head and the handle of the racket.
Head. End farthest away from where racket is held.

II. THE COURT

Base Line. The back line at either end of the court.
Side Line. The line at either side of the court marking the outside edge of the playing surface.
Service Line. The line 21 feet from the net on either side, which bounds the back of the service courts.
Center Service Line. The line that divides the service courts in half and separates the right and the left service courts.
Alley. The space between the side lines used in doubles.
Net. Netting across middle of court—3 feet high at the center.
Post. One of the metal or wooden uprights supporting the net.
Band. The strip of canvas at the top of the net.

III. THE GAME

Server. The player who serves.
Receiver. The player who receives the service.
Fault. A served ball that does not enter the proper service court, or is incorrectly served.
Ground Strokes. Strokes made after the ball has struck the ground, or playing surface.
Drive. A ground stroke, taken either on the forehand or backhand, in which the racket is swung parallel to the ground.
Volley. To make a return by hitting the ball before it has hit the ground, except when serving.
Lob. To hit a ball high into the air, over the head of an opponent who has come to the net.
Smash (Overhead). A ball hit forward and down from the highest point possible over the head.
Chop. To hit a ball from above, downward, so as to give back spin to the ball.
Drop Shot. To hit the ball in such a way that it barely clears the top of the net and drops close to the net.
Let. A ball on the service that touches the net and falls into the proper service court. Any stroke that does not count and may be played over is also called a "let."

Suggestions for Further Reading

Agutter, George: *Lessons in Tennis.* New York, A. S. Barnes & Co., 1939.
Anderson, Lou E.: *Tennis for Women.* New York, A. S. Barnes & Co., 1936.
Applewhaite, R. H. (Maj.): *Play the Game Lawn Tennis.* London, Educational Productions, Ltd., 1956.
Browne, Mary K.: *Streamline Tennis.* New York, American Sports Publishing Co., 1940.
———: *Design for Tennis.* New York, A. S. Barnes & Co., 1949.
Bruce and Bruce: *Tennis Fundamentals and Timing.* New York, Prentice-Hall, Inc., 1940.
Budge, Donald: *Budge on Tennis.* New York, Prentice-Hall, Inc., 1939.
Budge, L.: *Lawn Tennis.* London, Nicholas Kaye, Ltd., 1949.
Cochet, Henry: *The Art of Tennis.* New York, William Brendon & Son, Ltd., 1936.
Connolly, Maureen: *Power Tennis.* New York, A. S. Barnes & Co.
Cooke, Sarah P.: *Winning Tennis.* Garden City,

New York, Doubleday & Company, Inc., 1946.

Cummings, Parke: *American Tennis, the Story of a Game.* Boston, Little, Brown & Co.

Donnalley, Mary Jane: *Net Results.* A How-To Book for Beginners. New York, Pageant Press, 1961.

Driver, Helen: *Tennis for Teachers.* Madison, Wisconsin, Forest Woods, 1956.

Hart, Doris: *Tennis with Hart.* Philadelphia, J. B. Lippincott Co., 1955.

Hillas, Marjorie and Dorothy D. Randle: *Tennis Organized.* New York, A. S. Barnes & Co., 1932.

Jacobs, Helen H.: *Tennis.* New York, A. S. Barnes & Co., 1941.

———: *Beyond the Game.* Philadelphia, J. B. Lippincott Co., 1936.

———: *Improve Your Tennis.* London, Methuen & Co., Ltd., 1936.

Kramer, Jack: *How to Win at Tennis.* New York, Ziff-Davis Publishing Co., 1949.

Leighton, Harry: *How to Improve Your Tennis.* The Athletic Institute, 209 South State Street, Chicago 4, Illinois.

Leighton, Harry and Eloise Jaeger: *Teaching of Tennis for School and Recreation Programs.* Minneapolis, Minnesota, Burgess Publishing Company, 1959.

Murphy, Bill and Chet Murphy: *Tennis for Beginners.* New York, The Ronald Press, 1958.

Moss, T. (Maj.): *Lawn Tennis for Teachers and Players.* London, Unwin Brothers, Ltd., 1949.

Noel, Susan: *Tennis Without Tears.* London, Hutchinson's Library of Sports and Pastimes, 1949.

Olliff, John: *Romance of Wimbledon.* New York, Hutchinson & Co., 1949.

———: *Olliff on Tennis.* London, Eyre & Spottiswoode, 1948.

Patterson, Norman: *Lawn Tennis Courtcraft.* London, Adam & Charles Black, Ltd., 1947.

Riggs, Bobby: *Tennis is My Racket.* London, Stanley Paul & Co., Ltd., 1950.

Talbert, William F. and Bruce S. Olds: *The Game of Doubles.* New York, Henry Holt & Co., Inc., 1956.

Tilden, William T.: *Art of Lawn Tennis.* New York, Doran & Co., 1926.

———: *Match Play and the Spin of the Ball.* American Lawn Tennis Association, 461 8th Avenue, New York, 1925.

Wills, Helen: *Fifteen Thirty.* New York, Charles Scribner's Sons, 1937.

PERIODICALS

World Tennis. Box 3, Gracie Station, New York 28, New York. (Monthly, published and edited by Gladys Madalie Heldman.)

Tennis Guide. Division for Girls and Women's Sports, American Association for Health, Physical Education, and Recreation, 1201 16th Street, N.W., Washington, D.C.

U.S.L.T.A. Yearbook. Write: *World Tennis.*

FILMS

Fundamentals of Tennis. Donald Budge, Transfilm, Inc., 35 West 45th Street, New York.

Technique of Tennis. Lloyd Budge, Bell & Howell Co., 1801–1815 Larchmont Avenue, Chicago, Illinois.

Tennis for Everybody. 16 mm. Color and sound. U.S.L.T.A., 120 Broadway, New York 5, New York.

EQUIPMENT FOR TEACHING

Ball-Boy Co., Inc., 26 Milburn Street, Bronxville, New York.

Ball-Boy Machine throws the ball at pre-set height and speed, for individual or group practice.

Ball-Boy Server suspends a ball that flies free when hit.

Re-Bound Net is useful for stroke practice; both sides can be used at the same time.

Ready-Net can be set for tennis, badminton or volleyball.